D1450593

JOHN DEWEY

THE MIDDLE WORKS, 1899–1924

Volume 3: 1903—1906

Edited by Jo Ann Boydston
Associate Textual Editor, Patricia R. Baysinger
With an Introduction by Darnell Rucker

Carbondale and Edwardsville
SOUTHERN ILLINOIS UNIVERSITY PRESS
London and Amsterdam
FEFFER & SIMONS, INC.

CENTER FOR EDITIONS OF
AMERICAN AUTHORS
AN APPROVED TEXT
MODERN LANGUAGE
ASSOCIATION OF AMERICA

*Editorial expenses for this edition have been met in part by
grants from the National Endowment for the Humanities.
Publishing expenses have been met in part by grants from
the John Dewey Foundation and from Mr. Corliss Lamont.*

Library of Congress Cataloging in Publication Data   (Revised)

Dewey, John, 1859–1952.
    The middle works, 1899–1924.

    Bibliography: p.
    Includes indexes.
    CONTENTS: v. 1. 1899–1901.—v. 2. 1902–1903.—v 3.
1903–1906.
    1. Dewey, John, 1859–1952. 2. Education—Philosophy.
LB875.D34 1976   370.1′092′4   76–7231
ISBN 0–8093–0775–8 (v. 3)

The Middle Works, 1899–1924

Advisory Board

CONTENTS

INTRODUCTION

by Darnell Rucker

The third volume of Dewey's *Middle Works* seems an appropriate place to look at his philosophy in its whole range. The basic structure of the method, the general intent of the language and concepts, and the reach of the vision of that philosophy were evolved during the ten years at Chicago, under extraordinary conditions of intellectual cooperation among philosophers, psychologists, educators, sociologists, and others. Dewey's move to Columbia marked a moving out into a wider community far less homogeneous with and less immediately sympathetic to his pragmatic vision. Not that everyone at Chicago shared Dewey's vision or approved of his aims, by any means. But those of a pragmatic bent were sufficiently numerous, able, and respected to ward off those side battles that might have distracted them from the main line of the development going on. Columbia and New York provided quite a different milieu for Dewey from that of the university and city of Chicago.

The defining features of Dewey's philosophy were already clear, however, and well established enough to engage with profit a more cosmopolitan community. The method of inquiry that is Dewey's hallmark was outlined and fully operative, though he would continue to refine it for the next thirty years. His language in those early years of the century seems woefully old-fashioned now, especially that taken from the logic and psychology of the day. But the concepts and purposes are alive and significant, as the reader can see by noting that Dewey's revisions of the language of some of these works over a considerable span of time simply aim at making clearer ideas and purposes that were there from the start. The lifelong inquiry that is Dewey's philosophy takes its overall shape from the philosophic vision that informs to some degree every item in his considerable output and that is embodied strikingly both explicitly and implicitly in this volume.

Incorporated into that vision was the awareness Dewey developed, as he moved out of his early absolutism, of the danger that any overview of the human situation can become procrustean rather than guiding in making sense of whatever experience turns up. Yet in looking at the works from this crucial period of Dewey's philosophic life, it is important to emphasize the wholeness of purpose, the essential philosophic spirit, that makes of the entire body of his writings a philosophy and not merely a sequence of attempts at solutions of problems strung together by one person's biography. In spite of the prevalence in our time of narrowly focused research in the natural sciences, minimal expressions in art, and self-enclosed social experimentation, a philosophy still is obliged to try to see things whole; and necessary as are analyses of parts and conceptual distinctions to any sense of the world, no techniques of investigation, tools of formulation, or logical construction of systems are *philosophic* except as they contribute to some degree of understanding and realization in practice of the world as a continuum, without seam, despite the chasms and barriers we continue to create for ourselves. The thing that the lovers of the Absolute and the lovers of atomisms of whatever stripe most signally failed to comprehend in Dewey was the persistence of his striving to see—and to show—things whole.

In Dewey's assessment in 1930 of his development, he harks back to a physiology text by Huxley that brought into dim relief the inchoate dissatisfaction he felt as a very young man with what he calls the "divisions and separations that were . . . borne in upon me as a consequence of a heritage of New England culture, divisions by way of isolation of self from the world, of soul from body, of nature from God."[1] The "inward laceration" occasioned by those divisions marked in John Dewey the rise of that drive to know which chance so rarely produces, and which circumstances and character even more rarely sustain throughout a life. It is that dominant motivation that makes the true philosophic spirit stand out in the midst of intellectual fads

---

1. "From Absolutism to Experimentalism," in *Contemporary American Philosophy*, ed. George P. Adams and Wm. Pepperell Montague (New York: Macmillan Co., 1930), 2:19.

and fancies, scholarly politics, and personal cults. Even at this early date there is reason to believe that Dewey stands in that small group of the elect, much as he might have protested any such designation.

Almost every work in this volume evinces Dewey's painstaking effort to heal—intellectually—those rifts in life that continue to lacerate modern man. Nowhere is the philosophic problem of our time put more directly than in his address "Philosophy and American National Life," given at the University of Vermont in 1904:

If our civilization is to be directed, we must have such a concrete and working knowledge of the individual as will enable us to furnish on the basis of the individual himself substitutes for those modes of nurture, of restraint and of control which in the past have been supplied from authorizations supposedly fixed outside of and beyond individuality (p. 75).

This is the same insight into the predicament of humans in this century that has given such ready relevance to the otherwise unwelcome visions of Kierkegaard, Schopenhauer, Nietzsche, and others of the Continental European tradition. The common insight is into the problems presented by the juxtaposition of the collapse of those institutions men have looked to in the past for salvation and the sharply increasing self-consciousness and self-centeredness of the individual no longer meaningfully connected to the world he still depends upon for his being and his values. More important here, perhaps, is the contrast between Dewey's assessment of that insight and its implications and the characteristic European response.

The emergence of the isolated individual, cut off from comprehension of the corporate world that envelops and suffocates him, poses for Dewey the necessity for a social solution to the problems of the lost but still essentially social person. Hence the centrality for him of the problem of democracy—precisely the conception of a social order centered in and governed by the individuals who constitute it. Hence also the primary philosophic and practical importance of a philosophy of education; of a theory of inquiry broad enough and flexible enough to encompass the social, the intellectual, and the physical dimensions of the world; of

theories of the aesthetic, the religious, the moral, the metaphysical that serve to integrate human experience instead of
carving it up into personal and disciplinary enclaves within
which men huddle to protect themselves from awareness of
the real problem they fail to face.

Even so socially conscious a scion of the European
tradition as Sartre can justify no way of reconnecting the
severed ties of man to man and man to world when he interprets the obvious fact of our current isolation as final—
as he does, for example, in the following passage:

I want to grasp this being and I no longer find anything but
myself. This is because knowledge, intermediate between being
and non-being, refers me to absolute being if I want to make
knowledge subjective and refers me to myself when I think to
grasp the absolute. The very meaning of knowledge is what it is
not and is not what it is; for in order to know being such as it is,
it would be necessary to be that being. But there is this "such as
it is" only because I am not the being which I know; and if I
should become it, then the "such as it is" would vanish and could
no longer even be thought.[2]

This cosmic gap between the mind and the world is un-
bridgeable and fatal. Dewey's version of the gap, on the
other hand, is not so cosmic or so final as to be this per-
nicious; it is a gap *within* knowledge, not between man and
world, and is a less-debilitating recognition of our incapacity
to attain the absolute in knowledge or in anything else. Note
in particular the following from "The Experimental Theory
of Knowledge":

The thing meaning is one thing; the thing meant is another thing,
and is (as already pointed out) a thing presented as not given in
the same way as is the thing which means. It is something *to be*
so given. No amount of careful and thorough inspection of the
indicating and signifying things can remove or annihilate this
gap. The *probability* of correct meaning may be increased in
varying degrees—and this is what we mean by control. But final
certitude can never be reached except experimentally—except by
performing the operations indicated and discovering whether or
no the intended meaning is fulfilled *in propria persona* (pp. 122n–
23n).

2. Sartre, Jean Paul. *Being and Nothingness*, tr. Hazel Barnes
(New York: Philosophical Library, 1956), p. 218.

The certitude he mentions is practical and temporary, of course, being the result of a restoration of continuity in an interrupted process going on in the world.

The first essay in this volume appeared in the *Decennial Publications of the University of Chicago*, as did the *Studies in Logical Theory*.[3] But even though "Logical Conditions of a Scientific Treatment of Morality" was also published as a separate monograph, it received almost none of the attention paid to the logic volume. It remains, however, an important, perhaps a major, milestone in Dewey's thought; and he considered it significant enough to include it with only minor revisions in the collection of essays in 1946 in which everything else in the book dated from the mid-1930s. Although its language remains dated even after the revisions and its argument is difficult and perhaps over-subtle, it is of permanent importance in the corpus because it presents the most careful argument Dewey has worked out as a ground for his claim that ethics must become scientific if men are to gain that degree of control over their world necessary to supplant chance and the blind mechanism of institutions as governing forces. If science and values are unrelated, if the worth of the world is distinct from its existence, then the predicament of humans in the twentieth century appears hopeless because it is beyond the reach of intelligence. Despair or prayer to some unknown god is then the only possible response. For this reason, Dewey insisted that *the* problem of philosophy is that of the relation of science and values.

The basic distinctions in this essay are those between intellectual judgments and ethical judgments, on one hand, and between generic (abstract, general) judgments and individualized (concrete, particular) judgments, on the other. He argues that all sciences (physics, psychology, or ethics) require both generic and concrete judgments. We tend to regard the physical sciences as wholly composed of general propositions because there has been such a sizable ac-

3. Dewey, John. *Studies in Logical Theory* (Chicago: University of Chicago Press, 1903). Dewey's essays in that volume appear in *The Middle Works of John Dewey, 1899–1924*, ed. Jo Ann Boydston (Carbondale: Southern Illinois University Press, 1976), Vol. 2.

cumulation of established theory. And we think of ethics as composed of discrete particular propositions because there has been so little by way of established systematic theory in the area of our concerns with what is good and bad. Therefore, Dewey is concerned here to show that the difference between a science of physics (as we have it) and one of ethics (if we are to have it) is not the logical one between the generic and the particular but a substantive one between a subject matter into which the motives and character of the judger do *not* enter directly and one into which such motives and character do enter of necessity.

He defines science as "a mode of controlling our active relations with the world of experienced things" (p. 14n), hence as basically practical. The general propositions of a science are instruments, means for the control exercised in their *use* in concrete situations. The abstractions, as he puts it, are the tools of a science, while the concrete identifications in practice are its *life*—the location of its functions and growth. The only value a self-contained general proposition or theory could have would be an aesthetic value of the consummatory sort, having no logical import (p. 19). Knowing, whatever its level of abstraction or precision of statement, has its roots in human activity, and its being as knowledge depends upon the continual renewal of contact with that activity.

The character, the motivation, the disposition of the observer and judger are always and essentially factors in judgments of any sort. But, we have succeeded in instituting the required characteristics of the scientist in the intellectual realm so that we can take them for granted, by and large. Such institution is possible because the honesty and goodwill of the inquirer are general practical conditions for research and do not enter into the content of the research. It is certainly not the case that the motives of the physicist or any other scientist are irrelevant to his scientific activity. As Dewey says,

If the use made of scientific resources, of technique of observation and experiment, of systems of classification, etc., in directing the act of judging (and thereby fixing the content of the judgment) depends upon the interest and disposition of the judger, we have only to make such dependence explicit, and the so-called scientific judgment appears definitely as a moral judgment. If the physician is careless and arbitrary because of over-anxiety to get his work done, or if he lets his pecuniary needs influence his manner of judgment, we may say that he has failed both logically and morally (p. 19).

Those cases where scientists falsify data and results in research, thereby slowing down the growth of knowledge in that area and damaging the probity of research itself, make clear that there is no line to be drawn between research and ethics. We count upon the instituted processes of research in the natural sciences exposing such lapses of scientific integrity; and we usually take that integrity for granted so long as the process does not turn up such defections.

But a moral judgment is not just a judgment of the relations of external objects, as is an intellectual judgment; it is a judgment of both judger and objects judged. Thus the character of the judger is no longer simply a practical condition but becomes a logical matter. In fact, the character and preference of the judger is incorporated *into* the object judged.

The judger is engaged in judging himself; and thereby in so far is fixing the conditions of all further judgments of any type whatsoever. Put in more psychological terms, we may say the judgment realizes, through conscious deliberation and choice, a certain motive hitherto more or less vague and impulsive; or it expresses a habit in such a way as not merely to strengthen it practically, but as to bring to consciousness both its emotional worth and its significance in terms of certain kinds of consequences. But from the logical standpoint we say that the judger is consciously engaged in constructing as an object (and thereby giving objective form and reality to) the controlling condition of every exercise of judgment (p. 23).

We do not have an ethical science, however (as Dewey indicates in his *Encyclopedia Americana* article "Ethics"), and in order that one come into being, we must first have available *intellectual* judgments of the relations between disposition or character and actions, on one side, and similarly objective judgments of social situations that call out ethical judgments, on the other. A science of ethics, therefore, is dependent upon there being developed sciences of psychology and of sociology, but it will differ from both those sciences in that it will consist of generic propositions as to the conditions of action in its full sense: conditions of relations among character, attitude, conduct, and social conditions; whereas those sciences deal with partial aspects of action. In order for ethics to wield the control over ethical judgments necessary to call it a science, psychology and sociology must make available intellectual (objective) analyses of their respective subjective matters, in the same way that biology and physics must make their analyses available to psychology and sociology. The analyses will be intellectual in that psychology will treat motives, dispositions, emotions, sensations, etc., as objects in relation to other objects apart from any particular consideration of the motives, disposition, etc., of the psychologists making the analysis, and similarly for sociology and its subject matter. The ethical scientist, in contrast, will utilize such intellectual judgments to form his ethical judgments, judgments of worth, of better and worse, and thus his character and motives become part of the content of his propositions. His character is logically implicated, not just as a general practical condition, but as part of the logical structure of the judgment.

Intelligent, competent individuals and effective democratic institutions provide the only philosophic solution to the social problem of this century as Dewey and others recognize it. Quite obviously, unless intelligence can be applied effectively to the moral-political realm, and not just to the physical-biological, that solution remains a mere abstraction. "Logical Conditions of a Scientific Treatment of Morality" establishes the ground for moral science as a real possibility on the absolute principle of the continuum of habit,[4] and states as the postulate of that science the continuity of scientific judgments. The *Encyclopedia Americana* article referred to above not only makes clear that we do not have a science of ethics, but also indicates in historical terms why we require one.

---

4. Dewey seldom uses the word "absolute" in a positive way after his very early works, but it is noteworthy that his 1946 revisions of this essay did not alter this statement of principle.

Other essays in this volume draw further implications of this view of science as applicable in principle to all human problems. In "The Experimental Theory of Knowledge," for instance, Dewey shows that science not only can but often should be an end-in-itself for the scientist. Yet the significance as well as the life of science remains in its vital connections with ordinary experience.

We *employ* meanings in all intentional constructions of experience—in all anticipations, whether artistic, utilitarian or technological, social or moral. The success of the anticipation is found to depend upon the character of the meaning. Hence the stress upon a right determination of these meanings. Since they are the instruments upon which fulfilment depends *so far as that is controlled* or other than accidental, they become themselves objects of surpassing interest (p. 126).

Human intellect is a biological response to the evolution of environment; and at this stage of the evolution of self- and social-awareness, humans can no longer find a satisfactory existence in a social environment they cannot control to any significant degree. We can no more accept, at this point, what chance happens to impose upon us in social forms than we can what chance happens to provide in natural production of material goods.

The writings on education in the present volume represent well the scope of Dewey's concern (so central in the Chicago years) for the use of intelligence in education, the most obvious institution we must control, since it is in the education process that individuals develop or fail to develop habits of intelligent control of self and of environment. As with everything he wrote, what he is saying in his writings on education must be viewed in light of the particular audience he happens to be addressing at a given time. If the pieces in this collection are read in their contexts, they effectively answer most of the stock criticisms and misunderstandings that continue to prevent some educators from grasping the spirit of Dewey's philosophy of education. For example, his argument in "The Relation of Theory to Practice in Education" for the necessity in teacher education of concentration on scholarship and intellectual principles and methods should puzzle those who still blame Dewey for the contentless methods-approach to teacher training; especially when he says, "But I claim the facts mentioned prove that scholarship *per se* may itself be a most effective tool for training and turning out good teachers" (pp. 262–63). A reason for that claim also is found in "Education, Direct and Indirect," where he argues against artificial and isolated school tasks and external modes of grading on the ground that genuine interests and significant assessment of accomplishment must be attached to *subject matter*. And "Democracy in Education" stresses the importance of freeing *intelligence*, in contrast to the notion that freeing the child's external behavior from the rigid restrictions of traditional schools is an adequate reform. In fact, this last essay introduces a number of arguments against the kind of misguided progressivism for which Dewey also is blamed. The essay concludes with the observation that education brings together the three most powerful human motives: sympathy and affection for others (here, the child); social and institutional concerns (the well-being of society); and intellectual and scientific interests (truth valued for its own sake). This is education in its ideal sense, of course, but a sense growing out of the biological, social, and intellectual nature of the human being.

Except as education is instituted and pursued as continuous with the natural and social world in which it functions, education will continue to be a prime source of the sense of isolation and impotence that besets individuals today. The genetic method of child-study Dewey endorses in his introduction to Irving W. King's book is a method for seeing the child in a continuum—a method for looking to results as well as to causes. The importance of such method is illustrated in the articles on education problems in religion and in geometry. In both cases, Dewey points to the unfavorable results from imposing advanced concepts and methods upon a child into whose experience such concepts and methods cannot yet enter. The results are unfavorable for religion and geometry as well as for the growth of the child. This pair of articles is an interesting demonstration of the parallel treatment of moral and intellectual problems Dewey advocates in education and everywhere else.

The one education piece in the collection that was written after Dewey left Chicago, "Culture and Industry in Education," extends his notion of the necessity for the interconnection of education and society. The history of our inherited attitudes toward industry, the statement of our present situation as a business-dominated society, and the drawing out of the implications and possibilities for education in our situation are used to focus the teacher's awareness upon the need to humanize an increasingly impersonal, mechanized economic system—a humanization that will require a breaking down of the separations between theory and practice, rulers and workers, art and industry.

These attempts to convey the insights of his philosophic inquiry to educators and parents are not activities "in addition to" Dewey's philosophic enterprise, but are part and parcel of it. As he says in the Vermont address:

> Even were it not true (as I believe it to be true) that philosophical problems are in last analysis but definitions, objective statements, of problems which have arisen in a socially important way in the life of a people; it would still be true that to be "understood of men," to make its way, to receive confirmation or even the degree of attention necessary for doubt and discussion, a philosophy has to be conceived and stated in terms of conditions and factors that are moving generally in non-philosophic life (p. 73).

The more technical arguments, addressed primarily to fellow philosophers, serve as the warrant for those discussions addressed also to a variety of non-philosophic audiences. Among these arguments, the polemical writings that begin to appear with some regularity with Dewey's move to Columbia serve a double purpose: one of sharpening his thinking about his philosophy and the other of refining the language with which the philosophy is communicated. Nine of the 1905–6 articles,[5] in particular, constitute a careful working out of the distinctive character of Dewey's philosophy in relation to the problems of knowledge, of reality,

5. "Beliefs and Existences," "Reality as Experience," "The Experimental Theory of Knowledge," "Experience and Objective Idealism," "The Realism of Pragmatism," "The Postulate of Immediate Empiricism," "Immediate Empiricism," "The Knowledge Experience and Its Relationships," and "The Knowledge Experience Again."

and of ideals, as they existed in current academic discussion. And his articles on "The Meanings of the Term Idea" and "The Terms 'Conscious' and 'Consciousness'" are explicit examples of his sensitivity to the problems in communication of new ideas.

This group of articles emphasizes the comprehensiveness of Dewey's conception of experience. The real is what is experienced, as it is experienced—emotionally, aesthetically, cognitively, morally. Knowledge and truth or falsity are experienced relations among real things and, as such, are modes of experiencing necessarily among other modes. The fact that, so far as we know, only humans have experience in this sense does not therefore exclude nonhuman nature, either as it existed before there was human life or as it exists beyond the reach of our senses, from empirical reality. Any object, however distant in time or remote in space, is incomplete except as it is related to present reality as experienced. Experiencing an object *as* past or *as* remote in space is a common enough phenomenon for the ordinary man or the scientist. Similarly, ideals are live and functioning only as they grow out of problems with respect to natural satisfactions and as they connect with the intentional activities of experiencing agents. In general, the replies Dewey makes to the criticisms of his pragmatism rest upon the coherence and completeness of what he means by "experience."

But just as important as the works on philosophy, psychology, and education for seeing what philosophy is for Dewey are his discussions of other philosophers. And, again, a pairing of articles that occurs in the volume—the essays on Emerson and Spencer, in this case—is remarkably instructive. Dewey saw the wisdom of Emerson's attempt to read the human situation as honestly and sympathetically as he could. Logic, method, system—so dear to the hearts of academic philosophers—are subordinated in Emerson to his "natural transcripts of the course of events and of the rights of man" (p. 189). For Dewey, as for Plato, the difference between a sophist and a philosopher is not one of logic but of concern. And the critic who, as Dewey says, "needs the method separately propounded, and not finding his wonted

leading-string is all lost" (p. 184) has got his priorities confused. Not that Emerson lacks method, in Dewey's view:

I am not acquainted with any writer, no matter how assured his
position in treatises upon the history of philosophy, whose movement of thought is more compact and unified, nor one who combines more adequately diversity of intellectual attack with concentration of form and effect (p. 184).

For Emerson, as for Dewey, method and logic are tools; and
Dewey recognized in Emerson a true philosophic concern
that most philosophers refuse even yet to grant him.

The essay on Spencer conveys the same point from the
opposite pole. Dewey makes a keen assessment of Spencer's
meteoric rise to fame as a philosopher and an equally keen
prediction of the demise of that fame. As opposed to Emerson, who appears to other philosophers as a writer of sprays
of aphorisms, Spencer is a model of obtrusive system. Dewey
points out that what is wrong philosophically with that
model is that Spencer sat down "to achieve a preconceived
idea,—an idea, moreover, of a synthetic, deductive rendering of all that is in the Universe" (p. 194). "And," he adds,
"the more we compare the achievement with the announcement, the more we are struck with the way in which the
whole scheme stands complete, detached, able to go alone
from the very start." Such a scheme is contrasted with the
unity of other philosophies that is a *result* of a single mind
applied to a succession of problems, a unity gathered by
later minds but certainly not worked out in advance.

Spencer's philosophy was widely useful for a time, because it served to make systematically available a host of
the principal ideas developed in nineteenth-century social
thought, in biology, and in astronomy, physics, and geology.
Liberalism, individualism, evolutionism were coordinated
into a single system, but, as Dewey points out, the resultant
theory is dead, totally inert. It represents, in terms of
Dewey's analysis of inquiry, the deductive stage isolated
from the living process of inquiry. So any relation of the
formal scheme to the critical ongoing life of the world can
be only accidental. For Dewey,

It is upon the revelations that arise from the eternal mixture of
voluntary endeavor with the unplanned, the unexpected, that

most of us learn to depend for shaping thought and directing intellectual movement. We hang upon experience as it comes, not
alone upon experience as already formulated, into which we can
enter by "imitation" (p. 196).

Dewey certainly did not agree with all of Emerson's
perceptions of the world, but he knew the overwhelming
importance of Emerson's aims and methods. On the other
hand, Dewey no doubt concurred with any number of Spencer's propositions, yet he saw the fundamental fallacy of
Spencer's aims and methods. Spencer is, as a friend of mine
likes to put it, "dead as a dodo" philosophically. It remains
to be seen what will be made of Emerson as a philosopher.
Philosophers are still wary of this man who does not fit the
Anglo-American academic philosophic pattern. But Dewey,
for one, saw that Emerson knew what the problem of our
time is:

thinking of Emerson as the one citizen of the New World fit to
have his name uttered in the same breath with that of Plato, one
may without presumption believe that even if Emerson has no
system, none the less he is the prophet and herald of any system
which democracy may henceforth construct and hold by, and that
when democracy has articulated itself, it will have no difficulty
in finding itself already proposed in Emerson (p. 191).

The book reviews here further evidence Dewey's views
on the aim of philosophy, as does the exchange with Münsterberg on the St. Louis Congress. His treatment of authors
is characteristically generous, however minor the importance
of a book or however considerable the weight a book might
carry in the philosophical controversies of the day. He is
respectful of Professor Benedict's syllabus, and he defends
Santayana's style in the first two volumes of *The Life of
Reason* on the same basis as he defended Emerson. He
emphasizes the positive aspects he finds in Schiller's book,
being content merely to point out his "almost total dissent"
(p. 312) from the positions of two of the essays.[6] He credits

6. Dewey's disclaimer seems extraordinarily mild, considering such
   statements in Schiller as the following: "Let us, for instance,
   assume—as I think we must do in any case—the philosophic position of an idealistic experientialism. I use this clumsy phrase
   to designate the view that 'the world' is primarily 'my experience,' *plus* (secondarily) the supplementings of that experience
   which its nature renders it necessary to assume, such as, *e. g.*,
   other persons and a 'real' material world." F. C. S. Schiller,
   Humanism (London: Macmillan and Co., 1903), p. 281.

all these men with the same love of wisdom that moves him.

Men still think of mind as a thing, the world as given, and knowledge as mind somehow copying that world. And though our moral principles are imposed on us less and less by God or the church or our parents, they are nonetheless still largely imposed from without by our peers, by industry, and by business. Aesthetic reactions are mysteries; and art is what we are told is art (or what happens to land in a museum, theater, or concert hall); and taste is an accident of habit and circumstance. But, as Dewey knew, unexamined values are impoverished values; and the unexamined life in general is not only not worth living, we may not be *capable* of living it in this age of heightened consciousness and of institutions that grow like cancers.

In our attempt to understand Dewey's accomplishment, it is important to trace the sources of his problems, his ideas, his language, and his method—to Morris and Hegel, Hall and Darwin, James and Mill, for instance. But if we accept his own assessment of the true role of the past, it is more important to see the originality of his thought—that philosophic originality that results from a sincere, thoroughgoing, and competent search for the truth by a person profoundly rooted in his time and place as well as at home in the history of thought. All organized thought, of necessity, draws upon the accumulated thought of the past. The genetic method Dewey talks about and uses requires that origins, histories be viewed with an eye to their consequences and that those consequences be assessed as to their possibilities for the future. Hegel provided a holistic viewpoint of prime importance for Dewey, but he did not get trapped in the Hegelian apparatus that probably only Hegel could stay alive in. Darwin and the rapid developments in biology furnished a scientific starting point with connections still open to the whole world, unlike physics, which had grown so enormously at the expense of a formidable isolation from ordinary life. And Mill exemplified an empiricism that, at least, opened its eyes once more to experience.

The United States is a young culture, and most of its culture was borrowed wholesale to begin with. Most American academics, in the past and the present, have been content to expand, embroider, manipulate, rearrange, or repeat

European thought. Dewey and a few others were not. He stands as the most American of philosophers so far, because he is so consciously a product of American culture. Peirce was a man of awesome intellect—purely in terms of intellectual power, perhaps more awesome than Dewey. And James was a more engaging, more rhetorically effective exponent of pragmatism than Dewey was. But Peirce was too much an alien in his world and time—at Harvard, in Cambridge, in the United States—and James, at the other extreme, was too much a cosmopolitan, at home everywhere and with roots nowhere, for either of them to draw from his native soil a philosophic formulation both grounded in and explicitly cognizant of its present movement and potential.

Dewey is not, however, merely an *American* philosopher, because what he derived from his time and locale included a deep sense of the human situation at this time as epitomized in the United States and as the product of a long and complex history. In Europe, Sartre and Camus, among others, have given dramatic voice to the desperate plight of the individual caught in a hostile world, but their demand that the individual stand alone and shoulder the entire burden of that hostility over-stretches human power. Marcel saw the essential social nature and need of humans, but he made that nature mystical rather than real by such concepts as transcendence and the intersubjective nexus. Heidegger's *Dasein* and Jaspers's Encompassing have an even more chilling remoteness from the facts of their German culture and from the pressures of our world in general. And the positivists and analysts seem farther removed yet from the actualities of crumbling empires, burgeoning corporations, and marooned individuals.

The relation and distinction of the psychological and the sociological that appear in Dewey's earliest writings on ethics persist throughout his work because his ongoing thinking about our world verified the centrality of those aspects of the situation of men. What marks the development of Dewey's thought is the continuously more explicit and telling use of so many insights that came early on in his career. Others had those insights, too, of course, but few used them so widely, so consistently, and to such accurate effect. Learning from the past or the present is not a matter of intellectual archaeology, but rather of the fruitful, organized, successful utilization of instruments of inquiry, whatever the origin of those instruments. The having of genuine insights and the motivation to pursue their consequences are initially matters of pure chance, so far as the individual is concerned. Socrates was fortunate enough to be born a strong, intelligent, and ugly Athenian; Dewey was fortunate enough to encounter a sequence of men (Torrey, Harris, Morris) who encouraged his budding desire to understand, in a society that even yet little appreciates that desire. Once under way, however, only a conscious, courageous, increasingly ordered pursuit of knowledge could yield a philosophy (and a philosopher) of such power.

This introduction has aimed at showing the variety of materials gathered here under the arbitrary rubric of a time span as presenting in a compelling way a variety of facets of a single philosophy—not single in doctrine or in completeness—but single in purpose, in effort, and in power. This relatively small portion of his whole output is genuinely representative of that philosophic vision that carried Dewey through his long and productive life. I would suggest that one of the very last things Dewey wrote, an essay called "Modern Philosophy,"[7] states from the vantage point of 1952 the same basic themes and goals so clearly displayed in these pieces from 1903–6.

7. In *The Cleavage in our Culture*, ed. Frederick Burkhardt (Boston: Beacon Press, 1952), pp. 15–29.

ESSAYS

LOGICAL CONDITIONS OF A SCIENTIFIC TREATMENT OF MORALITY

I. The Use of the Term "Scientific"

The familiar notion that science is a body of systematized knowledge will serve to introduce consideration of the term "scientific" as it is employed in this article. The phrase "body of systematized knowledge" may be taken in different senses. It may designate a property which resides inherently in arranged facts, apart from the ways in which the facts have been settled upon to be facts, and apart from the way in which their arrangement has been secured. Or, it may mean the intellectual activities of observing, describing, comparing, inferring, experimenting, and testing, which are necessary in obtaining facts and in putting them into coherent form. The term should include both of these meanings. But since the static property of arrangement is dependent upon antecedent dynamic processes, it is necessary to make explicit such dependence. We need to throw the emphasis in using the term "scientific" first upon methods, and then upon results through reference to methods. As used in this article, "scientific" means regular methods of controlling the formation of judgments regarding some subject-matter.

The transition from an ordinary to a scientific attitude of mind coincides with ceasing to take certain things for granted and assuming a critical or inquiring and testing attitude. This transformation means that some belief and its accompanying statement are no longer taken as self-sufficing and complete in themselves, but are regarded as *conclusions*. To regard a statement as a conclusion, means (1) that its basis and ground lie outside of itself. This reference beyond

[First published in *Investigations Representing the Departments, Part II: Philosophy, Education.* University of Chicago, The Decennial Publications, first series, 3: 115–39 (Chicago: University of Chicago Press, 1903).]

itself sets us upon the search for prior assertions which are needed in order to make this one, *i.e.*, upon inquiry. (2) Such prior statements are considered with reference to their bearings or import in the determination of some further statement, *i.e.*, a consequent. The meaning or significance of a given statement lies, logically, in other statements to which we are committed in making the one in question. Thus we are set upon reasoning, the development of the assertions to which a particular assertion or view commits and entitles us. Our attitude becomes scientific in the degree in which we look in both directions with respect to every judgment passed; first, checking or testing its validity by reference to possibility of making other and more certain judgments with which this one is bound up; secondly, fixing its meaning (or significance) by reference to its use in making other statements. The determination of *validity* by reference to possibility of making other judgments upon which the one in question depends, and the determination of *meaning* by reference to the necessity of making other statements to which the one in question entitles us, are the two marks of scientific procedure.

So far as we engage in this procedure, we look at our respective acts of judging not as independent and detached, but as an interrelated system, within which every assertion entitles us to other assertions (which must be carefully deduced since they constitute its meaning) and to which we are entitled only through other assertions (so that they must be carefully searched for). "Scientific" as used in this article thus means the possibility of establishing an order of judgments such that each one when made is of use in determining other judgments, thereby securing control of their formation.

Such a conception of "scientific," throwing the emphasis upon the inherent logic of an inquiry rather than upon the particular form which the results of the inquiry assume, may serve to obviate some of the objections which at once suggest themselves when there is mention of a science of conduct. Unless this conception is emphasized, the term "science" is likely to suggest those bodies of knowledge which are most familiar to us in physical matters; and thus to give the impression that what is sought is reduction of matters of conduct to similarly physical or even quasi-mathematical form. It is, however, analogy with the method of inquiry, not with the final product, which is intended. Yet, while this explanation may preclude certain objections, it is far, in the present state of discussion, from removing all objections and thus securing a free and open field. The point of view expressly disclaims any effort to reduce the statement of matters of conduct to forms comparable with those of physical science. But it also expressly proclaims an identity of logical procedure in the two cases. This assertion will meet with sharp and flat denial. Hence, before developing the logic of moral science, it is necessary to discuss the objections which affirm such an inherent disparity between moral judgments and physical judgments that there is no ground in the control of the judging activity in one case for inferring the possibility of like control in the other.

II. *The Possibility of Logical Control of Moral Judgments*

In considering this possibility, we are met, as just indicated, by an assertion that there is something in the very nature of conduct which prevents the use of logical methods in the way they are employed in already recognized spheres of scientific inquiry. The objection implies that *moral* judgment is of such character that nothing can be systematically extracted from any one which is of use in facilitating and guaranteeing the formation of others. It denies, from the logical side, the continuity of moral experience. If there were such continuity, any one judgment could be dealt with in such a way as to make of it a conscious tool for forming other judgments. The ground of denial of continuity in moral experience rests upon the belief that the basis and justifying principle of the ethical judgment is found in transcendental conceptions, viz., considerations that do not flow from the course of experience as that is judged in terms of itself, but which have a significance independent of the course of experience as such.

The assertion of such logical disparity assumes a variety of forms, all coming back to pretty much the same presupposition. One way of putting the matter is that ethical judgments are immediate and intuitive. If this be true, an ethical judgment cannot be considered a conclusion; and hence there can be no question of putting it into orderly intellectual (or logical) relations with other like judgments. A merely immediate judgment is, by the nature of the case, incapable of either intellectual rectification or of intellectual application. This view finds expression in popular consciousness in the notion that scientific judgments depend upon reason, while moral valuations proceed from a separate faculty, conscience, having its own criteria and methods not amenable to intellectual supervision.

Another way of affirming radical disparity is that scientific judgments depend upon the principle of causation, which of necessity carries with it the dependence of one phenomenon upon another, and thus the possibility of stating every fact in connection with the statement of some other fact; while moral judgments involve the principle of final cause, of end and ideal. Hence to endeavor to control the construction and affirmation of any content of moral judgment by reference to antecedent propositions is to destroy its peculiar moral quality. Or, as it is popularly expressed, ethical judgment is ethical just because it is not scientific; because it deals with norms, values, ideals, not with given facts; with what *ought* to be, estimated through pure spiritual aspiration, not with what *is*, decided after investigation.

Pretty much the same point of view is expressed when it is said that scientific judgments, as such, state facts in terms of sequences in time and of coexistences in space. Wherever we are dealing with relations of this sort, it is apparent that a knowledge of one term or member serves as a guide and check in the assertion of the existence and character of the other term or member. But moral judgments, it is said, deal with actions which are still to be performed. Consequently in this case characteristic meaning is found only in the qualities which exist *after* and by means of the judgment. For this reason, moral judgment is thought essentially to transcend anything found in past experience; and so, once more, to try to control a moral judgment through the medium of other judgments is to eliminate its distinctive ethical quality. This notion finds its popular equivalent in the conviction that moral judgments relate to realities where freedom is implicated in such a way that no intellectual control is possible. The judgment is considered to be based, not upon objective facts, but upon arbitrary choice or volition expressed in a certain sort of approval or disapproval.

I have no intention of discussing these points in their full bearing. I shall reduce them to a single logical formulation, and then discuss the latter in its most general significance. The justification of the single statement as a formulation of the objections just set forth (and of other like ones) will not be attempted, for further discussion does not turn upon that point. When generalized, the various statements of the logical gulf between the moral judgment and the scientific reduces itself to an assertion of two antinomies: one, the separation between the universal and the individual; the other, between the intellectual and the practical. And these two antinomies finally reduce themselves to one: Scientific statements refer to *generic conditions* and relations, which are therefore capable of complete and objective statement; ethical judgments refer to an *individual act* which by its very nature transcends objective statement. The ground of separation is that scientific judgment is universal, hence only hypothetical, and hence incapable of relating to acts, while moral judgment is categorical, and thus individualized, and hence refers to acts. The scientific judgment states that where some condition or set of conditions is found, there also is found a specified other condition or set of conditions. The moral judgment states that a certain end has categorical value, and is thus to be realized without any reference whatsoever to antecedent conditions or facts. The scientific judgment states a connection of conditions; the moral judgment states the unconditioned claim of an idea to be made real.

This formulation of the logic of the problem under consideration fixes attention upon the two points which are in need of discussion. First: Is it true that scientific judgment deals with contents which have, in and of themselves, a universal nature—that its whole significance is exhausted in setting forth a certain connection of conditions? Secondly: Is it true that the attempt to regulate, by means of an intellectual technique, moral judgments—which, of course, are thoroughly individualized—destroys or in any way lessens distinctively ethical value?

In discussing the two questions just propounded, I shall endeavor to show: First, that scientific judgments have all the logical characteristics of ethical judgments; since they refer (1) to individual cases, and (2) to acts. I shall endeavor to show that the scientific judgment, the formulation of a connection of condition, has its origin, and is developed and employed for the specific and sole purpose of freeing and reinforcing acts of judgment that apply to unique and individual cases. In other words, I shall try to show that there is no question of eliminating the distinctive quality of ethical judgments by assimilating them to a different logical type, found in so-called scientific judgments; precisely because the logical type found in recognized scientific judgments is one which already takes due account of individualization and activity. I shall, then, secondly, endeavor to show that individualized ethical judgments require for their control generic propositions, which state a connection of relevant conditions in universal (or objective) form; and that it is possible to direct inquiry so as to arrive at such universals. And finally, I shall briefly set forth the three typical lines along which the construction of such generic scientific propositions must proceed, if there is to be a scientific treatment of ethics.

III. Nature of Scientific Judgments

The proposition that scientific judgments are hypothetic because they are universal is almost commonplace in recent logical theory. There is no doubt that there is a sense in which this proposition states an unquestioned truth. The aim of science is law. A law is adequate in the degree in which it takes the form, if not of an equation, at least of formulation of constancy, of relationship, or order. It is clear that any law, whether stated as formulation of order or as an equation, conveys, in and of itself, not an individualized reality, but a certain connection of conditions. Up to this point there is no dispute. When, however, it is argued that this direct and obvious concern of science with generic statements exhausts the logical significance of scientific method, certain fundamental presuppositions and certain fundamental bearings are ignored; and the logical question at issue is begged. The real question is not whether science aims at statements which take the form of universals, or formulae of connection of conditions, but *how* it comes to do so, and *what it does with* the universal statements after they have been secured.

In other words, we have, first, to ask for the logical import of generic judgments. Accordingly, not questioning the importance of general formulae as the objective content of the sciences, this section will endeavor to show that such importance lies in the development of "sciences" or bodies of generic formulae as instrumentalities and methods of controlling individualized judgments.

1. The boast and pride of modern science is its distinctly empirical and experimental character. The term "empirical" refers to origin and development of scientific statements out of concrete experiences; the term "experimental" refers to the testing and checking of the so-called laws and universals by reference to their application in further concrete experience. If this notion of science be correct, it shows, without further argument, that generic propositions occupy a purely intermediate position. They are neither initial nor final. They are the bridges by which we pass over from one particular experience to another; they are individual experiences put into such shape as to be available in regulating other experiences. Otherwise scientific laws would be only intellectual abstractions tested on the basis of their own reciprocal consistencies; and the trait which is supposed to demarcate science from mediaeval speculation would at once fade away.

Moreover, if the generic character of propositions of physical and biological sciences were ultimate, such propositions would be entirely useless from a practical point of view; they would be quite incapable of practical application because they would be isolated from intellectual continuity with the particular cases to which application is sought. No amount of purely deductive manipulation of abstractions brings a resulting conclusion any nearer a concrete fact than were the original premises. Deduction introduces in regular sequence new ideas, and thus complicates the universal content. But to suppose that by complicating the content of a universal we get nearer the individual of experience is the fallacy at once of mediaeval realism and of the ontological argument for the existence of God. No range of synthesis of universal propositions in chemistry, physics, and biology would (if such propositions were logically self-sufficing) assist us in building a bridge or in locating the source of an epidemic of typhoid fever. If, however, universal propositions and their deductive synthesis are to be interpreted in the sense of the manufacturing and employing of intellectual tools for the express purpose of facilitating our individual experiences, the outcome is quite other.

The empirical origin, the experimental test, and the practical use of the statements of science are enough of themselves to indicate the impossibility of holding to any fixed logical division of judgments into universal as scientific, and individual as practical. It suggests that what we term science is just the forging and arranging of instrumentalities for dealing with individual cases of experience—cases which, if individual, are just as unique and irreplaceable as are those of moral life. We might even say that the very fact which leads us upon a superficial view into believing in the logical separation of the generic judgment from the individual, viz., the existence of a large and self-contained body of universal propositions, is proof that as to some individual experiences we have already worked out methods of regulating our reflective transactions with them, while for another phase of experience this work remains to be done; i.e., is the problem of current ethical science.

The consideration of the technique by which the desired end of control is accomplished does not belong here. It suffices to note that the hypothetic judgment is a most potent instrumentality. If we inhibit the tendency to say, "This, A, is B," and can (1) find ground for saying, "Wherever there is mn there is B," and can (2) show that wherever there is op there is mn, and (3) have a technique for discovering the presence of *op* in *A*, we shall have warrant for identifying This, *A*, as *B*, even if all the outward and customary traits are lacking, and even if This, *A*, presents certain traits which, without the mediation of a generic proposition, would have inevitably led us to identify it as *C*. Identification, in other words, is secure only when it can be made through (1) breaking up the unanalyzed This of naïve judgment into determinate traits, (2) breaking up the predicate into a similar combination of elements, and (3) establishing uniform connection between some of the elements in the subject and some in the predicate. All judgments of everyday life, and indeed all judgments in such sciences as geology, geography, history, zoology, and botany (all sciences that have to do with historic narration or with description of space coexistences), come back ultimately to questions of identification. Even judgments in physics and chemistry, in their ultimate and concrete form, are concerned with individual cases. Of all the sciences, mathematics alone[1] is concerned with pure general propositions—hence the indispensable significance of mathematics as a *tool* for all judgments of technology and of the other sciences. It also is true in all the arts, whether commercial, professional, or artistic, that judgments reduce themselves to matters of correct identification. Observation, diagnosis, interpretation, and expert skill all display themselves in transactions with individual cases as such.

2. Thus far we have seen that the importance of generic statements in science is no ground for assuming a disparity in their logic from that of a scientific treatment of conduct. Indeed, since we have found that generic propositions originate, develop, and find their test in control of individual cases, the presumption is of similarity rather than of dissimilarity. Can we extend the parallelism farther? Does it apply equally well to the other characteristic trait of ethical judgment, viz., its reference to an act?

Just as modern logic has seized upon the hypothetic

1. If it were necessary for the purpose of this argument, it could of course be shown that reference to individual cases is involved in all mathematics. Within mathematical science, symbols (and diagrams are symbols) are individual objects of just the same logical nature as are metals and acids in chemistry and as are rocks and fossils in geology.

and universal character of scientific statements, relegating their bearing upon individual judgments into the background (but in truth so relegating them only because that bearing is always taken for granted), so modern logic has emphasized the aspect of content in judgment at the expense of the act of judging. I shall now try to show, however, that this emphasis also occurs because reference to act is so thoroughly taken for granted that it is possible to ignore it—that is, fail to give it explicit statement. I shall try to show that every judgment must be regarded as an act; that, indeed, the individual character of judgment proper, which has just been brought out, means, in final analysis, that the judgment is a unique act for which there is no substitute.

Our fundamental point is the control of the content or meaning which is asserted in any given judgment. How can such control be obtained? So far we have spoken as if the content of one judgment might be elaborated simply by reference to the content of another—particularly as if the content of an individual judgment, a judgment of identification, might be secured by reference to the content of a universal or hypothetic proposition. In truth, there is no such thing as control of one content by mere reference to another content as such. To recognize this impossibility is to recognize that the control of the formation of the judgment is always through the medium of an act by which the respective contents of both the individual judgment and of the universal proposition are selected and brought into relationship to each other. There is no road open from any generic formula to an individual judgment. The road leads through the habits and mental attitudes of the one concerned in judging. The universal gets logical force, as well as psychical reality, only in the acts by which it is invented and constructed as a tool and then is employed for the purpose for which it was intended.

I shall accordingly try to show that activity shows itself at every critical point in the formation of judgment: (a) that it shows itself in the genesis of the generic or universal employed; (b) that it shows itself in the selection of the particular subject-matter which is judged; and (c) that it shows itself in the way in which the validity of the hypothesis is tested and verified, and the significance of the particular subject-matter determined.

a) So far we have assumed the possibility of building up and selecting for use some generic principle which controls the identification reached in an individual case. We cannot, that is to say, regulate judgments of the type, "This is typhoid," or, "That is Bela's comet," unless we have certain generic concepts, which are defined as connection of particular conditions, and unless we know when and how to select from the stock of such concepts at our disposal the particular one required. The entire science considered as a body of formulae having coherent relations to one another is just a system of possible predicates—that is, of possible standpoints or methods to be employed in qualifying some particular experience whose nature or meaning is not clear to us. It furnishes us with a set of tools from which choice has to be made. The choice, of course, depends upon the needs of the particular facts which have to be discriminated and identified in the given case—just as the carpenter decides, on the basis of what he is going to do, whether he will take a hammer, a saw, or a plane from his tool-chest. One might as well suppose that the existence of possible candidates for office, plus the mathematically possible combinations and permutations of them, constitutes an election of one of them to office, as to suppose that a specific judgment follows from even an ideally exhaustive system of general principles. The logical process includes, as an organic part of itself, the selection and reference of that particular one of the system which is relevant to the particular case. This individualized selection and adaptation is an integral portion of the logic of the situation. And such selection and adjustment is clearly in the nature of an act.

Nor must we fail to make clear that we are concerned, not with selecting and adapting a ready-made universal, but with the *origin* of the universal absolutely for the sake of just such adaptation. If individual cases in experience never gave us any difficulty in identification, if they never set any problem, universals would simply not exist, to say nothing of being used. The universal is precisely such a statement of experience as will facilitate and guarantee the valuation of individualized experiences. It has no existence, as it has no check of validity, outside of such a function. In some case where science has already made considerable headway, we may, without error, speak as if universals were already at hand, and as if the only question were which one of them to pick out and employ. But such a way of speaking must not blind us to the fact that it was only because of the need of some more objective way of determining a given case that a universal ever originated and took on form and character. Did not the universal develop as medium of conciliation in just the same sort of situation of conflict as that in which it finds its use, such use would be absolutely arbitrary, and consequently without logical limit. The activity which selects and employs is logical, not extra-logical, just because the tool selected and employed has been invented and developed precisely for the sake of just such future selection and use.[2]

b) The individualized act (or choice) in judgments of identification shows itself not only in selection from a body of possibilities of the specific predicate required, but in the determination of the "This," or subject, as well. Students of logic are familiar with the distinction between the fact of particularity and the qualifications or distinguishing traits of a particular—a distinction which has been variously termed one between the "That" and the "What," or between "This" and "Thisness."[3] Thisness refers to a quality which, however

2. The point of view which is here presented is, of course, distinctly pragmatic. I am not quite sure, however, of the implications of certain forms of pragmatism. They sometimes seem to imply that a rational or logical statement is all right up to a certain point, but has fixed external limits, so that at critical points recourse must be had to considerations which are distinctly of an irrational or extra-logical order, and this recourse is identified with choice and "activity." The practical and the logical are thus opposed to each other. It is just the opposite which I am endeavoring to sustain, viz., that the logical is an inherent or organic expression of the practical, and hence is fulfilling its own logical basis and aim when it functions practically. I have no desire to show that what we term "science" is arbitrarily limited by out-side ethical considerations; and that consequently science cannot intrude itself into the ethical sphere; but precisely the contrary, viz., that just because science is a mode of controlling our active relations with the world of experienced things, ethical experience is supremely in need of such regulation. And by "practical" I mean only regulated change in experienced values.

3. This distinction in recent logic has been brought out with great force and clearness by Bradley, *Principles of Logic* (London, 1883), pp. 63–67.

sensuous it be (such as hot, red, loud), may yet in its own
meaning belong equally well to a large number of particulars. It is something a presentation *has*, rather than what it
just *is*. Such a variety of applications is involved in the very
notion of quality. It makes all qualities capable of consideration as degrees. It is responsible for the ease with which
names of qualities transform themselves into abstract terms,
blue into blueness, loud into loudness, hot into heat, etc.

The particularity, or better, singularity, of the judgment
is constituted by the immediate demonstrative reference of
the "This."[4] This demonstrative character means a preferential selection; it is a matter of action. Or, from the psychological side, the sensory quality becomes specific only in motor response. Red, blue, hot, etc., as immediate experiences,
always involve motor adjustments which determine them.
Change the kind of motor adjustment and the quality of the
experience changes; diminish it and the quality relapses
more and more into indefinite vagueness. The selection of
any particular "This" as the immediate subject of judgment
is not arbitrary, however, but is dependent upon the end involved in the interest which is uppermost. Theoretically, any
object within the range of perception, or any quality or any
element of any one object, may function as the "This," or the
subject-matter to be determined in judgment. Purely objectively, there is no reason for choosing any one of the infinite
possibilities rather than another. But the aim in view (which,
of course, finds its expression in the predicate of the judgment) gives a basis for deciding what object or what element
of any object is logically fit. The implication of selective activity is thus an organic part of the logical operation, and not
an arbitrary practical addition clapped on after the logical
activity as such is complete. The very same interest which
leads to the building up and selection of the universal leads
to the constructive selection of the immediate data or material with reference to which the universal is to be employed.[5]

4. It is hardly necessary to point out that the article "the" is a
weakened demonstrative, and that the pronouns, including "it,"
all have demonstrative reference.
5. Hence in accepting Bradley's distinction between "This" and
"Thisness" we cannot accept the peculiar interpretation which
he gives it. According to his way of looking at it, no strictly

c) The experimental character of all scientific identification is a commonplace. It is so commonplace that we are apt to overlook its tremendous import—the unconditional necessity of overt activity to the integrity of the logical process as such. As we have just seen, an act is involved in the determination of both the predicate, or the interpreting meaning, and of the "This," or fact to be identified. Were not both of these acts correlatives in a larger scheme of change of value in experience, they would both be arbitrary; and their ultimate appropriateness or adaptation to each other would be a sheer miracle. If one arbitrary act of choice reached forth to lay hold of some predicate from out the whole system of possible qualifications, while another act of choice, entirely independent in origin, reached out to seize a given area from the whole possible region of sense-perceptions, it would be the sheerest accident if the two selections thus made should fit into each other, should play into each other's hands.

But if one and the same end or interest operates in regulating both selections, the case stands quite otherwise. In such case, the experimental activity of verification is the carrying on of precisely the same purpose which found expression in the choice of subject and predicate respectively. It is in no sense a third process, but is the entire activity which we have already considered in two partial but typical aspects. The choice of meaning or predicate is always made with reference to the individual case to be interpreted; and the constitution of the particular objective case is always colored throughout by the point of view or idea with reference to which it is to be utilized. This reciprocal reference is the check or test continuously employed; and any particular more obvious experimental activity of verification means simply that conditions are such that the checking process is rendered overt.

I have now endeavored to show that if we take scientific

---

logical connection is possible between "This" and "Thisness." "Thisness" alone has logical significance; the "This" is determined by considerations entirely beyond intellectual control; indeed, it marks the fact that a reality lying outside of the act of judging has broken in upon, or forced itself into, a region of logical ideas or meanings, this peculiar and coercive irruption being an essential attendant of the *finite* extremely limited character of our experience.

judgment in its only ultimate form, viz., that which identifies or discriminates an individualized portion of experience, judgment appears as an act of judging; the act showing itself both in the selection and determination of the subject and the predicate, and in the determination of their values with reference or in respect to each other, and hence in deciding as to truth and validity.

Since in the discussion I have used a terminology which is hardly self-explanatory, and have introduced a variety of statements which to many will appear, in the present state or condition of logical discussion, to need rather than to afford support, I may point out that the force of the argument resides in matters capable of complete empirical confirmation. The truth or falsity of the conclusion reached depends upon these two notions:

First, every judgment is in its concrete reality an act of attention, and, like all attention, involves the functioning of an interest or end and the deploying of habits and impulsive tendencies (which ultimately involve motor adjustments) in the service of that interest. Hence it involves selection as regards both the object of attention and the standpoint and mode of "apperceiving" or interpreting. Change the interest or end, and the selected material (the subject of the judgment) changes, and the point of view from which it is regarded (and consequently the kind of predication) changes also.

Second, the abstract generalizing propositions of science have developed out of the needs of such individualized judgments or acts of attention; they have assumed their present form—that is, developed their characteristic structures or contents—as instrumentalities for enabling an individual judgment to do its work most effectively; that is to say, to accomplish most surely and economically the end for which it is undertaken. Consequently the value or validity of such concepts is constantly checked through a use which, by its success and failure, passes upon the competency of general principles, etc., to serve the regulative function for which they are instituted.[6]

6. It might check the prevalent tendency to draw sharp lines between philosophy as merely normative and the sciences as merely descriptive to realize that all generic scientific proposi-

So far as the scientific judgment is identified as an act, all *a priori* reason disappears for drawing a line between the logic of the material of the recognized sciences and that of conduct. We are thus free to proceed, if we can find any positive basis. The recognition that the activity of judging does not exist in general, but is of such a nature as to require reference to an initial point of departure and to a terminal fulfilment, supplies exactly this positive ground. The act of judging is not merely an active experience at large, but one which requires specific motivation. There must be some stimulus which moves to performing this particular sort of act rather than some other. Why engage in that particular kind of activity that we call judging? Conceivably some other activity might be going on—the sawing of wood, the painting of a picture, the cornering of the wheat market, the administering of reproof. There must be something outside the most complete and correct collection of intellectual propositions which induces to engage in the occupation of judging rather than in some other active pursuit. Science furnishes conditions which are to be used in the most effective execution of the judging activity, *if* one means to judge at all. But it presupposes the If. No theoretical system can settle that the individual shall at a given moment judge rather than do something else. Only the whole scheme of conduct as focusing in the interests of an individual can afford that determining stimulus.

Not only must a practical motive be found for the use of the organized scientific system, but a similar motive must be found for its correct and adequate use. The logical value of any intellectual proposition, its distinctively logical significance as distinct from existence as mere *ens rationis*, depends upon practical, and ultimately upon moral, considerations. The interest must be of a kind not only to move the individual to judge, but to induce him to judge critically,

---

tions, all statements of laws, all equations and formulae, are strictly normative in character, having as their sole excuse for being, and their sole test of worth, their capacity to regulate descriptions of individual cases. And the view that they are shorthand registers, or abstract descriptions, confirms instead of refuting this view. Why make a shorthand and unreal statement if it does not operate instrumentally in first-hand dealings with reality?

bringing into use all necessary precautions and all available resources which may insure the maximum probability of truth in the conclusion. The system of science (employing the term "science" to mean an organized intellectual content) is absolutely dependent for logical worth upon a moral interest: the sincere aim to judge truly. Remove such an interest, and the scientific system becomes a purely aesthetic object, which may awaken emotional response in virtue of its internal harmony and symmetry, but which has no logical import. If we suppose, once more, that it is a case of identification of typhoid fever, it is the professional, social, and scientific interests of the physician which lead him to take the trouble and pains to get all the data that bear upon the forming of judgment, and to consider with sufficient deliberateness as to bring to bear the necessary instrumentalities of interpretation. The intellectual contents get a logical function only through a specific motive which is outside of them barely as contents, but which is absolutely bound up with them in logical function.

If the use made of scientific resources, of technique of observation and experiment, of systems of classification, etc., in directing the act of judging (and thereby fixing the content of the judgment) depends upon the interest and disposition of the judger, we have only to make such dependence explicit, and the so-called scientific judgment appears definitely as a moral judgment. If the physician is careless and arbitrary because of overanxiety to get his work done, or if he lets his pecuniary needs influence his manner of judgment, we may say that he has failed both logically and morally. Scientifically he has not employed the methods at command for directing his act of judging so as to give it maximum correctness. But the ground for such logical failure lies in his own motive or disposition. The generic propositions or universals of science can take effect, in a word, only through the medium of the habits and impulsive tendencies of the one who judges. They have no *modus operandi* of their own.[7]

7. So far as I know, Mr. Charles S. Peirce was the first to call attention to this principle, and to insist upon its fundamental logical import (see *Monist*, Vol. II, pp. 534–36, 549–56). Mr.

The possibility of a distinctively moral quality attaching to an intellectual activity is due to the fact that there is no particular point at which one habit begins and others leave off. If a given habit could become entirely isolated and detached, we might have an act of judging dependent upon a purely intellectual technique, upon a habit of using specialized skill in dealing with certain matters, irrespective of any ethical qualifications. But the principle of the continuum is absolute. Not only through habit does a given psychical attitude expand into a particular case, but every habit in its own operation may directly or indirectly call up any other habit. The term "character" denotes this complex continuum of interactions in its office of influencing final judgment.

IV. *The Logical Character of Ethical Judgment*

We now recur to our original proposition: Scientific treatment of any subject means command of an apparatus which may be used to control the formation of judgments in all matters appertaining to that subject. We have done away with the *a priori* objection that the subject-matter to which recognized scientific judgments apply is so unlike that with which moral judgments are concerned that there is no common denominator. We are now free to revert to the original question: What are the differentiating logical conditions of a scientific treatment of conduct? Every sort of judgment has its own end to reach; and the instrumentalities (the categories and methods used) must vary as the end varies. If in general we conceive the logical nature of scientific technique, of formulae, universals, etc., to reside in their adaptation to guaranteeing the act of judging in accomplishing a purpose, we are thereby committed to the further proposition that the logical apparatus needed varies as the ends to be reached are

---

Peirce states it as the principle of continuity: A past idea can operate only so far as it is psychically continuous with that upon which it operates. A general idea is simply a living and expanding feeling, and habit is a statement of the specific mode of operation of a given psychical continuum. I have reached the above conclusion along such diverse lines that, without in any way minimizing the priority of Mr. Peirce's statement, or its more generalized logical character, I feel that my own statement has something of the value of an independent confirmation.

diverse. If, then, there is anything typically distinctive in the end which the act of ethical judging has to subserve, there must be equally distinctive features in the logic of its scientific treatment.

The question thus recurs to the characteristic differential features of the ethical judgment as such. These features readily present themselves if we return to those cases of scientific identification in which ethical considerations become explicit. There are cases, we saw, in which the nature of the identification—and its consequent truth or falsity—is *consciously* dependent upon the attitude or disposition of the judger. The term "consciously" differentiates a peculiar type of judgment. In all cases of individual judgment there is an act; and in all cases the act is an expression of motive, and thus of habit, and finally of the whole body of habit or character. But in many cases this implication of character remains a presupposition. It is not necessary to take notice of it. It is part of the practical conditions of making a judgment; but is no part of the logical conditions, and hence is not called upon to enter into a content—a conscious objectification in the judgment. To regard it as a practical instead of a logical condition means that while it is necessary to *any* judgment, the one act of judgment in question requires it no more than any other. It affects all *alike*; and this very impartiality of reference is equivalent to no reference at all as regards the truth or falsity of the particular judgment. Judging in such cases is controlled by reference to conditions of another quality than those of character; its presented data are judged in terms of objects of the same order or quality as themselves. Not only is there no conscious inclusion of motive and disposition within the content judged, but there is express holding off, inhibition, of all elements proceeding from the judger. From the standpoint of judgments of this type, such elements are regarded as logically merely subjective, and hence as disturbing factors with respect to the attainment of truth. It is no paradox to say that the activity of the agent in the act of judging expresses itself in effort to prevent its activity from having any influence upon the material judged. Accordingly through such judgments "external" objects are determined, the activity of the judger being kept absolutely neutral or indifferent as to its reference. The same idea is expressed by saying that the operation of motive and character may be presupposed, and hence left out of account, when they are so uniform in their exercise that they make no difference with respect to the *particular* object or content judged.

But whenever the implication of character, the operation of habit and motive, is recognized as a factor affecting the quality of the specific object judged, the logical aim makes it necessary to take notice of this fact by making the relationship an explicit element of content in the subject-matter undergoing judgment. When character is not an indifferent or neutral factor, when it qualitatively colors the meaning of the situation which the judger presents to himself, a characteristic feature is introduced into the very object judged; one which is not a mere refinement, homogeneous in kind with facts already given, but one which transforms their significance, because introducing into the very content judged the standard of valuation. In other words, character as a practical condition becomes *logical* when its influence is preferential in effect—when instead of being a uniform and impartial condition of any judgment it is, if left to itself (or unstated), a determinant of *this* content-value of judgment rather than that. Put from the other side, in the "intellectual" judgment, it makes no *difference* to character *what* object is judged, so be it the one judged is judged accurately; while in the moral judgment the nub of the matter is the difference which the determination of the content as this or that effects in character as a necessary condition of judging *qua* judging.

The conscious reference to disposition makes the object an active object, viz., a process defined by certain limits—given facts on one side and the same facts as transformed by agency of a given type on the other. The object judged is active, not "external," because it requires an act of judging, not merely as antecedent, but as a necessary element in its own structure. In judgments of the distinctively intellectual type, the assumption is that such activity as is necessary to effect certain combinations and distinctions will keep itself outside the material judged, retiring as soon as it has done its work in bringing together the elements that belong together and removing those that have no business. But in the ethical judgment the assumption is in the contrary sense; viz., that the situation is made what it is through the attitude which finds expression in the very act of judging. From the strictly logical standpoint (without reference, that is, to overtly moral considerations) the ethical judgment thus has a distinctive aim of its own: it is engaged with judging a subject-matter, a definitive element in whose determination is the attitude or disposition which leads to the act of judging.

It follows immediately that the aim of the ethical judgment may be stated as follows: Its purpose is to construct the act of judgment as itself a complex objective content. It goes back of the judging act as that is employed in distinctively intellectual processes, and makes its quality and nature (as distinct from its form—a question for psychology) an object of consideration. Just because character or disposition is involved in the material passed in review and organized in judgment, character is determined by the judgment. This is a fact of tremendous ethical significance; but here its import is not ethical, but logical. It shows that we are dealing, from the strictly logical point of view, with a characteristic type of judgment—that in which the conditions of judging activity are themselves to be objectively determined. The judger is engaged in judging himself; and thereby in so far is fixing the conditions of all further judgments of any type whatsoever. Put in more psychological terms, we may say the judgment realizes, through conscious deliberation and choice, a certain motive hitherto more or less vague and impulsive; or it expresses a habit in such a way as not merely to strengthen it practically, but as to bring to consciousness both its emotional worth and its significance in terms of certain kinds of consequences. But from the logical standpoint we say that the judger is consciously engaged in constructing as an object (and thereby giving objective form and reality to) the controlling condition of every exercise of judgment.

V. *The Categories of a Science of Ethics*

The ethical judgment is one which effects an absolutely reciprocal determination of the situation judged, and of the character or disposition which is expressed in the act of judging. Any particular moral judgment must necessarily reflect within itself all the characteristics which are essential to moral judgment *überhaupt*. No matter how striking or how unique the material of any particular ethical experience, it is at least an ethical experience; and as such its consideration or interpretation must conform to the conditions involved in the very act of judging. A judgment which institutes the reciprocal determination just described has its own characteristic structure or organization. The work that it has to do gives it certain limiting or defining elements and properties. These constitute the ultimate Terms or Categories of all ethical science. Moreover, since these terms are reflected in every moral experience that is in course of judgment, they do not remain formal or barren, but are instruments of analysis of any concrete situation that is subjected to scientific scrutiny.

The distinctively intellectual judgment, that of construing one object in terms of other similar objects, has necessarily its own inherent structure which supplies the ultimate categories of all physical science. Units of space, time, mass, energy, etc., define to us the limiting conditions under which judgments of this type do their work. Now, a type of judgment which determines a situation in terms of character, which is concerned with constructing what may be termed indifferently an active situation or a consciously active agency, has a like logical title to the standpoints and methods; the tools, which are necessary to its task. Ethical discussion is full of such terms: the natural and the spiritual, the sensuous and the ideal, the standard and the right, obligation and duty, freedom and responsibility, are samples. The discussion and use of these terms suffer, however, from a fundamental difficulty. The terms are generally taken as somehow given ready-made and hence as independent and isolated things. Then theory concerns itself, first, with debating as to whether the categories have validity or not; and, secondly, as to what their specific significance is. The discussion is arbitrary precisely because the categories are not taken as limiting terms; as constituent elements in a logical operation which, having its own task to perform, must have the means or tools necessary for its successful accomplishing. Consequently the primary condition of a scientific treatment of ethics is that the fundamental terms, the intellectual standpoints and instrumentalities, used, be discussed with reference to the position they occupy and the part they play in a judgment of a peculiar type, viz., one which brings about the reciprocal objective determination of an active situation and a psychical disposition.

When the categories receive the fate which is meted out to them in current discussion, when they are taken up in accidental because isolated ways, there is no method of controlling formation of judgment regarding them. Consequently other judgments which depend upon their use are in an increasing measure uncontrolled. The very tools which are necessary in order that more specific judgments may work economically and effectively are only vaguely known as to their own structure and modes of operation. Naturally they are bungled in employ. Because categories are discussed as if they had some ready-made independent meaning, each of its own, there is no check upon the meaning which is assigned to any one of them, and no recognized standard for judging the validity of any. Only reference to a situation within which the categories emerge and function can furnish the basis for estimation of their value and import. Otherwise the definition of ultimate ethical terms is left to argumentation based upon opinion, an opinion which snatches at some of the more obvious features of the situation (and thereby may always possess some measure of truth), and which, failing to grasp the situation as a whole, fails to grasp the exact significance of its characteristic terms. Discussion, for instance, about what constitutes the ethical standard— whether conduciveness to happiness, or approximation to perfection of being—must be relatively futile, until there is some method of determining by reference to the logical necessity of the case what *anything* must be and mean in order to be a standard at all. We lack a definition of standard in terms of the essential conditions of the ethical judgment and situation. Such a definition of standard would not indeed give us an off-hand view of the make-up of moral value such as might be utilized for forming moral precepts, but it will

set before us certain conditions which any candidate for the
office of moral standard must be capable of fulfilling; and
will thereby serve as an instrument in criticising the various
claimants for the position of standard, whether these offer
themselves in generic theory or in the affairs of concrete
conduct. Similarly, theorists have been attempting to tell
what the ideal of man is, what is *summum bonum*, what is
man's duty, what are his responsibilities, to prove that he is
possessed or not possessed of freedom, without any regulated
way of defining the content of the terms "ideal," "good,"
"duty," etc. If these terms have any verifiable proper meaning of their own, it is as limiting traits of that type of judgment which institutes the reciprocal identification of psychical attitude in judging and subject-matter judged. An
analysis of the make-up of judgment of this type must reveal
all the distinctions which have claim to the title of fundamental ethical categories. Whatever element of meaning reveals itself as a constituent part of such a judgment has all
the claim to validity which moral experience itself possesses;
a term which is not exhibited within such an analysis has no
title to validity. The differential meaning of any one of the
terms is dependent upon the particular part it plays in the
development and termination of judgments of this sort.

VI. *Psychological Analysis As a Condition of Controlling Ethical Judgments*

If it be true that a moral judgment is one in which the
content finally affirmed is affected at every point by the disposition of the judger (since he interprets the situation that
confronts him in terms of his own attitude), it follows at
once that one portion of the generic theory necessary for adequate control of individual moral judgments will consist
in an objective analysis of disposition as affecting action
through the medium of judgment. Everyone knows, as simple matter of fact, that a large part of existing treatises on
morals are filled with discussions concerning desirable and
undesirable traits of character—virtues and vices; with conscience as a function of character; with discussions of inten-

tion, motive, choice, as expressions of, and as ways of forming, character. Moreover, a concrete discussion of freedom,
responsibility, etc., is carried on as a problem of the relationship of character to the media of action. The reciprocal determination, already set forth, of character and the content
judged shows that such discussions are not mere practical
desiderata, nor yet a mere clearing up of incidental points,
but integral portions of any adequate ethical theory.

If character or disposition reflects itself at every point
in the constitution of the content finally set forth in judgment, it is clear that control of such judgment depends upon
ability to state, in universalized form, the related elements
constituting character an objective fact.[8] Our particular judgments regarding physical things are controlled only in so far
as we have, independent of and prior to any particular emergency in experience, a knowledge of certain conditions to be
observed in judging every physical object as physical. It is
through reference to such laws, or statements of connected
conditions, that we get the impartiality or objectivity which
enables us to judge in a particular crisis unswerved by purely
immediate considerations. We get away from the coercive
immediacy of the experience, and into a position to look at it
clearly and thoroughly. Since character is a fact entering
into any moral judgment passed, ability of control depends
upon our power to state character in terms of generic relation of conditions, which conditions are detachable from the
pressure of circumstance in the particular case. Psychological
analysis is the instrument by which character is transformed
from its absorption in the values of immediate experience
into an objective, scientific, fact. It is indeed a statement of
experience in terms of its modes of control of its own
evolving.

Even popular consciousness is aware of many ways in
which psychical dispositions modify judgment in a moral

8. Of course, the terms "object" and "objective" are used in a
logical sense, not as equivalent to "physical," which denotes
simply one form which the logical object may take. Dr. Stuart's
article on "Valuation as a Logical Process" in Studies in Logical
Theory (The University of Chicago Press, 1903) may be referred
to for a discussion of the study of the logical significance of the
term "object" and its bearing upon the objectivity of economic
and ethical judgments.

sense; and is accustomed to take advantage of its knowledge to regulate moral judgments. A score of proverbs could be collected expressing ways in which psychological attitudes affect moral valuation. The ideas in such statements as the following are commonplaces to the plain man: Habit, wont, and use dull the power of observation; passion blinds and confuses the power of reflection; self-interest makes the judger alert to certain aspects of the situation judged; impulse hurries the mind on uncritically to a conclusion; ends, ideals, arouse, when contemplated, emotions that tend to fill consciousness, and which, as they swell, first restrict and then eliminate power of judgment. Such statements, which might be indefinitely increased, are not only popularly known, but are commonly used in formation of a kind of hygiene of moral action.

Psychology proper differs from the aggregate of such statements through setting forth *how* various dispositions operate in bringing about the effects attributed to them. Just what are the various distinguishable psychical attitudes and tendencies? How do they hang together? How does one call forth or preclude another? We need an inventory of the different characteristic dispositions; and an account of how each is connected, both in the way of stimulation and inhibition, with every other. Psychological analysis answers this need. While it can answer this need only through development of scientific constructs which present themselves in experience only as results of the psychological examination, yet it is true that the typical attitudes and dispositions are familiar as functions of everyday experience. It is equally true that even the most atomic psychology employs generalized statements about the ways in which certain "states of consciousness" or elements (the constructs referred to) regularly introduce certain other "states." The theory of association is, indeed, just a generalization concerning an objective sequence of elements which reflects to the psychologist the sequence of attitudes or dispositions which are found in the immediate course of experience. In particular the sensationalists not only admit but claim that the association of other states of consciousness with states of pleasure and pain have uniform tendencies which may be reduced to universal propositions; and which may be employed to formulate principles exhibited in all conduct. If such is the case with psychological atomism, every step toward recognition of a more organized, or inherently complex, mental structure multiplies the number and range of possible propositions relating to connection of conditions among psychic states—statements which, if true at all, have exactly the same logical validity that is possessed by any "physical law." And in so far as these "states" are symbols of the attitudes and habits which operate in our immediate experience, every such proposition is at once translatable into one regarding the way in which character is constituted—just the type of generic statement required by a scientific ethics.

Psychology of course does not aim at reinstating the immediate experience of the individual; nor does it aim at describing that experience in its immediate values, whether aesthetic, social, or ethical. It reduces the immediate experience to a series of dispositions, attitudes, or states which are taken as either conditions or signatures of life-experience. It is not the full experience-of-seeing-a-tree it is concerned with, but the experience reduced by abstraction to an attitude or state of perception; it is not the concrete getting angry, with all its personal and social implications, but anger as one species of a generic psychic disposition known as emotion. It is not concerned with a concrete judgment as such —to say nothing of moral judgment. But psychological analysis finds in experience the typical attitudes it deals with, and only abstracts them so that they may be objectively stated.

Every statement of moral theory which purports to relate to our moral consciousness sets forth relations whose truth must ultimately be tested through psychological analysis—just as every judgment regarding a specific physical phenomenon must finally satisfy certain generic conditions of physical reality set forth in physical analysis.

Psychological analysis does not, for example, set before us an end or ideal actually experienced, whether moral or otherwise. It does not purport to tell us *what* the end or ideal is. But psychological analysis shows us just what forming and entertaining an end means. Psychological analysis ab-

stracts from the concrete make-up of an end, as that is found
as matter of direct experience, and because of (not in spite
of) that abstraction sets before us having-an-end in terms of
its conditions and its effects, that is, in terms of taking other
characteristic attitudes which are present in other experiences.

Hence purely psychologic propositions are indispensable
to any concrete moral theory. The logical analysis of the
process of moral judgment, setting forth its inherent organization or structure with reference to the peculiar logical
function it has to accomplish, furnishes the categories or
limiting terms of ethical science, and supplies their formal
meaning, their definition. But the logical category, say, of
end or ideal becomes concrete only as some individual has
actually experience of and with ends—and this involves the
act or attitude of forming and entertaining them. So the
category of standard becomes more than a possible intellectual tool only as some individual actually engages in an experience concerned with right and wrong, and which, when
viewed objectively, is regarded as a judgment. The entertaining of ends, the adjudging of values—such acts are
character-phenomena. Considered in abstraction from their
immediate matter in experience, viz., just as acts, states, or
dispositions, they are character-phenomena as these present
themselves to psychological analysis. Even to consider any
experience, or any phase of an experience, an ideal is to
reflect upon that experience; it is to abstract and to classify.
It involves passing judgment *upon* an experience; something
beyond the concrete experiencing. It is, as far as it goes,
psychological analysis—that is, it is a process of exactly the
same order and implying just the same distinctions and
terms as are found in psychological science. But the latter,
in making abstraction and classification conscious processes,
enables us to control them, instead of merely indulging in
them.

Hence it is futile to insist that psychology cannot "give"
the moral ideal, and that consequently there must be recourse
to transcendental considerations—to metaphysics. Metaphysics, in the sense of a logical analysis of that type of judgment
which determines the agent and the content of judgment in

complete reciprocity to each other, may "give" the ideal—
that is, it may show how the form or category of ideal is a
constitutive element in this type of judgment, and hence
has whatever of validity attaches to this mode of judging.
But such a logical analysis is far from transcendental metaphysics; and in any case we thus obtain only the category of
ideal as a standpoint or terminus of a *possible* moral judgment. There is no question here of ideal as immediately
experienced. Only living, not metaphysics any more than
psychology, can "give" an ideal in this sense. But when
ethical theory makes statements regarding the importance
of ideals for character and conduct, when it lays stress upon
the significance of this, rather than that, kind of ideal, it is
engaged in setting forth universal relations of conditions;
and there is absolutely no way of testing the validity of such
statements with respect to their claim of generality or objectivity save by an analysis of psychic dispositions which
shows what is ˌmeant by having-an-ideal in terms of its
antecedents and consequences. If any general statement
whatsoever can be made about ideals, it is because the
psychic attitude corresponding to conceiving an ideal can be
abstracted, and placed in a certain connection with attitudes
which represent abstracts of other experiences. To have an
ideal, to form and entertain one, must be a fact, or else
ideals are absolute non-existence and non-sense. To discuss
what it is to have an ideal is to engage in psychological
analysis. If the having-an-ideal can be stated in terms of
sequence with other similar attitudes, then we have a psychological generic statement (or law) which can be employed
as a tool of analysis in reflecting upon concrete moral experiences, just as the "law" of falling bodies is of use in
controlling our judgment of pile-drivers, the trajectory of
shells, etc. The possibility of *generalized propositions* regarding any character-phenomenon stands and falls with the
possibility of psychological analysis revealing regular association or coordination of certain tendencies, habits, or dispositions with one another. Hence the continued reiteration
that psychology as a natural science deals only with facts,
while ethics is concerned with values, norms, ideals which
ought to be whether they exist or no, is either aside from

the point, or else proves the impossibility of making any general statements, metaphysical as well as practical and scientific, about such matters.

VII. *Sociological Analysis As a Condition of Controlling Ethical Judgments*

We revert once more to our fundamental consideration: the reciprocal determination in moral judgment of the act of judging and the content judged. As we have just seen, adequate control of an act as determining a content involves the possibility of making character an object of scientific analysis—of stating it as a system of related conditions or an object complete in itself—a universal. We have now to recognize the converse, viz., that we can control the judgment of the act, hence of character as expressed in act, only as we have a method of analyzing the *content* in itself—that is, in abstraction from its bearings upon action.

The ethical problem needs to be approached from the point of view of the act as modifying the content, and of the content as modifying the act; so that, on one hand, we require, prior to a particular moral crisis, a statement in universal terms of the mechanism of the attitudes and dispositions which determine judgment about action; while, on the other hand, we need a similar prior analysis and classification of the situations which call forth such judgment. Which portion of the scientific apparatus we bring most prominently into play in any given case depends upon the circumstances of that case as influencing the probable source of error. If the situation or scene of action (by which we mean the conditions which provoke or stimulate the act of moral judging) is fairly familiar, we may assume that the source of error in judgment lies in the disposition which is back of the experience—that if we can only secure the right motive on the part of the judger, the judgment itself will be correct. In other cases circumstances are reversed. We can fairly presuppose or take for granted a right attitude on the part of the judger; the problematic factor has to do with the interpretation of the situation. In this case what is needed for right judgment is a satisfactory knowledge of the "facts of the case." Given that, the existing motive will take care of the rest. It is this latter aspect of the matter that we now have to discuss.

The only way in which the agent can judge himself as an agent, and thereby control his act—that is, conceive of himself as the one who is to do a certain thing—is by finding out the situation which puts upon him the necessity of judging it in order that he may decide upon a certain course of action. As soon as a conclusion is reached as to the nature of the scene of action, a conclusion is also reached as to what the agent is to do, and this decides in turn what sort of an agent he is to be. The merely intellectual judgment may be marked off as one in which a content or object is fixed in terms of some other object or content, homogeneous in worth, and where accordingly it is a necessary part of the procedure to suppress participation in judging of traits which proceed from, or refer to, the disposition of the judger. But judgments which are ethical (not merely intellectual) make no such abstraction. They expressly and positively include the participation of the judger in the content judged, and of the object judged in the determination of the judger. In other words, the object judged or situation constructed in moral judgment is not an external object, cold, remote, and indifferent, but is most uniquely, intimately, and completely the agent's own object, or is the agent *as object*.

Such being the case, what is required in order to form such a judgment of the scene or conditions of action as will facilitate the most adequate possible construing of the agent? I reply: A social science which will analyze a content as a combination of elements in the same way that psychological analysis determines an act as a set of attitudes. It is assumed that the situation which calls forth distinctively moral judgment is a social situation, which accordingly can be adequately described only through methods of sociological analysis. I am aware that (even admitting the necessity of some sort of scientific interpretation of the scene of action) it is something of a jump to say that such science must be sociological in character. The logical gap could be covered only by carrying the discussion of the categories of moral

judgment to the point where their social value would explicitly show itself. Such analysis is apart from my present
purpose. Here I need only recur to the proposition of the
reciprocal determination, in the ethical judgment, of the
judger and the content judged, and suggest that this idea
requires in its logical development the conclusion that, since
the judger is personal, the content judged must ultimately
be personal too—so that the moral judgment really institutes
a relationship between persons, relationship between persons
being what we mean by "social."

But in any case, some way of getting an objective statement of the situation, a statement in terms of connection of
conditions, is necessary. Certain descriptive sciences are
necessary and in many cases no one would deny that elements of associated life enter into the facts to be described.
But even if it be admitted that the scene is social, this
characterization does not exhaust the description. Any scene
of action which is social is *also* cosmic or physical. It is also
biological. Hence the absolute impossibility of ruling out the
physical and biological sciences from bearing upon ethical
science. If ethical theory require, as one of its necessary conditions, ability to describe in terms of itself the situation
which demands moral judgment, any proposition, whether
of mechanics, chemistry, geography, physiology, or history,
which facilitates and guarantees the adequacy and truth of
the description, becomes in virtue of that fact an important
auxiliary of ethical science.

In other words, the postulate of moral science is the
continuity of scientific judgment. This proposition is denied
by both the materialistic and transcendental schools of
metaphysics. The transcendental school draws such a fixed
line between the region of moral and of cosmic values that
by no possibility can propositions which refer to the latter
become auxiliary or instrumental with respect to the former.
The fact that advance of physical and biological science so
profoundly modifies moral problems, and hence moral judgments, and hence once more moral values, may serve as an
argument against transcendental ethics—since, according to
the latter, such obvious facts would be impossibilities.
Materialism denies equally the principle of continuity of

judgment. It confuses continuity of method, the possibility of using a general statement regarding one object as a tool in the determination of some other, with immediate identity of subject-matter. Instead of recognizing the *continuity* of ethical with other forms of experience, it wipes out ethical experience by assimilating it not simply with reference to logical method, but in its own ontological structure, to another form of objects defined in judgment—that is, the physical form. If it is once recognized that *all* scientific judgments, physical as well as ethical, are ultimately concerned with getting experience stated in objective (that is, universal) terms for the sake of the direction of further experience, there will, on the one hand, be no hesitation in using any sort of statement that can be of use in the formation of other judgments, whatever be their topic or reference; and, on the other hand, there will be no thought of trying to explain away the *distinctive* traits of any type of experience. Since conscious life is continuous, the possibility of using any one mode of experience to assist in the formation of any other is the ultimate postulate of *all* science—non-ethical and ethical alike. And this possibility of use, of application, of instrumental service, makes it possible and necessary to employ materialistic science in the construction of ethical theory, and also protects in this application ethical values from deterioration and dissolution.

In conclusion, it may avoid misapprehension if I say that the considerations set forth in this paper do not involve any pedantic assumption regarding the necessity of using science, or logical control, in any particular instance of moral experience. The larger part, infinitely the larger part, of our concrete contact with physical nature takes place without conscious reference to the methods, or even the results, of physical science. Yet no one questions the fundamental importance of physical science. This importance discovers itself in two ways:

First, when we come to peculiarly difficult problems (whether of interpretation or of inventive construction), physical science puts us in possession of tools of conscious analysis and of synthesis. It enables us to economize our time and effort, and to proceed with the maximum probability of success to solution of the problem which confronts us. This use is conscious and deliberate. It involves the critical application of the technique and already established conclusions of science to cases of such complexity and perplexity that they would remain unsolved and undealt with, were it not for scientific resources.

In the second place, physical science has a wide sphere of application which involves no conscious reference whatsoever. Previous scientific methods and investigations have taken effect in our own mental habits and in the material dealt with. Our unconscious ways of apprehending, of interpreting, of deliberating, are saturated with products of prior conscious critical science. We thus get the benefit, in our intellectual commerce with particular situations, of scientific operations which we have forgotten, and even of those which we individually have never performed. Science has become incarnate in our immediate attitude toward the world about us, and is embodied in that world itself. Every time that we solve a difficulty by sending a telegram, crossing a bridge, lighting the gas, boarding a railroad train, consulting a thermometer, we are controlling the formation of a judgment by use of so much precipitated and condensed science. Science has pre-formed, in many of its features, the situation with reference to which we have to judge; and it is this objective delimitation and structural reinforcement which, answering at every point to the conformation of habit, most assists intelligence in the details of its behavior.

There is every reason to suppose that the analogy holds with reference to a science of conduct. Such a science can be built up only through reference to cases which at the outset need conscious critical direction in judgment. We need to know what the social situation is in which we find ourselves required to act, so that we may know what it is right to do. We need to know what is the effect of some psychical disposition upon our way of looking at life and thereby upon our conduct. Through clearing up the social situation, through making objective to ourselves our own motives and their consequences, we build up generic propositions: statements of experience as a connection of conditions, that is, in the form of objects. Such statements are

used and applied in dealing with further problems. Gradually
their use becomes more and more habitual. The "theory"
becomes a part of our psychical apparatus. The social situation takes on a certain form or organization. It is pre-
classified as of a certain sort, as of a certain genus and even
species of this sort; the only question which remains is
discrimination of the particular variety. Again, we get into
the habit of taking into account certain sources of error in
our own disposition as these affect our judgments of behavior, and thereby bring them sufficiently under control so
that the need of conscious reference to their intellectual
formulation diminishes. As physical science has brought
about an organization of the physical world along with an
organization of practical habits of dealing with that world,
so ethical science will effect an organization of the social
world and a corresponding organization of the psychical
habits through which the individual relates himself to it.
With this clearing up of the field and organs of moral action,
conscious recourse to theory will, as in physical cases, limit
itself to problems of unusual perplexity and to constructions
of a large degree of novelty.

Summary

1. By "scientific" is meant methods of control of formation of judgments.

2. Such control is obtained only by ability to abstract
certain elements in the experience judged, and to state them
as connections of conditions, *i.e.*, as "objects," or universals.

3. Such statements constitute the bulk of the recognized
sciences. They are generic propositions, or laws, put, as a
rule, in the hypothetic form if M, then N. But such generic
propositions are the instruments of science, not science itself.
Science has its life in judgments of identification, and it is
for their sake that generic propositions (or universals, or
laws) are constructed and tested or verified.

4. Such judgments of concrete identification are individualized, and are also acts. The presence of action as a
logical element appears indirectly in (a) the selection of the

subject, (b) the determination of the predicate, and (c) most directly in the copula—the entire process of the reciprocal forming and testing of tentative subjects and predicates.

5. Judgments are "intellectual" in logical type so far as this reference to activity may be presupposed, and thereby not require to be consciously set forth or exposed. This happens whenever the action involved is impartial in its influence upon the quality of the content judged. Judgments are "moral" in logical type so far as the presence of activity in affecting the content of judgment is seen consciously to affect itself—or whenever the reciprocal determination of activity and content becomes itself an object of judgment whose determination is a prerequisite for further successful judgments.

6. Control of moral judgment requires ability to constitute the reciprocal determination of activity and content into an object. This has three phases: First, a statement of the limiting forms of that type of judgment which is concerned with construing an activity and a content in terms of each other. The limiting terms of such a type of judgment constitute the characteristic features, or categories, of the object of ethical science, just as the limiting terms of the judgment which construes one object in terms of another object constitute the categories of physical science. A discussion of moral judgment from this point of view may be termed "The Logic of Conduct." Second, an abstraction of the activity, which views it as a system of attitudes or dispositions involved in having experiences, and states it (since a system) as an object constituted by definite connections of diverse attitudes with the attitude of judging—viz., the science of psychology. Third, a similar abstraction of the "content," which views it as a system of social elements which form the scene or situation in which action is to occur, and with reference to which, therefore, the actor is to be formed—viz., sociological science.

7. The whole discussion implies that the determination of objects as objects, even when involving no conscious reference whatever to conduct, is, after all, for the sake of the development of further experience. This further development is change, transformation of existing experience, and

thus is *active*. So far as this development is intentionally directed through the construction of objects as objects, there is not only active experience, but *regulated activity, i.e.*, conduct, behavior, practice. Therefore, all determination of objects as objects (including the sciences which construct physical objects) has reference to change of experience, or experience as activity; and, when this reference passes from abstraction to application (from negative to positive), has reference to conscious control of the nature of the change (*i.e.*, conscious change), and thereby gets ethical significance. This principle may be termed *the postulate of continuity of experience.* This principle on the one hand protects the integrity of the moral judgment, revealing its supremacy and the corresponding instrumental or auxiliary character of the intellectual judgment (whether physical, psychological, or social); and, upon the other, protects the moral judgment from isolation (*i.e.*, from transcendentalism), bringing it into working relations of reciprocal assistance with all judgments about the subject-matter of experience, even those of the most markedly mechanical and physiological sort.

ETHICS

Ethics (from Gr. ἠθικά, having to do with conduct, from ἦθος, character, lengthened form of ἔθος, custom, manners; *cf.* morals, from Latin, *mos, mores*, customs), that branch of the theory of conduct which is concerned with the formation and use of judgments of right and wrong, and with intellectual, emotional, and executive, or overt, phenomena, which are associated with such judgments, either as antecedents or consequents. As a branch of the theory of conduct, it is generically akin to the sciences of jurisprudence, politics and economics; but it is marked off from such sciences in that it considers the common subject-matter of human conduct from the standpoint of rightness and wrongness. Such terms as good and evil, the dutiful or obligatory, might be used in the definition as substitutes for the terms "right" and "wrong," but good and evil are somewhat too wide in scope, including, for instance, economic utilities, commodities and satisfactions; while duty is somewhat too narrow an idea, emphasizing the notion of control at the expense of the idea of the good and desirable. "Right" and "wrong" designate exactly those phases of good and evil to which the idea of the obligatory is also applicable. The terms moral philosophy, moral science, and morals have also been used to designate the same subject of inquiry.

In its historical development, ethics has been regarded as a branch of philosophy, as a science, and as an art—often as a composite of two or all of these in varying proportions. As a branch of philosophy, it is the business of ethics to investigate the nature and reality of certain conceptions in connection with fundamental theories of the universe. It is the theory of reality in its moral aspect. The term good is taken to denote or describe a property of ultimate and abso-

[First published in *Encyclopedia Americana* (New York: Scientific American, 1904).]

lute being. As such, it is usually coordinated with two other fundamental properties of reality, the true and the beautiful; and the three philosophic disciplines are defined as ethics, logic, and aesthetics. Even when so much emphasis is not thrown upon the place of the good in the general scheme of the universe, ethics may still be regarded as a branch of philosophy, because concerned with the ideal, with what ought to be, or with what is absolutely desirable, as distinct from the actual, the existent, the phenomenal. From this point of view, ethics is regarded as *normative* in character, that is, concerned with establishing and justifying certain ultimate norms, standards, and rules of action.

In contrast with such functions, ethics as a science is concerned with collecting, describing, explaining and classifying the facts of experience in which judgments of right and wrong are actually embodied or to which they apply. It is subdivided into social, or sociological, ethics, and individual, or psychological, ethics. (*a*) The former deals with the habits, practices, ideas, beliefs, expectations, institutions, etc., actually found in history or in contemporary life, in different races, peoples, grades of culture, etc., which are outgrowths of judgments of the moral worth of actions or which operate as causes in developing such judgments. Up to the present, social ethics has been developed mainly in connection, (1) with discussion of the evolution of morality, either by itself or in connection with institutions of law and judicial procedure, or of religious cult and rite; or (2) with problems of contemporary social life, particularly with questions of philanthropy, penology, legislation, regarding divorce, the family and industrial reform—such as child-labor, etc. In both aspects it is closely connected with the science of sociology. It is sometimes called inductive, or in its second aspect, applied ethics. (*b*) Psychological ethics is concerned with tracing in the individual the origin and growth of the moral consciousness, that is, of judgments of right and wrong, feelings of obligation, emotions of remorse, shame, of desire for approbation; of the various habits of action which are in accord with the judgment of right, or the virtues; with the possibility and nature, from the standpoint of the psychical structure of the individual, of free, or voluntary, action. It gathers and organizes psychological data bearing upon the nature of intention, and motive; desire, effort and choice; judgments of approbation and disapprobation; emotions of sympathy, pity in relation to the impulse of self-preservation and the formation and reformation of habit in its effect upon character, etc. In other words, it treats behavior as an expression of certain psychical elements and groupings, or associations: psychological analysis.

Ethics as an art is concerned with discovering and formulating rules of acting in accordance with which men may attain their end. These rules may be considered as of the nature either of injunctions or commands, which prescribe as well as instruct; or as technical formulae which indicate to the individual the best way of proceeding toward a desired result, thus not different in kind from rules of painting, or of carpentry. Which view is taken depends usually upon the kind of philosophy with which ethics as an art is associated. Ethics as an art may also be an outgrowth of either a general philosophy of conduct, or of a scientific analysis of it. Thus, from the philosophic point of view, a recent writer, Sorley, in the *Dictionary of Philosophy and Psychology* (Vol. I, p. 346, 1901), says of ethics: "It has to do not merely with actual conduct, but with right or good conduct, and accordingly with an ideal from which rules may be laid down for actual conduct." It is clear that the philosophical establishment of the ideal is considered to terminate in rules for its attainment. On the other hand, Jeremy Bentham in his *Principles of Legislation* (1789), having before insisted that ethics is a science whose truths are to be discovered "only by investigations as severe as mathematical ones, and beyond all comparison more intricate and extensive," goes on to define ethics "as the art of directing men's actions to the production of the greatest possible quantity of happiness," and says it is the business of private ethics "*to instruct* each individual in what manner to govern his own conduct in the details of life." Thus as an art ethics may be grounded upon either a philosophy or a science.

As may readily be inferred from the above account, some of the most serious problems of ethics at present are concerned with defining and delimiting its own scope, basis and aims. From a purely abstract point of view, all three conceptions can exist harmoniously side by side. It is possible theoretically to regard certain topics as assigned to ethics as a branch of philosophy, others to its scientific phase, and others to the practical, or to ethics as an art. But no consensus as to these various possible assignments exists. Usually those who insist that ethics is a branch of philosophy deny that it can be anything else; they deny that any descriptive and explanatory account of *actual*, as distinct from ideal, conduct, deserves the name of ethics. What we have above treated as belonging to the science of ethics is by them treated as really a matter of history, sociology and psychology, not of ethics proper at all. Thus Green, *Prolegomena to Ethics* (1883), begins by attempting to prove that a natural science of ethics is inherently impossible, because moral conduct by its nature implies an ideal that transcends actual conduct which alone can be made a matter of observation and experiment, and sets up an obligation which in its absoluteness transcends all the sanctions of experience. On the other hand, those who have occupied themselves with the scientific analysis of moral behavior and character, have usually denied the legitimacy of the philosophic aspect. Thus Bentham expressly regards all philosophical inquiries as doomed to result in sterility, in mere dogmatic personal assertions, or, as he calls them, *"ipse dixits."* A more recent writer, Leslie Stephen, *Science of Ethics* (1882), without absolutely denying the possibility in the remote future of a metaphysics of conduct, says that the metaphysical view is entirely irrelevant to a scientific treatment. Along with this uncertainty as to the defining aim and characteristic methods of ethics, are naturally found a large number of subordinate and secondary controversies and divisions of opinion.

As a matter of fact, however, in every historical period there have been found in ethical theories some connection with general philosophic thought, and with the data of behavior exhibited in experience (or the scientific aspect) and with the further direction and conduct of life—the practical aspect. Historically, ethics has passed through three epochs: (1) the Graeco-Roman; (2) the Patristic-Mediaeval; (3) the

Early Modern; terminating with say the French Revolution, and may now be regarded as having entered upon a fourth stage. In each period, a certain practical interest is uppermost in social life, and this interest serves to concentrate and direct attention toward certain relevant theoretic problems. An adequate account of ethical thought accordingly is possible only in connection with the larger civilization and culture of which it is a part. Brief characterizations of the main problem of each epoch in its wider social tendencies will serve, however, to point out (*a*) the philosophic, (*b*) the scientific, (*c*) the practical centre of ethics in each period.

The Graeco-Roman period was characterized by the disintegration of local custom, tradition and institution, civil and religious, coincident with the spread of cosmopolitan learning and the formation of an inclusive political organization taking effect in both legislation and administration—Greek culture and the Roman empire. With the disintegration of the habits and modes of life which had previously defined the sphere of legitimate individual satisfaction, and which supplied the sanctions of the moral life, there was necessarily coincident an inquiry which attempted to establish through reflection adequate substitutes for the waning institutional modes of control. One of the results of modern historical science is the proof of the extent and stringency of the force of custom in early life. It is custom which defines the morally right and obligatory, and it is custom which enforces its own demands. In it are bound together morals, law, and religion, and all are bound into the very life of the people, emotional and intellectual, as well as practical. Where custom rules, moral theory is unnecessary and indeed impossible. In the 6th and 5th centuries before Christ, this régime of custom was irretrievably shaken in the Greek world, and with a twofold result upon morals. Many thought that all sanctions for morality had disappeared, or at least lost validity, and that pure individualism in thought and conduct—tempered at best only by some judicious regard to consequences—was the proper outcome. Others, prevented by what they regarded as the low moral standards of customary morality from coming to its defense, were also shocked by the demoralization attendant upon ethical individualism, and set to work to dis-

cover a universal and unassailable basis for a higher type of
ideal morality. In this conflict, ethical theory was born.

   The Graeco-Roman Period (6th century B.C. to 5th century A.D.)—The controversy originated in a discussion as to
whether morality exists by convention ($\nu\acute{o}\mu\omega$), by arbitrary
enactment ($\theta\acute{\epsilon}\sigma\epsilon\iota$), or in reality, that is (in the terminology
of the time), "by nature," ($\theta\acute{v}\sigma\epsilon\iota$), or in the nature of things.
Some of the Sophists taught that morality was a creature of
the efforts of the rulers of a community, being a device on
their part to keep others in subjection for the better indulgence of their own desires—much as many of the "free-
thinkers" of the 18th century (in many respects the modern
congeners of the Sophists) taught that religion was an invention of state-craft and priest-craft. Others taught that it
was a product of social agreement or institution. Some of
the nobler Sophists (like Protagoras, see the Platonic dialogue
of the same name) interpreted this as praise of the state of
civilization and culture as against the raw, crude state of
nature; while others taught that it was merely a conventional
means to personal satisfaction, and hence had no binding
force when short-cuts to happiness were available. In the
meantime, the actual moral discipline of the Greek city-state
was much relaxed, partly because of the interminable dis-
sensions of party strife, and partly because the religious
beliefs which were the foundation of civic life were fast
becoming incredible. Socrates (about 470 B.C.–399 B.C.) was
apparently the first to undertake a positive and constructive
analysis of moral ideas. He made the following contributions:
(1) All things have to be considered with reference to their
end, which indeed constitutes their real "nature"; the end of
each thing is its good. Man must therefore have his own
end, or good; this is real and inherent, not conventional nor
the product of law. (2) To know is to grasp the essential,
real being of a thing—its "nature," or end; "know thyself" is
the essence of morality; it means that man must base his
activity upon comprehension of the true end of his own
being. All evil is really involuntary, based on ignorance, or
misconception of man's true good. To be ignorant of the good
is the one disgrace. If a man does not know it—and Socrates
professed that he did not—he can at least devote himself

seriously to inquiring, to the effort to learn. If not wise (a sophist) he can at least be a lover of wisdom (a philosopher). And until he attains knowledge, the individual will be loyal to the responsibilities of his own civic life.

The two conceptions of the good as somehow the fulfilment of man's true nature or reality, and as attainable only under conditions of rational insight are the bases of all later Greek thought. Opinions differed to what man's end is, and as to the character of true knowledge of it. The extreme division was between the Cynic school, the forerunner of the Stoics, founded by Antisthenes (about 444 B.C.–369 B.C.), and the Cyrenaic (the precursor of Epicureanism), founded by Aristippus (about 435 B.C.–360 B.C.). The former taught that virtue, manifested in temperance or self-control, is the one and only good, pleasure as an end being evil, and that it is known by pure reason. The latter taught that pleasure, known only in feeling (the sensation of a gentle and continuous change), is the good. The wise man of Socrates is he who knows this moderate and enduring pleasure and is not captured by sudden and violent passion. Both schools take a somewhat antagonistic attitude toward the state; the Cynic emphasizing the superiority of the sage to government and authority, well illustrated in the anecdotes of Diogenes and Alexander the Great; the Cyrenaic holding that the pleasures of friendship and social companionship of the congenial are superior to those of participation in public life. These schools thus set two of the fundamental problems of subsequent ethical theory, namely, the nature of the good, and the nature of knowledge of it; and supplied the framework of later schools of thought. Those who hold that pleasure is the good are termed Hedonists (Gr. ἡδονή, pleasure), those who held to its residence in the virtuous will Perfectionists, or (with certain qualifications added) Rigorists. Those who hold that it is known through reason are Intuitionalists, the other school, Sensationalists or Empiricists.

Plato (q.v.) (about 427 B.C.–347 B.C.) attempted a synthesis of the conceptions of the two schools just referred to, with a constructive program of social, political and educational reform, and with a reinterpretation of earlier philosophic theories of the universe and of knowledge. His most characteristic doctrines are (1) the generalization of the Socratic conception of the good as constituting the true essence or nature of man. Under the influence of philosophic concepts derived from a variety of sources, Plato conceived man as essentially a microcosm; as the universe in miniature. He is composed of a certain arrangement of the elements of reality itself; hence he can be truly known only as the real nature of the universal reality which constitutes him is known; his good is ultimately one with the final cause or good of the universe. Thus Plato goes even farther than Socrates in asserting that morality is by nature—it is by the nature not only of man but of absolute reality itself, which is thus given an ethical or spiritual interpretation. Thus he grounded ethics on general philosophic conceptions and has been the model for all since who have distinctly conceived ethics to be a branch of philosophy. Moreover, since he regards the ultimate good of the universe as one with God and as the animating purpose in the creation of physical nature, he brings ethics into connection with religion, and with man's relations to the world about him. (2) Plato regarded the state in its true or ideal form as the best embodiment or expression of the essential nature of individual man; as indeed more truly man than any one individual. In its true organization, it reflects or images the constitution of the ultimate good. Thus Plato brings ethics back into connection with politics as the theory of ideal social organization. Practically, he delineates this state in outline (especially in his *Republic*, and, with greater attention to feasible detail in his *Laws*), and proposes in view of this ideal a specific reform of the existing order, instead of disregard of it as with Cynic and Cyrenaic. (3) He sets forth a scheme of the good as realizable in human nature, which endeavors to combine the one-sided extremes of mere pleasure, and mere virtue. He conceives the good to be the fulfilment of all capacities, faculties or functions of human nature, the fulfilment of each power being accompanied with its own appropriate pleasure, and all being ordered and bound together in a harmonious whole by a law of measure or proportion which assigns to each its proper place; at the head, the pleasure of pure knowledge; at the bottom, the appetites; between, the pleasures of the nobler senses (sight and hearing), and of the higher impulses—ambition, honor, etc. The right functioning of each is virtue; its product is pleasure. The system of pleasures according to virtue is the good. Moreover, he specifies four cardinal virtues which result—wisdom, the knowledge of the good or organized whole; justice, the law of proportion or measure; courage, the assertion of the higher tendencies against the pleasures and pains arising from the contemplation or imagination of the lower; temperance, the law of subordination in accordance with which each lower function is restrained from usurping the place of the higher. Plato's system of ethics remains the standard of ethical theories of the "self-realization" type.

Aristotle (q.v.) (384 B.C.–322 B.C.) gave the philosophic considerations of Plato a more scientific and empirical turn —a contrast, however, which is often exaggerated. He protested against the identification by Plato of human end or good with that of the universe, and consequently attached less importance to knowledge in the form of philosophic insight, and more to practical insight or wisdom. But, in the main assuming the Platonic basis, he carried into detail the analysis of human faculties or functions involved in conduct, giving a careful analysis of desire, pleasure and pain, of the various modes of knowledge, of voluntary action, and making a remarkable analysis of the various forms of virtue and vice actually current. In a word, he emphasized in detail psychological and social aspects, merely sketched by Plato. On the social side, it had become obvious that the comprehensive scheme of reform entertained by Plato was impossible; and here, also, Aristotle is free to undertake a more empirical description and analysis of various forms of government and organization in their moral bases and bearings. When, in the 12th and 13th centuries A.D. the works of Aristotle were again made known to the European world, first through translations from the Arabic and then from the Greek, Aristotle's ethics became embodied in the official philosophy of the Roman Catholic Church, especially in the writings of St. Thomas Aquinas (1225–74), and found literary expression in the *Divine Comedy* of Dante. His ethical writings have more profoundly affected common speech and thought than those of any other writer, and to a large extent have become a part of the moral common sense of civilized humanity.

The details of later ethical philosophy in Greece and Rome form an interesting part of the history of ethics, but, with one exception, supply no new idea of sufficient importance to need mention here. The exception is the Stoic conception of virtue as "living in accordance with nature," and the conception of the "law with nature" which grew out of this. This idea, under the form of *jus naturale*, was taken up into Roman jurisprudence, and became the ideal of a common moral law which underlies all differences of positive municipal law, and which, accordingly, forms an ethical standard by which positive law can be tried, and its diversities reduced to a common denominator. It reappeared in the Middle Ages in the form of the natural law (as distinct from revealed or supernatural law), written on the "fleshly tablets of the heart," and was thus indirectly influential in forming the still current notion of *conscience* as a moral legislative force. It came out in continental ethical thought of the 17th and 18th centuries in the conception of moral law as something analogous to a system of mathematical axioms, definitions and demonstrations, discoverable by reason, and forming the framework of both individual and political ethics.

Patristic Mediaeval Period (5th to 15th centuries A.D.) —The second period of ethical history is characterized by the subordination of ethics, as a branch of philosophy, to theology. The distinctive features contributed in this period to subsequent ethics are the emphasis laid upon ideas of law, authority, obligation or duty, and merit or demerit, namely, the good as religious salvation involving a knowledge and love of God as supreme perfection, possible only in the next world; and evil as sin, guilt also needing supernatural expiation. Because of the emphasis upon law and authority, moral ideas are largely assimilated to forensic and juridical conceptions. Most significant, however, for ethical theory is the transfer of theoretical interest from the conception of the good, the central idea of ancient ethics, to that of obligation. Not the natural end of man, but the duty of absolute submission of will to transcendent moral authority was the keynote. And even when ethics was freed from subservience to theology, it still remained easier for the modern mind to conceive of morality in terms of the nature and authority of duty than as the process of realizing the good. On the more concrete, empirical side, the great contribution of mediaeval theory was in depicting the moral drama, the struggle of good and evil, as it goes on in the individual soul. The fact that this was fraught with significance for an endless future life made it a subject of anxious and minute attention; and here, too, even when the moral region was later marked off more or less definitely from the religious, modern thought owes its consciousness of the subtle perplexities, temptations and shades of moral effort and issue to mediaeval rather than to ancient ethics.

Early Modern Period (The Reformation to the French Revolution)—The complexity and variety of moral theory and inquiry since the 15th century, as well as its relative nearness, make it difficult to secure the perspective necessary to its proper characterization. It is all more or less connected, however, with the struggle toward greater individual freedom, and with the problem of maintaining a stable associated and institutional life, on the basis of recognition of individuality —the democratic movement. In its earliest period, modern ethics was largely characterized by reaction against scholasticism; it was an effort to secure a basis for ethics free from subordination to theology and to mediaeval philosophy, and the schoolmen's versions of Aristotle. Moreover so much of energy was expended in the practical effort to get freedom of thought, of political action, of religious creed, of commercial life, that moral theory turned largely upon detailed questions arising out of the practical struggle. This accounts to a considerable extent for the scattered, fragmentary condition of modern ethics as compared with the systematic character of either Greek or mediaeval thought. Moreover, the very gaining of intellectual freedom of inquiry opened up countless fields of interest. Ethical problems sprang into existence at every turn; every new movement in industry, in politics, national and international, and in art, brought with it a new ethical problem. Social life was itself undergoing such rapid change, and in such tentative, uncertain ways, that each of these problems had to be attacked independently. The result is a critical, controversial and individualistic, rather than a constructive and systematized ethics—with the advantage, however, of remarkable richness in detail.

Continental ethics followed the prevailing philosophic method of rationalism: the attempt to build up a theory of conduct, individual and social, on the basis of pure reason, independent of revelation of ecclesiastic authority, or positive institutions. While the method was *a priori* in name, as matter of fact it drew largely upon the inheritance of generalized Roman law, attempting to harmonize and purify it in accordance with ideals of unity and comprehensiveness which were supposed to represent the demands of reason. Grotius (1583–1645) was the founder of this movement, and, in his *De Jure Belli et Pacis,* used the idea of law which is founded upon man's rational nature, which in turn is inherently social, to place international relations of comity, commerce and war upon a more humane and enlightened basis. His German successors, Puffendorf (1632–94), Leibniz (1646–1716), Thomasius (1655–1728), Wolff (1679–1754), carried on with greater critical acumen and more adequate philosophic instruments, the same work, and finally developed a complete system of rights and duties (called *Naturrecht* after *Jus Naturale*) applicable to all spheres of private, domestic, civil, political and international life—a *code* of morals, positive in effect, but supposed all to be drawn deductively from rational first principles. Upon the whole, the influence of German ethical rationalism was conservative; the result in fundamentals was the justification of the existing social order, purged of inconsistencies and reformed of abuses in detail. French rationalism took a different turn. It attempted a synthesis of the more basal notions of the newly arisen physical science with psychological ideas borrowed from Locke and his English successors. It was rationalistic not so much in attempting to deduce an ethical system from the conceptions of reason, as in subjecting the existing order of belief and institutions to unsparing criticism as antiscientific. In its extreme forms it seemed to demand an abrogation of existing institutions, the erection of the same *tabula rasa* in social matters, that Descartes had postulated in intellectual, and a creation, *de novo*, by sheer voluntary action, of a new social order, aiming at universal happiness. Reason gives an ideal of society in which all men shall be free and equal, and in which economic want and misery shall be abolished, and a widely diffused intelligence and wealth shall be instituted. Pessimistic to the extreme as regards the existing order, it was equally optimistic as to the possibilities of social organization, culminating in the conception of the infinitely progressive perfectibility of human nature; thus Helvétius, 1715–71 (*De l'esprit,* 1758; *De l'homme,* published 1772); Diderot (1713–84); Condillac (1715–80); D'Holbach (1723–89), especially *Système· Social* (1773); Condorcet (1743–94). While German ethics had emphasized the conception of natural law which is social in nature, French thought culminated in a deification of natural rights which are individual in their import and location. Certain characteristic features of not only the French Revolution but of the thought of American publicists in the latter half of the 18th century are directly traceable to this influence.

English ethical theory received its impetus from Hobbes (1588–1679). He begins with an analysis of the make-up of the individual, and resolves the latter into a bundle of egotistic impulses, all aiming at unrestricted satisfaction. He denies the existence of any inherent social tendency, or of anything "rational" in the individual save as deliberation may be involved in the individual's efforts after satisfaction. The social counterpart of this unlimited individualism is chaos, anarchy, conflict—the war of all against all. Hence the individual's quest for happiness is self-contradictory. It is possible of fruition only within the state of absolute power which prescribes to each individual the proper sphere of the exercise of his powers. The state is thus the author and sanction of all moral distinctions and obligations. The authority of this state with respect to individuals is absolute; since the source of moral law, it cannot be subject to anything beyond itself. There are thus three strains in Hobbes's teaching. The psychological, which teaches pure· egotism and hedonism; the ethical, which makes the state the source of moral values and relations; the political, which makes its authority unlimited. Each strain evoked profound and instant reaction. John Locke (1632–1704) taught that the individual has a natural right to a life of personal security, possession of property and social activity, subject only to limits of the similar rights of others, and that the state comes into existence to protect and secure these rights by settling cases of dispute or aggression, and hence is null and void when it goes beyond this province and encroaches upon individual rights. A succession of writers, notably Shaftesbury (1671–1713); Hutcheson (1694–1746); Butler (1692–1752); Adam Smith (1723–90), undertook a re-analysis of human nature, and endeavored to justify the presence of disinterested, benevolent impulses, of tendencies to regard the welfare of others. Cudworth (1617–88); More (1614–87); Cumberland (1631–1718); Clarke (1675–1729); Price (1723–91), took up the question of the origin of moral distinctions, and tried to show that they were based not in the state but in immutable laws of reason, or upon a science as abstract and certain as mathematics; or else were made known in intuition, etc. But during these inquiries, new problems came to light, and led to a rearrangement of forces. These problems were: (1) the relation of happiness—the expression of the self-seeking tendencies of man—to virtue, the expression of his benevolent tendencies; (2) the nature of the test or standard of right and wrong; (3) the nature of moral knowledge. The first problem led in Butler to the attempt to introduce "conscience" as a third and balancing authoritative factor in human nature; and in Smith and Hume (1711–76) to a peculiarly rich and significant theory of sympathy as a central principle through which distinctively moral sentiments are generated and whose exercise is intimately bound up with individual happiness. The second and third problems taken together lead to the conflict of utilitarianism and intuitionalism, the former holding that conduciveness to the maximum of possible happiness is the standard of right, the basis of obligation, and the source of all moral rules; this conduciveness to be determined by actual experience; the latter holding that there are moral values, which are inherently and absolutely such, without reference to consequences. Each school has a theological and a non-theological variety. Among theological utilitarians are prominent: Gay (1686–1761), and Paley (1743–1805); among the non-theological Jeremy Bentham (1748–1832) outranks all the others. Without adding much that is fundamentally new to the theoretical analysis, he makes an analysis of happiness in connection with a discussion of the various impulses (or motives as he termed them) of human nature the basis of a thorough-going scheme of judicial and penal reform. Through him utilitarianism became the most potent instrument of the first half of the 19th century of social reform; conduciveness to general and equally distributed happiness being the test by which all customs, traditions and institutions were tried—and by which most of them in their existent forms were condemned.

Recent Modern (From the French Revolution)—The last 20 years of the 18th century signalize a turning point in the history of thought. Bentham's and Kant's chief works are dated in this period. The French Revolution, carrying into effect the naturalistic rationalism and its optimistic faith in the possibilities of the individual, compelled a reconsideration of the intellectual premises from which it set forth. The problem of 19th century ethics was to get back from the individual to the social whole which includes him and within which he functions; but to do this in a way which should take due account of the deepened significance given to individual initiative and freedom—without, that is, a return to pure institutionalism, or to arbitrary external authority. The following schools or main tendencies are easily distinguishable:

(*a*) *English Liberalism.*—In Bentham, utilitarianism, as we have seen, became a program of social reform. The attempt to stretch an individualistic hedonism which taught that the end of desire is always the agent's own pleasure into a theory which taught that the individual should always judge his motives and acts from the standpoint of their bearing upon the happiness of all beings, brought out all the weaknesses of the theory. James Mill (q.v.) (1773–1836) strove valiantly to overcome these weaknesses by a systematic use of the principle of association, in virtue of which individual states become indissolubly connected, through punishment or commerce, with the welfare of others—the theory of "enlightened selfishness," for which Hartley (1705–57) had previously provided the psychological machinery. His son, John Stuart Mill (1806–73) while extending the same idea, introduced into utilitarianism two innovations, which were seized upon by his intuitional opponents as virtual abandonments of the entire hedonistic position. These were that quality of pleasure is more important than quantity, and that the individual is naturally social and so instinctively judges his own welfare from the standpoint of society, instead of *vice versa.* J. S. Mill also severely criticised the other utilitarians for their neglect of the ideal elements in education, and for neglect of the culture element in historical development. Without abandoning the individualistic basis he was much influenced by schools (*b*) and (*c*) below. From (*b*) came the influence of Coleridge (1772–1834); Maurice (1805–72), and Sterling (1806–44). Bain (1818–1903) belongs to the same empirical and utilitarian school. Sidgwick (1838–1900) in his *Methods of Ethics* attempted a fusion of the utilitarian standard with an intuitional basis and method.

(*b*) German rationalism culminated in Kant (1724–1804), who reduced the function of moral reason in man to a single principle; the consciousness of the moral law as the sole and sufficing principle of action. Since the claims of this principle are opposed by those of self-love—the desire for personal happiness—the presence of moral reason in us takes the form of a "categorical imperative," or the demand that duty alone, without any influence from inclination, desire or affection, be the motive of conduct. Upon the consciousness of duty are built the ideas of freedom, God and immortality—that is, by moral action is opened to us a sphere of reasonable faith in transcendental realities which are shut to scientific and philosophic cognition. Kant brought rationalism to a turn much as Bentham had affected empiricism. Subsequent German thought attempted to overcome the formalism of Kant's bare reason making itself known only in a consciousness of obligation. Hegel (1770–1831) attempted a synthesis of the Kantian idealism with the ideas of Schiller, of Spinoza (especially through the medium of Goethe), and of the rising historical school founded by Savigny. He endeavored to show that the social order is itself an objective embodiment of will and reason, and that the regions of civil law, of family life, social and commercial intercourse and above all the state, constitute an ethical world (as real as the physical) from which the individual must take his cue. He anticipated in many particulars from the standpoint of a different method and terminology, doctrines of recent anthropology and social psychology. German moral influence has been felt in English thought chiefly through Coleridge, Carlyle (who was mainly affected by Kant's successor, Fichte, 1762–1814), and more recently, T. H. Green (1836–82). The New England Transcendentalists were also affected by this school of thought, Ralph Waldo Emerson (q.v.) (1803–82) giving a highly original version of it, blending it with factors of his own personality and with ideas drawn from Puritanism.

(c) In France, the reaction from the individualism of the Revolution was most marked. At the head of the reaction stands Comte (1798–1857), who attempted to build up a theory of ethics upon an organized social basis, similar in many respects to that of Hegel, but relying upon a systematization of sciences rather than upon philosophy, for method, his system accordingly being termed positivism. Comte sought to show how such an ethical-social science could replace metaphysics and theology, the latter in the form of a religion of humanity. He influenced G. H. Lewes and the latter's wife, George Eliot, and also John Stuart Mill.

(d) In the latter half of the 19th century the theory of evolution has been dominant in ethical as well as in other forms of philosophic and scientific thought. Herbert Spencer's application is the best known to English readers. It is, however, generally recognized that his fundamental ethical conceptions were worked out before he became an evolutionist, and that the attachments between his ethics and the theory of evolution are of a somewhat external character. Indeed, it is now clear that the further development of the science of ethics waits upon the more thorough clearing up of the evolutionary ideas themselves, and upon more complete application to biology, psychology and sociology (including anthropology and certain phases of the history of man) in order to supply the auxiliary sciences necessary for ethical science. Through the conception of evolution it is probable that ethics will be emancipated from the survival of the idea that it is an art whose business is to lay down rules. The practical aspect of the theory of ethics will necessarily remain (since it is theory of practice or conduct), but it will take the form of providing *methods* for analyzing and resolving concrete individual and social situations, rather than of furnishing injunctions and precepts. The coincidence of the evolutionary tendency with the growth of democracy will relieve ethics in its philosophic aspects from its dependence upon fixed values, ideals, standards and laws, and constitute ethics more and more a working method for the self-regulation of the individual and of society.

Every period of ethical theory has been associated, as we have seen, with some corresponding epoch of human development, having its own characteristic problem. Upon the whole, however, ethics has not as yet adequately outgrown the conditions of its origin, and the supposed necessity they imposed of finding something as fixed and unchanging as custom. Consequently, philosophic inquiry has been devoted to finding *the* good, *the* law of duty, etc.; that is, something unchanging, all inclusive. Even the empirical school, in its emphasis upon pleasure, has tried to find something free from conditions of development, something fixed in the sense of being everywhere and at all times the same single unchanging standard and end. Even Spencer distinguishes present ethical codes as merely relative, and anticipates a period in which evolution will reach its goal—a period in which an unchanging set of rules shall be uniformly binding. But as ethical writers become more habituated to evolutionary ideas, they will cease setting up ideals of a Utopian millennium, with only one end and law; and will devote themselves to studying the conditions and effects of the changing situations in which men actually live, and to enabling men to use their best intelligence to find out just what the specific ends and specific duties are which characterize just those situations.

Consult the works of the authors already mentioned and also Clifford, W. K., *The Scientific Basis of Morals* (New York 1884); Croce, B., *Philosophy of the Practical* (London 1913); Dewey and Tufts, *Ethics* (New York 1908); Mackenzie, J. S., *Manual of Ethics* (New York 1901); Mezes, S. E., *Ethics* (London 1901); Palmer, G. H., *The Field of Ethics* (Boston 1901); Paulsen, F., *System of Ethics* (New York 1899); Royce, J., *Philosophy of Loyalty* (New York 1908); Sorley, R., *Recent Tendencies in Ethics* (Edinburgh 1904); Stephen, Sir Leslie, *The Science of Ethics* (2d ed., New York 1907); Thilly, Frank, *Introduction to Ethics* (New York 1900); Wundt, W. M., *Ethics* (London 1897–1901).

PSYCHOLOGICAL METHOD IN ETHICS

It is commonly agreed that the most generic distinction between philosophy and the sciences is that the former deals primarily with values, and the latter with facts or presented phenomena. Or, in rough but convenient phraseology, the philosophic disciplines are normative, the scientific descriptive. From this general premise it is argued that since psychology is a science concerned with facts and events (states of consciousness, and their physiological correlations), it can have no essential bearing upon ethics, a branch of philosophy concerned with a particular sphere of value. I wish to point out that one may accept both the generic distinction referred to and the placing of psychology as a purely natural science, and yet maintain that psychology furnishes an indispensable phase of method in ethics.

1. While affairs of conduct are primarily matters of value, viz., functions and attitudes, not of mere presentations in the stream of conscious states, and hence not a part of direct psychological data, it yet remains true that every such conduct-value has its signature or correspondent in the body of immediate data or presentations. That is to say, an end or ideal of behavior is not to be sought for as a mere psychological presentation; but since it marks a positive distinction within conscious experience there must be a conscious state which somehow corresponds to it, and, for the psychologist's purpose, *carries* it.

2. The psychologist can study the particular conditions in the stream of presentations of that particular content which represents the having of a moral ideal; and he can trace the influence, in the way of stimulation and inhibition, which such content exercises upon further presentations in the stream. Psychology as genetic is concerned precisely with

[First published in *Psychological Review* 10 (1903): 158–60.]

just such problems of origin and subsequent career; the matter of further career being a strict part of genetic psychology in so far as any one presentation is found to furnish specific conditions.

3. It is practically impossible to see how any control of the interpretation of the meaning to be justly assigned to the category of, say, "ideal" is to be secured without recourse to just such a device as this. Just because the ideal in actual moral experience is a matter of immediate personal worth, it is unanalyzed. Just because the presentation is not the moral reality, but gives it in an abstract and detached form, it renders the ideal capable of objective analysis and statement, or lends itself to the needs of intellectual control. Normative philosophy is not concerned with a mere reproduction of the original, vital experience. To object to the employment of psychology because it does not constitute or present the value with which it is concerned, would, therefore, so far as its logic is concerned, rule out any philosophic interpretation whatsoever. The only way to have the value is to have it as a matter of personal experience, and that is no more philosophy than it is science. To say then that psychology cannot give the ideal is entirely aside from the point. Philosophy cannot "give" it either. What psychology can do is to study in a definite and analytic way the meaning of a value as determined by its origin and function in the stream of experience.

4. It is clear that the use of psychology in this way is formal rather than material. That is to say, it does not tell what the concrete ethical ideal is; it tells what any experience must be if it is to be qualified as ideal. It shows the conditions of origin and use to which any qualitative experience must conform if it can be properly characterized as aim, end or purpose. It is quite clear, however, that such determination is not *merely* formal. The very fact that there are certain specific conditions of origin and career to which the candidate for ideal value must submit itself, gives a definite intellectual base line from which to measure the claims of such a candidate. In other words, if it is said that pleasure of perfection and self-realization, or recognition of duty, is the ideal, we have at once a definite method to

pursue. Can they fulfil the conditions of origin and functioning which are demanded? Or, putting the matter more positively, the knowledge of these circumstances of genesis and subsequent career enables us to delineate the main features of anything which has legitimate claim to be considered as end or ideal. If we assume for the moment that an anticipatory image is the psychological counterpart of the moral ideal, our problem is defined as the discovery of the adequate stimulus and the adequate use of functioning of such an image in experience. Such an analysis carried to its end would certainly leave us with a very positive notion regarding the generic traits of the ethical ideal. The form thus determined is not a form separate from all matter of experience, but is the form or framework of a certain kind of actual experience.

NOTES UPON LOGICAL TOPICS

I. A Classification of Contemporary Tendencies[1]

It is an interesting example of the irony of history that it was Kant who remarked, about a century and a quarter ago, that since Aristotle logical theory has neither lost nor gained an inch—that it appeared complete and settled. To-day the greatest difficulty students of logic have to contend with is the variety of independent and specialized points of view, a variety so great that it is almost impossible for any one person to be at home in all of them, independently of the diversity of opinion found in any one of them. A rough attempt to catalogue these various points of view and tendencies, even when undertaken by one quite ignorant in some of the fields, may be of use at least in defining some problems which are pressing in the further development of logic. Accordingly, a rough scheduling of tendencies follows.

1. *Formal Logic.*—The logic of scholastic tradition. It was, of course, formal logic which Kant, wrongly ascribing to Aristotle, regarded as finished and settled. But Kant's very insistence upon the purely formal character of thinking as such—his insistence that pure logic has nothing to do with any of the objects or contents of knowledge, being confined to analytic consistency with reference to identity and non-contradiction, was one of the chief forces in calling out by reaction other conceptions of logic.[2] The more rigorously one

1. I am glad to take advantage of the foundation of a publication of this type to record notes which are too informal to justify publication in more finished shape, and yet which, as notes of a student, may be of some use to other students of the same subject.
2. See, for example, how Hamilton and Mansel, who followed Kant in applying logic to formal laws of thinking, evoked the reaction of Mill on the one side, and of T. H. Green on the other. Mill, *An Examination of Sir William Hamilton's Philosophy,* 1865, and T. H. Green, *Works,* Vol. II, "Logic of the Formal Logicians." (Lectures delivered in 1874–75.)

[First published in *Journal of Philosophy, Psychology and Scientific Methods* 1 (1904): 57–62, 175–78.]

carries out the program of excluding from logical theory all
reference to truth, belief and the evidential value of data,
the more apparent the emptiness of such logic becomes, and
the more the mind seeks for some other conception of thought
to serve as a basis for logic of another type.

2. *Empirical Logic.*—Hence it was inevitable that when
the rationalistic school went to seed in its doctrine of a purely
empty thinking process, empiricism strove to build up a
constructive logic of "experience" as a source and guarantee
of practical and scientific truths. John Stuart Mill was, of
course, explicit in teaching that true logic is concerned with
adequacy of evidence and proof, with the validating and discrediting of belief—with, in a word, all the processes which
have to do with the consideration of any truth which is not
self-evident. Rarely has any piece of intellectual work met
so fully the need which called it out, and imposed itself so
overmasteringly upon its generation, as did the logic of Mill.
The empiricist, since Mill, repeats by his actions, if not by
his words, what Kant said of Aristotle, that logic is henceforth complete and settled.[3]

The tendency of current textbooks to incorporate within
themselves both the formal and the empirical logics, as if
they simply amicably divided the field between them, is a
good illustration of the capacities of the human mind. The
assumption that thought has a deductive and an inductive
process, which work by different laws, and that the formal,
syllogistic logic adequately describes the deductive function,
while the empirical logic as adequately represents the inductive, furnishes as striking an instance as one could find
of the catholic willingness of the human mind to accommodate itself even to diametrically opposite assumptions provided that will save the trouble of systematic, reconstructive
thinking.

3. *Real Logic.*—I use this term not as assuming that
this sort of logical theory is "real," while others are artificial,
but as a phrase, in the absence of any commonly recognized
designation, with which to refer to those tendencies which
give thought itself a content, and which reach their limit in

3. Nevertheless, the work of John Venn, *Principles of Empirical or
Inductive Logic*, London, 1889, is such an independent rendering
of Mill as to be worthy of more attention than it receives in the
current Teutophile philosophy.

the assumption that truth itself is just the perfected content
of thought. The irony of history, to which I alluded at the
outset, is, of course, the fact that it was Kant's transcendental
logic which brought to an end the settled and fixed condition
he attributed to logic. His so-called transcendental logic was
nothing more nor less than an attempt to show the positive
part played by thought in the determination of any experience which is capable of having attributed to itself the
distinctions of truth and falsity.

Under this head come all who have been positively influenced by the Kantian theory of judgment as involving an
objective synthesis, possible only through certain thought
functions. It is a term, therefore, which has to be applied
largely by way of contrast. It includes almost all those who
do not believe in the purely formal notion of thought, and
yet are unwilling to accept empiricism. It names certain
tendencies rather than any very homogeneous or defined body
of thought. To take some of the best known writers, the
names of Bradley, Bosanquet, Lotze, Sigwart and Wundt
would all appear here, much as they differ from one another.

These three captions refer to movements that are
sufficiently well defined to be termed schools of logical
thought. They represent, that is to say, intellectual standpoints which have become sufficiently conscious of themselves to get formulation, and to be aware of their incompati-
bilities with one another. The tendencies that I am about to
schedule are rather just tendencies. They are forces at work
rather than schools of doctrine. Consequently, they are not
necessarily incompatible either with one another or in all
respects with the three tendencies just mentioned.

4. Attempts to reform the traditional syllogistic and
inductive logics so as to bring them into greater accord with
"common sense" and with the methods and results of scientific inquiry. Such attempts, in the main, start from the
accepted terminology of logical theory and try to free it from
those connotations which attach to it in virtue of either the
scholastic or the empirical standpoints; and to show how,
without accepting any particular philosophical standpoint,
logical conceptions must be interpreted in order to meet the
working logic of practical life, and of scientific investigation

and verification. To my mind the best representative of this tendency is Professor Alfred Sidgwick, and as I hope to devote one of my later notes specially to his reformatory work, I shall say nothing more about it here.

5. *Mathematical Logic.*—Under this head two tendencies are to be noted. One is the disposition to interpret and to construct logic as mathematics, and the other to build up the system of mathematical science as itself the adequate representative of logic. Most systems of symbolic logic illustrate the former. By the latter I mean the work which has been done primarily by mathematicians as mathematicians under the conception that mathematical science is in no sense limited by the concept of quantity, but has to do with all reasoning which may be exhibited in necessary form or that deals with necessary conclusions. I am not enough of a mathematician to characterize this movement closely, but I am sure I am not far out of the way in referring to the work of Benjamin Pierce, and of the recent Italian school of Peano as typical examples. I suppose this strictly logical tendency has been much more influential in building up the hyperspace geometry and the modern theory of numbers than the layman recognizes. In our present condition of specialization it is somewhat difficult for one and the same person to be well posted on the more general and philosophical aspects of logical theory, and at the same time to be at home in the recent development of scientific mathematics. I am inclined to believe that a person who should be properly equipped on both sides, and who was also at home in recent psychology, could render the logic of reasoning a very great service. Professor Royce has already given us some tantalizing specimens of what is possible in this direction.[4]

Among those who are interested in logic from the mathematical side there seems to be a further division of tendency. One school seems explicitly or implicitly to hold by

4. I refer especially to parts IV and V of the second chapter of his *World and the Individual*, Second Series, and to his presidential address upon "Recent Logical Inquiries," *The Psychological Review*, Vol. IX, p. 105. I do not include his supplementary essay in the first volume of his *World and the Individual*, because he has (unfortunately, it seems to me) given his interpretation an ontological rather than a logical turn.

the traditional formal logic, and to be engaged in making it more rigorous by the use of symbols, thus carrying out the program of more strict formalism, eliminating ambiguities arising from context and putting the formulae of logic into a more compact and sequential form.

But, on the other hand, Mr. C. S. Peirce (if I interpret him aright) believes that one of the chief advantages of the mathematical, or symbolic statement is that logic may transcend thereby the limitations of mere formalism and become a potent instrumentality in developing a system which has inherent reference to the pursuit of truth and the validation of belief.

6. *Psychological Logic.*—Without in any way prejudging in advance the question as to whether logic and psychology are independent disciplines which can be brought into contact with each other only at the risk of corruption to both, one may note the fact that there is a renaissance of interest in the psychology of the reflective processes. This psychological development is giving at once such a novel and such a significant interpretation of the nature of thought in general, and of its various phenomena in particular, that it is hard to see how it can continue without in time affecting somewhat profoundly the consideration of strictly logical problems. If, for example, psychologists should come to a pretty definite consensus that thinking is originally conditioned by inhibited and, therefore, postponed action, it would seem as if such a view could not fail to modify the details of logical theory. Professor James's identification of abstraction with a selective function, taking place on the basis of interest, which runs through all psychical processes whatsoever, and his theory of the teleological nature of conception, if accepted in psychology, can hardly fail to carry with them some kind of moral for logic. And, to take an instance that is seemingly somewhat more remote from logic proper, his conception of the stream of consciousness as involving a rhythm of substantive and transitive sort, and of carrying with it necessarily a certain relationship between the more or less definite (or, what is the same thing, the more or less vague) must be either true or false in psychology —and if true in psychology must modify in some way or other the conception of thought that obtains in logic.

7. *Logic in Connection with Comparative and General Grammar.*—It goes without saying that logic in its beginnings, logic at the hands of Plato and Aristotle, went along with and was largely dependent upon an analysis of the sentential structures in which thought is embodied. Logic more than repaid what it borrowed from its analysis of language, fixing the categories of grammar and language study for many centuries. The science of language had practically no independent existence, but was a mode of phrasing the recognized distinctions of classic logical theory. But, as everyone knows, within the last hundred years the study of language has entered upon an independent development of its own, and has now practically shaken itself free from the incubus of its externally imposed categories, which in turn originated from a more superficial study of linguistic phenomena. The time has about come, I think, when logic may again borrow from the extensive and profound analysis of language in as significant and important a way as the logic of Aristotle borrowed from the narrow and obvious language data at command.

Up to the present those who have attempted to make the connections between general grammar and logic have, for the most part, been already committed to a certain psychology. I do not wish to be ungrateful to the services rendered by Steinthal and his followers, but it seems to me, nevertheless, true that their efforts have been very much compromised (and this is true also in some degree, I should say, of Wundt) by the attempt to fit the results of philology into the *cadres* of a preexistent psychology, the Herbartian. The situation will be more promising in the degree in which students of language, working freely with their own data, and using psychology only as a working tool, make their own logical renderings and translations. It would not be difficult to gather from modern grammarians of the comparative and historical schools, a large body of data of great significance for the logical theory of propositions and terms—that is, of judgment and ideas.

8. *Logic and Scientific Methods.*—Of course, the status of scientific method has always had reflex influence upon logic; but in the main this has taken effect in the past through the efforts of those who were already logicians in

utilizing the methods of experimental science in connection with the building up of their own systems. Without ignoring the tremendous fluctuation that has come to logic from such endeavors, we may expect, I think, still more fertilization when scientific men undertake an independent statement of the logical bearings of their own modes of procedure. We clearly are entering upon this stage of development. It is necessary only to refer to such names as Poincaré, Boltzmann and Mach.

II. The Meanings of the Term Idea

In this note I venture to set forth some results concerning the development of the meanings of the term "idea" gained from reading Murray's Oxford Dictionary. I believe it will be found that the actual succession of meanings of this term put before us a life-history of a thought which is quite as significant in its way as is the series of morphological changes gone through in the life-history of any animal.

(1) The original and primary signification of the term is definitely objective. The word is a straight transliteration of the Platonic ἰδέα. No psychological, not even a conceptual, sense attaches to the term. The idea is a real essence or substance of a spiritual as distinct from a material sort. But the Platonic idea is also, of course, an archetype, and as such serves the purpose of an exemplar and model. This sense introduces the subjective rift into the lute; and the further history of the term represents the evolution of this shade of meaning until as thoroughly psychical it dominates; and displaces, even not only the original ontological sense of spiritual essence, but apparently all objective reference.

A perfect archetype, being an ideal, serves to introduce (2) idea as the conception of an objective end to be realized —"the plan or design according to which something is created or constructed." Here objective meaning is still dominant. The plan or design is not mental; it is a real plan of real construction which is meant, something, say, like the architect's design for a house. But there is now an easy road to a more subjective sense, since we have (3) the idea as a plan in the sense of *intention*, an attitude of consciousness to be fulfilled in the thing to be done or executed. The plan of the house need not be the objective scheme in accordance with the specifications of which the builder is working; it may be the notion of a house as a desirable thing suggesting itself in an inchoate condition and not yet having taken shape in any definite mode of construction. The volitional reference, however, is so marked as clearly to preserve objective import and reference; the objective is the goal, the object.

(4) Idea in Greek as well as in English means shape, image, figure. This meaning also is quite objective at the outset. A picture, for example, is an idea. So we have a quotation, as late as Shakespeare, to this effect—

I do infer your lineaments, being the right idea of your father,
Both in your form and nobleness of mind.

Now let this sense of an objective picture or representation blend with the sense of idea as desirable end entertained as a purpose or intention, and we get a distinctly new turn of thought. Such fusion, moreover, is practically bound to occur, since in many cases the idea as intention (for instance, the entertaining the project of building a house) is sure to take the form of an image of the house which is wanted. Through this fusion there arises (5) the sense of idea which is probably the popularly current one at present: idea as a mental picture or representative of anything whatsoever, past, present or future. Here the meaning is, so to speak, just on the dividing line between the subjective and the objective. It is subjective in so far as the picture or representation is taken to be mental, part of the possessions of a personal life. But it is objective in content and reference. It is a mental scheme or portraiture *of* something or other. It is just *something* in the mind instead of in space. For example, the idea of a cow is, in the intellectual realm, just what the thing cow is in the physical—so, at least, it seems to naïve consciousness. The idea is subjective in existence, but not in import or worth. For certain purposes the idea is just as good as the real thing, and indeed under certain circumstances better. A picture is often a convenience where the thing of which it is a picture would be a nuisance. If the picture serves the purposes for which a picture is usually intended, we do not regard it as any reflection upon its reality or objectivity to say that it is just a picture. What else should it be? The greenback is not a beefsteak; it can not, like beefsteak, be eaten and so nourish the body; but it may be much more convenient and useful in the pocket than would be the beefsteak. Now it seems to me that to the naïve, non-philosophical consciousness, ideas are in just about such a situation as this. They are felt to be representatives of certain realities; thus they are not the realities of which they are representative. But they have a reality of their own, which, moreover, like that of the portrait, is just as good as, and for certain purposes better than, that of their originals or objectives.

But a portrait may be a poor one. It may misrepresent the original. Ideas frequently turn out to be misreports, misconceptions; they are mis-takings of the object; hence we get (6) the sense of *mere* idea; fancy as opposed to fact, chimera as opposed to solid thing. Here the subjective sense is peculiarly to the fore, but, after all, is prominent only because of an implied objective function and worth which the idea has failed to subserve. This meaning could not originate without at least a prior sense of objective worth which has failed in a given case to make good. Anyway, the idea now becomes something peculiarly and distinctively mental. This meaning of idea as a product of pure mental activity, cut loose from any object, the idea as the affair of arbitrary imagination, seems historically to have been the transition to our next sense, (7) where the idea signifies any product of mental activity when so regarded, that is, *qua* mental. Or in dictionary phrase, the idea is "an item of knowledge or belief as existing in the mind; a thought, conception, notion, way of thinking." To conceive an idea as an item of knowledge existing in the mind or intellect is a remarkable achievement, the importance of which is disguised from us only by its familiarity and constant employ. As an item of knowledge, it must be objective in import. But as existing in the mind it is subjective. It is just a thought, a "notion," a fancy. It is (a) a way of thinking *objects*, but (b) it is only a *way of*

thinking. Ideas in this sense become a tremendous resource
for science. By this device we succeed in storing up, so to
say, all the things and objects which we have known; and
yet store them in such a way that we can readily discard
them in case we find reason to suspect their validity, and
can modify and transform them so far as further experience
indicates the desirability of reconstruction. Ideas in this
sense are past knowledge organized with special reference
to its own correction, further verification, the taking in of
new meanings, and for use as tools of discovery.

(8) But the matter of knowledge, the truth or fact, the
plan, the original spiritual substance, is finally unambigu-
ously "in the mind." It has to accept the coloring given to it
by its new habitat and companions—which corrupt its naturally good (objective) manners. Now we have the full-
fledged Lockeian meaning. It is "that Term which serves
best to stand for whatsoever is the Object of the Understanding when a Man thinks." It is used "to express whatever is
meant by phantasm, notion, species, or whatever it is that
the mind can be employed about in thinking." Thus Locke.
The life-history of the term has consummated itself. The idea
is now a *subjective object* as such. That is to say, it is an
object which is simply the construct and content of mental
activity as such. The world of objects has not only passed
over into mind so as to have certain representatives of itself
there which can be manipulated and managed for the mind's
own purposes; but it has got so completely domesticated in
mind that its representatives there have lost all consciousness of their family relationships in the world of facts and
truths. The idea sets up in business as itself an object, but
an object of a peculiar and unique sort, the object of consciousness as consciousness, and only of "consciousness"—
mere mental entity. It is now a short-cut to Hume's "every
distinct idea is a separate existence," and to the denial of all
possibility of converse with things and of causal connections
—since our only tools are just states of consciousness.

In leaving this summary, I will content myself with one
question. Are there really and truly any such independent
psychical entities as the Lockeian ideas, or have we in ideas
as just psychical simply a more adequate methodological

device for facilitating and controlling knowledge—that is to say, acquaintance and transactions with objects? The account of ideas in James's *Psychology* would, if the latter view be correct, give sense (9) of idea—the idea as a mental state for the sake of referring easily and fluidly to *any* object in *any* phase, and thus freeing and facilitating our intercourse with things. The idea as purely psychical is the object in solution, moving towards re-precipitation in some object which is more anticipated, which thus satisfies more, and hence has increase of meaning. Although wholly subjective, subjective is a phrase which refers to objectivity undergoing liberation from pre-committed, and hence limited, modes of significance, and by solution in the medium of personality getting varied worths.

PHILOSOPHY AND AMERICAN NATIONAL LIFE

It is today generally recognized that systems of philosophy however abstract in conception and technical in exposition, lie, after all, much nearer the heart of social, and of national, life than superficially appears. If one were to say that philosophy is just a language, one would doubtless give occasion for rejoicing to those who already believe that philosophy is "words, words, words"; that it is only an uncouth terminology invented and used for the mystification of common sense. Yet mathematics, too, is only a language. Much, most, depends upon what the language is of and about. And, speaking roundly, philosophy is a language in which the deepest social problems and aspirations of a given time and a given people are expressed in intellectual and impersonal symbols. It has been well said that philosophy is a reflective self-consciousness of what first exists spontaneously, effectively, in the feelings, deeds, ideas of a people.

Even were it not true (as I believe it to be true) that philosophical problems are in last analysis but definitions, objective statements, of problems which have arisen in a socially important way in the life of a people, it would still be true that to be "understood of men," to make its way, to receive confirmation or even the degree of attention necessary for doubt and discussion, a philosophy has to be conceived and stated in terms of conditions and factors that are moving generally in non-philosophic life. It is not a futile question to ask after the reciprocal influences of American national life and American philosophy.

It is reasonably sure, however, that the answer is not to be sought in some special philosophic -ism. We may dis-

[First published in University of Vermont, *Centennial Anniversary of the Graduation of the First Class, July Third to Seventh 1904* (Burlington, Vermont, 1905), pp. 106–13.]

count the belief current in Europe that American philosophy is bound to be a system if not of Materialism, at least of Mechanicalism; a highly "positive," non-spiritual type of thought. We may dismiss the idea of an American author that our philosophy is sure to be Realism, because the Americans are so essentially a hard-headed people. Not in such wholesale and exclusive labels are we to look for what we are after, but rather in certain features which color the atmosphere, and dye the spirit of all our thinking. American philosophy must be born out of and must respond to the demands of democracy, as democracy strives to voice and to achieve itself on a vaster scale, and in a more thorough and final way than history has previously witnessed. And democracy is something at once too subtle and too complex and too aspiring to be caught in the meshes of a single philosophical school or sect.

It is, then, to the needs of democracy in America that we turn to find the fundamental problems of philosophy; and to its tendencies, its working forces, that we look for the points of view and the terms in which philosophy will envisage and solve these problems. The relation of the individual to the universal is one of the oldest, one of the most controverted, at some periods seemingly one of the most barren and merely metaphysical, of all problems. But the question gets a new force and a new meaning with us. It is born again. It is the question of the possibility and the validity of the way of life to which we have committed ourselves. To the individual we have appealed; to the court of the individual we must go. Is the individual capable of bearing this strain? What is there in his make-up that justifies such dependence? Is the attempt inherently foredoomed to failure because of the feebleness and corruptness of the instrumentality and the instability of the end we have set up? Such questions are, indeed, to the forefront of all thinking since the origin of Protestantism and of political and industrial liberty. But in a country which is externally detached, which has physically severed the ties and traditions that bind it to systems of action and belief which give the individual a subordinate and incidental, or else a merely transcendental and, as it were, Pickwickian, place in the scheme of things, such questions take on at once a more vital and a changed significance.

It is no longer primarily a question of the logical individual, but of the concrete individuality; not of Socrates as just a stock example or sample about which discussion may turn, but of a living John Smith, his wife and his children and his neighbors. If our civilization is to be justified we must reach a conception of the individual which shows, in general and in detail, the inherently significant and worthful place which the psychical, which the doubting, hoping, striving, experimenting individual occupies in the constitution of reality. We must know why and how it is that it is neither the way nor the end of the individual fitfully and imperfectly to reproduce some universe of reality already externally constituted and externally complete in itself, and set as a model for him to copy and conform to. We must know it is his method and his aim to add to, to complete and to perfect, even in his faiths and strivings and errors, a reality which he is needed to fulfill.

If our civilization is to be directed, we must have such a concrete and working knowledge of the individual as will enable us to furnish on the basis of the individual himself substitutes for those modes of nurture, of restraint and of control which in the past have been supplied from authorizations supposedly fixed outside of and beyond individuality. It is no accident that American philosophy is even in its present incipient and inchoate style permeated with psychological data and considerations. This, I take it, is not accounted for by saying that the American mind is interested more in positive observation than in metaphysical speculation, in phenomena rather than in ultimate explanations. It means that in some very true sense the individual with which psychology deals now is an ultimate; and that henceforth the metaphysical question of the nature and significance of the individual is bound up with the scientific problem of his actual structure and behavior. Because the concrete individuality is a body as well as a soul, because through his body he is in multiple and complicated relations of stimulation and response to a natural and social environment, such psychology, moreover, must include the physiological and the experimental methods along with the more directly introspective. This again is not materialism nor display of talent of mechanical ingenuity. It is a sincere, even while subconscious, recognition of the fundamental ethical importance attaching to the actual play of individuality in the conditions of our life.

So we might go through, one by one, the historic problems of philosophy with a view to indicating that American philosophy does not cut loose from the past to begin a provincial career on its own account; nor yet settles the historic problems offhand in the terms of some one philosophical school; but that it has inevitably to reconceive and to rebeget them in the light of the demands and the ideals contained in our own national life-spirit. One might suggest, for example, that the question of the relation of mind and matter is revised when it is seen as the abstract form of the problem of the relation of the so-called material, that is, industrial and economic life, to the intellectual and ideal life of a democracy, and particularly to the ethical demands of democracy for a just distribution of economic opportunity and economic reward. One might even show how the entire dualism of mind and matter haunting the footsteps of historic philosophy is, at bottom, a reflex of a separation of want, of appetite, from reason, from the ideal, which in turn was the expression of non-democratic societies in which the "higher" and spiritual life of the few was built upon and conditioned by the "lower" and economic life of the many.

But since any detailed treatment of philosophic questions is not here in place, I conclude with a few words upon the subject of method. An absence of dogmatism, of rigidly fixed doctrines, a certain fluidity and socially experimental quality must characterize American thought. Philosophy may be regarded as primarily either system or method. As system, it develops, justifies and delivers a certain definite body of doctrine. It is taken to discover, or at least to guarantee, a more or less closed set of truths which are its peculiar and exclusively appropriate object. Its worth is measured by the finality and completeness of this independent and exclusive body of doctrines. Mediaeval philosophy is a typical example of what I mean, but the idea did not pass away with the

waning of scholasticism. It animates as an ideal most philosophic thought of later times. Or, if questioned, it is questioned only in the interests of scepticism. But there is also
struggling for articulation a conception of philosophy as
primarily *method*: —system only in the sense of an arrangement of problems and ideas which will facilitate further inquiry, and the criticism and constructive interpretation of a
variety of life-problems. This point of view is not sceptical.
It is not undogmatic in the sense of mere looseness of definition and avoidance of classification, nor yet in the sense of a
careless eclecticism. But it aims at a philosophy which shall
be instrumental rather than final, and instrumental not to
establishing and warranting any particular set of truths, but
instrumental in furnishing points of view and working ideas
which may clarify and illuminate the actual and concrete
course of life.

Such a conception of the aim and worth of philosophy
is alone, I take it, appropriate to the inherent logic of our
America. Philosophers are not to be a separate and monopolistic priesthood set apart to guard, and, under certain
conditions, to reveal, an isolated treasury of truths. It is
theirs to organize—such organization involving, of course,
criticism, rejection, transformation—the highest and wisest
ideas of humanity, past and present, in such fashion that
they may become most effective in the interpretation of
certain recurrent and fundamental problems, which humanity, collectively and individually, has to face. For this
reason philosophers must be teachers as well as inquirers.
The association of these two functions is organic, not accidental. Hence the connection of philosophy with the work
and function of the university is natural and inevitable. The
university is the fit abode of philosophy. It is in the university that philosophy finds the organ, the working agency,
through which it may realize its social and national aim.

I recognize that this treatment of the relation of philosophy to university teaching and to national life has con-
veyed only vague, although unfortunately not glittering, generalities. Generalities, indeed, are all the occasion permits or
requires. But vagueness, in the present formative condition
of national life and of philosophy, inheres in the very situa-

tion. It were all too easy to gain a seeming definiteness and finality by paying the price of a certain falsity and unreality. It is, however, unsuitable to the occasion and to the filial gratitude due my *Alma Mater* to conclude otherwise than with a recognition of the profound and vital consciousness evinced by the University of Vermont from the day of its foundation, of the import of philosophy,—directly for its own students and through them for the nation.

THE TERMS "CONSCIOUS" AND "CONSCIOUSNESS"

In an early number of the *Journal of Philosophy, Psychology and Scientific Methods*[1] I gave a brief account of the historical evolution of the significations of the term "idea" in the English language. I wish now to consider the terms "conscious" and "consciousness"; not, however, so much with reference to their historical development as to the different types of meaning they represent and convey. I think this discrimination will be found not altogether irrelevant to current problems and discussions. I take my material again from Murray's Oxford Dictionary.

1. An early use emphasizes the "con-" factor: a social fact. Consciousness means joint, or mutual, awareness. "To be a friend and to be conscious are terms equivalent" (South, 1664).[2] While this use is obsolete, it persists in poetic metaphor as attributed to things, *e.g.*, the "conscious air," etc. It also clearly influences the next sense, which is,

2. That of being "conscious *to* one's self": having the witness to something within one's self. This is naturally said especially of one's own innocence, guilt, frailties, etc., that is of personal activities and traits, where the individual has peculiar or unique evidence not available to others. "Being so conscious unto my selfe of my great weaknesse" (Ussher, 1620). Here is a distinctively personal adaptation of the social, or joint, use. The agent is, so to speak, reduplicated. In one capacity, he does certain things; in another, he is cognizant of these goings-on. A connecting link between 1

1. Vol. I, No. 7, p. 175. [See this volume, pp. 68–72.]
2. I owe to the editor of the *Journal* this interesting reference to Hobbes (*Leviathan*, Ch. 7): "When two, or more, men know of one and the same fact, they are said to be Conscious of it one to another; which is as much as to know it together." Hobbes then uses this to explicate the moral meaning of conscience.

[First published in *Journal of Philosophy, Psychology and Scientific Methods* 3 (1906): 39–41.]

and 2 is found in a sense (obsolete like 1) where conscious means "privy to," a cognizant accomplice of,—usually, a guilty knowledge. It is worth considering whether "self-consciousness," in both the moral and the philosophic sense, does not involve this distinction and relation between the self doing and the self reflecting upon its past or future (anticipated) doings to see what sort of an agent is implicated; and whether, in short, many of the difficulties of self-consciousness as a "subject-object" relation are not due to a failure to keep in mind that it establishes connection between a practical and a cognitional attitude, not between two cognitional terms.

3. "Conscious" is also used to discriminate a certain kind of being or agent, one which knows what it is about, which has emotions, etc., e.g., a *personal* being or agent, as distinct from a stone or a plant. "Consciousness" is then used as short for such a being. It denotes all the knowledges, intentions, emotions, etc., which make up the differential being or activity of such a being or agent. This practical and empirical reference to a specific thing is seen clearly in sub-sense (a) where "conscious" means intentional, purposive, and (b) where it means undue preoccupation with what concerns, invidiously, one's self (the bad sense of "self-consciousness"). "Consciousness" thus marks off in general the difference of persons from things, and in particular the characteristic differences between persons,—since each has his own emotions, informations, intentions, etc. No *technically* philosophical sense is involved.

4. "Conscious" means *aware*: "consciousness," the state of being aware. This is a wide, colorless use; there is no discrimination nor implication as to contents, as to what there is awareness of,—whether mental or physical, personal or impersonal, etc.

5. The distinctively philosophical use (that defined as such in the dictionary) appears to be a peculiar combination of 2, 3 and 4. It is, in the words of the dictionary, "the state or faculty of being conscious, as a *condition and concomitant* of all thought, feeling and volition." The words I have italicized bring out the difference between thoughts, etc., characterizing the peculiar quality of a specific being or agent, and

something which in general lies back of and conditions all
such thoughts. Consciousness is now one with mind, or soul,
or subject, as an underlying condition hypostasized into a
substance. This identification of "mind" and "consciousness"
leads to Locke's familiar doctrine (1690), "Consciousness is
the perception of what passes in one's own mind." Awareness
is borrowed from sense 4, but is limited to what is "in the
mind" only. Meanwhile the "private witness" sense of 3 more
or less intentionally colors the resultant meaning. Consciousness is distinctly "one's own" perception of "one's own" mind.
As a net result, we get a private type of existence (as distinct
from private cognizance); of which *alone* one is directly or
immediately aware (as distinct from the anything and everything of 4), while, moreover, enough is retained of the con-
creteness, the *thingness*, of 3 to make this a *special* stuff or
entity, although the specific and practical character of the
personal agent is eliminated, a "condition" back of particular
purposes, emotions, etc., being substituted.

6. Then we have a comparatively modern adaptation of
3, illustrated in a quotation from Dickens (1837): "When
the fever left him and consciousness returned, he found,"
etc. The formal definition given is, "The state of being conscious regarded as the *normal condition of a healthy, waking
life*." (Italics naturally mine.) The corresponding term "conscious" is defined as "having one's mental faculties actually
in an active and waking state." (It is interesting to note that
here, too, the earliest quotation dates no further back than
1841.)

I hardly think that anyone who is aware of the ambiguous senses in which the term consciousness is habitually used
in philosophical discussions and of the misunderstandings
that result, possibly of one's self and certainly of others, will
regard the foregoing as a merely linguistic contribution. It
is no part of my present intention to note the implied philosophical bearings, save to suggest that meaning 5 begs as
many metaphysical problems as is likely ever to be the privi-
lege of any one word; that considerations based exclusively
on 4 are not likely to be conclusive against positions that
have 3 especially in mind, and *vice versa*; and that 6 seems
to give the sense which underlies the psychological use of

the term and to give (either by itself or in connection with 3) a standpoint from which the psychological sense can be kept free from the logical implications of the "awareness" problem in general, and from the metaphysics of 5. To take the term "by itself" is perhaps more appropriate for "structural" psychology, while to take it in connection with a person or agent (sense 3) is appropriate for "functional" psychology. But in the latter case, it should be understood that "consciousness" means not a stuff, nor an entity by itself, but is short for *conscious* animal or agent,—for something *which is* conscious.

In making these suggestions I do not mean to indicate a belief that the different senses have no common qualities or appropriate cross-references. On the contrary, I believe that the connection of the logical meaning of "awareness" with the facts involved empirically and practically in the existence of a certain sort of agent (especially as the latter itself becomes the subject-matter of natural science) determines one of the most real problems of present philosophy. But in discussing these problems nothing but good could come from stating explicitly the *prima facie* or immediate denotation of the terms used.

BELIEFS AND EXISTENCES[1]
[BELIEFS AND REALITIES]

I

Beliefs look both ways, towards persons and toward things. They are the original Mr. Facing-both-ways. They form or judge—justify or condemn—the agents who entertain them and who insist upon them. They are of things whose immediate meanings form their content. To believe is to ascribe value, impute meaning, assign import. The collection and interaction of these appraisals and assessments is the world of the common man,—that is, of man as an individual and not as a professional being or class specimen. Thus things are characters, not mere entities; they behave and respond and provoke. In the behavior that exemplifies and tests their character, they help and hinder; disturb and pacify; resist and comply; are dismal and mirthful, orderly and deformed, queer and commonplace; they agree and disagree; are better and worse.

Thus the human world, whether or no it have core and axis, has presence and transfiguration. It means here and now, not in some transcendent sphere. It moves, of itself, to varied incremental meaning, not to some far off event, whether divine or diabolic. Such movement constitutes conduct, for conduct is the working out of the commitments of

1. Read as the Presidential Address at the fifth annual meeting of the American Philosophical Association, at Cambridge, December 28, 1905, and reprinted with verbal revisions from the *Philosophical Review*, Vol. XV, March, 1906. The substitution of the word "Existences" for the word "Realities" (in the original title) is due to a subsequent recognition on my part that the eulogistic historic associations with the word "Reality" (against which the paper was a protest) infected the interpretation of the paper itself, so that the use of some more colorless word was desirable.

[First published in *Philosophical Review* 15 (1906): 113–19. Revised and reprinted as "Beliefs and Existences" in *The Influence of Darwin on Philosophy* (New York: Henry Holt and Co., 1910), pp. 169–97.]

belief. That believed better is held to, asserted, affirmed, acted upon. The moments of its crucial fulfilment are the natural "transcendentals"; the decisive, the critical, standards of further estimation, selection, and rejection. That believed worse is fled, resisted, transformed into an instrument for the better. Characters, in being condensations of belief, are thus at once the reminders and the prognostications of weal and woe; they concrete and they regulate the terms of effective apprehension and appropriation of things. This general regulative function is what we mean in calling them characters, forms.

For beliefs, made in the course of existence, reciprocate by making existence still farther, by developing it. Beliefs are not made *by* existence in a mechanical or logical or psychological sense. "Reality" naturally instigates belief. It appraises itself and through this self-appraisal manages its affairs. As things are surcharged valuations, so "consciousness" means ways of believing and disbelieving. It is interpretation; not merely existence aware of itself as fact, but existence discerning, judging itself, approving and disapproving.

This double outlook and connection of belief, its implication, on one side, with beings who suffer and endeavor, and, its complication on the other, with the meanings and worths of things, is its glory or its unpardonable sin. We cannot keep connection on one side and throw it away on the other. We cannot preserve significance and decline the personal attitude in which it is inscribed and operative, any more than we can succeed in making things "states" of a "consciousness" whose business is to be an interpretation of things. Beliefs are personal affairs, and personal affairs are adventures, and adventures are, if you please, shady. But equally discredited, then, is the universe of meanings. For the world has meaning as somebody's, somebody's at a juncture, taken for better or worse, and you shall not have completed your metaphysics till you have told whose world is meant and how and what for—in what bias and to what effect. Here is a cake that is had only by eating it, just as there is digestion only *for* life as well as *by* life.

So far the standpoint of the common man. But the pro-

fessional man, the philosopher, has been largely occupied
in a systematic effort to discredit the standpoint of the common man, that is, to disable belief as an ultimately valid
principle. Philosophy is shocked at the frank, almost brutal,
evocation of beliefs by and in natural existence, like witches
out of a desert heath—at a mode of production which is
neither logical, nor physical, nor psychological, but just
natural, empirical. For modern philosophy is, as every college
senior recites, epistemology; and epistemology, as perhaps
our books and lectures sometimes forget to tell the senior,
has absorbed Stoic dogma. Passionless imperturbability, absolute detachment, complete subjection to a ready-made and
finished reality—physical it may be, mental it may be, logical
it may be—is its professed ideal. Forswearing the reality of
affection, and the gallantry of adventure, the genuineness of
the incomplete, the tentative, it has taken an oath of alle-
giance to Reality, objective, universal, complete; made perhaps of atoms, perhaps of sensations, perhaps of logical
meanings. This ready-made reality, already including everything, must of course swallow and absorb belief, must produce it psychologically, mechanically or logically, according
to its own nature; must in any case, instead of acquiring aid
and support from belief, resolve it into one of its own preordained creatures, making a desert and calling it harmony,
unity, totality.[2]

Philosophy has dreamed the dream of a knowledge
which is other than the propitious outgrowth of beliefs that
shall develop aforetime their ulterior implications in order to

2. Since writing the above I have read the following words of a
candidly unsympathetic friend of philosophy: "Neither philosophy nor science can institute man's relation to the universe,
because such reciprocity must have existed before any kind of
science or philosophy can begin; since each investigates phenomena by means of the intellect, and independent of the position and feeling of the investigator; whereas the relation of man
to the universe is defined, not by the intellect alone, but by his
sensitive perception aided by all his spiritual powers. However
much one may assure and instruct a man that all real existence
is an idea, that matter is made up of atoms, that the essence of
life is corporality or will, that heat, light, movement, electricity,
are different manifestations of one and the same energy, one
cannot thereby explain to a being with pains, pleasures, hopes,
and fears his position in the universe." Tolstoi, essay on "Religion and Morality," in Essays, Letters, and Miscellanies.

recast them, to rectify their errors, cultivate their waste places, heal their diseases, fortify their feeblenesses: — the dream of a knowledge that has to do with objects having no nature save to be known.

Not that their philosophers have admitted the concrete realizability of their scheme. On the contrary, the assertion of the absolute "Reality" of what is empirically unrealizable is a part of the scheme; the ideal of a universe of pure, cognitional objects, fixed elements in fixed relations. Sensationalist and idealist, positivist and transcendentalist, materialist and spiritualist, defining this object in as many differing ways as they have different conceptions of the ideal and method of knowledge, are at one in their devotion to an identification of Reality with something that connects monopolistically with passionless knowledge, belief purged of all personal reference, origin, and outlook.[3]

What is to be said of this attempt to sever the cord which naturally binds together personal attitudes and the meaning of things? This much at least: the effort to extract meanings, values, from the beliefs that ascribe them, and to give the former absolute metaphysical validity while the latter are sent to wander as scapegoats in the wilderness of mere phenomena, is an attempt which, as long as "our interest's on the dangerous edge of things," will attract an admiring, even if suspicious, audience. Moreover, we may admit that the attempt to catch the universe of immediate experience, of action and passion, coming and going, to damn it in its present body in order expressly to glorify its spirit to all eternity, to validate the meaning of beliefs by discrediting their natural existence, to attribute absolute worth to the intent of human convictions just because of the absolute worthlessness of their content — that the performance

3. Hegel may be excepted from this statement. The habit of interpreting Hegel as a Neo-Kantian, a Kantian enlarged and purified, is a purely Anglo-American habit. This is no place to enter into the intricacies of Hegelian exegesis, but the subordination of both logical meaning and of mechanical existence to *Geist*, to life in its own developing movement, would seem to stand out in any unbiased view of Hegel. At all events, I wish to recognize my own personal debt to Hegel for the view set forth in this paper, without, of course, implying that it represents Hegel's own intention.

of this feat of virtuosity has developed philosophy to its present wondrous, if formidable, technique.

But can we claim more than a *succès d'estime*? Consider again the nature of the effort. The world of immediate meanings, or the world empirically sustained in beliefs, is to be sorted out into two portions, metaphysically discontinuous, one of which shall alone be good and true "Reality," the fit material of passionless, beliefless knowledge; while the other part, that which is excluded, shall be referred exclusively to belief and treated as mere appearance, purely subjective, impressions or effects in consciousness, or as that ludicrously abject modern discovery—an epiphenomenon. And this division into the real and the unreal is accomplished by the very individual whom his own "absolute" results reduce to phenomenality, in terms of the very immediate experience which is infected with worthlessness, and on the basis of preference, of selection, that are declared to be unreal! Can the thing be done?

Anyway, the snubbed and excluded factor may always reassert itself. The very pushing it out of "Reality" may but add to its potential energy, and invoke a more violent recoil. When affections and aversions, with the beliefs in which they record themselves, and the efforts they exact, are reduced to epiphenomena, dancing an idle attendance upon a reality complete without them, to which they vainly strive to accommodate themselves by mirroring, then may the emotions flagrantly burst forth with the claim that, as a friend of mine puts it, reason is *only* a fig leaf for *their* nakedness. When one man says that need, uncertainty, choice, novelty, and strife have no place in Reality, which is made up wholly of established things behaving by foregone rules, then may another man be provoked to reply that all such fixities, whether named atoms or God, whether they be fixtures of a sensational, a positivistic or an idealistic system, have existence and import only in the problems, needs, struggles and instrumentalities of conscious agents and patients. For home rule may be found in the unwritten efficacious constitution of experience.

That contemporaneously we are in the presence of such a reaction is apparent. Let us in pursuit of our topic inquire how it came about and why it takes the form that it takes. This consideration may not only occupy the hour, but may help diagram some future parallelogram of forces. The account calls for some sketching (1) of the historical tendencies which have shaped the situation in which a Stoic theory of knowledge claims metaphysical monopoly, and (2) of the tendencies that have furnished the despised principle of belief opportunity and means of reassertion.

II

Imagination readily travels to a period when a gospel of intense, and, one may say, deliberate passionate disturbance appeared to be conquering the Stoic ideal of passionless reason; when the demand for individual assertion by faith against the established, embodied objective order was seemingly subduing the idea of the total subordination of the individual to the universal. By what course of events came about the dramatic reversal, in which an ethically conquered Stoicism became the conqueror, epistemologically, of Christianity?

How are our imaginations haunted by the idea of what might have happened if Christianity had found ready to its hand intellectual formulations corresponding to its practical proclamations!

That the ultimate principle of conduct is affectional and volitional; that God is love; that access to the principle is by faith, a personal attitude; that belief, surpassing logical basis and warrant, works out through its own operation its own fulfilling evidence: such was the implied moral metaphysic of Christianity. But this implication needed to become a theory, a theology, a formulation; and in this need, it found no recourse save to philosophies that had identified true existence with the proper object of logical reason. For, in Greek thought, after the valuable meanings, the meanings of industry and art that appealed to sustained and serious choice, had given birth and status to reflective reason, reason denied its ancestry of organized endeavor, and proclaimed itself in its function of self-conscious logical thought to be the author and warrant of all genuine things. Yet how nearly Christianity had found prepared for it the needed means of its own intellectual statement! We recall Aristotle's account of moral knowing, and his definition of man. Man as man, he tells us, is a principle that may be termed either desiring thought or thinking desire. Not as pure intelligence does *man* know, but as an organization of desires effected through reflection upon their own conditions and consequences. What if Aristotle had only assimilated his idea of theoretical to his notion of practical knowledge! Because practical thinking was so human, Aristotle rejected it in favor of pure, passionless cognition, something superhuman. Thinking desire is experimental, is tentative, not absolute. It looks to the future, and to the past for help in the future. It is contingent, not necessary. It doubly relates to the individual: to the individual thing as experienced by an individual agent; not to the universal. Hence desire is a sure sign of defect, of privation, of non-being, and seeks surcease in something which knows it not. Hence desiring reason culminating in beliefs relating to imperfect existence, stands forever in contrast with passionless reason functioning in pure knowledge, logically complete, of perfect being.

I need not remind you how through Neo-Platonism, St. Augustine, and the Scholastic renaissance, these conceptions became imbedded in Christian philosophy; and what a reversal occurred of the original practical principle of Christianity. Belief is henceforth important because it is the mere antecedent, in a finite and fallen world, a temporal and phenomenal world infected with non-being, of true knowledge to be achieved only in a world of completed Being. Desire is but the self-consciousness of defect striving to its own termination in perfect possession, through perfect knowledge of perfect being. I need not remind you that the *prima facie* subordination of reason to authority, of knowledge to faith, in the mediaeval code, is, after all, but the logical result of the doctrine that man as man (since only reasoning desire) is merely phenomenal; and has his reality in God, who as God is the complete union of rational insight and being—the term of man's desire, and the fulfillment of his feeble attempts at knowing. Authority, "faith" as it then had to be

conceived, meant just that this Being comes externally to
the aid of man, otherwise hopelessly doomed to misery in
long drawn out error and non-being, and disciplines him till,
in the next world under more favoring auspices, he may have
his desires stilled in good, and his faith may yield to knowledge: — for we forget that the doctrine of immortality was
not an appendage, but an integral part of the theory that
since knowledge is the *true* function of man, happiness is
attained only in knowledge, which itself exists only in
achievement of perfect Being or God.

For my part, I can but think that mediaeval absolutism,
with its provision for authoritative supernatural assistance
in this world and assertion of supernatural realization in the
next, was more logical, as well as more humane, than the
modern absolutism, that, with the same logical premises, bids
man find adequate consolation and support in the fact, that,
after all, his strivings are already eternally fulfilled, his errors already eternally transcended, his partial beliefs already
eternally comprehended.

The modern age is marked by a refusal to be satisfied
with the postponement of the exercise and function of reason
to another and supernatural sphere, and by a resolve to practice itself upon its present object, nature, with all the joys
thereunto appertaining. The pure intelligence of Aristotle,
thought thinking itself, expresses itself as free inquiry directed upon the present conditions of its own most effective
exercise. The principle of the inherent relation of thought to
being was preserved intact, but its practical locus was moved
down from the next world to this. Spinoza's "God or Nature"
is the logical outcome; as is also his strict correlation of the
attribute of matter with the attribute of thought; while his
combination of thorough distrust of passion and faith with
complete faith in reason and all-absorbing passion for knowledge is so classic an embodiment of the whole modern
contradiction that it may awaken admiration where less
thorough-paced formulations call out irritation.

In the practical devotion of present intelligence to its
present object, nature, science was born, and also its philosophical counterpart, the theory of knowledge. Epistemology
only generalized in its loose, although narrow and technical

way, the question practically urgent in Europe: How is science possible? How can intelligence actively and directly get at its object?

Meantime, through Protestantism, the values, the meanings formerly characterizing the next life (the opportunity for full perception of perfect being), were carried over into present-day emotions and responses.

The dualism between faith authoritatively supported as the principle of this life, and knowledge supernaturally realized as the principle of the next, was transmuted into the dualism between intelligence now and here occupied with natural things, and the affections and accompanying beliefs, now and here realizing spiritual worths. For a time this dualism operated as a convenient division of labor. Intelligence, freed from responsibility for and preoccupation with supernatural truths, could occupy itself the more fully and efficiently with the world that now is; while the affections, charged with the values evoked in the mediaeval discipline, entered into the present enjoyment of the delectations previously reserved for the saints. Directness took the place of systematic intermediation; the present of the future; the individual's emotional consciousness of the supernatural institution. Between science and faith, thus conceived, a bargain was struck. Hands off; each to his own, was the compact; the natural world to intelligence, the moral, the spiritual world to belief. This (natural) world for knowledge; that (supernatural) world for belief. Thus the antithesis, unexpressed, ignored, *within experience*, between belief and knowledge, between the purely objective values of thought and the personal values of passion and volition, was more fundamental, more determining, than the opposition, explicit and harassing, *within knowledge*, between subject and object, mind and matter.

This latent antagonism worked out into the open. In scientific detail, knowledge encroached upon the historic traditions and opinions with which the moral and religious life had identified itself. It made history to be as natural, as much its spoil, as physical nature. It turned itself upon man, and proceeded remorselessly to account for his emotions, his volitions, his opinions. Knowledge, in its general theory, as philosophy, went the same way. It was pre-committed to the old notion: the absolutely real is the object of *knowledge*, and hence is something universal and impersonal. So, whether by the road of sensationalism or rationalism, by the path of mechanicalism or objective idealism, it came about that concrete selves, specific feeling and willing beings, were relegated with the beliefs in which they declare themselves to the "phenomenal."

III

So much for the situation against which some contemporary tendencies are a deliberate protest.

What of the positive conditions that give us not mere protest, like the unreasoning revolt of heart against head found at all epochs, but something articulate and constructive? The field is only too large, and I shall limit myself to the evolution of the knowledge standpoint itself. I shall suggest, first, that the progress of intelligence directed upon natural materials has evolved a procedure of knowledge that renders untenable the inherited conception of knowledge; and, secondly, that this result is reinforced by the specific results of some of the special sciences.

1. First, then, the very use of the knowledge standpoint, the very expression of the knowledge preoccupation, has produced methods and tests that, when formulated, intimate a radically different conception of knowledge, and of its relation to existence and belief, than the orthodox one.

The one thing that stands out is that thinking is inquiry, and that knowledge as science is the outcome of systematically directed inquiry. For a time it was natural enough that inquiry should be interpreted in the old sense, as just change of subjective attitudes and opinions to make them square up with a "reality" that is already there in ready-made, fixed, and finished form. The rationalist had one notion of the reality, *i.e.*, that it was of the nature of laws, genera, or an ordered system, and so thought of concepts, axioms, etc., as the indicated modes of representation. The empiricist, holding reality to be a lot of little discrete particular lumps, thought of disjointed sensations as its appropriate counter-part. But both alike were thorough conformists. If "reality" is already and completely given, and if knowledge is just submissive acceptance, then, of course, inquiry is only a sub-jective change in the human "mind" or in "consciousness,"— these being subjective and "unreal."

But the very development of the sciences served to reveal a peculiar and intolerable paradox. Epistemology, having condemned inquiry once for all to the region of sub-jectivity in an invidious sense, finds itself in flat opposition in principle and in detail to the assumption and to the re-sults of the sciences. Epistemology is bound to deny to the results of the special sciences in detail any ulterior objectivity just because they always *are* in a process of inquiry—*in* solution. While a man may not be halted at being told that his mental activities, since his, are not genuinely real, many men will draw violently back at being told that all the dis-coveries, conclusions, explanations and theories of the sciences share the same fate, being the products of a dis-credited mind. And, in general, epistemology, in relegating human thinking as inquiry to a merely phenomenal region, makes concrete approximation and conformity to objectivity hopeless. Even if it did square itself up to and by "reality" it never could be sure of it. The ancient myth of Tantalus and his effort to drink the water before him seems to be ingeni-ously prophetic of modern epistemology. The thirstier, the needier of truth the human mind, and the intenser the efforts put forth to slake itself in the ocean of being just beyond the edge of consciousness, the more surely the living waters of truth recede!

When such self-confessed sterility is joined with con-sistent derogation of all the special results of the special sciences, someone is sure to raise the cry of "dog in the manger," or of "sour grapes." A revision of the theory of thinking, of inquiry, would seem to be inevitable; a revision which should cease trying to construe knowledge as an at-tempted approximation to a reproduction of reality under conditions that condemn it in advance to failure; a revision which should start frankly from the fact of thinking as in-quiring, and purely external realities as terms in inquiries, and which should construe validity, objectivity, truth, and the test and system of truths, on the basis of what they actually mean and do within inquiry.

Such a standpoint promises ample revenge for the long damnation and longer neglect to which the principle of belief has been subjected. The whole procedure of thinking as developed in those extensive and intensive inquiries that constitute the sciences, is but rendering into a systematic technique, into an art deliberately and delightfully pursued, the rougher and cruder means by which practical human beings have in all ages worked out the implications of their beliefs, tested them and endeavored in the interests of economy, efficiency, and freedom, to render them coherent with one another. Belief, sheer, direct, unmitigated belief, reappears as the working hypothesis; action that at once develops and tests belief reappears in experimentation, deduction, demonstration; while the machinery of universals, axioms, *a priori* truths, etc., becomes a systematization of the way in which men have always worked out, in anticipation of overt action, the implications of their beliefs with a view to revising them in the interests of obviating unfavorable, and securing welcome consequences. Observation, with its machinery of sensations, measurements, etc., is the resurrection of the way in which agents have always faced and tried to define the problems that face them; truth is the union of abstract postulated meanings and of concrete brute facts in a way that circumvents the latter by judging them from a new standpoint, while it tests concepts by using them as methods in the same active experience. It all comes to experience personally conducted and personally consummated.

Let consciousness of these facts dawn a little more brightly over the horizon of epistemological prejudices, and it will be seen that nothing prevents admitting the genuineness both of thinking activities and of their characteristic results, except the notion that belief itself is not a genuine ingredient of existence—a notion which itself is not only a belief, but a belief which, unlike the convictions of the common man and the hypotheses of science, finds its proud proof in the fact that it does not demean itself so unworthily as to work.

Once believe that beliefs themselves are as "real" as anything else can ever be, and we have a world in which uncertainty, doubtfulness, really inhere; and in which personal attitudes and responses are real both in their own distinctive existence, and as the only ways in which an as yet undetermined factor of reality takes on shape, meaning, value, truth. If "to wilful men the injuries that they themselves procure, must be their schoolmasters"—and all beliefs are wilful—then by the same token the propitious evolutions of meaning, which wilful men secure to an expectant universe, must be their compensation and their justification. In a doubtful and needy universe elements must be beggarly, and the development of personal beliefs into experimentally executed systems of actions, is the organized bureau of philanthropy which confers upon a travailling universe the meaning for which it cries out. The apostrophe of the poet is above all to man the thinker, the inquirer, the knower:

> O Dreamer! O Desirer, goer down
> Unto untravelled seas in untried ships,
> O crusher of the unimagined grape,
> On unconceivèd lips.

2. Biology, psychology, and the social sciences proffer an imposing body of concrete facts that also point to the rehabilitation of belief—to the interpretation of knowledge as a human and practical outgrowth of belief, not to belief as the state to which knowledge is condemned in a merely finite and phenomenal world. I need not, as I cannot, here summarize the psychological revision which the notions of sensation, perception, conception, cognition in general have undergone, all to one intent. "Motor" is writ large on their face. The testimony of biology is unambiguous to the effect that the organic instruments of the whole intellectual life, the sense-organs and brain and their connections, have been developed on a definitely practical basis and for practical aims, for the purpose of such control over conditions as will sustain and vary the meanings of life. The historic sciences are equally explicit in their evidence that knowledge as a system of information and instruction is a cooperative social achievement, at all times socially toned, sustained, and directed;

and that logical thinking is a reweaving through individual activity of this social fabric at such points as are indicated by prevailing needs and aims.

This bulky and coherent body of testimony is not, of course, of itself philosophy. But it supplies, at all events, facts that have scientific backing, and that are as worthy of regard as the facts pertinent to any science. At the present time these facts seem to have some peculiar claim just because they present traits largely ignored in prior philosophic formulations, while those belonging to mathematics and physics have so largely wrought their sweet will on systems. Again, it would seem as if, in philosophies built deliberately upon the knowledge principle, any body of known facts should not have to clamor for sympathetic attention.

Such being the case, the reasons for ruling psychology and sociology and allied sciences out of competency to give philosophic testimony have more significance than the bare denial of jurisdiction. They are evidences of the deep-rooted preconception that whatever concerns a particular conscious agent, a wanting, struggling, satisfied and dissatisfied being, must of course be only "phenomenal" in import.

This aversion is the more suggestive when the professed idealist appears as the special champion of the virginity of pure knowledge. The idealist, so content with the notion that consciousness determines reality, provided it be done once for all, at a jump and in lump, is so uneasy in presence of the idea that empirical conscious beings genuinely determine existences now and here! One is reminded of the story told, I think, by Spencer. Some committee had organized and contended, through a long series of parliaments, for the passage of a measure. At last one of their meetings was interrupted with news of success. Consternation was the result. What was to become of the occupation of the committee? So, one asks, what is to become of idealism at large, of the wholesale unspecifiable determination of "reality" by or in "consciousness," if specific conscious beings, John Smiths and Susan Smiths (to say nothing of their animal relations), beings with bowels and brains, are found to exercise influence upon the character and existence of reals?

One would be almost justified in construing idealism as

a Pickwickian scheme, so willing is it to idealize the principle of intelligence at the expense of its specific undertakings, were it not that this reluctance is the necessary outcome of the Stoic basis and tenor of idealism—its preoccupation with logical contents and relations in abstraction from their *situs* and function in conscious living beings.

IV

I have suggested to you the naïve conception of the relation of beliefs to realities: that beliefs are themselves real without discount, manifesting their reality in the usual proper way, namely, by modifying and shaping the reality of other things, so that they connect the bias, the preferences and affections, the needs and endeavors of personal lives with the values, the characters ascribed to things:—the latter thus becoming worthy of human acquaintance and responsive to human intercourse. This was followed by a sketch of the history of thought, indicating how beliefs and all they insinuate were subjected to preconceived notions of knowledge and of "reality" as a monopolistic possession of pure intellect. Then I traced some of the *motifs* that make for reconsideration of the supposed uniquely exclusive relation of logical knowledge and "reality"; *motifs* that make for a less invidiously superior attitude towards the convictions of the common man.

In concluding, I want to say a word or two to mitigate —for escape is impossible—some misunderstandings. And, to begin with, while possible doubts inevitably troop with actual beliefs, the doctrine in question is not particularly sceptical. The radical empiricist, the humanist, the pragmatist, label him as you will, believes not in fewer but in more "realities" than the orthodox philosophers warrant. He is not concerned, for example, in discrediting objective realities and logical or universal thinking; he is interested in such a reinterpretation of the sort of "reality" which these things possess as will accredit, without depreciation, concrete empirical conscious centres of action and passion.

My second remark is to the opposite effect. The intent is

not especially credulous, although it starts from and ends with the radical credulity of all knowledge. To suppose that because the sciences are ultimately instrumental to human beliefs, we are therefore to be careless of the most exact possible use of extensive and systematic scientific methods, is like supposing that because a watch is made to tell present time, and not to be an exemplar of transcendent, absolute time, watches might as well be made of cheap stuffs, casually wrought and clumsily put together. It is the task of telling present time, with all its urgent implications, that brings home, steadies and enlarges the responsibility for the best possible use of intelligence, the instrument.

For one, I have no interest in the old, old scheme of derogating from the worth of knowledge in order to give an uncontrolled field for some *special* beliefs to run riot in,—be these beliefs even faith in immortality, in some special sort of a Deity, or in some particular brand of freedom. Any one of our beliefs is subject to criticism, revision and even ultimate elimination through the development of its own implications by intelligently directed action. Because reason is a scheme of working out the meanings of convictions in terms of one another and of the consequences they import in further experience, convictions are the more, not the less, amenable and responsible to the full exercise of reason.[4]

Thus we are put on the road to that most desirable thing,—the union of acknowledgment of moral powers and demands with thoroughgoing naturalism. No one really wants to lame man's practical nature; it is the supposed exigencies of natural science that force the hand. No one really bears a grudge against naturalism for the sake of ob-

---

4. There will of course come in time with the development of this point of view an organon of beliefs. The signs of a genuine as against a simulated belief will be studied; belief as a vital personal reaction will be discriminated from habitual, incorporate, unquestioned (because unconsciously exercised) traditions of social classes and professions. In his *Will to Believe* Professor James has already laid down two traits of genuine belief (viz., "forced option," and acceptance of responsibility for results) which are almost always ignored in criticisms (really caricatures) of his position. In the light of such an organon, one might come to doubt whether *belief* in, say, immortality (as distinct from hope on one side and a sort of intellectual balance of probability of opinion on the other) can genuinely exist at all.

scurantism. It is the need of some sacred reservation for moral interests that coerces. We all want to be as naturalistic as we can be. But the "can be" is the rub. If we set out with a fixed dualism of belief and knowledge, then the uneasy fear that the natural sciences are going to encroach and destroy "spiritual values" haunts us. So we build them a citadel and fortify it; that is, we isolate, professionalize, and thereby weaken beliefs. But if beliefs are the most natural, and in that sense, the most metaphysical of all things, and if knowledge is an organized technique for working out their implications and interrelations, for directing their formation and employ, how unnecessary, how petty the fear and the caution. Because freedom of belief is ours, free thought may exercise itself; the freer the thought the more sure the emancipation of belief. Hug some special belief and one fears knowledge; believe in belief and one loves and cleaves to knowledge.

We have here, too, the possibility of a common understanding, in thought, in language, in outlook, of the philosopher and the common man. What would not the philosopher give, did he not have to part with some of his common humanity in order to join a class? Does he not always when challenged justify himself with the contention that all men naturally philosophize, and that he but does in a conscious and orderly way what leads to harm when done in an indiscriminate and irregular way? If philosophy be at once a natural history *and* a logic—an art—of beliefs, then its technical justification is at one with its human justification. The natural attitude of man, said Emerson, is believing; "the philosopher, after some struggle, having only reasons for believing." Let the struggle then enlighten and enlarge beliefs; let the reasons kindle and engender new beliefs.

Finally, it is not a solution, but a problem which is presented. As philosophers, our disagreements as to conclusions are trivial compared with our disagreement as to problems. To see the problem another sees, in the same perspective and at the same angle—that amounts to something. Agreement in solutions is in comparison perfunctory. To experience the same problem another feels—that perhaps is agreement. In a world where distinctions are as invidious as comparisons

are odious, and where intellect works only by comparison
and distinction, pray what is one to do?

But beliefs are personal matters, and the person, we
may still believe, is social. To be a man is to be thinking
desire; and the agreement of desires is not in oneness of
intellectual conclusion, but in the sympathies of passion and
the concords of action: — and yet significant union in affection and behavior may depend upon a consensus in thought
that is secured only by discrimination and comparison.

REALITY AS EXPERIENCE

There are those who find that the assimilation to each other of the ideas of experience and reality is seriously hampered or even put out of court by the fact that science makes known a chronological period in which the world managed to lead a respectable existence in spite of not including conscious organisms. Under such conditions there was no experience, yet there was reality. Must we not, then, either give up the identification of the two conceptions, or else admit we are denying and sophisticating the plain facts of knowledge?

One is entitled to enter a *caveat* against any attempt to impose science, whether physical or psychological, *as* philosophy. One is moved to suggest that the greater the accumulation of interesting and professedly important details, the more urgent the question of what the import and interest are: the philosophic meaning of it all. Yet most empiricists would hardly be willing to adopt any philosophic position of which it could be clearly shown that it depends upon ignoring, denying or perverting scientific results.

Let us, then, analyze the situation which is offered to justify such charges. *It is a situation of which, by scientific warrant, it always is to be said that it is on its way to the present situation, that is, to "experience," and that this way is its own way.* The conditions which antecede experience are, in other words, already *in transition* towards the state of affairs in which they are experienced. Suppose one keep in mind the fact of *qualitative-transformation-towards*, and keep in mind that *this* fact has the same objective warrant as any other assigned trait (mechanical and chemical characteristics and relations, etc.). What, then, becomes of the force of the objection?

[First published in *Journal of Philosophy, Psychology and Scientific Methods* 3 (1906): 253–57.]

If, at some point, one shoves a soul-substance, a mind or even *a* consciousness[1] in between the prior condition of reality and experience, then, of course, the suggested implication—of identification of reality and experience—does not hold. Reality and experience are separable, because this heterogeneous factor interposes and *makes* their difference. *It*, not reality, is responsible for the transformation; *it* somehow modifies reality and makes experience out of it, the resultant experience being heterogeneous to reality in the degree in which the intervening mind, subject, or substance, is interjective in its nature, and sudden or catastrophic in its workings. I am not concerned here with all the hopeless puzzles that now emerge—puzzles which constitute "metaphysics" in the popular, pejoristic sense of that word. I am not even concerned with pointing out the difficulty, with respect to an experience so constituted, of picking out the features which belong to reality pure and uncontaminated, and those for which mind or consciousness, or whatever, is held accountable. I am only pointing out that such a conception is incompatible with the idea that the earlier chronological condition of reality is for philosophic purposes henceforth identifiable with reality. For philosophy, reality, on this basis, must include "mind," "consciousness," or whatever, along with the scientifically warranted early-dated world; and philosophy must worry through, as best it may, with the questions of a reality so hopelessly divided, by conception and definition, within and against itself. It is in any case a notion irrelevant to the particular problem under discussion.

I return to the supposedly strictly scientific objection. Unless some heterogeneous kind of reality is shoved in, then the early reality is at any and every point on its way to experience. It is only the earlier portion, historically speaking, of what later is experience. So viewed, the question of reality versus experience turns out to be only the question of an earlier version of reality against a later version,—or if the term "version" be objected to, then, of an

---

1. Consciousness is "the faint rumor left behind by the disappearing 'soul' upon the air of philosophy," James, *Journal of Philosophy, Psychology and Scientific Methods*, Vol. I, p. 477.

earlier rendering or expression or state of reality compared with its own later condition.

We can not, however, say an earlier reality versus a later reality, because this denies the salient point of *transition towards*. Continual-transformation-in-the-direction-of — this is the fact which excludes on the basis of science (to which we have agreed to appeal) any chopping off of the non-contemporaneously[2] experienced earlier reality from later experience. So viewed, the question for philosophy reduces itself to this: What is the better index, for philosophy, of reality: its earlier or its later form?

The question answers itself: the property or quality of transition-towards, change-in-the-direction-of, which is, to say the least, as objectively real as anything else, *can not* be included in the statement of reality qua earlier, but is only apprehended or realized *in* experience. In a very real sense, the present experience of the veriest unenlightened ditch-digger does philosophic justice to the earlier reality in a way which the scientific statement does not and can not: can not, that is, as formulated knowledge. As itself vital or direct experience, as *man's* experience (which as geologist's or physicist's or astronomer's formulation is ignored), the latter is more valuable; and is truer in the sense of worth more for other interpretations, for the construction of other objects

---

2. I insert this word because it is essential. By hypothesis, this prior state now *is* experienced, namely, in science, or so far as experience becomes critical. This is the scientific fact on which are wrecked all strictly objectivistic realisms. It is also the fact which, on the basis of a *psychological* analysis of reality and the substitution of psychological science for physical science as a methodological clue, is perverted into idealisms. Of course, it may be pointed out that this psychological procedure always starts from the body and its organs, the senses, brain, muscles, etc.; so that, as Santayana says, idealisms hold that because we get our experience through a body, therefore we have no body. But, on the other hand, it may be pointed out that this body, the organism and the behaviors characteristic of it, is just as real as anything else, and hence that an account of reality based upon systematically ignoring its curious attitudes and responses (that is, a philosophy based preferentially upon physical sciences) is also self-contradictory. In such a situation, the important point would seem to be the significance of science or experience in its critically controlled forms, whether physically or psychologically directed. And here is where the pragmatic variety of empiricism with its interpretation of the place of reflective knowledge, or thought, in control of experience, seems to have the call.

and the basing of projects upon them. The reason the scientist can suppress in his *statement* of the reality factors which the reality possesses, is just because (1) he is not interested in the total reality, but in such phases of it as serve as trustworthy indications of imports and projects, and because (2) the elements suppressed are not totally suppressed, but are right there in his *experience*: in its extrascientific features. In other words, the *scientist* can ignore some part of the *man's* experience just because that part is so irremediably there in experience.

Suppose a theoretically adequate cognition of the early reality as early (prior to the existence of conscious beings) is attained: call this O. Call its properties *a*, *b*, *c*, *d*, etc. Call its laws, the constant relations of these elements, A, B, C, D, etc. Now since, by the evolutionary theory to which appeal is made, this O is in qualitative transformation towards experience, O is not reality complete, is not R, but is a selection of certain conditions of R. But, it may be replied, the theory of *evolution* does recognize and state these factors of transformation. So be it. But where is the *locus* of this recognition? If these factors are referred to O, to the prior object, we have the same situation over again. We just have certain additional properties, *e*, *f*, *g*, etc., with additional functions, E, F, G, etc., which as referred to O are still in qualitative transformation. Something essential to reality is still omitted.

Recognize that this transformation is realized in present experience, and the contradiction vanishes. Since the qualitative transformation was towards experience, where else *should* its nature be realized save in experience—and in the very experience in which O, the knowledge object, is present.

The O as scientifically known is thus contained in an experience which is not exhausted in its quality of presenting O as object. And the surplusage is not irrelevant, but supplies precisely the factors of reality which are suppressed in the O taken as the chronologically prior thing. The only reason this is not universally recognized is just because it is inevitable and universally so. Only in philosophy does it require recognition; elsewhere it is taken for granted. The very motive and basis for formulating R as O is in those features of the experience which are not formulated, and which can be formulated only in a subsequent experience. What is omitted from reality in the O is always restored in the experience in which O is present. The O is thus really taken as what it is—a condition of reality as experience.

This immersion of a knowledge-object in an inclusive, vital, direct experience (which terms, like "immediate," are tautological, serving only as warnings against taking experience partially or abstractly) is the solution, I take it, of the problem of the transcendent aspect of knowledge. What is said of the overreaching, diaphanous character of knowledge in relation to its object is something which holds of the experience in which knowledge-and-its-object is sustained, and whose schematized, or structural, portion it is. Every experience thus holds in suspense within itself knowledge with its entire object-world, however big or little. And the experience here referred to is *any* experience in which cognition enters. It is not some ideal, or absolute, or exhaustive experience.

Thus, the knowledge-object always carries along, contemporaneously with itself, an other, something to which it is relevant and accountable, and whose union with it affords the condition of its testing, its correction and verification. This union is intimate and complete. The distinction in experience between the knowledge portion, as such, and its own experienced context, as non-cognitional, is a reflective, analytic distinction—itself real in *its* experienced content and function. In other words, we can not dispose of the "margin" or "surplus" of the experience in which knowledge is immersed as being emotional and volitional (and therefore just psychological, and hence philosophically irrelevant) because the distinction between knowledge-in-relation-to-its-object, qua known, and other, supposedly irrelevant, features is constituted in one and the same subsequent reflective experience. The experience in which O is presented is one in which O is distinguished from other elements of the experience as well as held in vital connection with them; but it is not one in which the knowledge-function is discriminated from other functions, say, the emotional and volitional. If the later experience in which this discrimination is made is purely psychological, then the knowledge-function itself, as well as the emotional and volitional, is merely a psychological distinction, and again the whole case falls. In other words, whether taken directly as the scientist's experience or later as the philosopher's (or logician's) experience, we have the same type of situation: that of something discriminated as a condition of experience over against and along with those features of experience of which it is the condition.

If one is inclined to deny this, let him ask himself how it is possible to correct (supposed) knowledge of the earlier history of the globe. If O is not all the time in most real connection with the extra-scientific features of its experience, then is it isolated and final. If, however, it has to square itself up with them, if it enters as just one factor into a more inclusive present reality, then there are conditions present which make for accountability, testing and revision. To take O as an *adequate* statement of reality (adequate, that is, for philosophy) is to exalt one scientific product at the expense of the entire scientific procedure by which that product is itself legitimated and corrected.

THE EXPERIMENTAL THEORY
OF KNOWLEDGE[1]

It should be possible to discern and describe a knowing as one identifies any object, concern or event. It must have its own marks; it must offer characteristic features—as much so as a thunder-storm, the constitution of a State, or a leopard. In the search for this affair, we are first of all desirous for something which is for itself, contemporaneously with its occurrence, a cognition, not something called knowledge by another and from without—whether this other be logician, psychologist or epistemologist. The "knowledge" may turn out false, and hence no knowledge; but this is an after-affair; it may prove to be rich in fruitage of wisdom, but if this outcome be only wisdom after the event, it does not concern us. What we want is just something which takes itself as knowledge, rightly or wrongly.

I

This means a specific case, a sample. Yet instances are proverbially dangerous—so naïvely and graciously may they beg the questions at issue. Our recourse is to an example so simple, so much on its face as to be as innocent as may be of assumptions. This case we shall gradually complicate, mindful at each step to state just what new elements are introduced. Let us suppose a smell, just a floating odor. This odor may be anchored by supposing that it moves to action; it starts changes that end in picking and enjoying a rose. This description is intended to apply to the course of events

1. Reprinted, with considerable change in the arrangement and in the matter of the latter portion, from *Mind*, Vol. XV, N.S., July, 1906.

[First published in *Mind*, n.s. 15 (1906): 293–307. Revised and reprinted in *The Influence of Darwin on Philosophy* (New York: Henry Holt and Co., 1910), pp. 77–111.]

witnessed and recounted from without. What sort of a course must it be to constitute a knowledge, or to have somewhere within its career that which deserves this title? The smell, *imprimis*, is there; the movements that it excites are there; the final plucking and gratification are experienced. But, let us say, the smell is not the smell *of* the rose; the resulting change of the organism is not a sense of walking and reaching; the delicious finale is not the fulfilment of the movement, and, through that, of the original smell; "is not," in each case meaning is "not experienced as" such. We may take, in short, these experiences in a brutely serial fashion. The smell, S, is replaced (and displaced) by a felt movement, K, this is replaced by the gratification, G. Viewed from without, as we are now regarding it, there is S-K-G. But from within, for itself, it is now S, now K, now G, and so on to the end of the chapter. Nowhere is there looking before and after; memory and anticipation are not born. Such an experience neither is, in whole or in part, a knowledge, nor does it exercise a cognitive function.

Here, however, we may be halted. If there is anything present in "consciousness" at all, we may be told (at least we constantly are so told) there must be knowledge of it as present—present, at all events, in "consciousness." There is, so it is argued, knowledge at least of a simple apprehensive type, knowledge of the acquaintance order, knowledge *that*, even though not knowledge *what*. The smell, it is admitted, does not know *about* anything else, nor is anything known *about* the smell (the same thing, perhaps); but the smell is known, either by itself, or by the mind, or by some subject, some unwinking, unremitting eye. No, we must reply; there is no apprehension without some (however slight) context; no acquaintance which is not either recognition or expectation. Acquaintance is presence honored with an escort; presence is introduced as familiar, or an associate springs up to greet it. Acquaintance always implies a little friendliness; a trace of re-knowing, of anticipatory welcome or dread of the trait to follow.

This claim cannot be dismissed as trivial. If valid, it carries with it the distance between being and knowing: and the recognition of an element of mediation, that is, of art, in all knowledge. This disparity, this transcendence, is not something which holds of *our* knowledge, of finite knowledge, just marking the gap between our type of consciousness and some other with which we may contrast it after the manner of the agnostic or the transcendentalist (who hold so much property in joint ownership!), but exists because knowing is knowing, that way of bringing things to bear upon things which we call reflection—a manipulation of things experienced in the light one of another.

"Feeling," I read in a recent article, "feeling is immediately acquainted with its own quality, with its own subjective being."[2] How and whence this duplication in the inwards of feeling into feeling the knower and feeling the known? into feeling as being and feeling as acquaintance? Let us frankly deny such monsters. Feeling *is* its own quality; is its own *specific* (whence and why, once more, *subjective*?) being. If this statement be dogmatism, it is at least worth insistent declaration, were it only by way of counter-irritant to that other dogmatism which asserts that being in "consciousness" is always presence for or in knowledge. So let us repeat once more, that to *be* a smell (or anything else) is one thing, to be *known* as smell, another; to be a "feeling" one thing, to be *known* as a "feeling" another.[3] The first is thinghood; existence indubitable, direct; in this way all things *are* that are in "consciousness" at all.[4] The second is *reflected* being, things

2. I must remind the reader again of a point already suggested. It is the identification of presence in consciousness with knowledge as such that leads to setting up *a* mind (*ego*, subject) which has the peculiar property of knowing (only so often it knows wrong!), or else that leads to supplying "sensations" with the peculiar property of surveying their own entrails. Given the correct feeling that knowledge involves relationship, there being, by supposition, no other *thing* to which the thing in consciousness is related, it is forthwith related to a soul substance, or to its ghostly offspring, a "subject," or to "consciousness" itself.

3. Let us further recall that this theory requires either that things present shall already be psychical things (feelings, sensations, etc.), in order to be assimilated to the knowing mind, subject to consciousness; or else translates genuinely naïve realism into the miracle of a mind that gets outside itself to lay its ghostly hands upon the things of an external world.

4. This means that things may be present *as* known, just as they be present as hard or soft, agreeable or disgusting, hoped for or dreaded. The mediacy, or the art of intervention, which characterizes knowledge, indicates precisely the way in which known things as known are immediately present.

indicating and calling for other things—something offering
the possibility of truth and hence of falsity. The first is genuine immediacy; the second is (in the instance discussed) a
pseudo-immediacy, which in the same breath that it proclaims its immediacy smuggles in another term (and one
which is unexperienced both in itself and in its relation) the
subject, or "consciousness," to which the immediate is related.[5]

But we need not remain with dogmatic assertions. To
be acquainted with a thing or with a person has a definite
empirical meaning; we have only to call to mind what it is
to be genuinely and empirically acquainted, to have done forever with this uncanny presence which, though bare and simple presence, is yet known, and thus is clothed upon and
complicated. To be acquainted with a thing is to be assured
(from the standpoint of the experience itself) that it is of
such and such a character; that it will behave, if given an opportunity, in such and such a way; that the obviously and
flagrantly present trait is associated with fellow traits that
will show themselves, if the leadings of the present trait are
followed out. To be acquainted is to anticipate to some extent, on the basis of prior experience. I am, say, barely acquainted with Mr. Smith: then I have no extended body of
associated qualities along with those palpably present, but
at least some one suggested trait occurs; his nose, his tone
of voice, the place where I saw him, his calling in life, an
interesting anecdote about him, etc. To be acquainted is to
know what a thing is *like* in some particular. If one is acquainted with the smell of a flower it means that the smell is
not just smell, but reminds one of some other experienced
thing which stands in continuity with the smell. There is thus
supplied a condition of control over or purchase upon what

5. If Hume had had a tithe of the interest in the *flux* of perceptions
and in *habit*—principles of continuity and of organization—
which he had in distinct and isolated existences, he might have
saved us both from German *Erkenntnisstheorie*, and from that
modern miracle play, the psychology of elements of consciousness, that under the aegis of science, does not hesitate to have
psychical elements compound and breed, and in their agile in-
tangibility put to shame the performances of their less acrobatic
cousins, physical atoms.

is present, the possibility of translating it into terms of some other trait not now sensibly present.

Let us return to our example. Let us suppose that S is not just displaced by K and then by G. Let us suppose it persists; and persists not as an unchanged S alongside K and G, nor yet as fused with them into a new further quale J. For in such events, we have only the type already considered and rejected. For an observer the new quale might be more complex, or fuller of meaning, than the original S, K, or G, but might not be experienced *as* complex. We might thus suppose a composite photograph which should suggest nothing of the complexity of its origin and structure. In this case we should have simply another picture.

But we may also suppose that the blur of the photograph suggests the superimposition of pictures and something of their character. Then we get another, and for our problem, much more fruitful kind of persistence. We will imagine that the final G assumes this form: Gratification-terminating-movement-induced-by-smell. The smell is still present; it has persisted. It is not present in its original form, but is represented with a quality, an office, that of having excited activity and thereby terminating its career in a certain quale of gratification. It is not S, but Σ; that is S with an increment of meaning due to maintenance and fulfilment through a process. S is no longer just smell, but smell which has excited and thereby secured.

Here we have a cognitive, but not a cognitional thing. In saying that the smell is finally experienced as *meaning* gratification (through intervening handling, seeing, etc.) and meaning it not in a hapless way, but in a fashion which operates to effect what is meant, we retrospectively attribute intellectual force and function to the smell—and this is what is signified by "cognitive." Yet the smell is not cognitional, because it did not knowingly intend to mean this; but is found, after the event, to have meant it. Nor again is the final experience, the Σ or transformed S, a knowledge.

Here again the statement may be challenged. Those who agree with the denial that bare presence of a quale in "consciousness" constitutes acquaintance and simple apprehension, may now turn against us, saying that experience of fulfilment of meaning is just what we mean by knowledge, and this is just what the Σ of our illustration is. The point is fundamental. As the smell at first was presence or being, less than knowing, so the fulfilment is an experience that is more than knowing. Seeing and handling the flower, enjoying the full meaning of the smell as the odor of just this beautiful thing, is not knowledge because it is more than knowledge.

As this may seem dogmatic, let us suppose that the fulfilment, the realization, experience, is a knowledge. Then how shall it be distinguished from and yet classed with other things called knowledge, viz., reflective, discursive cognitions? Such knowledges are what they are precisely because they are not fulfilments, but intentions, aims, schemes, symbols of overt fulfilment. Knowledge, perceptual and conceptual, of a hunting dog is prerequisite in order that I may really hunt with the hounds. The hunting in turn may increase my knowledge of dogs and their ways. But the knowledge of the dog, *qua* knowledge, remains characteristically marked off from the use of that knowledge in the fulfilment experience, the hunt. The hunt is a *realization* of knowledge; it alone, if you please, verifies, validates, knowledge, or supplies tests of truth. The prior knowledge of the dog, was, if you wish, hypothetical, lacking in assurance or categorical certainty. The hunting, the fulfilling, realizing experience alone *gives* knowledge, because it alone completely assures; makes faith good in works.

Now there is and can be no objection to this definition of knowledge, *provided it is consistently adhered to*. One has as much right to identify knowledge with complete assurance, as I have to identify it with anything else. Considerable justification in the common use of language, in common sense, may be found for defining knowledge as complete assurance. But even upon this definition, the fulfilling experience is not, as such, complete assurance, and hence not a knowledge. Assurance, cognitive validation, and guaranteeship, follow from it, but are not coincident with its occurrence. It *gives*, but *is* not, assurance. The concrete construction of a story, the manipulation of a machine, the hunting with the dogs, is not, so far as it *is* fulfilment, a confirmation of meanings previously entertained as cognitional; that is, is not contemporaneously experienced as such. To think of prior schemes, symbols, meanings, as fulfilled in a subsequent experience, is reflectively to present in their relations to one another both the meanings and the experiences in which they are, as a matter of fact, embodied. This reflective attitude cannot be identical with the fulfilment experience itself; it occurs only in retrospect when the worth of the meanings, or cognitive ideas, is critically inspected in the light of their fulfilment; or it occurs as an interruption of the fulfilling experience. The hunter stops his hunting as a fulfilment to reflect that he made a mistake in his idea of his dog, or again, that his dog is everything he thought he was—that his notion of him is confirmed. Or, the man stops the actual construction of his machine and turns back upon his plan in correction or in admiring estimate of its value. *The fulfilling experience is not of itself knowledge*, then, even if we identify knowledge with fulness of assurance or guarantee. Moreover it gives, affords, assurance only in reference to a situation which we have not yet considered.[6]

Before the category of confirmation or refutation can be introduced, there must be something which *means* to mean something and which therefore can be guaranteed or nullified by the issue—and this is precisely what we have not as yet found. We must return to our instance and introduce a further complication. Let us suppose that the smell quale recurs at a later date, and that it recurs neither as the original S nor yet as the final Σ, but as an S' which is fated or charged with the sense of the possibility of a fulfilment like unto Σ. The S' that recurs is aware of something else which it means, which it intends to effect through an operation incited by it and without which its own presence is abortive, and, so to say, unjustified, senseless. Now we have an experience which is *cognitional*, not merely cognitive; which is contemporaneously aware of meaning something beyond itself, instead of having this meaning ascribed by another at a later period. *The odor knows the rose; the rose is known by the odor; and the import of each term is constituted by the rela-*

6. In other words, the situation as described is not to be confused with the case of hunting on purpose to test an idea regarding the dog.

tionship in which it stands to the other. That is, the import
of the smell is the indicating and demanding relation which
it sustains to the enjoyment of the rose as its fulfilling experience; while this enjoyment is just the content or definition
of what the smell consciously meant, *i.e.,* meant to mean.
Both the thing meaning and the thing meant are elements
in the same situation. Both are present, but both are not present in the same way. In fact, one is present as-*not*-present-in-
the-same-way-in-which-the-other-is. It is present as something
to be rendered present in the same way through the intervention of an operation. We must not balk at a purely verbal
difficulty. It suggests a verbal inconsistency to speak of a
thing present-as-absent. But all ideal contents, all aims (that
is, things aimed at) are present in just such fashion. Things
can be presented as absent, just as they can be presented as
hard or soft, black or white, six inches or fifty rods away
from the body. The assumption that an ideal content must be
either totally absent, or else present *in just the same fashion*
as it will be when it is realized, is not only dogmatic, but self-
contradictory. The only way in which an ideal content can
be experienced at all is to be presented as *not-present-in-the-
same-way* in which something else is present, the latter kind
of presence affording the standard or type of *satisfactory*
presence. When present in the same way it ceases to be an
ideal content. Not a contrast of bare existence over against
non-existence, or of present consciousness over against reality out of present consciousness, but of a satisfactory with
an unsatisfactory mode of presence makes the difference between the "really" and the "ideally" present.

In terms of our illustration, handling and enjoying the
rose are present, but they are not present in the same way
that the smell is present. They are present as *going* to be
there in the same way, through an operation which the smell
stands sponsor for. The situation is inherently an uneasy one
—one in which everything hangs upon the performance of
the operation indicated; upon the adequacy of movement as
a connecting link, or real adjustment of the thing meaning
and the thing meant. Generalizing from the instance, we get
the following definition: An experience is a knowledge, if in
its quale there is an experienced distinction and connection

of two elements of the following sort: *one means or intends the presence of the other in the same fashion in which itself is already present, while the other is that which, while not present in the same fashion, must become so present if the meaning or intention of its companion or yoke-fellow is to be fulfilled through the operation it sets up.*

II

We now return briefly to the question of knowledge as acquaintance, and at greater length to that of knowledge as assurance, or as fulfilment which confirms and validates. With the recurrence of the odor as meaning something beyond itself, there is apprehension, knowledge *that*. One may now say I know what a *rose* smells like; or I know what *this* smell is like; I am acquainted with the rose's agreeable odor. In short, on the basis of a present quality, the odor anticipates and forestalls some further trait.

We have also the conditions of knowledge of the confirmation and refutation type. In the working out of the situation just described, in the transformation, self-indicated and self-demanded, of the tensional into a harmonious or satisfactory situation, fulfilment *or* disappointment results. The odor either does or does not fulfil itself in the rose. The smell as intention is borne out by the facts, or is nullified. As has already been pointed out, the subsequent experience of the fulfilment type is not primarily a confirmation or refutation. Its import is too vital, too urgent to be reduced *in itself* just to the value of testing an intention or meaning.[7] But it gets *in*

7. Dr. Moore, in an essay in *Studies in Logical Theory* has brought out clearly, on the basis of a criticism of the theory of meaning and fulfilment advanced in Royce's *World and Individual*, the full consequences of this distinction. I quote one sentence (p. 350): "Surely there is a pretty discernible difference between experience as a purposive idea, and the experience which fulfils this purpose. To call them both 'ideas' is at least confusing." The text above simply adds that there is also a discernible and important difference between experiences which, *de facto*, are purposing and fulfilling (that is, are seen to be such *ab extra*), and those which meant to be such, and are found to be what they meant.

reflection just such verificatory significance. If the smell's intention is unfulfilled, the discrepancy may throw one back, in reflection, upon the original situation. Interesting developments then occur. The smell meant a rose; and yet it did not (so it turns out) mean a rose; it meant another flower, or something, one can't just tell what. Clearly there is *something else* which enters in; something else beyond the odor as it was first experienced determined the validity of its meaning. Here then, perhaps, we have a transcendental, as distinct from an experimental reference? *Only if this something else makes no difference, or no detectable difference, in the smell itself.* If the utmost observation and reflection can find no difference in the smell quales that fail and those that succeed in executing their intentions, then there is an outside controlling and disturbing factor, which, since it is outside of the situation, can never be utilized in knowledge, and hence can never be employed in any concrete testing or verifying. In this case, knowing depends upon an extra-experimental or transcendental factor. But this very transcendental quality makes both confirmation and refutation, correction, criticism, of the pretensions or meanings of things, impossible. For the conceptions of truth and error, we must, upon the transcendental basis, substitute those of accidental success or failure. Sometimes the intention chances upon one, sometimes upon another. Why or how, the gods only know —and they only if to them the extra-experimental factor is not extra-experimental, but makes a concrete difference in the concrete smell. But fortunately the situation is not one to be thus described. The factor that determines the success or failure, does institute a difference in the thing which means the object, and this difference is detectable, once attention, through failure, has been called to the need of its discovery. At the very least, it makes this difference: the smell is infected with an element of uncertainty of meaning —and this as a part of the thing experienced, not for an observer. This additional *awareness* at least brings about an additional *wariness*. Meaning is more critical, and operation more cautious.

But we need not stop here. Attention may be fully directed to the subject of smells. Smells may become the object of knowledge. They may take, *pro tempore*,[8] the place which the rose formerly occupied. One may, that is, observe the cases in which odors mean other things than just roses, may voluntarily produce new cases for the sake of further inspection, and thus account for the cases where meanings had been falsified in the issue; discriminate more carefully the peculiarities of those meanings which the event verified, and thus safeguard and bulwark to some extent the employing of similar meanings in the future. Superficially, it may then seem as if odors were treated after the fashion of Locke's simple ideas, or Hume's "distinct ideas which are separate existences." Smells apparently assume an independent, isolated status during this period of investigation. "Sensations," as the laboratory psychologist and the analytic psychologist generally studies them, are examples of just such detached things. But egregious error results if we forget that this seeming isolation and detachment is the outcome of a deliberate scientific device—that it is simply a part of the scientific technique of an inquiry directed upon securing *tested* conclusions. Just and only because odors (or any group of qualities) are parts of a connected world are they signs of things beyond themselves; and only because they are signs is it profitable and necessary to study them *as if* they were complete, self-enclosed entities.

In the reflective determination of things with reference to their specifically meaning other things, experiences of fulfilment, disappointment and going astray inevitably play an important and recurrent *rôle*. They also are realistic facts, related in realistic ways to the things that intend to mean other things and to the things intended. When these fulfilments and refusals *are reflected upon* in the determinate relations in which they stand to their relevant meanings, they obtain a quality which is quite lacking to them in their immediate occurrence as just fulfilments or disappointments; *viz.*, the property of affording assurance and correction—of

8. The association of science and philosophy with leisure, with a certain economic surplus, is not accidental. It is practically worth while to postpone practice; to substitute theorizing, to develop a new and fascinating mode of practice. But it is the excess achievement of practice which makes this postponement and substitution possible.

confirming and refuting. Truth and falsity are not properties of any experience or thing, in and of itself or in its first intention; *but of things where the problem of assurance consciously enters in. Truth and falsity present themselves as significant facts only in situations in which specific meanings and their already experienced fulfilments and non-fulfilments are intentionally compared and contrasted with reference to the question of the worth, as to reliability of meaning, of the given meaning or class of meanings.* Like knowledge itself, truth is an experienced relation of things, and it has no meaning outside of such relation,[9] any more than such adjectives as comfortable applied to a lodging, correct applied to speech, persuasive applied to an orator, etc., have worth apart from the *specific* things to which they are applied. It would be a great gain for logic and epistemology, if we were always to translate the noun "truth" back into the adjective "true," and this back into the adverb "truly"; at least, if we were to do so until we have familiarized ourselves thoroughly with the fact that "truth" is an abstract noun, summarizing a quality presented by specific affairs in their own specific contents.

III

I have attempted, in the foregoing pages, a description of the function of knowledge in its own terms and on its merits—a description which in intention is realistic, if by realistic we are content to mean naturalistic, a description undertaken on the basis of what Mr. Santayana has well called "following the lead of the subject-matter." Unfortunately at the present time all such undertakings contend with a serious extraneous obstacle. Accomplishing the undertaking has difficulties enough of its own to reckon with; and first attempts are sure to be imperfect, if not radically wrong. But at present the attempts are not, for the most part, even

9. It is the failure to grasp the coupling of truth of meaning with a *specific* promise, undertaking or intention expressed by a thing which underlies, so far as I can see, the criticisms passed upon the experimental or pragmatic view of the truth. It is the same failure which is responsible for the wholly *at large* view of truth which characterizes the absolutists.

listened to on their own account, they are not examined and criticised as naturalistic attempts. *They are compared with undertakings of a wholly different nature, with an epistemological theory of knowledge, and the assumptions of this extraneous theory are taken as a ready-made standard by which to test their validity.* Literally of course, "epistemology" means only theory of knowledge; the term *might* therefore have been employed simply as a synonym for a descriptive logic; for a theory that takes knowledge as it finds it and attempts to give the same kind of an account of it that would be given of any other natural function or occurrence. But the mere mention of what *might* have been only accentuates what is. The things that pass for epistemology all assume that knowledge is not a natural function or event, but a mystery.

Epistemology starts from the assumption that certain conditions lie back of knowledge. The mystery would be great enough if knowledge were constituted by non-natural conditions back of knowledge, but the mystery is increased by the fact that the conditions are defined so as to be incompatible with knowledge. Hence the primary problem of epistemology is: How is knowledge *überhaupt*, knowledge at large, *possible*? Because of the incompatibility between the concrete occurrence and function of knowledge and the conditions back of it to which it must conform, a second problem arises: How is knowledge in general, knowledge *überhaupt, valid*? Hence the complete divorce in contemporary thought between epistemology as theory of knowledge and logic as an account of the specific ways in which particular beliefs that are better than other alternative beliefs regarding the same matters are formed; and also the complete divorce between a naturalistic, a biological and social psychology, setting forth how the function of knowledge is evolved out of other natural activities, and epistemology as an account of how knowledge is possible anyhow.

It is out of the question to set forth in this place in detail the contrast between transcendental epistemology and an experimental theory of knowledge. It may assist the understanding of the latter, however, if I point out, baldly and briefly, how, *out of the distinctively empirical situation*, there arise those assumptions which make knowledge a mystery, and hence a topic for a peculiar branch of philosophizing.

As just pointed out, epistemology makes the possibility of knowledge a problem, because it assumes back of knowledge conditions incompatible with the obvious traits of knowledge as it empirically exists. These assumptions are that the organ or instrument of knowledge is not a natural object, but some ready-made state of mind or consciousness, something purely "subjective," a peculiar kind of existence which lives, moves, and has its being in a realm different from things to be known; and that the ultimate goal and content of knowledge is a fixed, ready-made thing which has no organic connections with the origin, purpose, and growth of the attempt to know it, some kind of *Ding-an-sich* or absolute, extra-empirical "Reality."

(1) It is not difficult to see at what point in the development of natural knowledge, or the signifying of one thing by another, there arises the notion of the knowing medium as something radically different in the order of existence from the thing to be known. It arises subsequent to the repeated experience of non-fulfilment, of frustration and disappointment. The odor did not after all mean the rose; it meant something quite different; and yet its indicative function was exercised so forcibly that we could not help—or at least *did* not help—believing in the existence of the rose. This is a familiar and typical kind of experience, one which very early leads to the recognition that "things are not what they seem." There are two contrasted methods of dealing with this recognition: one is the method indicated above (pp. 116–17). We go more thoroughly, patiently, and carefully into the facts of the case. We employ all sorts of methods, invented for the purpose, of examining the things that are signs and the things that are signified, and we experimentally produce various situations, in order that we may tell *what* smells mean roses *when* roses are meant, what it is about the smell and the rose that led us into error; and that we may be able to discriminate those cases in which a suspended conclusion is all that circumstances admit. We simply do the best we can to regulate our system of signs so that they become as instructive as possible, utilizing for this purpose (as indicated above) all possible experiences of success and of failure, and deliberately instituting cases which will throw light on the specific empirical causes of success and failure.

Now it so happens that when the facts of error were consciously generalized and formulated, namely in Greek thought, such a technique of specific inquiry and rectification did not exist—in fact, it hardly could come into existence until *after* error had been seized upon as constituting a fundamental anomaly. Hence the method just outlined of dealing with the situation was impossible. We can imagine disconsolate ghosts willing to postpone any professed solution of the difficulty till subsequent generations have thrown more light on the question itself; we can hardly imagine passionate human beings exercising such reserve. At all events, Greek thought provided what seemed a satisfactory way out: there are two orders of existence, one permanent and complete, the noumenal region, to which alone the characteristic of Being is properly applicable, the other transitory, phenomenal, sensible, a region of non-Being, or at least of mere Coming-to-be, a region in which Being is hopelessly mixed with non-Being, with the unreal. The former alone is the domain of knowledge, of truth; the latter is the territory of opinion, confusion, and error. In short, the contrast *within* experience of the cases in which things successfully and unsuccessfully maintained and executed the meanings of other things was erected into a wholesale difference of status in the intrinsic characters of the things involved in the two types of cases.

With the beginnings of modern thought, the region of the "unreal," the source of opinion and error, was located exclusively in the individual. The object was *all* real and *all* satisfactory, but the "subject" could approach the object only through his own subjective states, his "sensations" and "ideas." The Greek conception of two orders of existence was retained, but instead of the two orders characterizing the "universe" itself, one *was* the universe, the other was the individual mind trying to know that universe. This scheme would obviously easily account for error and hallucination; but how could *knowledge*, truth, ever come about on such a basis? The Greek problem of the possibility of error became the modern problem of the possibility of knowledge.

Putting the matter in terms that are independent of history, experiences of failure, disappointment, non-fulfilment of the function of meaning and contention may lead the individual to the path of science—to more careful and extensive investigation of the things themselves, with a view to detecting specific sources of error, and guarding against them, and regulating, so far as possible, the conditions under which objects are bearers of meanings beyond themselves. But impatient of such slow and tentative methods (which insure not infallibility but increased probability of valid conclusions), by reason of disappointment a person may turn epistemologist. He may then take the discrepancy, the failure of the smell to execute its own intended meaning, as a wholesale, rather than as a specific fact: as evidence of a contrast in general between things meaning and things meant, instead of as evidence of the need of a more cautious and thorough inspection of odors and execution of operations indicated by them. One may then say: Woe is me; smells are only *my* smells, subjective states existing in an order of being made out of consciousness, while roses exist in another order made out of a radically different sort of stuff; or odors are made out of "finite" consciousness as their stuff, while the real things, the objects which fulfil them, are made out of an "infinite" consciousness as their material. Hence some purely metaphysical tie has to be called in to bring them into connection with each other. And yet this tie does not concern knowledge; it does not make the meaning of one odor any more correct than that of another, nor enable us to discriminate relative degrees of correctness. As a principle of control, this transcendental connection is related to all alike, and hence condemns and justifies all alike.[10]

10. The belief in the *metaphysical* transcendence of the object of knowledge seems to have its real origin in an *empirical* transcendence of a very specific and describable sort. The thing meaning is one thing; the thing meant is another thing, and is (as already pointed out) a thing presented as not given in the same way as is the thing which means. It is something *to be* so given. No amount of careful and thorough inspection of the indicating and signifying things can remove or annihilate this gap. The *probability* of correct meaning may be increased in varying degrees—and this is what we mean by control. But final certitude can never be reached except experimentally—except by performing the operations indicated and discovering whether or

It is interesting to note that the transcendentalist almost invariably first falls into the psychological fallacy; and then having himself taken the psychologist's attitude (the attitude which is interested in meanings as themselves self-enclosed "ideas") accuses the empiricist whom he criticises of having confused mere psychological existence with logical validity. That is, he begins by supposing that the smell of our illustration (and all the cognitional objects for which this is used as a symbol) is a purely mental or psychical state, so that the question of logical reference or intention is the problem of how the merely mental can "know" the extra-mental. But from a strictly empirical point of view, the smell which knows is no more merely mental than is the rose known. We may, if we please, say that the smell when involving conscious meaning or intention is "mental," but this term "mental" does not denote some separate type of existence—existence as a state of consciousness. It denotes only the fact that the smell, a real and non-psychical object, now exercises an intellectual *function*. This new property involves, as James has pointed out, an *additive* relation—a new property possessed by a non-mental object, when that object, occurring in a new context, assumes a further office and use.[11] To be "in the mind" means to be in a situation in which the function of intending is directly concerned.[12] Will not someone who believes that the knowing experience is *ab origine* a strictly "mental" thing, explain how, as matter of fact, it does get a specific, extra-mental reference, capable of being tested, confirmed or refuted? Or, if he believes that viewing it as merely mental expresses only the form it takes for psychological analysis, will he not explain why he so persistently attributes

no the intended meaning is fulfilled *in propria persona*. In this experimental sense, truth or the object of any given meaning is always beyond or outside of the cognitional thing that means it. Error as well as truth is a necessary function of knowing. But the non-empirical account of this transcendent (or beyond) relationship puts *all* the error in one place (*our* knowledge), and *all* the truth in another (absolute consciousness or else a thing-in-itself).

11. Compare his essay, "Does 'Consciousness' Exist?" in the *Journal of Philosophy, Psychology and Scientific Methods*, Vol. I, p. 480.
12. Compare the essay on the "Problem of Consciousness," by Professor Woodbridge, in the Garman Memorial Volume, entitled *Studies in Philosophy and Psychology*.

the inherently "mental" characterization of it to the empiricist whom he criticises? An object *becomes* meaning when used empirically in a certain way; and, under certain circumstances, the exact character and worth of this meaning *becomes* an object of solicitude. But the transcendental epistemologist with his purely psychical "meanings" and his purely extra-empirical "truths" assumes a *Deus ex Machina* whose mechanism is preserved a secret. And as if to add to the arbitrary character of his assumption, he has to admit that the transcendental *a priori* faculty by which mental states get objective reference does not in the least help us to discriminate, *in the concrete*, between an objective reference that is false and one that is valid.

(2) The counterpart assumption to that of pure aboriginal "mental states" is, of course, that of an Absolute Reality, fixed and complete in itself, of which our "mental states" are bare transitory hints, their true meaning and their transcendent goal being the Truth *in rerum natura*. If the organ and medium of knowing is a self-enclosed order of existence different in kind from the Object to be known, then that Object must stand out there in complete aloofness from the concrete purpose and procedure of knowing it. But if we go back to the knowing as a natural occurrence, capable of description, we find that just as a smell does not mean Rose in general (or anything else at large), but means a *specific* group of qualities whose experience is intended and anticipated, so the function of knowing is always expressed in connections between a given experience and a specific possible wanted experience. The "rose" that is meant in a particular situation *is* the rose of that situation. When this experience is consummated, it is achieved as the fulfilment of the conditions in which just *that* intention was entertained—not as the fulfilment of a faculty of knowledge or a meaning in general. Subsequent meanings and subsequent fulfilments may increase, may enrich the consummating experience; the object or content of the rose as known may be other and fuller next time and so on. But we have no right to set up "a rose" at large or in general as the object of the knowing odor; the object of a knowledge is always strictly correlative to that particular thing which means it. It is not something

which can be put in a wholesale way over against that which
cognitively refers to it, as when the epistemologist puts the
"real" rose (object) over against a merely phenomenal or
empirical rose which *this* smell happens to mean. As the
meaning gets more complex, fuller, more finely discriminated, the object which realizes or fulfils the meaning grows
similarly in quality. But we cannot set up a rose, an object
of fullest, complete and exhaustive content as that which is
really meant by any and every odor of a rose, whether it consciously meant to mean it or not. The test of the cognitional
rectitude of the odor lies in the *specific* object which it sets
out to secure. This is the meaning of the statement that the
import of *each* term is found in its relationship to the other.
It applies to object meant as well as to the meaning. Fulfilment, completion are always relative terms. *Hence the criterion of the truth or falsity of the meaning, of the adequacy,
of the cognitional thing lies within the relationships of the
situation and not without.* The thing that means another by
means of an intervening operation either succeeds or fails in
accomplishing the operation indicated, while this operation
either gives or fails to give the object meant. Hence the truth
or falsity of the original cognitional object.

IV

From this excursion, I return in conclusion to a brief
general characterization of those situations in which we are
aware that things mean other things and are so critically
aware of it that, in order to increase the probability of fulfilment and to decrease the chance of frustration, all possible
pains are taken to regulate the meanings that attach to
things. These situations define that type of knowing which
we call *scientific*. There are things that claim to mean other
experiences; in which the trait of meaning other objects is
not discovered *ab extra*, and after the event, but is part of
the thing itself. This trait of the thing is as realistic, as specific, as any other of its traits. It is, therefore, as open to
inspection and determination as to its nature, as is any other
trait. Moreover, since it is upon this trait that assurance (as

distinct from accident) of fulfilment depends, an especial interest, an absorbing interest, attaches to its determination. Hence the scientific type of knowledge and its growing domination over other sorts.

We *employ* meanings in all intentional constructions of experience—in all anticipations, whether artistic, utilitarian or technological, social or moral. The success of the anticipation is found to depend upon the character of the meaning. Hence the stress upon a right determination of these meanings. Since they are the instruments upon which fulfilment depends *so far as that is controlled* or other than accidental, they become themselves objects of surpassing interest. For all persons at some times, and for one class of persons (scientists) at almost all times, the determination of the meanings employed in the control of fulfilments (of acting upon meanings) is central. The experimental or pragmatic theory of knowledge explains the dominating importance of science; it does not depreciate it or explain it away.

Possibly pragmatic writers are to blame for the tendency of their critics to assume that the practice they have in mind is utilitarian in some narrow sense, referring to some preconceived and inferior use—though I cannot recall any evidence for this admission. But what the pragmatic theory has in mind is precisely the fact that all the affairs of life which need regulation—*all values of all types*—depend upon utilizations of meanings. Action is not to be limited to anything less than the carrying out of ideas, than the execution, whether strenuous or easeful, of meanings. Hence the surpassing importance which comes to attach to the careful, impartial construction of the meanings, and to their constant survey and resurvey with reference to their value as evidenced by experiences of fulfilment and deviation.

That truth denotes *truths*, that is, specific verifications, combinations of meanings and outcomes reflectively viewed, is, one may say, the central point of the experimental theory. Truth, in general or in the abstract, is a just name for an experienced relation among the things of experience: that sort of relation in which intents are retrospectively viewed from the standpoint of the fulfilment which they secure through their own natural operation or incitement. Thus the experimental theory explains directly and simply the absolutistic tendency to translate concrete true things into the general relationship, Truth, and then to hypostatize this abstraction into identity with real being, Truth *per se* and *in se*, of which all transitory things and events—that is, all experienced realities—are only shadowy futile approximations. This type of relationship is central for man's will, for man's conscious endeavor. To select, to conserve, to extend, to propagate those meanings which the course of events has generated, to note their peculiarities, to be in advance on the alert for them, to search for them anxiously, to substitute them for meanings that eat up our energy in vain, defines the aim of rational effort and the goal of legitimate ambition. The absolutistic theory is the transfer of this moral or voluntary law of selective action into a quasi-physical (that is, metaphysical) law of indiscriminate being. Identify metaphysical being with *significant excellent* being—that is, with those relationships of things which, in our moments of deepest insight and largest survey, we would continue and reproduce—and the experimentalist, rather than the absolutist, is he who has a right to proclaim the supremacy of Truth, and the superiority of the life devoted to Truth for its own sake over that of "mere" activity. But to read back into an order of things which exists without the participation of our reflection and aim, the quality which defines the purpose of our thought and endeavor is at one and the same stroke to mythologize reality and to deprive the life of thoughtful endeavor of its ground for being.

EXPERIENCE AND OBJECTIVE IDEALISM[1]

I

Idealism as a philosophic system stands in such a delicate relation to experience as to invite attention. In its subjective form, or sensationalism, it claims to be the last word of empiricism. In its objective, or rational form, it claims to make good the deficiencies of the subjective type, by emphasizing the work of thought that supplies the factors of objectivity and universality lacking in sensationalism. With reference to experience *as it now is*, such idealism is half opposed to empiricism and half committed to it,—antagonistic, so far as existing experience is regarded as tainted with a sensational character; favorable, so far as this experience is even now prophetic of some final, all-comprehensive, or absolute experience, which in truth is one with reality.

That this combination of opposition to present experience with devotion to the cause of experience in the abstract leaves objective idealism in a position of unstable equilibrium from which it can find release only by euthanasia in a thorough-going empiricism seems evident. Some of the reasons for this belief may be readily approached by a summary sketch of three historic episodes in which have emerged important conceptions of experience and its relation to reason. The first takes us to classic Greek thought. Here experience means the preservation, through memory, of the net result of a multiplicity of particular doings and sufferings; a preservation that affords positive skill in maintaining further practice, and promise of success in new emergencies. The craft

1. Reprinted, with slight verbal changes, from the *Philosophical Review*, Vol. XV (1906).

[First published in *Philosophical Review* 15 (1906): 465–81. Revised and reprinted in *The Influence of Darwin on Philosophy* (New York: Henry Holt and Co., 1910), pp. 198–225.]

of the carpenter, the art of the physician are standing examples of its nature. It differs from instinct and blind routine or servile practice because there is some knowledge of materials, methods, and aims, in their adjustment to one another. Yet the marks of its passive, habitual origin are indelibly stamped upon it. On the knowledge side it can never aspire beyond opinion, and if true opinion be achieved, it is only by happy chance. On the active side it is limited to the accomplishment of a special work or a particular product, following some unjustified, because assumed, method. Thus it contrasts with the true knowledge of reason, which is direct apprehension, self-revealing and self-validating, of an eternal and harmonious content. The regions in which experience and reason respectively hold sway are thus explained. Experience has to do with production, which, in turn, is relative to decay. It deals with generation, becoming, not with finality, being. Hence it is infected with the trait of relative nonbeing, of mere imitativeness; hence its multiplicity, its logical inadequacy, its relativity to a standard and end beyond itself. Reason, *per contra*, has to do with meaning, with significance (ideas, forms), that is eternal and ultimate. Since the meaning of anything is the worth, the good, the end of that thing, experience presents us with partial and tentative efforts to achieve the embodiment of purpose, under conditions that doom the attempt to inconclusiveness. It has, however, its meed of reality in the degree in which its results *participate* in meaning, the good, reason.

From this classic period, then, comes the antithesis of experience as the historically achieved *embodiments* of meaning, partial, multiple, insecure, to reason as the source, author, and container of *meaning*, permanent, assured, unified. Idealism means ideality, experience means brute and broken facts. That things exist because of and for the sake of meaning, and that experience gives us meaning in a servile, interrupted, and inherently deficient way—such is the standpoint. Experience gives us meaning in process of becoming; special and isolated instances in which it *happens*, temporally, to appear, rather than meaning pure, undefiled, independent. Experience presents purpose, the good, struggling against obstacles, "involved in matter."

Just how much the vogue of modern Neo-Kantian idealism, professedly built upon a strictly epistemological instead
of upon a cosmological basis, is due, in days of a declining
theology, to a vague sense that affirming the function of reason in the constitution of a knowable world (which in its
own constitution as logically knowable may be, morally and
spiritually, anything you please), carries with it an assurance
of the superior reality of the good and the beautiful as well as
of the "true," it would be hard to say. Certainly unction seems
to have descended upon epistemology, in apostolic succession, from classic idealism; so that Neo-Kantianism is rarely
without a tone of edification, as if feeling itself the patron of
man's spiritual interests in contrast to the supposed crude-
ness and insensitiveness of naturalism and empiricism. At
all events, we find here one element in our problem: Experience considered as the summary of past episodic adventures
and happenings in relation to fulfilled and adequately expressed meaning.

The second historic event centres about the controversy
of innate ideas, or pure concepts. The issue is between empiricism and rationalism as theories of the origin and validation of scientific knowledge. The empiricist is he who feels
that the chief obstacle which prevents scientific method from
making way is the belief in pure thoughts, not derived from
particular observations and hence not responsible to the
course of experience. His objection to the "high *a priori* road"
is that it introduces in irresponsible fashion a mode of presumed knowledge which may be used at any turn to stand
sponsor for mere tradition and prejudice, and thus to nullify
the results of science resting upon and verified by observable
facts. Experience thus comes to mean, to use the words of
Peirce, "that which is forced upon a man's recognition will-he,
nill-he, and shapes his thoughts to something quite different
from what they naturally would have been."[2] The same definition is found in James, in his chapter on Necessary Truths:
"Experience means experience of something foreign supposed
to impress us whether spontaneously or in consequence of
our own exertions and acts."[3] As Peirce points out, this no-

2. C. S. Peirce, *Monist*, Vol. XVI, p. 150.
3. *Psychology*, Vol. II, p. 618.

tion of experience as the foreign element that forces the hand of thought, and controls its efficacy, goes back to Locke. Experience is "observation employed either about external sensible objects, or about the internal operations of our minds"[4] —as furnishing in short all the valid data and tests of thinking and knowledge. This meaning, thinks Peirce, should be accepted "as a landmark which it would be a crime to disturb or displace."

The contention of idealism, here bound up with rationalism, is that perception and observation cannot guarantee knowledge in its honorific sense (science); that the peculiar differentia of scientific knowledge is a constancy, a universality, and necessity that contrast at every point with perceptual data, and that indispensably require the function of conception.[5] In short, *qualitative transformation* of *facts* (data of perception), not their mechanical subtraction and recombination, is the difference between scientific and perceptual knowledge. Here the problem which emerges is, of course, the significance of perception and of conception in respect to experience.[6]

The third episode reverses in a curious manner (which confuses present discussion) the notion of experience as a foreign, alien, coercive material. It regards experience as a fortuitous association, by merely psychic connections, of individualistic states of consciousness. This is due to the Humian development of Locke. The "objects" and "operations," which to Locke were just given and secured in observation, become shifting complexes of subjective sensations and ideas, whose apparent permanency is due to discoverable illusions. This, of course, is the empiricism which made Kant so uneasily toss in his dogmatic slumbers (a tossing that he took

4. *Essay concerning Human Understanding*, Bk. II, Ch. 2, Sec. 2. Locke doubtless derived this notion from Bacon.
5. It is hardly necessary to refer to the stress placed upon mathematics, as well as upon fundamental propositions in logic, ethics and cosmology.
6. Of course there are internal historic connections between experience as effective "memory," and experience as "observation." But the motivation and stress, the problem, has quite shifted. It may be remarked that Hobbes still writes under the influence of the Aristotelian conception "Experience is nothing but Memory" (*Elements of Philosophy*, Part One, Ch. 1, Sec. 2), and hence is opposed to science.

for an awakening); and which, by reaction, called out the conception of thought as a function operating both to elevate perceptual data to scientific status, and also to confer objective status, or knowable character, upon even sensational data and their associative combinations.[7] Here emerges the third element in our problem: The function of thought as furnishing objectivity to any experience that claims cognitive reference or capacity.

Summing up the matter, idealism stands forth with its assertion of thought or reason as (1) the sponsor for all significance, ideality, purpose, in experience,—the author of the good and the beautiful as well as the true; (2) the power, located in pure conceptions, required to elevate perceptive or observational material to the plane of science; and (3) the constitution that gives objectivity, even the semblance of order, system, connection, mutual reference, to sensory data that without its assistance are mere subjective flux.

II

I begin the discussion with the last-named function. Thought is here conceived as *a priori*, not in the sense of particular innate ideas, but of a function that constitutes the

7. There are, of course, anticipations of Hume in Locke. But to regard Lockeian experience as equivalent to Humian is to pervert history. Locke, as he was to himself and to the century succeeding him, was not a subjectivist, but in the main a common-sense objectivist. It was this that gave him his historic influence. But so completely has the Hume-Kant controversy dominated recent thinking that it is constantly projected backward. Within a few weeks I have seen three articles, all insisting that the meaning of the term experience must be subjective, and stating or implying that those who take the term objectively are subverters of established usage! But a casual study of the dictionary will reveal that experience has always meant "*what* is experienced," observation as a source of knowledge, as well as the act, fact or mode of experiencing. In the Oxford Dictionary, the (obsolete) sense of "experimental testing," of actual "observation of facts and events," and "the fact of being consciously affected by an act" have almost contemporaneous datings, viz., 1384, 1377, and 1382 respectively. A usage almost more objective than the second, the Baconian use, is "what has been experienced; the events that have taken place within the knowledge of an individual, a community, mankind at large, either during a particular period or generally." This dates back to 1607. Let us have no more captious criticisms and plaints based on ignorance of linguistic usage. [This pious wish has not been met. J. D., 1909.]

very possibility of any objective experience, any experience involving reference beyond its own mere subjective happening. I shall try to show that idealism is condemned to move back and forth between two inconsistent interpretations of this *a priori* thought. It is taken to mean both the organized, the regulated, the informed, established character of experience, an order immanent and constitutional; and an agency which organizes, regulates, forms, synthesizes, a power operative and constructive. And the oscillation between and confusion of these two diverse senses is necessary to Neo-Kantian idealism.

When Kant compared his work in philosophy to that of the men who introduced construction into geometry, and experimentation into physics and chemistry, the point of his remarks depends upon taking the *a priori* worth of thought in a regulative, directive, controlling sense, thought as consciously, intentionally, making an experience *different* in a *determinate* sense and manner. But the point of his answer to Hume consists in taking the *a priori* in the other sense, as something which is *already* immanent in *any* experience, and which accordingly makes no determinate difference to any one experience as compared with any other, or with any past or future form of itself. The concept is treated first as that which makes an experience actually different, controlling its evolution towards consistency, coherency, and objective reliability; then, it is treated as that which has already effected the organization of any and every experience that comes to recognition at all. The fallacy from which he never emerges consists in vibrating between the definition of a concept as a rule of constructive synthesis in a *differential* sense, and the definition of it as a static endowment lurking in "mind," and giving automatically a hard and fixed law for the determination of every experienced object. The *a priori* conceptions of Kant as immanent fall, like the rain, upon the just and the unjust; upon error, opinion, and hallucination. But Kant slides into these *a priori* functions the preferential values exercised by empirical reflective thought. The concept of triangle, taken geometrically, means doubtless a determinate method of construing space elements; but to Kant it also means something that exists in the mind *prior* to all such geometrical constructions and that unconsciously lays down the law not only for their conscious elaboration, but also for any space perception, even for that which takes a rectangle to be a triangle. The first of the meanings is intelligible, and marks a definite contribution to the logic of science. But it is not "objective idealism"; it is a contribution to a revised empiricism. The second is a dark saying.

That organization of some sort exists in every experience I make no doubt. That isolation, discrepancy, the fragmentary, the incompatible, are brought to recognition and to logical function only with reference to some prior existential mode of organization seems clear. And it seems equally clear that reflection goes on with profit only because the materials with which it deals have already some degree of organization, or exemplify various relationships. As against Hume, or even Locke, we may be duly grateful to Kant for enforcing acknowledgment of these facts. But the acknowledgment means simply an improved and revised empiricism.

For, be it noted, this organization, first, is not the work of reason or thought, unless "reason" be stretched beyond all identification; and, secondly, it has no sacrosanct or finally valid and worthful character. (1) Experience always carries with it and within it certain systematized arrangements, certain classifications (using the term without intellectualistic prejudice), coexistent and serial. If we attribute these to "thought" then the structure of the brain of a Mozart which hears and combines sounds in certain groupings, the psychophysical visual habit of the Greek, the locomotor apparatus of the human body in the laying-out and plotting of space is "thought." Social institutions, established political customs, effect and perpetuate modes of reaction and of perception that compel a certain grouping of objects, elements, and values. A national constitution brings about a definite arrangement of the factors of human action, which holds even physical things together in certain determinate orders. Every successful economic process, with its elaborate divisions and adjustments of labor, of materials and instruments, is just such an objective organization. Now it is one thing to say that thought has played a part in the origin and development of such organizations, and continues to have a rôle in their judicious employment and application; it is another to say that these organizations *are* thought, or are its exclusive product. Thought that functions in these ways is distinctively *reflective* thought, thought as practical, volitional, deliberately exercised for specific aims—thought as an act, an art of skilled mediation. As *reflective* thought, its end is to terminate its own first and experimental forms, and to secure an organization which, while it may evoke new reflective thinking, puts an end to the thinking that secured the organization. As *organizations*, as established, effectively controlling arrangements of objects in experience, their mark is that they are not thoughts, but habits, customs of action.[8]

Moreover, such reflective thought as does intervene in the formation and maintenance of these practical organizations harks back to prior practical organizations, biological and social in nature. It serves to *valuate* organizations already existent as biological functions and instincts, while, as itself a biological activity, it redirects them to new conditions and results. Recognize, for example, that a geometric concept is a practical locomotor function of arranging stimuli in reference to maintenance of life activities *brought into consciousness*, and then serving as a centre of reorganization of such activities to freer, more varied flexible and valuable forms; recognize this, and we have the truth of the Kantian idea, without its excrescences and miracles. The concept is the practical activity doing consciously and artfully what it had aforetime done blindly and aimlessly, and thereby not only doing it better but opening up a freer world of significant activities. Thought as such a reorganization of natural functions does naturally what Kantian forms and schematizations do only supernaturally. In a word, the constructive or organizing activity of "thought" does not inhere in thought as a transcendental function, a form or mode of some supraempirical ego, mind or consciousness, but in thought as itself vital activity. And in any case we have passed to the

---

8. The relationship of organization and thought is precisely that which we find psychologically typified by the rhythmic functions of habit and attention, attention being always, *ab quo*, a sign of the failure of habit, and, *ad quem*, a reconstructive modification of habit.

idea of thought as reflectively reconstructive and directive, and away from the notion of thought as immanently constitutional and organizational. To make this passage and yet to ignore its existence and import is essential to objective idealism.

(2) No final or ultimate validity attaches to these original arrangements and institutionalizations in any case. Their value is teleological and experimental, not fixedly ontological. "Law and order" are good things, but not when they become rigidity, and create mechanical uniformity or routine. Prejudice is the acme of the *a priori*. Of the *a priori* in this sense we may say what is always to be said of habits and institutions: They are good servants, but harsh and futile masters. Organization as already effected is always in danger of becoming a *mortmain*; it may be a way of sacrificing novelty, flexibility, freedom, creation to static standards. The curious inefficiency of idealism at this point is evident in the fact that genuine thought, empirical reflective thought, is required precisely for the purpose of re-forming established and set formations.

In short, (*a*) *a priori* character is no exclusive function of thought. Every biological function, every motor attitude, every vital impulse as the carrying vehicle of experience is thus *apriorily* regulative in prospective reference; what we call apperception, expectation, anticipation, desire, demand, choice, are pregnant with this constitutive and organizing power. (*b*) In so far as "thought" does exercise such reorganizing power, it is because thought is itself still a *vital* function. (*c*) Objective idealism depends not only upon ignoring the existence and capacity of vital functions, but upon a profound confusion of the constitutional *a priori*, the unconsciously dominant, with empirically reflective thought. In the sense in which the *a priori* is worth while as an attribute of thought, thought cannot be what the objective idealist defines it as being. Plain, ordinary, everyday empirical reflections, operating as centres of inquiry, of suggestion, of experimentation, exercise the valuable function of regulation, in an auspicious direction, of subsequent experiences.

The categories of accomplished systematization cover

alike the just and the unjust, the false and the true, while (unlike God's rain) they exercise no *specific* or *differential* activity of stimulation and control. Error and inefficiency, as well as value and energy, are embodied in our objective institutional classifications. As a special favor, will not the objective idealist show how, in some one single instance, his immanent "reason" makes any difference as respects the detection and elimination of error, or gives even the slightest assistance in discovering and validating the truly worthful? This practical work, the life blood of intelligence in everyday life and in critical science, is done by the despised and rejected matter of concrete empirical contexts and functions. Generalizing the issue: If the immanent organization be ascribed to thought, why should its work be such as to demand continuous correction and revision? If specific reflective thought, as empirical, be subject to all the limitations supposed to inhere in experience as such, how can it assume the burden of making good, of supplementing, reconstructing, and developing meanings? The logic of the case seems to be that Neo-Kantian idealism gets its status against empiricism by first accepting the Humian idea of experience, while the express import of its positive contribution is to show the *non-existence* (not merely the cognitive invalidity) of anything describable as mere states of subjective consciousness. Thus in the end it tends to destroy itself and to make way for a more adequate empiricism.

III

In the above discussion, I have unavoidably anticipated the second problem: the relation of conceptual thought to perceptual data. A distinct aspect still remains, however. Perception, as well as apriority, is a term harboring a fundamental ambiguity. It may mean (1) a distinct type of activity, predominantly practical in character, though carrying at its heart important cognitive and aesthetic qualities; or (2) a distinctively cognitional experience, the function of observation as explicitly logical—a factor in science *qua* science.

In the first sense, as recent functional empiricism (working in harmony with psychology, but not itself peculiarly psychological) has abundantly shown, perception is primarily an act of adjustment of organism and environment, differing from a mere reflex or instinctive adaptation in that, in order to compensate for the failure of the instinctive adjustment, it requires an objective or discriminative presentation of conditions of action: the negative conditions or obstacles, and the positive conditions or means and resources.[9] This, of course, is its cognitive phase. In so far as the material thus presented not only serves as a direct cue to further successful activity (successful in the overcoming of obstacles to the maintenance of the function entered upon) but presents auxiliary collateral objects and qualities that give additional range and depth of meaning to the activity of adjustment, perceiving is aesthetic as well as intellectual.[10]

Now such perception cannot be made antithetical to thought, for it may itself be surcharged with any amount of imaginatively supplied and reflectively sustained ideal factors —such as are needed to determine and select relevant stimuli and to suggest and develop an appropriate plan and course of behavior. The amount of such saturating intellectual material depends upon the complexity and maturity of the behaving agent. Such perception, moreover, is strictly teleological, since it arises from an experienced need and functions to fulfill the purpose indicated by this need. The cognitional content is, indeed, carried by affectional and intentional contexts.

Then we have perception as scientific observation. This involves the deliberate, artful exclusion of affectional and purposive factors as exercising mayhap a vitiating influence upon the cognitive or objective content; or, more strictly

9. Compare, for example, Dr. Stuart's paper in the *Studies in Logical Theory*, pp. 253–56. I may here remark that I remain totally unable to see how the *interpretation* of objectivity to mean controlling conditions of action (negative and positive as above) derogates at all from its naïve objectivity, or how it connotes cognitive subjectivity, or is in any way incompatible with a common-sense realistic theory of perception.
10. For this suggested interpretation of the aesthetic as surprising, or unintended, gratuitous collateral reinforcement, see Gordon, *Psychology of Meaning.*

speaking, a transformation of the more ordinary or "natural" emotional and purposive concomitants, into what Bain calls "neutral" emotion, and a purpose of finding out what the present conditions of the problem are. (The practical feature is not thus denied or eliminated, but the overweening influence of a present dominating end is avoided, so that *change of the character of the end* may be effected, if found desirable.) Here observation may be opposed to thought, in the sense that exact and minute description may be set over against interpretation, explanation, theorizing, and inference. In the wider sense of thought as equaling reflective process, the work of observation and description forms a constituent division of labor *within* thought. The impersonal demarcation and accurate registration of what is objectively there or present occurs for the sake (*a*) of eliminating meaning which is habitually but uncritically referred, and (*b*) of getting a basis for a meaning (at first purely inferential or hypothetical) that may be consistently referred; and that (*c*), resting upon examination and not upon mere *a priori* custom, may weather the strain of subsequent experiences. But in so far as thought is identified with the conceptual phase as such of the entire logical function, observation is, of course, set over against thought: deliberately, purposely, and artfully so.

It is not uncommon to hear it said that the Lockeian movement was all well enough for psychology, but went astray because it invaded the field of logic. If we mean by psychology a natural history of what at any time *passes* for knowledge, and by logic conscious control in the direction of grounded assurance, this remark appears to reverse the truth. As a natural history of knowledge in the sense of opinion and belief, Locke's account of discrete, simple ideas or meanings, which are compounded and then distributed, does palpable violence to the facts. But every line of Locke shows that he was interested in knowledge in its honorific sense— controlled certainty, or, where this is not feasible, measured probability. And to logic as an account of the way in which we by art build up a *tested* assurance, a rationalized conviction, Locke makes an important positive contribution. The pity is that he inclined to take it for the whole of the logic of science,[11] not seeing that it was but a correlative division of labor to the work of hypotheses or inference; and that he tended to identify it with a natural history or psychology. The latter tendency exposed Locke to the Humian interpretation and permanently sidetracked the positive contribution of his theory to logic, while it led to that confusion of an untrue psychology with a logic, valid within limits, of which Mill is the standard example.

In analytic observation, it is a positive object to strip off all inferential meaning so far as may be—to reduce the facts as nearly as may be to derationalized data, in order to make possible a new and better rationalization. In and because of this process, the perceptual data approach the limit of a disconnected manifold, of the brutely given, of the merely sensibly present; while meaning stands out as a searched for principle of unification and explanation, that is, as a thought, a concept, an hypothesis. The extent to which this is carried depends wholly upon the character of the specific situation and problem; but, speaking generally, or of limiting tendencies, one may say it is carried to mere observation, pure brute description, on the one side, and to mere thought, that is hypothetical inference, on the other.

So far as Locke ignored this instrumental character of observation, he naturally evoked and strengthened rationalistic idealism; he called forth its assertion of the need of reason, of concepts, of universals, to constitute knowledge in its eulogistic sense. But two contrary errors do not make a truth, although they suggest and determine the nature of some relevant truth. This truth is the empirical origin, in a determinate type of situation, of the contrast of observation and conception; the empirical relevancy and the empirical worth of this contrast in controlling the character of subsequent experiences. To suppose that perception as it concretely exists, either in the early experiences of the animal, the race, or the individual, or in its later refined and expanded experiences, is identical with the sharply analyzed, objectively discriminated and internally disintegrated elements of scientific ob-

11. This, however, is not strictly true, since Locke goes far to supply the means of his own correction in his account of the "workmanship of the understanding."

servation, is a perversion of experience; a perversion for which, indeed, professed empiricists set the example, but which idealism must perpetuate if it is not to find its end in an improved, functional empiricism.[12]

IV

We come now to the consideration of the third element in our problem; ideality, important and normative value, in relation to experience; the antithesis of experience as a tentative, fragmentary, and ineffectual embodiment of meaning over against the perfect, eternal system of meanings which experience suggests even in nullifying and mutilating.

That from the *memory* standpoint experience presents itself as a multiplicity of episodic events with just enough continuity among them to suggest principles true "on the whole" or usually, but without furnishing instruction as to their exact range and bearing, seems obvious enough. Why should it not? The motive which leads to reflection on *past* experience could be satisfied in no other way. Continuities, connecting links, dynamic transitions drop out because, for the purpose of the recollection, they would be hindrances if now repeated; or because they are now available only when themselves objectified in definite terms and thus given a *quasi*-independent, a *quasi*-atomistic standing of their own. This is the only alternative to what the psychologists term "total reminiscence," which, so far as total, leaves us with an elephant on our hands. Unless we are going to have a wholesale revivification of the past, giving us just another embarrassing present experience, illusory because irrelevant, memory must work by retail—by summoning *distinct* cases, events, sequences, precedents. Dis-membering is a positively necessary part of re-membering. But the resulting *disjecta membra* are in no sense experience as it was or is; they are simply elements held apart, and yet tentatively implicated together, in

12. Plato, especially in his *Theaetetus*, seems to have begun the procedure of blasting the good name of perceptive experience by identifying a late and instrumental distinction, having to do with logical control, with all experience whatsoever.

present experience for the sake of its most favorable evolution; evolution in the direction of the most excellent meaning or value conceived. If the remembering is efficacious and pertinent, it reveals the possibilities of the present; that is to say, it clarifies the transitive, transforming character that belongs inherently to the present. The dismembering of the vital present into the disconnected past is correlative to an anticipation, an idealization of the future.

Moreover, the contingent character of the principle or rule that emerges from a survey of cases, instances, as distinct from a fixed or necessary character, secures just what is wanted in the exigency of a prospective idealization, or refinement of excellence. It is just this character that secures flexibility and variety of outlook, that makes possible a consideration of alternatives and an attempt to select and to execute the more worthy among them. The fixed or necessary law would mean a future like the past—a dead, an unidealized future. It is exasperating to imagine how completely different would have been Aristotle's valuation of "experience" with respect to its contingency, if he had but once employed the function of developing and perfecting value, instead of the function of knowing an unalterable object, as the standard by which to estimate and measure intelligence.

The one constant trait of experience from its crudest to its most mature forms is that its contents undergo change of meaning, and of meaning in the sense of excellence, value. Every experience is in-course,[13] in course of becoming worse or better as to its contents, or in course of conscious endeavor to sustain some satisfactory level of value against encroachment or lapse. In this effort, both precedent, the reduction of the present, and idealization, the anticipation of the possible, though doubtful, future, emerge. Without idealization, that is, without conception of the favorable issue that the present, defined in terms of precedents, may portend in its transition,

13. Compare James, "Continuous transition is one sort of conjunctive relation; and to be a radical empiricist means to hold fast to this conjunctive relation of all others, for this is the strategic point, the position through which, if a hole be made, all the corruptions of dialectics and all the metaphysical fictions pour into our philosophy."—*Journal of Philosophy, Psychology and Scientific Methods*, Vol. I, p. 536.

the recollection of precedents and the formulation of tentative rules are nonsense. But without the identification of the present in terms of elements suggested by the past, without recognition, the ideal, the value projected as end, remains inert, helpless, sentimental, without means of realization. Resembling cases and anticipation, memory and idealization, are the corresponding terms in which a present experience has its transitive force analyzed into reciprocally pertinent means and ends.

That an experience will change in content and value is the one thing certain. *How* it will change is the one thing naturally uncertain. Hence the import of the art of reflection and invention. Control of the character of the change in the direction of the worthful is the common business of theory and practice. Here is the province of the episodic recollection of past history and of the idealized foresight of possibilities. The irrelevancy of an objective idealism lies in the fact that it totally ignores the position and function of ideality in sustained and serious endeavor. Were values automatically injected and kept in the world of experience by any force not reflected in human memories and projects, it would make no difference whether this force were a Spencerian environment or an Absolute Reason. Did purpose ride in a cosmic automobile toward a predestined goal, it would not cease to be physical and mechanical in quality because labelled Divine Idea, or Perfect Reason. The moral would be "let us eat, drink and be merry," for to-morrow—or if not this to-morrow, then upon some to-morrow, unaffected by our empirical memories, reflections, inventions, and idealizations—the cosmic automobile arrives. Spirituality, ideality, meaning as purpose, would be the last things to present themselves if objective idealism were true. Values cannot be both ideal and given, and their "given" character is emphasized, not transformed, when they are called eternal and absolute. But natural values become ideal the moment their maintenance is dependent upon the intentional activities of an empirical agent. To suppose that values are ideal because they are so eternally given is the contradiction in which objective idealism has entrenched itself. Objective ontological teleology spells machinery. Reflective and volitional, experimental teleology alone

spells ideality.[14] Objective, rationalistic idealism breaks upon
the fact that it can have no intermediary between a brutally
achieved embodiment of meaning (physical in character or
else of that peculiar quasi-physical character which goes generally by the name of metaphysical) and a total opposition
of the given and the ideal, connoting their mutual indiffer-
ence and incapacity. An empiricism that acknowledges the
transitive character of experience, and that acknowledges
the possible control of the character of the transition by
means of intelligent effort, has abundant opportunity to cele-
brate in productive art, genial morals, and impartial inquiry
the grace and the severity of the ideal.

14. One of the not least of the many merits of Santayana's *Life of
    Reason* is the consistency and vigor with which is upheld the
    doctrine that significant idealism means idealization.

THE ST. LOUIS CONGRESS OF
THE ARTS AND SCIENCES

To the Editor of Science: In the May number of the *Atlantic Monthly* there appeared an article by Dr. Hugo Münsterberg, giving, in a quasi-official manner, a statement of the plans for the St. Louis Congress of the Arts and Sciences.* The fact that a literary rather than a scientific journal has been selected as a means of communication to the public, and that the plan itself as there set forth is philosophical rather than scientific, affords my justification for writing on a matter which my own technical scientific qualifications would under ordinary circumstances hardly entitle me to discuss, excepting possibly as respects one group of the sciences.

That the article bases the working plans of the St. Louis Congress of Arts and Sciences upon a particular methodology emanating from a particular school of metaphysics, not as yet numbering among its adherents any great number of either scientific men or philosophers, naturally arouses certain apprehensions. I write chiefly in the hope that some explanation may be forthcoming which will allay these apprehensions, which I find I am far from alone in feeling. Even after the explicit statements of the article, one can hardly believe one's own eyes, and is sceptical of one's right to attribute to the distinguished committee the notion of basing the Congress upon a particular scheme of metaphysical logic. One is sure the plan must be capable of construction in some other way. Accordingly I beg in advance the pardon of the committee if I should attribute to it in my following remarks a plan which as a matter of fact it has not fathered.

1. The article begins by setting forth an idea which is rational and feasible, and which would probably command general if not unanimous assent: the idea that the Congress

* See pp. 352–73, this volume.

[First published in *Science*, n.s. 18 (1903): 275–78.]

should concern itself with the general aspects and bearings of the sciences, their relations to each other and to the unity of human knowledge and endeavor, rather than with purely specialized questions and researches.

2. Apprehension begins when we read: "The necessary condition would be a plan in which every possible striving for truth, every theoretical and practical science would find its exact place. . . . It must be really a plan which brings the inner relation of all branches of knowledge to light . . . a ground plan which would give to every section its definite position in the whole system" (p. 674 of the *Atlantic Monthly* for May, 1903). It is repeatedly stated that the chief feature of the plan is that the arrangement of the sciences chosen is not one of practical convenience or effectiveness, but is one based upon a logical theory of knowledge. It is hardly necessary to point out the radical difference between a Congress which should work along the lines of the generalized aspects and interests of the sciences, and a Congress based upon a previously formulated and predetermined scheme of the unity of knowledge, or to dwell upon the *non sequitur* from the first notion to the second. It is not the Congress of scientific and philosophical workers which is to bring to light (or bring nearer to the light) the unity and interrelation of the various movements of contemporary intellectual life. No, a necessary precondition of the work of the Congress is that it follow the lines of a predetermination of what the unity really is, a notion foreordained by a committee in charge of the Congress! One naturally asks the pardon of the committee for attributing to it even the passing fancy of a scheme at once so presumptuous and so futile.

3. As we read further we learn that this precondition of a "ground plan" has been met, the committee having officially adopted a "ground plan." From the historical point of view, we learn from the article that contemporary intellectual life is officially decreed by the committee to have got beyond materialism, positivism, psychologism, indeed beyond any scheme in which the mental and physical sciences are coordinated with each other. The practical bearing of this appears when we are told that each department is to have an address on the historical development of its own line of work in the last century. It will certainly tend to decrease intellec-

tual labor that each speaker know in advance the "ground plan" of development which his own group of sciences has followed in the last century. There are still those, however (of whom I confess myself one), who would prefer to gather their ideas of what the actual historical movement of the century has been from the results of the deliberate investigations of scientific leaders in a large number of fields, rather than to accept the conclusions of even so distinguished a body as the committee which has framed the plan for the Congress.

4. The "ground plan" is also set forth in its logical scope and symmetry. There are five classes of sciences; the divisions being based upon the distinction, first between "purposes" and "phenomena," and then between such purposes and phenomena as hold good for the individual and those which are more than individual in quality. There is we learn a radical gulf between purposes and phenomena. Purposes are "not to be explained but to be interpreted" (sic, p. 677); they represent values which are to be appreciated, not described; they are to be approached by teleological not by causal methods (pp. 676–77). The student of art, history, literature, politics, jurisprudence, education, is, we are told, occupied with matters of this sort. Just what will happen to those students of art, history, politics, education, etc., who persist in considering that their concern is with phenomena, with their description and explanation, and who are desirous of employing psychological methods in this description and explanation, we are not told. Then "phenomena and purposes" both subdivide themselves; each branches into those facts which are individual or hold only for one subject, and those which hold for every possible subject. The sciences which deal with the individual *phenomena* are the mental; those which deal with individual *purposes* are the historical. The sciences which deal with more than individual phenomena are the physical; those which deal with more than individual purposes are the normative, viz., metaphysics, logic, ethics and mathematics. Then we have a fifth class of sciences: those which deal with the relations between "physical or mental, normative or historical facts on one side, and practical ends of ours on the other" (p. 678).

While it is somewhat confusing to discover in this fifth

classification that purposes and norms turn out to be only facts, after all, and that even after we have gone through the sciences devoted to norms and purposes there still remain practical ends to be dealt with, yet the point that I here raise is not that of the ultimate value or final truth of this classification. The point is that it is a scheme characteristic of one limited school of philosophical thought. The real question at issue is the wisdom of basing a world's congress of arts and sciences upon any sectarian intellectual idea representing some particular *a priori* logic. Why should the committee take it upon itself to define the constitution of the unity of human knowledge, and to provide ready-made a plan or map of the interrelation of all its parts? Why is it not the business of the scientific and philosophical workers called together from all parts of the earth to consider, collate and present their own ideas about the structure and the divisions of the unity of human knowledge? Is it not the business of such a congress to further a consensus of judgment, or at least of inquiry, regarding just the features which the committee, according to the *Atlantic* article, has seen fit to prejudge and forestall?

One might also raise the question whether any scheme has a right to arrogate to itself the title of a "ground plan" of the *unity* of human knowledge whose final result is to separate the psychological sciences from logic, aesthetics and ethics, to separate all of these from the historical sciences, and the historical sciences in turn from the sociological sciences, and then to set up a fifth division of practical sciences to furnish "links" for what has thus been chopped up! It would involve discussion of the merits of the particular plan proposed to argue that any plan which terminates in such arbitrary divisions has thereby experienced a *reductio ad absurdum*. But it is within the scope of the present discussion to indicate that such divisions, if they have any effect at all, can only operate prejudicially to the freedom and completeness of the intellectual discussions of the Congress. The essential trait of the scientific life of to-day is its democracy, its give-and-take, its live-and-let-live character. Scientific men of to-day are struggling hard and successfully to break down previously existing artificial walls separating different sciences, and to secure a continuous open and free field of inquiry. The most active sciences of the day have bifold names—astro-physics, physical chemistry, geo-physics, physiological chemistry, psycho-physics, social psychology, to take the first names that suggest themselves. Pick up the first authority that comes to hand upon the science of language: we read that language has two sides, meaning and form; that the explanation of meaning is a matter of psychology and of logic, while the problems of form are treated by phonetics and phonology which are a combination of physics and physiology. Turn to the committee's classification and we find that the science of language is officially recognized as a science of "purposes," not "phenomena," and hence excludes psychology. It is a science of *individual* purposes, and hence excludes logic. As a science of purposes, not phenomena, it also excludes physics or physiology or any combination of them. The case is typical, and conclusive of the fated practical inefficiency of a plan which attempts to arrange sciences—*i.e.*, branches of inquiry—according to *a priori* logic. The "chance combinations of the university catalogue" in the laying off of the fields of inquiry may not conform to any existing "ground plan" of metaphysical logic; but they have at least the modest merit of representing the vital activities of those engaged in the cooperative pursuit of truth and the building up of the working system of human knowledge.

The dilemma that presents itself after reading the article is the following: Either the scheme is one for presentation and discussion in literary and philosophical journals, not intended to have any influence upon the practical conduct of the Congress, or else it represents a theory of the constitution and divisions of human knowledge to which the various sections and subsections are really expected to conform themselves. In the first case, it is impossible to see why, in the *Atlantic* article, so much stress is laid upon the philosophical basis and aim of the Congress, upon the fact that it is an arrangement based not upon considerations of practical convenience, but upon a logic of knowledge. In the second case, the effect upon the Congress itself can only be disastrous. The imagining of someone invited to speak who does not accept the scheme, either in general or in its bearings upon the particular group of sciences which he is called upon to discuss, will serve as a convenient symbol for presenting the practical logic of the situation. Is he to decline because he can not accept the preordained formulations of the committee? If so, is such a result regarded as desirable from any point of view? Or is he to accept and to proceed with a complete ignoring of the "ground plan" set forth? If so, what is the significance of the "ground plan," and how does the scheme in any way differ from one which should have based itself purely upon an empirical grouping of current lines of research made upon the basis of convenience?

[REJOINDER TO MÜNSTERBERG]

The St. Louis Congress of Arts and Science

To the Editor of Science: In the number of *Science* for August 28 [*Middle Works* 3:145–50], I occupied considerable space in raising certain questions suggested by Dr. Münsterberg's article on the St. Louis Congress in the May number of the *Atlantic Monthly*. I objected

1. To Dr. Münsterberg's basing the working classification and grouping of the schedule or program of that Congress upon a scheme of philosophical methodology (of which he himself happened to be the author), and

2. To the representation made in the article that the Committee on the Congress had given his methodology an official sanction and endorsement by arranging a program upon its basis.

In what purports to be a reply in *Science* for October 30,* Dr. Münsterberg elaborately ignores the objection I raised and as elaborately attributes and refutes a position which I neither took nor even suggested. The objection which he attributes to me is upon its face either a matter of minor importance or else is absurd. This is an objection to the actual working classification and grouping adopted for the conduct of the Congress. It does not require two pages of *Science* to point out that such an objection is trivial if taken to mean an objection to just this or that number and set of divisions, departments and sections; and absurd if taken to mean objection to any classification and grouping whatsoever. Nor does it require a careful reading of my *Science* article to discover that I never entertained such objections.

While I regret that Dr. Münsterberg has raised an ir-

* See pp. 374–81, this volume.

[First published in *Science*, n.s. 18 (1903): 665.]

relevant issue, instead of discussing the matter on its merits, I yet take one consolation from his article. His ignoring the real point of my objection suggests that as a matter of fact the philosophical methodology set forth in such a prominent way in the May *Atlantic* has ceased to have (if it ever had) any bearing upon the actual conduct of the Congress; and that what now exists is just a certain working classification, whose exact merits, as I have just indicated, are a matter of detail and not of principle. In that case, while some explanation would seem to be due the editor and readers of the *Atlantic Monthly*, the scientific men of the country may rest reasonably content.

THE REALISM OF PRAGMATISM

Professor Colvin in his instructive article on Subjective Idealism and Psychology,[1] lets drop this significant remark: "It is an extremely fascinating doctrine, this radical subjectivism, which becomes solipsism when interpreted in terms of the intellect, *and pragmatism when formulated in the categories of the will.*" The words I have italicized are significant because, thrown in incidentally and not in an argument *pro* or *con* as to pragmatism, they reveal what seems to be the general assumption. Accordingly this may offer a fit and uncontroversial opportunity for making a somewhat personal and dogmatic *Auseinandersetzung.*

Speaking of the matter only for myself, the presuppositions and tendencies of pragmatism are distinctly realistic; not idealistic in any sense in which idealism connotes or is connoted by the theory of knowledge. (Idealistic in the ethical sense is another matter, and one whose associations with epistemological idealism, aside from the accidents of history, are chiefly verbal.) Pragmatism believes that in knowledge as a fact, an accomplished matter, things are "representative of one another," to employ Woodbridge's happy, because correct, phrase.[2] Ideas, sensations, mental states, are, in their cognitive significance, media of so adjusting things to one another, that they *become* representative of one another. When this is accomplished, they drop out;[3] and things are present to the agent in the most naïvely realistic fashion.

1. "Is Subjective Idealism a Necessary Point of View for Psychology?" *Journal of Philosophy, Psychology and Scientific Methods*, Vol. II, No. 9, April 27, 1905, p. 225. [See pp. 382–89, this volume.]
2. See *Science*, N. S., Vol. XX, p. 587; and *Journal of Philosophy, Psychology and Scientific Methods*, Vol. II, No. 5, March 2, 1905, p. 119.
3. The sense in which their value remains will be spoken of later.

[First published in *Journal of Philosophy, Psychology and Scientific Methods* 2 (1905): 324–27.]

"States of consciousness" refer to *getting* knowledge; to the situation when things as objective fail us; have, so to speak, gone back on us; when accordingly we neither have them to know nor yet to *know with*. It is in this situation, and only in this situation, that "states of consciousness" exist or have meaning, cognitively speaking. And if I put in the phrase, "cognitively speaking," it is only to take account of the emotions; and with reference to the emotions the significant point is that they also arise and function in problematic situations; in situations whose objective determination or character is not known, not presented.

Instrumentalism is thus thoroughly realistic as to the objective or fulfilling conditions of knowledge. States of consciousness, sensations and ideas as cognitive, exist as tools, bridges, cues, functions—whatever one pleases—to affect a realistic presentation of things, in which there are no intervening states of consciousness as veils, or representatives. Known things, as known, are direct presentations in the most diaphanous medium conceivable. And if getting knowledge, as distinct from having it, involves representatives, pragmatism carries with it a reinterpretation, and a realistic interpretation, of "states of consciousness" *as* representations. They are practically or effectively, not transcendentally, representative. They represent in the sense in which a signature, for legal purposes, represents a real person in a contract; or as money, for economic purposes, represents beefsteak or a night's lodging. They are symbols, in short, and are known and used as such.

Knowledge, even *getting* knowledge, must rest on facts, or things. But the need of truth, of cognitively assured things, means once more that such things are *not* present— just as the beefsteak is not eating, in the situation in which money stands for it. Things in problematic situations must operate through representatives, ministerial agents, through psychical things, which, *for the purpose in hand and for that only*, stand for and thus accomplish what things would accomplish—viz., mutually realistic significance—if they were only there. Psychical things are thus themselves realistically conceived; they can be described and identified in biological and physiological terms, in terms (with adequate science) of chemicophysical correspondents.[4] Psychologically, they are themselves literal emotions and felt impulses. Moreover, they are realistically conditioned from the genetic side. Their origin as existences can be stated and must be stated in terms of adjustments and maladjustments among habits, biological functions.[5] The reproach that has been brought against "pragmatism" of utilizing biological evolutionary data, might, it would seem, at least have preserved it from the reproach of subjectivism.

In short, the point that the critics of pragmatism have missed with a surprising unanimity, is that in giving a reinterpretation of the nature and function of knowledge, pragmatism gives necessarily a thoroughgoing reinterpretation of all the cognitive machinery—sensations, ideas, concepts, etc.; one which inevitably tends to take these things in a much more literal and physically realistic fashion than is current. What pragmatism takes from idealism is just and only *empiricism*. That, to it, is the real lesson of the subjectivism which has held sway since the time of Descartes and Locke. This lesson learned, we can think freely and naïvely in terms of things—because things are no longer entities in a world set over against another world called "mind" or "consciousness," with some sort of mysterious ontological tie between them. Again, pragmatism has learned that the true meaning of subjectivism is just *anti*-dualism. Hence philosophy can enter again into the realistic thought and conversation of common sense and science, where dualisms are just dualities, distinctions having an instrumental and practical, but not ultimate, metaphysical worth; or rather, having metaphysical worth in a practical and experimental sense, not in that of indicating a radical existential cleavage in the nature of things.

4. This possibility of objective statement is, I take it, the meaning of the psychophysical parallelism—if it has any meaning. There is no sense that I am aware of in which their description is to be limited to brain terms rather than to chemical terms, or to terms of changes among extra-organic objects, or to terms of changes among social objects, persons. The point is simply that psychical changes do correspond to changes in reality.
5. Pragmatism would thus deny absolutely that psychology rests upon the idealistic presupposition. The psychologist has the same naïve right to things and bodies as has the geologist or zoologist.

I speak only for myself, but in giving my hearty assent to what Professor James has said about the nature of truth (see *Journal of Philosophy, Psychology and Scientific Methods*, p. 118, Vol. II), I venture to express the hope that he also conceives the matter in some such way as I have suggested. Certainly it is the obvious deduction from his denial of the existence of consciousness. It is the witness borne by Professor Mead in his *Definition of the Psychical*. It is what I had supposed to be the only possible outcome of my essays in the *Studies in Logical Theory*—though I am glad to have this opportunity of expressing my indebtedness to conversations with Professor Woodbridge, as well as to his published articles, for making me aware of the full force of their realistic implications.

In conclusion, I wish to say a word upon the ethical idealism involved. Speaking from the cognitive standpoint, it is difficult to conceive of anything stranger, more curious, more wholly unanticipatable, than that certain things—emotions, sensations—which are biologically conditioned as to their origin, should become bearers of the transformation of things into things mutually representative or significant of one another. But such is the empirical fact. It demonstrates that while ideas, states of consciousness, drop out in our assured aesthetic, intellectual and practical transactions with things, leaving a face-to-face or realistic situation, yet their worth, their value, remains in the significance which things have gained as representative of one another. *The increments of meaning which things are constantly taking on is as much the product of psychical existences, as the added significance of words is the result of their use in propositions, i.e., with a context.* They are the media of effecting the transformation of conflicting, unsatisfactory, and consequently fragmentarily significant situations, into situations where things are surely and reciprocally (in an all-around way) significant of one another. Hence the free, the indeterminate, the growing, the potential factor in reality. Meaning, significance is never just predetermined. It is always hanging upon the operation of the psychical, of the peculiarly individual. *Hence morality: the recognition of responsibility for the use of the psychical, as the ultimate determiner of the ways in which the world of all (you and me) who live among things grows in significance.* It is because the psychical is, cognitively, realistic, that morality has an empirically real sanction and yet an ideal bearing of infinite import. It never gets in the way of things of knowledge to obstruct or pervert; but its prior operations control what things become representative of one another, and hence the experienced meaning, or value, of those things.

THE POSTULATE OF IMMEDIATE EMPIRICISM[1]

The criticisms made upon that vital but still unformed movement variously termed radical empiricism, pragmatism, humanism, functionalism, according as one or another aspect of it is uppermost, have left me with a conviction that the *fundamental* difference is not so much in matters overtly discussed as in a presupposition that remains tacit: a presupposition as to what experience is and means. To do my little part in clearing up the confusion, I shall try to make my own presupposition explicit. The object of this paper is, then, to set forth what I understand to be the postulate and the criterion of *immediate empiricism*.[2]

Immediate empiricism postulates that things—anything, everything, in the ordinary or non-technical use of the term "thing"—are what they are experienced as. Hence, if one wishes to describe anything truly, his task is to tell what it is experienced as being. If it is a horse that is to be described, or the *equus* that is to be defined, then must the horse-trader, or the jockey, or the timid family man who wants a "safe

1. Reprinted, with very slight change, from the *Journal of Philosophy, Psychology and Scientific Methods*, Vol. II, No. 15, July, 1905.
2. All labels are, of course, obnoxious and misleading. I hope, however, the term will be taken by the reader in the sense in which it is forthwith explained, and not in some more usual and familiar sense. Empiricism, as herein used, is as antipodal to sensationalistic empiricism, as it is to transcendentalism, and for the same reason. Both of these systems fall back on something which is defined in non-directly-experienced terms in order to justify that which is directly experienced. Hence I have criticized such empiricism (*Philosophical Review*, Vol. XI, No. 4, p. 364 [*Middle Works* 2:31]) as essentially absolutistic in character; and also (*Studies in Logical Theory*, pp. 30, 58 [*Middle Works* 2:322, 344]) as an attempt to build up experience in terms of certain methodological checks and cues of attaining *certainty*.

[First published in *Journal of Philosophy, Psychology and Scientific Methods* 2 (1905): 393–99. Reprinted in *The Influence of Darwin on Philosophy* (New York: Henry Holt and Co., 1910), pp. 226–41.]

driver," or the zoologist or the paleontologist tell us what the horse is which is experienced. If these accounts turn out different in some respects, as well as congruous in others, this is no reason for assuming the content of one to be exclusively "real," and that of others to be "phenomenal"; for each account of what is experienced will manifest that it is the account *of* the horse-dealer, or *of* the zoologist, and hence will give the conditions requisite for understanding the differences as well as the agreements of the various accounts. And the principle varies not a whit if we bring in the psychologist's horse, the logician's horse or the metaphysician's horse.

In each case, the nub of the question is, *what sort of experience* is denoted or indicated: a concrete and determinate experience, varying, when it varies, in specific real elements, and agreeing, when it agrees, in specific real elements, so that we have a contrast, not between *a* Reality, and various approximations to, or phenomenal representations of Reality, but between different reals of experience. And the reader is begged to bear in mind that from this standpoint, when "an experience" or "some sort of experience" is referred to, "some thing" or "some sort of thing" is always meant.

Now, this statement that things are what they are experienced to be is usually translated into the statement that things (or, ultimately, Reality, Being) *are* only and just what they are *known* to be or that things are, or Reality *is*, what it is for a conscious knower—whether the knower be conceived primarily as a perceiver or as a thinker being a further and secondary question. This is the root-paralogism of all idealisms, whether subjective or objective, psychological or epistemological. By our postulate, things are what they are experienced to be; and, unless knowing is the sole and only genuine mode of experiencing, it is fallacious to say that Reality is just and exclusively what it is or would be to an all-competent all-knower; or even that it *is*, relatively and piecemeal, what it is to a finite and partial knower. Or, put more positively, knowing is one mode of experiencing, and the primary philosophic demand (from the standpoint of immediatism) is to find out *what* sort of an experience knowing is—or, concretely how things are experienced when

they are experienced *as* known things.[3] By concretely is
meant, obviously enough (among other things), such an account of the experience of things as known that will bring
out the characteristic traits and distinctions they possess as
things of a knowing experience, as compared with things experienced aesthetically, or morally, or economically, or technologically. To assume that, because from the *standpoint of
the knowledge experience* things *are* what they are known
to be, therefore, metaphysically, absolutely, without qualification, everything in its reality (as distinct from its "appearance," or phenomenal occurrence) is what a knower would
find it to be, is, from the immediatist's standpoint, if not the
root of all philosophic evil, at least one of its main roots. For
this leaves out of account what the knowledge standpoint is
itself *experienced as*.

I start and am flustered by a noise heard. Empirically,
that noise *is* fearsome; it *really* is, not merely phenomenally
or subjectively so. That *is what* it is experienced as being.
But, when I experience the noise as a *known* thing, I find it
to be innocent of harm. It is the tapping of a shade against
the window, owing to movements of the wind. The experience has changed; that is, the thing experienced has changed
—not that an unreality has given place to a reality, nor that
some transcendental (unexperienced) Reality has changed,[4]
not that truth has changed, but just and only the concrete
reality experienced has changed. I now feel ashamed of my
fright; and the noise as fearsome is changed to noise as a
wind-curtain fact, and hence practically indifferent to my

3. I hope the reader will not therefore assume that from the empiricist's standpoint knowledge is of small worth or import. On
   the contrary, from the empiricist's standpoint it has *all* the
   worth which it is concretely experienced as possessing—which
   is simply tremendous. But the exact *nature* of this worth is a
   thing to be found out in describing what we mean by experiencing objects as known—the actual differences made or found in
   experience.

4. Since the non-empiricist believes in things-in-themselves (which
   he may term "atoms," "sensations," transcendental unities, *a
   priori* concepts, *an* absolute experience, or whatever), and since
   he finds that the empiricist makes much of change (as he must,
   since change is continuously experienced) he assumes that the
   empiricist means *his own* non-empirical Realities are in continual
   flux, and he naturally shudders at having his divinities so violently treated. But, once recognize that the empiricist doesn't
   have any such Realities at all, and the entire problem of the
   relation of change to reality takes a very different aspect.

welfare. This is a change of experienced existence effected through the medium of cognition. The content of the latter experience cognitively regarded is doubtless *truer* than the content of the earlier; but it is in no sense more real. To call it truer, moreover, must, from the empirical standpoint, mean a concrete *difference* in actual things experienced.[5] Again, in many cases, only in retrospect is the prior experience cognitionally regarded at all. In such cases, it is only in regard to contrasted content *in* a subsequent experience that the determination "truer" has force.

Perhaps some reader may now object that as matter of fact the entire experience *is* cognitive, but that the earlier parts of it are only imperfectly so, resulting in a phenomenon that is not real; while the latter part, being a more complete cognition, results in what is relatively, at least, more real.[6] In short, a critic may say that, when I was frightened by the noise, I *knew* I was frightened; otherwise there would have been no experience at all. At this point, it is necessary to make a distinction so simple and yet so all-fundamental that I am afraid the reader will be inclined to pooh-pooh it away as a mere verbal distinction. But to see that to the empiricist this distinction is not verbal, but genuine, is the precondition of any understanding of him. The immediatist must, by his postulate, ask what is the fright experienced *as*. Is what is actually experienced, I-know-I-am-frightened, or I-*am*-frightened? I see absolutely no reason for claiming that the experience *must* be described by the former phrase. In all probability (and all the empiricist logically needs is just one case of this sort) the experience is simply and just of fright-

5. It would lead us aside from the point to try to tell just what is the nature of the experienced difference we call truth. Professor James's recent articles may well be consulted. The point to bear in mind here is just what sort of a thing the empiricist must mean by true, or truer (the noun Truth is, of course, a generic name for all cases of "Trues"). The adequacy of any particular account is not a matter to be settled by general reasoning, but by finding out what sort of an experience the truth-experience actually is.

6. I say "relatively," because the transcendentalist still holds that finally the cognition is imperfect, giving us only some symbol or phenomenon of Reality (which *is* only in the Absolute or in some Thing-in-Itself)—otherwise the curtain-wind fact would have as much ontological reality as the existence of the Absolute itself: a conclusion at which the non-empiricist perhorresces, for no reason obvious to me—save that it would put an end to his transcendentalism.

at-the-noise. Later one may (or may not) have an experience describable *as* I-know-I-am- (or-was) and improperly or
properly, frightened. But this is a different experience—
that is, a different *thing*. And if the critic goes on to urge that
the person *"really"* must have known that he was frightened,
I can only point out that the critic is shifting the venue. He
may be right, but, if so, it is only because the "really" is
something not concretely experienced (whose nature accordingly is the critic's business); and this is to depart from
the empiricist's point of view, to attribute to him a postulate
he expressly repudiates.

The material point may come out more clearly if I say
that we must make a distinction between a thing as *cognitive*,
and one as *cognized*.[7] I should define a cognitive experience
as one that has certain bearings or implications which induce and fulfill themselves in a subsequent experience in
which the relevant thing is experienced *as* cognized, *as* a
known object, and is thereby transformed, or reorganized.
The fright-at-the-noise in the case cited is obviously *cognitive*, in this sense. By description, it induces an investigation or inquiry in which both noise and fright are objectively
stated or presented—the noise as a shade-wind fact, the
fright as an organic reaction to a sudden acoustic stimulus,
a reaction that under the given circumstances was useless
or even detrimental, a maladaptation. Now, pretty much all
of experience is of this sort (the "is" meaning, of course, is
experienced *as*), and the empiricist is false to his principle
if he does not duly note this fact.[8] But he is equally false to
his principle if he permits himself to be confused as to the
concrete differences in the two things experienced.

There are two little words through explication of which
the empiricist's position may be brought out—*"as"* and *"that."*
We may express his presupposition by saying that things are
what they are experienced *as* being; or that to give a just ac-

7. In general, I think the distinction between *-ive* and *-ed* one of
   the most fundamental of philosophic distinctions, and one of the
   most neglected. The same holds of *-tion* and *-ing*.
8. What is criticized, now as "geneticism" (if I may coin the word)
   and now as "pragmatism" is, in its truth, just the fact that the
   empiricist does take account of the experienced "drift, occasion
   and contexture" of things experienced—to use Hobbes's phrase.

count of anything is to tell what *that* thing is experienced to
be. By these words I want to indicate the absolute, final, ir-
reducible and inexpugnable concrete *quale* which everything
experienced not so much *has* as *is*. To grasp this aspect of
empiricism is to see what the empiricist means by objectivity,
by the element of control. Suppose we take, as a crucial case
for the empiricist, an out and out illusion, say of Zöllner's
lines. These are experienced as convergent; they are "truly"
parallel. If things are what they are experienced as being,
how can the distinction be drawn between illusion and the
true state of the case? There is no answer to this question
except by sticking to the fact that the experience of the lines
as divergent is a concrete qualitative thing or *that*. It is *that*
experience which it is, and no other. And if the reader rebels
at the iteration of such obvious tautology, I can only reiterate
that the realization of the *meaning* of this tautology is the
key to the whole question of the objectivity of experience, as
that stands to the empiricist. The lines of *that* experience *are*
divergent: not merely *seem* so. The question of truth is not
as to whether Being or Non-Being, Reality or mere Appearance, is experienced, but as to the *worth* of a certain concretely experienced thing. The only way of passing upon this
question is by sticking in the most uncompromising fashion
to *that* experience as real. *That* experience is that two lines
with certain cross-hatchings are apprehended as convergent;
only by taking that experience as real and as fully real, is
there any basis for or way of going to an experienced knowledge that the lines are parallel. It is in the concrete thing *as
experienced* that all the grounds and clues to its own intellectual or logical rectification are contained. It is because this
thing, afterwards adjudged false, is a concrete *that*, that it
develops into a corrected experience (that is, experience of
a corrected thing—we reform things just as we reform ourselves or a bad boy) whose full content is not a whit more
real, but which is true or truer.[9]

9. Perhaps the point would be clearer if expressed in this way:
Except as subsequent estimates of *worth* are introduced, "real"
means only existent. The eulogistic connotation that makes the
term Reality equivalent to *true* or *genuine* being has great pragmatic significance, but its confusion with reality as existence is
the point aimed at in the above paragraph.

If *any* experience, then a *determinate* experience; and this determinateness is the only, and is the adequate, principle of control, or "objectivity." The experience may be of the vaguest sort. I may not see any thing which I can identify as a familiar object—a table, a chair, etc. It may be dark; I may have only the vaguest impression that there is something which looks like a table. Or I may be completely befogged and confused, as when one rises quickly from sleep in a pitch-dark room. But this vagueness, this doubtfulness, this confusion is the thing experienced, and, *qua* real, is as "good" a reality as the self-luminous vision of an Absolute. It is not just vagueness, doubtfulness, confusion, at large or in general. It is *this* vagueness, and no other; absolutely unique, absolutely what *it* is.[10] Whatever gain in clearness, in fullness, in trueness of content is experienced must grow out of some element in the experience of *this* experienced *as* what it is. To return to the illusion: If the experience of the lines as convergent is illusory, it is because of some elements in the thing as experienced, not because of something defined in terms of externality to this particular experience. If the illusoriness can be detected, it is because the thing experienced is real, having within its experienced reality elements whose *own mutual* tension effects its reconstruction. Taken concretely, the experience of convergent lines contains within itself the elements of the transformation of its own content. It is *this* thing, and not some separate truth, that clamors for its own reform. There is, then, from the empiricist's point of view, no need to search for some aboriginal *that* to which all successive experiences are attached, and which is somehow thereby undergoing continuous change. Experience is always of *thats*; and the most comprehensive and inclusive experience of the universe that the philosopher himself can obtain is the experience of a characteristic *that*. From the empiricist's point of view, this is as true of the exhaustive and complete insight of a hypothetical all-knower as of the vague, blind experience of the awakened

---

10. One does not so easily escape medieval Realism as one thinks. Either every experienced thing has its own determinateness, its own unsubstitutable, unredeemable reality, or else "generals" *are* separate existences after all.

sleeper. As reals, they stand on the same level. As trues, the latter has by definition the better of it; but if this insight is in any way the truth of the blind awakening, it is because the latter has, in its *own* determinate *quale*, elements of real continuity with the former; it is, *ex hypothesi*, transformable through a series of experienced reals without break of continuity, into the absolute thought-experience. There is no need of logical manipulation to effect the transformation, nor *could* any logical consideration effect it. If effected at all it is just by immediate experiences, each of which is just as real (no more, no less) as either of the two terms between which they lie. Such, at least, is the meaning of the empiricist's contention. So, when he talks of experience, he does not mean some grandiose, remote affair that is cast like a net around a succession of fleeting experiences; he does not mean an indefinite total, comprehensive experience which somehow engirdles an endless flux; he means that *things* are what they are experienced to be, and that every experience is *some* thing.

From the postulate of empiricism, then (or, what is the same thing, from a *general* consideration of the concept of experience), nothing can be deduced, not a single philosophical proposition.[11] The reader may hence conclude that all this just comes to the truism that experience is experience, or is what it is. If one attempts to draw conclusions from the bare concept of experience, the reader is quite right. But the real significance of the principle is that of a method of philosophical analysis—a method identical in kind (but differing in problem and hence in operation) with that of the scientist. If you wish to find out what subjective, objective, physical, mental, cosmic, psychic, cause, substance, purpose, activity,

11. Excepting, of course, some negative ones. One could say that certain views are certainly *not* true, because, by hypothesis, they refer to nonentities, *i.e.*, non-empiricals. But even here the empiricist must go slowly. From his own standpoint, even the most professedly transcendental statements are, after all, real as experiences, and hence negotiate some transaction with facts. For this reason, he cannot, in theory, reject them *in toto*, but has to show concretely how they arose and how they are to be corrected. In a word, his logical relationship to statements that profess to relate to things-in-themselves, unknowables, inexperienced substances, etc., is precisely that of the psychologist to the Zöllner lines.

evil, being, quality—any philosophic term, in short—means, go to experience and see what the thing is experienced *as*.

Such a method is not spectacular; it permits of no off-hand demonstrations of God, freedom, immortality, nor of the exclusive reality of matter, or ideas, or consciousness, etc. But it supplies a way of telling what all these terms mean. It may seem insignificant, or chillingly disappointing, but only upon condition that it be not worked. Philosophic conceptions have, I believe, outlived their usefulness considered as stimulants to emotion, or as a species of sanctions; and a larger, more fruitful and more valuable career awaits them considered as specifically experienced meanings.

[NOTE: The reception of this essay proved that I was unreasonably sanguine in thinking that the foot-note of warning, appended to the title, would forfend radical misapprehension. I see now that it was unreasonable to expect that the word "immediate" in a philosophic writing could be generally understood to apply to anything except *knowledge*, even though the body of the essay is a protest against such limitation. But I venture to repeat that the essay is not a denial of the necessity of "mediation," or reflection, in knowledge, but is an assertion that the inferential factor must *exist*, or must occur, and that all existence is direct and vital, so that philosophy can pass upon its nature—as upon the nature of all of the rest of its subject-matter—only by first ascertaining what it exists or occurs *as*.

I venture to repeat also another statement of the text: I do not mean by "immediate experience" any aboriginal stuff out of which things are evolved, but I use the term to indicate the necessity of employing in philosophy the direct descriptive method that has now made its way in all the natural sciences, with such modifications, of course, as the subject itself entails.

There is nothing in the text to imply that things exist in experience atomically or in isolation. When it is said that a thing as cognized is *different* from an earlier non-cognitionally experienced thing, the saying no more implies lack of continuity between the things, than the obvious remark that a seed is different from a flower or a leaf denies their continuity. The amount and kind of continuity or discreteness that exists is to be discovered by recurring to what actually occurs in experience.

Finally, there is nothing in the text that denies the existence of things temporally prior to human experiencing of them. Indeed, I should think it fairly obvious that we experience most things *as* temporally prior to our experiencing of them. The import of the article is to the effect that we are not entitled to draw philosophic (as distinct from scientific) conclusions as to the meaning of prior temporal existence till we have ascertained what it is to experience a thing as past. These four disclaimers cover, I think, all the misapprehensions disclosed in the four or five controversial articles (noted below) that the original essay evoked. One of these articles (that of Professor Woodbridge), raised a point of fact, holding that cognitional experience tells us, without alteration, just what the things of other types of experience are, and in that sense transcends other experiences. This is too fundamental an issue to discuss in a note, and I content myself with remarking that with respect to it, the bearing of the article is that the issue must be settled by a careful descriptive survey of things as experienced, to see whether modifications do not occur in existences when they are experienced *as* known; *i.e.*, as true or false in character. The reader interested in following up this discussion is referred to the following articles: Vol. II of the *Journal of Philosophy, Psychology and Scientific Methods*, two articles by Bakewell, p. 520 and p. 687; one by Bode, p. 658; one by Woodbridge, p. 573; Vol. III of the same Journal, by Leighton, p. 174.]

IMMEDIATE EMPIRICISM

Professor Bakewell writes as follows, in an open letter to me in the *Journal of Philosophy, Psychology and Scientific Methods* concerning "Immediate Empiricism":[1] "My difficulty, in short, is simply this: Either everything experienced is real exactly as, and no further than, it is then and there experienced—and then there is no occasion to speak of correcting or rectifying experience; or, there is in every experience a self-transcendency which points beyond that thing *as experienced* for *its own* reality—and then good-by to immediatism." And in a foot-note he says that my view is atomistic, chopping reals off from one another, and that if "this consequence is avoided by making the earlier experience contain implicitly the later to which it leads, immediatism gives way to a doctrine of mediation."

There was once a botanist who suggested that instead of deducing botany from the concept of plants (and from certain allied concepts) the proper method was to study plants to see what each was in itself. Whereupon an opponent replied that such a doctrine destroyed botany. "Take the case of a seed"; he urged, "either you mean that this seed just as it now is, and no further, is real, and then growth is impossible; or else there is in the seed a self-transforming somewhat which changes it first into a sprouting plant, and then, finally, into a mature plant with seed of its own—and then good-by to the idea that the reality of the seed is to be sought in just what the seed now, and no further, is. Moreover," he continued, "since each plant in itself is something different from every other, the doctrine makes relation of

1. Vol. II, No. 19, p. 521 [*Middle Works* 3:390–92]. See also the *Journal of Philosophy, Psychology and Scientific Methods*, Vol. II, No. 15, p. 393 [*Middle Works* 3:158–67].

[First published in *Journal of Philosophy, Psychology and Scientific Methods* 2 (1905): 597–99.]

plants to one another, and hence generalization, and hence science, impossible."

Whereupon the first-mentioned botanist replied that either a given seed is alive and capable of growth, or, dead and incapable of becoming a plant, and that the actual state of affairs in this respect is precisely one of the things to be determined by a study of the particular seed; that it is of the very essence of the method that the question of "further" or "no further" should be settled by reference not to general notions, but by reference to the *determinate* character of the particular seed. Moreover, it was just by a study of each plant "in itself" that one would find out whether it was something unrelated, atomistic, or something genetically and responsibly connected with other plants, relationship being precisely an affair of the determinate character of the seed.

In other words, while I expressly state in my article (1) that a thing which is rectified in a subsequent cognitive experience "contains within itself" (that is as part of its own concrete determinate thinghood) "the elements of the transformation of its own content," and (2) expressly disclaim the possibility of deriving any conclusions whatever from the concept of immediate experience, Professor Bakewell expressly assumes (1) that the very *concept* of immediate experience carries with it some necessary implication regarding the character or nature of *what* is experienced, and (2) that it precludes any continuity of experienced things. As an immediate empiricist, I can only reply that it is to things *as* experienced that I go for instruction as to continuity, transformation and mediation; and that it is just because I find things immediately experienced *as* continuous, and *as* self-rectifying that I believe in continuity and self-rectification. Compare the distinction of cognitive and cognized in the former article, and the reference to the importance of the "drift, occasion and contexture" of things—distinctions which are inherent and not external to the things. Does the transcendentalist believe that things *as* experienced are continuous? If yes, why should he charge an empiricist with *ex officio* denial of this empirical fact? But if he holds that a transcendental principle or function is required to give continuity to what as experienced is "chopped-off," then *he*

would seem to be the one denying actual, empirical, continuity. I am always wishing that some transcendentalist
would expound and expose his own positive doctrine about
the problems which he accuses the empiricist of maltreating,
instead of assuming that the transcendental position is self-
evident, or at least thoroughly understood. Perhaps Professor
Bakewell will help in this illumination, bearing in mind that
an important motive in developing the newer philosophy has
been the conviction that mediation, continuity, reconstruction and growth are facts which transcendentalism has failed
consistently to define and account for. I do not understand
the notion that because things of immediate experience are
real, mediation can not be real. I am quite sure that the
logic of immediate empiricism would include mediation
along with the categories "subjective, objective, physical,
mental, psychic, etc." (see Vol. II, p. 399 [*Middle Works*
3:161–62]) and say, "if you wish to find out what it means, go
to experience and see what it is experienced *as*." I find difficulty in realizing the difficulty which one has with immediately experiencing something *as* mediate. I don't see *any*
way of experiencing the mediate (any more than of experiencing a cat or a dog) excepting that of immediately experiencing it *as* what it is, viz., mediate. If I were to make a
guess as to the origin of the difficulty, I should refer it to a
mental habit of employing a conceptual, instead of an empirical, philosophy,[2] a habit so inveterate as to display itself
even when one is attempting to appreciate the position of an
empiricist.

I conclude with a question and a remark: Does Professor Bakewell mean to deny (1) that all philosophic conceptions must somehow enter into experience, or (2) that
all experience is, *as existence*, immediate? The remark is,
that I quite meant my earlier statement, (Vol. II, p. 399
[*Middle Works* 3:161–62]), that from the postulate I gave,
not a single philosophical proposition could be deduced—that
its significance was that of affording a method of philosophical analysis.

2. Lest I be charged with intimating that concepts are unreal and
   unempirical, I say forthwith that I believe meanings may be and
   are immediately experienced *as* conceptual.

THE KNOWLEDGE EXPERIENCE
AND ITS RELATIONSHIPS

Professor Woodbridge's recent article in the *Journal of Philosophy, Psychology and Scientific Methods*[1] raises clearly and effectively certain questions involved in the conception of philosophy and its problems, which, in my mind, associate themselves with the ideas set forth in the first chapter of *Studies in Logical Theory* [*Middle Works* 2:298–315]. At all events, I am going to make some points in his article an excuse for reverting to the position there taken, *viz.*, that the characteristic problem of philosophy is the relationships to one another borne by certain typical functions or modes of experience, *e.g.*, the practical, cognitional, aesthetic, etc. Objectively put, philosophy arises because the reals which are the distinctively appropriate subject-matters of these different types get into conflict with one another, a conflict so thorough as to leave us no choice except (*a*) to doubt all, (*b*) somewhat arbitrarily to select one as the standard and norm for valuing the others, or (*c*) to effect a harmonization of their respective claims through a more thorough consideration of their respective historic and working positions and relationships.[2]

Woodbridge's article presents a special case of the general problem, *viz.*, how to justify the peculiar claims of knowledge to provide a valid account of other modes of experience. "If reality as true is but one sort of reality or one sort of experience, how can it possibly be affirmed that the nature of reality is most fittingly defined, when we have that

1. Vol. II, No. 21, p. 573 [*Middle Works* 3:393–97].
2. One of the many merits of Bradley's *Appearance and Reality* is the way in which it thrusts this conception virtually, if not intentionally, to the foreground. It leaves but three alternatives: to accept Bradley's result; to explain *away* satisfactorily the seeming discrepancies of the various functions; or to find another method and scheme of harmonization than his.

[First published in *Journal of Philosophy, Psychology and Scientific Methods* 2 (1905): 652–57.]

sort, when, that is, reality is experienced as true?" (p. 394). And again: "We attempt to give an account of experience which will commend itself to thought. How can we succeed if we raise the suspicion that any account for thought must necessarily be not only partial and inadequate, but radically different from what experience is?" (p. 397).

1. Certainly any empirical statement which ends up in the implication that the knowledge account is radically different "from what experience is" has committed suicide. But when we say, with Woodbridge, (1) that "the real is simply *that* which is experienced and *as* it is experienced" (p. 393), and (2) that "there are many sorts of experience of which the cognitive sort is only one" (p. 396), we seem to be committed to the conviction that the knowledge-experience is of things which, in some sense, are different from what the things of other experiences *were*, and from what they would continue to be in the future were it not for an intervening knowledge-experience. As I interpret the history of thought, it is precisely the fact that the knowledge account *is* different from what the things of other experiences are, contemporaneously with those experiences, which has been the main motivation of the transcendental non-empirical conception of knowledge.

Because the things of experience *are* so many different things, it has been thought that reality to be one, single and comprehensive, must be *exclusively* identifiable with the content of the perfected knowledge account; and this is then set over against the things of other experiences (of all experience *qua* experience), as the absolute against the phenomenal, the really real against the world of appearances. Hence the attacks made by the transcendentalists upon recent empiricisms (however denominated), because they deny exclusive or isolated jurisdiction to the knowledge function. Hence also the charges by the empiricists upon the "transcendent" concept of knowledge, claiming that the isolation in which knowledge is placed leaves it an arbitrary, brute dictum (none the less arbitrary and even solipsistic because referred to a knower *termed* Absolute), or else a subjectivistic aesthetic indulgence, since such isolation excludes verification in all the senses of verification hitherto employed by man.

When, therefore, we have, as in Professor Woodbridge's account, a "transcendence" notion of knowledge put forth with an empiristic motivation and basis, we have the problem in an especially interesting form: How can the knowledge-experience connect with other experiences in such a way as not to justify itself at *their* expense? How can, at one and the same time, knowledge be transcendent of other experiences, and the things of other experiences be real?

2. What, concretely, is the knowledge-experience? Three sets of facts are designated by the term knowledge: (1) It may denote the *de facto* presence in experience of a discriminate or outstanding quale or content. Some degree of distinction is necessary to any experienced thing, and such determinateness in experience one may agree to call knowledge. This sort of thing can hardly be referred to as transcendent—for what does it transcend? Not the things of other experiences, for it *is* the things of all experiences. It is a name for them in their determinate character. If transcendence refers to the relationships between such things, and things not *at all* determinately present in experience, then it has an intelligible meaning, but appears to involve a theory of the existence of reals apart from experience—or to be non-empirical. And transcendence as a relationship of that which is in experience to out-of-experience things would certainly make wholly meaningless *any* statement as to whether knowledge does or does not modify the out-of-experience. Such a statement can have intelligible meaning only when said of the things of knowledge in contrast and connection with other experienced things. Knowledge in this sense (apart from the question of the appropriateness of the term) does not seem, then, to be anything more than a restatement of the postulate of immediate empiricism: that things are that which they are experienced to be, recognizing that some sort of distinctiveness is necessary to any thing. All things, truth and error, the obscure and the clear, the practical, the logical, the aesthetic, are thus present, and all equally real—though *not* equally valuable and valid.

(2) Reference as a contemporaneous empirical trait is not an inevitable accompaniment of presence as just defined. The quale or content which discriminates a thing may not

be referred explicitly to any other, nor any other to it. Connection may exist, however, practically: one thing may be found subsequently to affect, influence or control, favorably or unfavorably, the quality of some other present thing. Reference as an empirical fact is then established—that is, becomes a discriminate element in the constitution of something which is complex. Hence a second sense of knowledge. It is the experience in which the nature of such reference is investigated and defined. This involves such transformation of the character of antecedent things as makes possible the ascription to them and the maintenance by them of the relevant references.

Recognize that practical bearing or influence becomes explicit as reference in case of conflicting and therefore uncertain and contradictory bearings, and we get knowledge as Woodbridge has defined it when he says: "It is of such a sort that it enables us to tell what the others actually are when *we ask the question about their sort*."

The practical conflict of experiences in bringing to light the problem of their reference, also brings to light the question of their nature as fitted to sustain such and such a reference; it makes their old characters suspicious, doubtful, precarious—in a word, problematic. This inherent dissentience is always, as to its *terminus ad quem*, a movement of inquiry, of institution or definition. This constitutes an answering or "telling" experience in which an unquestioned thing replaces the dubious thing. Hence, while it would not do to say that the statement quoted above is an innocuous truism—there are too many subjectivistic theories of knowledge abroad to render its realistic implication other than important—it may do to say that its excellence lies in the fact that it identifies knowledge as a doubt-inquiry-answer experience.

When Woodbridge adds (to what was last quoted): "The question may not be asked and may not be answered. In that case no one sort of experience is identified or distinguished. And what sort of an experience would that be if not precisely what we should mean by an unconscious experience?" (p. 396), there appears to be a relapse to the first sense of knowledge set forth. It is one thing to say that distinctive character is necessary to any experience, in order not to fall into the contradiction of an unconscious experience; it is another thing to say that *that kind* of identification and distinction, namely, of reference, which follows from express questioning and constitutes express answering, is necessary to a conscious experience. Only of the first sense of knowledge can the contradiction be relevant; only of the second sense is the reference to question and answer relevant.

Bearing these things in mind, I do not appreciate the difficulty in the statement that reality is most fittingly defined as true "because defined in a way which most usefully meets the needs that raise the demand for definition" (p. 394, the "needs," however, do not "raise" the demand, they *are* the demand). For the "needs" and their "usefully meeting" are neither of them extrinsic to the situation. The needs *are* the unstable, dissentient characters constituting an intolerable condition; while "usefully" *is* the meeting of this demand, that is, their transformation into a stable, dependable state of affairs. Needs are not met more or less usefully; they are met more or less successfully, and the successful fulfillment defines the useful thing of the situation. There is no other measure of use.

I am convinced that the charges of subjectivism and of an arbitrarily utilitarian practicalism brought against current empiricism are due to the fact that the critic, because he himself retains a belief in the independent existence of a subject, ego, consciousness or whatever, external to the subject-matters, ascribes similar beliefs to the one criticized; and hence suppose that the latter, when he talks about genesis in needs, and outcome in success or fulfillment, is talking about something resident in a subject or consciousness which arbitrarily pounces in, picks out its plum and withdraws triumphant. But to the thoroughgoing empiricist, the self, the ego, consciousness, needs and utility, are all alike interpreted in terms of functions, contexts or contents in and of the things experienced.

3. The empiricist (of the immediate type) will prefer to use the term knowledge-experience, or cognitional experience, concerning the sort just described. For here things are *contemporaneously* experienced as known things. It is now

and here that they have "knownness" as one of their discriminated properties—just as they may have that of hard-
ness or unpleasantness or monetary value. But "knowledge"
is also used to denote the function or result of the doubt-
inquiry-answer experience in its outcome of critically assured
presence, with respect to further experiences. By the nature
of the case, dissentiency of conflicting things reaches an end
when the nature of reference is defined, and the character
of things altered so that they may sustain such reference.
Hence, when Woodbridge says (p. 396) "in cognitive experience all other sorts may exist without alteration," he says
something which seems obviously false if said of knowledge
in the second sense discussed (since transformation is the
salient trait of *its* things), but ideally true of knowledge in
this third sense. That is, the precise and defining aim of
knowledge in the second sense is to *secure* things which are
permanent or stable objects of reference; which may be persistently employed without thereby introducing further con-
flicts. Unalterability means precisely capacity to enter into
further things as secured points of regard, established contents and quales, guaranteed methods.[3]

We are thus enabled to give a precise statement of the
relationship of the knowledge-experience to alteration and to
validity. In its second sense, knowledge arises because of the
inherent discrepancy and consequent alteration of things.
But it gives that alteration a particular turn which it would
not take without knowledge—it directs alteration toward a
result of security and stability. Hence it is because knowledge is an experience, in organic connections of genesis and
destiny with other experiences, that the validity of knowledge
or truth has an assignable meaning. Because it is an affair
of meeting the concrete demands of things, the demand of
dissentient things for consensus, harmony, through defining
reference and through redefining things which sustain the
reference in question, validity or invalidity is a trait or property of facts which may be empirically investigated and instituted. But validity is not definable or measurable in terms

3. Knowledge might thus be roughly defined as the function of
economically (or efficiently) securing increasing complexity in
experienced things.

of the knowledge-content if *isolated*, but only of the *function* of the knowledge-experience in subsequent experiences. So knowledge tells us the nature of the real "when it is most fittingly and appropriately defined," because it is only when a real is ambiguous and discrepant that it needs definition. Its peculiar fitness is functional, relative and empirical, not absolutistic and transcendental. Yet we may admit a certain empirical transcendence. The outcome of the doubt-inquiry-answer experience literally goes beyond the state of suspense and dissentience out of which it originates. So far as the knowledge experience fulfills its function, it permanently transcends its own originating conditions. It puts certain things out of doubt, rendering them reliable, economical and fruitful constituents in other more complex things. *This* transcendence is the very essence of the pragmatic empiricist's account of truth.

THE KNOWLEDGE EXPERIENCE AGAIN

I owe an apology to the editor and to the readers of the *Journal of Philosophy, Psychology and Scientific Methods* for returning a third time to the defense of my article on "Immediate Empiricism,"[1] but Dr. Bode's recent article[2] is so clear and compact that I can not refrain from again taking a hand.

Dr. Bode points out that since I recognize that an experience (which is not itself a knowledge experience) may be cognitive, *i.e.*, have bearings which lead out into a distinctively knowledge experience, I can not readily be charged with making such a gap between the (dominantly) non-knowledge experience and the knowledge experience as deprives the latter of all point when it comes. But he claims (1) that this later experience which identifies the thing of the first as being thus and so (a fearsome noise as a wind-curtain fact) is essentially a "pointing" experience, a "knowledge about," and hence does not give the full meaning or truth of the first, which can be found only (2) in an experience which is wholly of the "acquaintance with" type, having neither the "leadings" of the first nor the "pointings" of the second. And this he claims must be (3) an "unconscious experience," a term which can have no other meaning assigned to it than the implication or presupposition of an object out of experience, conscious experience being then confined (on this basis) to relations between final out-of-consciousness terms. This position is (4) acutely identified with Woodbridge's definition of consciousness as a continuum, with its realistic implications.

I agree wholly with the first two points (save that em-

1. Vol. II, No. 15, p. 393 [*Middle Works* 3:158–67].
2. Vol. II, No. 24, p. 658 [*Middle Works* 3:398–404].

[First published in *Journal of Philosophy, Psychology and Scientific Methods* 2 (1905): 707–11.]

pirically the "complete acquaintance" thing need not necessarily be an entire experience, but may be an element in a more complex experience, and this, *as a whole*, may have cognitive leadings). But if this third point is correct, empiricism, in presupposing things which can not be experienced, has hanged itself on the topmost bough of the tree whose seed and fruit it meant and pretended to be. I marvel that Dr. Bode, in seeing so clearly the first two implications, did not follow the empirical clue; and, instead of arguing conceptually that the terminal experience *must* refer to something unexperienced, did not look about for some experience which should meet the conditions of complete cognitive fulfillment in a thing which itself is neither a "leading on" nor a "pointing back." Take again the case of the fearsome noise which develops into a wind-curtain fact. What is its appropriate career? Surely not into an "unconscious experience," but into an experience which in so far forth is practical (or moral) and aesthetic. The complete acquaintance which is self-adequate is, one might say, a relationship of friendship or affection (or of contempt and disregard) and of assurance or control. The complete "acquaintance" determines the attitude of, say, management of the thing as a means to an end; or of, say, amused recollection—not remembrance as logical pointing; *i.e.*, you are what once fooled me (an S-P experience, or judgment), but remembrance as recreation, or revival, in their literal immediate senses.

I am enough of a Hegelian to believe that "perfect" knowledge is not knowledge (in its intellectual or logical connotation) at all, but such a thing as religionists and practical people have in mind; an attitude of possession and of satisfaction,—the peace that *passes* understanding. It means control of self, because control of the object on which the status of the self contemporaneously depends. Here, if anywhere, the pragmatic is justified, like wisdom, of its children; and if we have something more than the pragmatic, it is because this attitude of attained adjustment is so saturated with emotional, or morally and aesthetically conscious, content. If one will realize how largely discursive knowledge empirically fulfills itself in a coloring or toning—an immediate value element—in subsequent experiences,[3] one will, I think, be fully guarded against supposing that "unconscious experience" is the sole alternative to intellectualized experience. "Unconscious" the experience is with respect to logical determinations; but immediate experience is saturated with values that are not logical determinations. The epistemological idealist can not deny this as a fact, because it is precisely this fact which makes him discredit immediate experience, and insist, therefore, upon its absorption into an "absolute" which is just and wholly logical.

Such a position also differentiates itself from the realism which Bode criticizes. If consciousness were just cognitional awareness, Woodbridge would seem to have said the last word in calling it a "continuum of objects"—of objects which are, as objects, out of consciousness. For as cognitional or intellectual, it is surely the business, so to say, of consciousness to be determined (that is, determinate) solely in and through objects. Otherwise common sense is crazy and science an organized insanity. But the "things" of which knowledge constitutes a continuum may be precisely immediate values which are not constituted by logical considerations, but by attitudes, adjustments, coordinations of personal activities. Knowledge, in the strict or logical sense, mediates these activities (which include, of course, passivities), establishing certain "leadings" and "pointings," certain equivalences, and thereby certain intermediaries and transitional points of immediate valences or worths; and, when it has completely wrought out a certain equivalence, finds its own surcease in a new value, expressive of a new aesthetic-moral attitude. From this point of view, knowledge is not, but develops, a continuum; an emotional content being, as substrate, the continuum of which knowledge "pointings," or discriminated-identities, are the discretes.[4]

Have we not the elements of a reconciliation of what is significant in realism and in idealism? We have something

3. There is much in Dr. Gordon's articles on "Feeling" (*Journal of Philosophy, Psychology and Scientific Methods*, Vol. II, Nos. 23 and 24) which I should gladly adopt as exegetical of my position.

4. See, again, Dr. Gordon's articles, and also her thesis, *The Psychology of Meaning*, pp. 22–26.

which is beyond consciousness *as cognitional* and which determines consciousness as cognitional—*literally* determines
it in the sense that the practical-aesthetic attitude, in order
to maintain itself, evokes the reflective attitude; and *logically*
determines it, in that the content of knowledge must conform to conditions which the knowledge consciousness does
not itself supply.[5] But this "efficient" and "formal" cause
presents a situation in which a conscious agent or person is
indispensably present. It is not a non-empirical thing-in-
itself (against which idealism has stood as a protest); and
it is something in which a conscious being plays a part. Is
epistemological idealism anything but a transfer into the
knowledge situation of a relation which actually holds in the
practical-aesthetic situation—a mistranslation which always
calls out "realism" as a counterbalance; which tends, in the
end, to destroy the peculiar individuality that is the essence
of such situations (resolving individuality into terms of the
universal, objective content which is alone appropriate to
knowledge); and which hopelessly complicates the treatment
of the knowledge situation itself by deliberately throwing
away the key to its interpretation?

I wish to take this occasion to say a few words also
about Professor Bakewell's interesting contribution to this
discussion.[6] My original contribution was intended, as Bakewell sees, to bring into sharper relief what seemed to be the
fundamental point at issue, so that the artillery of the opponents of recent empiricism (for whose range and shot I
profess the greatest respect) might fire there, rather than at
bogey-men or side-issues. I must confess I did not succeed in
so presenting it to Professor Bakewell. He says the idealist
denies that "any single actual experience, as existent or as
known, is immediate, and simply immediate" (p. 690). By
turning to p. 394 of my original article, it will be seen that
I there declare the nub of *immediate* empiricism to be precisely the thoroughgoing fallacy of the absolute identification, for metaphysics, of experience "*as known*" with experi-

5. See *Studies in Logical Theory*, p. 85, and, for a statement in
   psychological language, pp. 253–56.
6. *Journal of Philosophy, Psychology and Scientific Methods*, Vol.
   II, No. 25, p. 687. The preceding paragraphs stand as written
   prior to the appearance of Professor Bakewell's article.

ence "*as existent.*" This is the point at issue; hence objections which rest upon the fact that all *knowledge* involves a mediate element, are just non-relevant. That the distinction between the immediate *content* and the mediate *content* (together with their reference to one another) is necessary in and to the knowledge experience *as such*, I not only fully accept, but have been at considerable pains to expound and to attempt to explain (in *Studies in Logical Theory*).

So when "the idealist" (p. 688 of Bakewell's article) says that "experience is always a complex of the immediately perceived and the mediately conceived" he is saying something which the empiricist accepts so far as the content of a *distinctively* knowledge, or logical, experience is concerned, while he (1) takes fundamental issue with the implication that experience is "always" distinctively logical, and also (2) points out that even the distinctively logical experience is still "always" *in toto* an immediate experience; or, more specifically, that the distinction between "immediate perception" and its material ("data") and "mediate conception" and its methods ("thinking") is always within and for the sake of a value in experience which is "pragmatic" (personally, I should add aesthetic), not reducible to cognitional terms. Since it is only *as elements in the content* of an immediate experience that the distinction between the immediately perceived (the sensibly given) and the mediately conceived (the relationally thought) occurs, it is obvious that immediate empiricism does not identify the immediacy for which it stands with one of the *terms* of its own content at a special juncture.[7]

When Professor Bakewell says that "immediacy in this enlarged and general sense, as noting that aspect of direct ownership, of personal appropriation, which is always found in concepts and principles of mediation . . . is a fact fully taken into consideration by idealism," he is saying something which doubtless *his* idealism takes due account of, but which many of us believe epistemological idealism is wholly im-

---

7. I repeat what I have said before: it is the essential vice of *sensationalistic* empiricism to make this identification between a *functionally determined instrument and test of knowledge* and experience as such.

potent to take account of. It gladly assumes the benefit of such facts, but only by introducing elements which are not, and can not be reduced to, cognitional terms and relations; which connote emotional and volitional values; and to which "humanism," "pragmatism," "radical empiricism," are desirous of assigning their metaphysical weight. If Professor Bakewell's idealism takes *such* facts into consideration, then, I believe, he is, for all intents and purposes, an immediate empiricist, though seemingly one not yet entirely free from epistemological bondage.

EMERSON–THE PHILOSOPHER OF DEMOCRACY[1]

It is said that Emerson is not a philosopher. I find this denegation false or true according as it is said in blame or praise—according to the reasons proffered. When the critic writes of lack of method, of the absence of continuity, of coherent logic, and, with the old story of the string of pearls loosely strung, puts Emerson away as a writer of maxims and proverbs, a recorder of brilliant insights and abrupt aphorisms, the critic, to my mind, but writes down his own incapacity to follow a logic that is finely wrought. "We want in every man a long logic; we cannot pardon the absence of it, but it must not be spoken. Logic is the procession or proportionate unfolding of the intuition; but its virtue is as silent method; the moment it would appear as propositions and have a separate value, it is worthless." Emerson fulfills his own requisition. The critic needs the method separately propounded, and not finding his wonted leading-string is all lost. Again, says Emerson, "There is no compliment like the addressing to the human being thoughts out of certain heights and presupposing his intelligence"—a compliment which Emerson's critics have mostly hastened to avert. But to make this short, I am not acquainted with any writer, no matter how assured his position in treatises upon the history of philosophy, whose movement of thought is more compact and unified, nor one who combines more adequately diversity of intellectual attack with concentration of form and effect. I recently read a letter from a gentleman, himself a distinguished writer of philosophy, in which he remarked that philosophers are a stupid class, since they want every reason

1. A paper read at the Emerson Memorial Meeting, the University of Chicago, May 25, 1903.

[First published in *International Journal of Ethics* 13 (1903): 405–13. Reprinted as "Ralph Waldo Emerson" in *Characters and Events* 1:69–77 (New York: Henry Holt and Co., 1929).]

carefully pointed out and labelled, and are incapable of taking anything for granted. The condescending patronage by literary critics of Emerson's lack of cohesiveness may remind us that philosophers have no monopoly of this particular form of stupidity.

Perhaps those are nearer right, however, who deny that Emerson is a philosopher, because he is more than a philosopher. He would work, he says, by art, not by metaphysics, finding truth "in the sonnet and the play." "I am," to quote him again, "in all my theories, ethics and politics, a poet"; and we may, I think, safely take his word for it that he meant to be a maker rather than a reflector. His own preference was to be ranked with the seers rather than with the reasoners of the race, for he says, "I think that philosophy is still rude and elementary; it will one day be taught by poets. The poet is in the natural attitude; he is believing; the philosopher, after some struggle, having only reasons for believing." Nor do I regard it as impertinent to place by the side of this utterance, that other in which he said "We have yet to learn that the thing uttered in words is not therefore affirmed. It must affirm itself or no forms of grammar and no plausibility can give it evidence and no array of arguments." To Emerson, perception was more potent than reasoning; the deliverances of intercourse more to be desired than the chains of discourse; the surprise of reception more demonstrative than the conclusions of intentional proof. As he said "Good as is discourse, silence is better, and shames it. The length of discourse indicates the distance of thought betwixt the speaker and the hearer." And again, "If I speak, I define and confine, and am less." "Silence is a solvent that destroys personality and gives us leave to be great and universal."

I would not make hard and fast lines between philosopher and poet, yet there is some distinction of accent in thought and of rhythm in speech. The desire for an articulate, not for silent, logic is intrinsic with philosophy. The unfolding of the perception must be stated, not merely followed and understood. Such conscious method is, one might say, the only thing of ultimate concern to the abstract thinker. Not thought, but reasoned thought, not things, but

the ways of things, interest him; not even truth, but the paths
by which truth is sought. He construes elaborately the symbols of thinking. He is given over to manufacturing and
sharpening the weapons of the spirit. Outcomes, interpretations, victories, are indifferent. Otherwise is it with art. That,
as Emerson says, is "the path of the creator to his work";
and again "a habitual respect to the whole by an eye loving
beauty in detail." Affection is towards the meaning of the
symbol, not to its constitution. Only as he wields them, does
the artist forge the sword and buckler of the spirit. His affair
is to uncover rather than to analyze; to discern rather than
to classify. He reads but does not compose.

One, however, has no sooner drawn such lines than one
is ashamed and begins to retract. Euripides and Plato, Dante
and Bruno, Bacon and Milton, Spinoza and Goethe, rise in
rebuke. The spirit of Emerson rises to protest against exag-
gerating his ultimate value by trying to place him upon a
plane of art higher than a philosophic platform. Literary
critics admit his philosophy and deny his literature. And if
philosophers extol his keen, calm art and speak with some
depreciation of his metaphysic, it also is perhaps because
Emerson knew something deeper than our conventional
definitions. It is indeed true that reflective thinkers have
taken the way to truth for their truth; the method of life for
the conduct of life—in short, have taken means for end. But
it is also assured that in the completeness of their devotion,
they have expiated their transgression; means become identified with end, thought turns to life, and wisdom is justified
not of herself but of her children. Language justly preserves
the difference between philosopher and sophist. It is no
more possible to eliminate love and generation from the definition of the thinker than it is thought and limits from the
conception of the artist. It is interest, concern, caring, which
makes the one as it makes the other. It is significant irony
that the old quarrel of philosopher and poet was brought off
by one who united in himself more than has another individual the qualities of both artist and metaphysician. At
bottom the quarrel is not one of objectives nor yet of methods, but of the affections. And in the divisions of love, there
always abides the unity of him who loves. Because Plato

was so great he was divided in his affections. A lesser man could not brook that torn love, because of which he set poet and philosopher over against one another. Looked at in the open, our fences between literature and metaphysics appear petty—signs of an attempt to affix the legalities and formularies of property to the things of the spirit. If ever there lived not only a metaphysician but a professor of metaphysics it was Immanuel Kant. Yet he declares that he should account himself more unworthy than the day laborer in the field if he did not believe that somehow, even in his technical classifications and remote distinctions, he too, was carrying forward the struggle of humanity for freedom—that is for illumination.

And for Emerson of all others, there is a one-sidedness and exaggeration, which he would have been the first to scorn, in exalting overmuch his creative substance at the expense of his reflective procedure. He says in effect somewhere that the individual man is only a method, a plan of arrangement. The saying is amply descriptive of Emerson. His idealism is the faith of the thinker in his thought raised to its nth power. "History," he says, "and the state of the world at any one time is directly dependent on the intellectual classification then existing in the minds of men." Again, "Beware when the great God lets loose a thinker on this planet. Then all things are at risk. The very hopes of man, the thoughts of his heart, the religion of nations, the manners and morals of mankind are all at the mercy of a new generalization." And again, "Everything looks permanent until its secret is known. Nature looks provokingly stable and secular, but it has a cause like all the rest; and when once I comprehend that, will these fields stretch so immovably wide, these leaves hang so individually considerable?" And finally, "In history an idea always overhangs like a moon and rules the tide which rises simultaneously in all the souls of a generation." There are times, indeed, when one is inclined to regard Emerson's whole work as a hymn to intelligence, a paean to the all-creating, all-disturbing power of thought.

And so, with an expiatory offering to the Manes of Emerson, one may proceed to characterize his thought, his method, yea, even his system. I find it in the fact that he takes the distinctions and classifications which to most philosophers are true in and of and because of their systems, and makes them true of life, of the common experience of the everyday man. To take his own words for it, "There are degrees in idealism. We learn first to play with it academically, as the magnet was once a toy. Then we see, in the heyday of youth and poetry, that it may be true, that it is true in gleams and fragments. Then, its countenance waxes stern and grand, and we see that it must be true. It now shows itself ethical and practical." The idealism which is a thing of the academic intellect to the professor, a hope to the generous youth, an inspiration to the genial projector, is to Emerson a narrowly accurate description of the facts of the most real world in which all earn their living.

Such reference to the immediate life is the text by which he tries every philosopher. "Each new mind we approach seems to require," he says, "an abdication of all our past and present possessions. A new doctrine seems at first a subversion of all our opinions, tastes and manner of living." But while one gives himself "up unreservedly to that which draws him, because that is his own, he is to refuse himself to that which draws him not, because it is not his own. I were a fool not to sacrifice a thousand Aeschyluses to my intellectual integrity. Especially take the same ground in regard to abstract truth, the science of the mind. The Bacon, the Spinoza, the Hume, Schelling, Kant, is only a more or less awkward translator of things in your consciousness. Say, then, instead of too timidly poring into his obscure sense, that he has not succeeded in rendering back to you your consciousness. Anyhow, when at last, it is done, you will find it is not recondite, but a simple, natural state which the writer restores to you." And again, take this other saying, "Aristotle or Bacon or Kant propound some maxim which is the key-note of philosophy thenceforward, but I am more interested to know that when at last they have hurled out their grand word, it is only some familiar experience of every man on the street." I fancy he reads the so-called eclecticism of Emerson wrongly who does not see that it is reduction of all the philosophers of the race, even the prophets like Plato and Proclus whom Emerson holds most dear, to the test of trial by the service rendered the present and immediate experience. As for those who contemn Emerson for superficial pedantry because of the strings of names he is wont to flash like beads before our eyes, they but voice their own pedantry, not seeing, in their literalness, that all such things are with Emerson symbols of various uses administered to the common soul.

As Emerson treated the philosophers, so he treats their doctrines. The Platonist teaches the immanence of absolute ideas in the World and in Man, that every thing and every man participates in an absolute Meaning, individualized in him and through which one has community with others. Yet by the time this truth of the universe has become proper and fit for teaching, it has somehow become a truth of philosophy, a truth of private interpretation, reached by some men, not others, and consequently true for some, but not true for all, and hence not wholly true for any. But to Emerson all "truth lies on the highway." Emerson says, "We lie in the lap of immense intelligence which makes us organs of its activity and receivers of its truth," and the Idea is no longer either an academic toy nor even a gleam of poetry, but a literal report of the experience of the hour as that is enriched and reinforced for the individual through the tale of history, the appliance of science, the gossip of conversation and the exchange of commerce. That every individual is at once the focus and the channel of mankind's long and wide endeavor, that all nature exists for the education of the human soul—such things, as we read Emerson, cease to be statements of a separated philosophy and become natural transcripts of the course of events and of the rights of man.

Emerson's philosophy has this in common with that of the transcendentalists; he prefers to borrow from them rather than from others certain pigments and delineations. But he finds truth in the highway, in the untaught endeavor, the unexpected idea, and this removes him from their remotenesses. His ideas are not fixed upon any Reality that is beyond or behind or in any way apart, and hence they do not have to be bent. They are versions of the Here and the Now, and flow freely. The reputed transcendental worth of an

overweening Beyond and Away, Emerson, jealous for spiritual democracy, finds to be the possession of the unquestionable Present. When Emerson, speaking of the chronology of
history, designated the There and Then as "wild, savage
and preposterous," he also drew the line which marks him
off from transcendentalism—which is the idealism of a Class.
In sorry truth, the idealist has too frequently conspired with
the sensualist to deprive the pressing and so the passing Now
of value which is spiritual. Through the joint work of such
malign conspiracy, the common man is not, or at least does
not know himself for, an idealist. It is such disinherited of
the earth that Emerson summons to their own. "If man is
sick, is unable, is mean-spirited and odious, it is because
there is so much of his nature which is unlawfully with-
holden from him."

Against creed and system, convention and institution,
Emerson stands for restoring to the common man that which
in the name of religion, of philosophy, of art and of morality,
has been embezzled from the common store and appropri-
ated to sectarian and class use. Beyond anyone we know of,
Emerson has comprehended and declared how such malver-
sation makes truth decline from its simplicity, and in becoming partial and owned, become a puzzle of and trick for
theologian, metaphysician and litterateur—a puzzle of an
imposed law, of an unwished for and refused goodness, of a
romantic ideal gleaming only from afar, and a trick of
manipular skill, of specialized performance.

For such reasons, the coming century may well make
evident what is just now dawning, that Emerson is not only
a philosopher, but that he is the Philosopher of Democracy.
Plato's own generation would, I think, have found it difficult
to class Plato. Was he an inept visionary or a subtle dia-
lectician? A political reformer or a founder of the new type
of literary art? Was he a moral exhorter, or an instructor
in an Academy? Was he a theorist upon education, or the
inventor of a method of knowledge? We, looking at Plato
through the centuries of exposition and interpretation, find
no difficulty in placing Plato as a philosopher and in attributing to him a system of thought. We dispute about the
nature and content of this system, but we do not doubt it is

there. It is the intervening centuries which have furnished
Plato with his technique and which have developed and
wrought Plato to a system. One century bears but a slender
ratio to twenty-five; it is not safe to predict. But at least,
thinking of Emerson as the one citizen of the New World
fit to have his name uttered in the same breath with that of
Plato, one may without presumption believe that even if
Emerson has no system, none the less he is the prophet and
herald of any system which democracy may henceforth construct and hold by, and that when democracy has articulated
itself, it will have no difficulty in finding itself already proposed in Emerson. It is as true to-day as when he said it: "It
is not propositions, not new dogmas and the logical exposition
of the world that are our first need, but to watch and ten-
derly cherish the intellectual and moral sensibilities and
woo them to stay and make their home with us. Whilst they
abide with us, we shall not think amiss." We are moved to
say that Emerson is the first and as yet almost the only
Christian of the Intellect. From out such reverence for the
instinct and impulse of our common nature shall emerge in
their due season propositions, systems and logical expositions
of the world. Then shall we have a philosophy which religion
has no call to chide and which knows its friendship with
science and with art.

Emerson wrote of a certain type of mind: "This tranquil,
well-founded, wide-seeing soul is no express-rider, no at-
torney, no magistrate. It lies in the sun and broods on the
world." It is the soul of Emerson which these words describe. Yet this is no private merit nor personal credit. For
thousands of earth's children, Emerson has taken away the
barriers that shut out the sun and has secured the un-
impeded, cheerful circulation of the light of heaven, and
the wholesome air of day. For such, content to endure without contriving and contending, at the last all express-riders
journey, since to them comes the final service of all com-
modity. For them, careless to make out their own case, all
attorneys plead in the day of final judgment; for though
falsehoods pile mountain high, truth is the only deposit that
nature tolerates. To them who refuse to be called "master,
master," all magistracies in the end defer, for theirs is the

common cause for which dominion, power and principality is put under foot. Before such successes, even the worshipers of that which to-day goes by the name of success, those who bend to millions and incline to imperialisms, may lower their standard, and give at least a passing assent to the final word of Emerson's philosophy, the identity of Being, unqualified and immutable, with Character.

THE PHILOSOPHICAL WORK OF
HERBERT SPENCER

I do not know whether it may have occurred to anyone else to associate the work of Émile Zola in fiction and of Herbert Spencer in philosophy. I find myself, however, mentally running together the careers of these two men, different as they were in surroundings, interests, aims, and personalities. The two somehow associate themselves in my mind, at least to such an extent that I find no words of my own so apt to characterize the larger features of the work of Herbert Spencer as these borrowed from the remarkable critical appreciation by Henry James of Émile Zola, published in the August, 1903, number of the *Atlantic Monthly*. Mr. James begins by referring to "the circumstance that, thirty years ago, a young man of extraordinary brain and indomitable purpose, wishing to give the measure of these endowments in a piece of work supremely solid, conceived and sat down to Les Rougon-Macquart, rather than to an equal task in physics, mathematics, politics, economics. He saw his undertaking, thanks to his patience and courage, practically to a close. . . . No finer act of courage and confidence, I think, is recorded in the history of letters. The critic in sympathy with him returns again and again to the great wonder of it, in which something so strange is mixed with something so august. Entertained and carried out almost from the threshold of manhood, the high project, the work of a lifetime, announces beforehand its inevitable weakness, and yet speaks in the same voice for its admirable, its almost unimaginable, strength."

With few verbal changes, this surely sets forth the case of Mr. Spencer; and in saying the word of criticism which must inevitably shadow all mortal attempts, I again find

[First published in *Philosophical Review* 13 (1904): 159–75. Reprinted in *Characters and Events*, ed. Joseph Ratner (New York: Henry Holt and Co., 1929), 1:45–62.]

nothing more appropriate than some further sentences of
Mr. James. "It was the fortune, it was in a manner the doom,
of Les Rougon-Macquart to deal with things almost always
in gregarious form, to be a picture of *numbers*, of classes,
crowds, confusions, movements. . . . The individual life is,
if not wholly absent, reflected in coarse and common, in
generalized terms; whereby we arrive . . . at the circumstance that, looking out somewhere, and often woefully
athirst, for the taste of fineness, we find it not in the fruits
of our author's fancy, but in a different matter altogether.
We get it in the very history of his effort, the image itself of
his lifelong process, comparatively so personal, so spiritual
even . . . through all its patience and pain."

The point that seems to me so significant (and, indeed,
so absolutely necessary to take into the reckoning), when
we balance accounts with the intellectual work of Mr.
Spencer, is this sitting down to achieve a preconceived idea,
—an idea, moreover, of a synthetic, deductive rendering of
all that is in the Universe. The point stands forth in all its
simplicity and daring every time we open our *First Principles*.
We find there republished the prospectus of 1860, the program of the entire Synthetic Philosophy. And the more we
compare the achievement with the announcement, the
more we are struck with the way in which the whole scheme
stands complete, detached, able to go alone from the very
start.

Spencer and his readers are committed in advance to a
definitely wrought out, a rounded and closed interpretation
of the Universe. Further discovery and intercourse are not to
count; it remains only to fill in the *cadres*. Successive volumes
are outlined; distinctive sections of each set forth. All the
fundamental generalizations are at hand, which are to apply
to *all* regions of the Universe with the exception of inorganic
nature, attention being especially called to this exception as
a gap unavoidable but regrettable. There is but one thing
more extraordinary than the conception which this program
embodies: the fact that it is carried out. We are so accustomed to what we call systems of philosophy; the "systems" of Plato, Aristotle, Descartes, Kant, or Hegel, that I
suspect we do not quite grasp the full significance of such a

project as this of Mr. Spencer's. The other systems are such
after all more or less *ex post facto*. In themselves they have
the unity of the *development* of a single mind, rather than
of a predestined *planned achievement*. They are systems
somewhat in and through retrospect. Their completeness
owes something to the mind of the onlooker gathering together parts which have grown up more or less separately
and in response to felt occasions, to particular problems. Our
reflection helps bind their parts into one aggregative whole.
But Spencer's system *was* a system from the very start. It
was a system in conception, not merely in issue. It was one
by the volition of its author, complete, compact, coherent,
not in virtue of a single personality which by ways mainly
unconscious continually and restlessly reattempts to attain to
some worthy and effective embodiment of itself. We are almost inclined to believe in the identification of conscious will
with physical force as we follow the steady, unchanging mo-
mentum of Spencer's thought.

It is this fore-thought, foreclosed scheme which makes
so ominous that phrase of James to the effect that "the high
project announces beforehand its inevitable weakness." It is
this which makes so unavoidable the appropriation of the
phrase regarding absence of the *individual* life. It is this fact
which gives jurisdiction to the further remark that "vision
and opportunity reside in a personal sense, and in a personal
history, and no short cut to them has ever been discovered."
It is this same fact that moves me to transfer to Spencer a
further phrase, that the work went on in "the region that I
qualify as that of experience by imitation." It may seem
harsh to say Spencer occupies himself in any such way as
to justify the phrase "experience by imitation." Or, on the
other hand, one may say, however the case stands in arts
and letters, that in philosophy one must perforce work in
and with a region of experience which it is but praise to call
"experience by imitation," since it is experience deperson-
alized, from which the qualities of individual contact and
career, with their accidents of circumstance, and corresponding emotional entanglements, have been intentionally shut
out. But whether one regard the phrase as harsh, or as defining an indispensable trait of all philosophizing, it remains

true that one who announces in advance a system in all its characteristic conceptions and applications has discounted, in a way which is awful in its augustness, all individual contingencies, all accidents of time and place, personal surroundings and personal intercourse, new ideas from new contacts and new expansions of life. It is upon the revelations that arise from the eternal mixture of voluntary endeavor with the unplanned, the unexpected, that most of us learn to depend for shaping thought and directing intellectual movement. We hang upon experience as it comes, not alone upon experience as already formulated, into which we can enter by "imitation." To assure to the world a comprehensive system of the Universe, in a way which precludes further development and shapings of this personal sort, is a piece of intellectual audacity of the most commanding sort. It is this extraordinary objectivity of Spencer's work, this hitherto unheard of elimination of the individual and the subjective, which gives his philosophy its identity, which marks it off from other philosophic projects, and is the source at once of its power and of its "inevitable weakness."

The austere devotion, the singleness, simplicity, and straightforwardness of Spencer's own life, and its seclusion, its remoteness, its singular immunity from all intellectual contagion, are chapters in the same story. Here, we may well believe, is the revenge of nature. The element of individual life so lacking in the philosophy, both in its content and in its style, is the thing that strikes us in the history of Spencer's personal effort. No system, after all, has ever been more thoroughly conditioned by the intellectual and moral personality of its author. The impersonal content of the system is the register of the personal separation of its author from vital participation in the moving currents of history.

The seclusion and isolation necessary to a system like Spencer's appear from whatever angle we approach him. Doubtless his autobiography will put us in possession of one of the most remarkable educational documents the world has yet seen. But even without this, we know that his intellectual life was early formed in a certain remoteness. The relative absence of the social element in his education, and his own later conscious predilection for non-institutionalized instruction, for education of the tutorial sort apart from schools and classes, at once constitute and reflect his aloofness from the ordinary give and take processes of development. The lack of university associations is another mark on the score. The lack of knowledge of ancient languages and comparative ignorance of modern languages and literature have to be reckoned with. Nor was Spencer (in this unlike Bacon, Locke, Berkeley, Hume, and John Mill) a man of affairs, one who continually renewed the region of "experience by imitation," of formulated knowledge, by engaging in those complications of life which force a man to re-think, re-feel, and re-choose; to have, in a word, first-hand experience. It would be hard to find another intellect of first class rank so devoid of historical sense and interest as was Spencer's; incredible as is this fact taken alongside authorship of a system of evolution! Certainly the world may wait long for another example of a man who dares to conceive and has the courage and energy to execute a system of philosophy, in almost total ignorance of the entire history of thought. We have got so used to it that we hardly pause, when we read such statements as that of Spencer, that after reading the first few pages of Kant's *Critique* he laid the book down. "Twice since then the same thing has happened; for, being an impatient reader, when I disagree with the cardinal propositions of a work I can go no further."[1]

It is not Spencer's ignorance to which I am calling attention. Much less am I blaming him for his failure to run hither and yon through the fields of thought; there is something almost refreshing, in these days of subjugation by the mere overwhelming mass of learning, in the naïve and virgin attitude of Spencer. What I am trying to point out is the absence in Spencer of any interest in the history of human ideas and of acts prompted by them, considered simply as history,—as affairs of personal initiation, discovery, experimentation, and struggle. His insulation from the intellectual currents of the ages as moving processes (apart, that is, from their impersonal and factual deposit in the form of

1. *Essays Scientific, Political, and Speculative*, Vol. III, p. 206, note.

"science") is the mirror of the secludedness of his early education, and of his entire later personal life. I do not think it necessary to apologize even for referring to the little device by which, when wearied of conversation, he closed his ears and made himself deaf to what was going on about him. There are not two facts here, but only one. His isolation was necessary in carrying out his gigantic task, not merely as a convenience for securing the necessary leisure, protection against encroachment, and the nursing of inadequate physical strength against great odds; but it was an organic precondition of any project which assigns the Universe to volumes in advance, and then proceeds steadily, irresistibly, to fill them up chapter by chapter. Such work is possible only when one is immune against the changing play of ideas, the maze of points of view, the cross-currents of interests, which characterize the world historically viewed,—seen in process as an essentially moving thing.

We have to reckon with the apparent paradox of Spencer's rationalistic, deductive, systematic habit of mind over against all the traditions of English thought. How could one who thought himself the philosopher of experience *par excellence*, revive, under the name of a "universal postulate," the fundamental conception of the formal rationalism of the Cartesian school, which even the philosophers whom Spencer despised as purely *a priori*, had found it necessary, under the attacks of Kant (whom Spencer to his last day regarded as a sort of belated supernaturalist), long since to abandon? It is too obvious to need mention that Spencer is in all respects a thoroughgoing Englishman,—indeed what, without disrespect and even with admiration, we may term a "Britisher." But how could the empirical and inductive habit of the English mind so abruptly, so thoroughly, without any shadow of hesitation or touch of reserve, cast itself in a system whose professed aim was to deduce all the phenomena of life, mind, and society from a single formula regarding the redistribution of matter and motion?

Here we come within sight of the problem of the technical origins and structure of Spencer's philosophy, a problem, however, which may still be approached from the standpoint of Spencer's own personal development. We must

not forget that Spencer was by his environment and education initiated into all the characteristic tenets of English
political and social liberalism, with their individualistic connotations. It is significant that Spencer's earliest literary
contribution,—written at the age of twenty-two,—was upon
the proper sphere of government, and was intended (I speak
only from second-hand information, never having seen the
pamphlet) to show the restrictions upon governmental action
required in the interests of the individual. I know no more
striking tribute to the thoroughness and success with which
earlier English philosophic thought did its work than the
fact that Spencer was completely saturated with, and possessed by, the characteristic traditions of this individualistic
philosophy, simply, so to speak, by absorption, by respiration
of the intellectual atmosphere, with a minimum of study and
reflective acquaintance with the classic texts of Hobbes,
Hume, and (above all) John Locke. So far as we can tell,
Spencer's ignorance of the previous history of philosophy extended in considerable measure even to his own philosophic
ancestry; and I am inclined to believe that even such reading
as he did of his predecessors left him still with a delightful
unconsciousness that in them were the origin and kin of his
own thought. The solid body and substantiality of Spencer's
individualism is made not less but more comprehensible on
the supposition that it came to him not through conscious
reading and personal study, but through daily drafts upon
his intellectual environment; the results being so unconsciously and involuntarily wrought into the fibre of his being
that they became with him an instinct rather than a reflection or theory.

It is this complete incorporation of the results of prior
individualistic philosophy, accompanied by total unconsciousness that anything was involved in the way of philosophic preliminaries or presuppositions, which freed Spencer
from the lurking scepticism regarding systems and deductive
syntheses which permeate the work of Locke, Berkeley,
Hume, and John Stuart Mill. It was this thoroughgoing unconscious absorption that gave him a confident, aggressive,
dogmatic individualism,—which enabled him to employ individualism as a deductive instrument, instead of as a point

of view useful in the main for criticising undue intellectual pretensions, and for keeping the ground cleared for inductive, empirical inquiries. The eighteenth century, indeed, exhibits to us the transformation of the sceptically colored individualism of the seventeenth century, taking effect mainly in a theory of the nature and limits of human knowledge, and employed most effectively to get rid of dogma in philosophy, theology, and politics,—the transformation of this, I say, into an individualism which aims at social reform, and thereby is becoming positive, constructive, rationalistic, optimistic.

Spencer is the heir not of the psychological individualism of Locke direct, but of this individualism after exportation and reimportation from France. It was the individualism of the French Encyclopedist, with its unwavering faith in progress, in the ultimate perfection of humanity, and in "nature" as everywhere beneficently working out this destiny, if only it can be freed from trammels of church and state, which in Spencer mingles with generalizations of science, and is thereby reawakened to new life. Seen in this way, there is no breach of continuity. The paradox disappears. Spencer's work imposes itself upon us all precisely because it so remarkably carries over the net result of that individualism which (contend against it as we may) represents the fine achievement of the seventeenth and eighteenth centuries. It preserves it in the only way in which it could be conserved, by carrying it over, by translating it into the organic, the systematic, the universal terms which report the presence of the nineteenth century spirit. And if a certain constitutional incoherency results, if the compound of individualism and organicism shows cleavages of fundamental contradictions, none the less without this restatement the old would have been lost, and a certain thinness and remoteness would characterize the new. The earlier and more thoroughgoing formulations of the organic standpoint in post-Kantian thought were, and had to remain, transcendental (in the popular, if not technical sense of the term) in language and idea just because the expression, though logically more adequate, was socially and psychologically premature. It did not and could not at once take up into itself the habits of thought and feeling characteristic of

earlier individualism and domesticate them in the social and
moral attitude of the modern man.

In the struggle of adjustment, Spencer is without a rival
as a mediator, a vehicle of communication, a translator. It
is, as we shall see, the successful way in which he exercises
this function that gives him his hold upon the culture of our
day, and which makes his image stand out so imposingly
that to many he is not one creator with many others of the
theory of evolution, but its own concrete incarnation. In
support of the idea that Spencer's work was essentially that
of carrying over the net earlier social and ethical individualism into the more organic conceptions characteristic of the
nineteenth century science and action, we can here only
refer to the *Social Statics* of 1851,—this being in my judgment one of the most remarkable documents, from the
standpoint of tracing the origins of an intellectual development, ever produced. This book shows with considerable
detail the individualistic method of the English theory of
knowledge in process of transformation into something
which is no longer a method of regulating belief, but is an
attained belief in a method of action, and hence itself a substantial first principle, an axiom, an indisputable, absolute
truth, having within itself substantial resources which may
in due order—that is, by use of a deductive method—be delivered and made patent. It shows the individualistic creed
dominant, militant; no longer a principle of criticism, but
of reform and construction in social life, and, therefore, of
necessity a formula of construction in the intellectual sphere.
In this document, the world-formula of "evolution" of later
philosophy appears as the social formula of "progress." It
repeats as an article of implicit faith the creed of revolutionary liberalism in the indefinite perfectibility of mankind.
"Man has been, is, and will long continue to be, in process of
adaptation, and the belief in human perfectibility merely
amounts to the belief that in virtue of these processes, man
will eventually become completely suited to his mode of life.
Progress, therefore, is not an accident, but a necessity."[2]

In this characteristic sentence we have already present
the conception: first, of evolution; second, of the goal of the

2. *Social Statics*, pp. 31 f., edn. of 1892.

evolution as adaption of human life to certain conditions beyond itself; and third (although implicitly—the notion, however, being made explicit in other portions of the same book), the conception that it is the conditions to which life is to be adapted which are the causally operating forces in bringing about the adaptation, and hence the progress. The "organism" of the Synthetic Philosophy is the projection of the individual man of the thought of 1850. The "environment" of the latter system appears in the earlier sketch as "conditions of life." The "evolution" of later systematic philosophy is the "progress" figuring in the early social creed as the continual adaptation of human life to the necessities of its outward conditions. In all, and through all, runs the idea of "nature,"—that nature to which the social and philosophical reformation of the eighteenth century appealed with such unhesitating and sublime faith. Load down the formula by filling "nature" with the concrete results of physical and biological science, and the transformation scene is complete. The years between 1850 and 1862 (the date of the *First Principles*) are the record of this loading. "Nature" never parts with its eighteenth century function of effecting approximation to a goal of ultimate perfection and happiness, but nature no longer proffers itself as a pious reminiscence of the golden age of Rousseau, or a prophetic inspiration of the millennium of Condorcet, but as that most substantial, most real of all forces guaranteed and revealed to us at every turn by the advance of scientific inquiry. And "science" is in turn but the concrete rendering of the "reason" of the Enlightenment.

Spencer's faith in this particular article of the creed never faltered. Eighteenth century liberalism, after the time of Rousseau, was perfectly sure that the only obstacles to the fulfillment of the beneficent purpose of nature in effecting perfection have their source in institutions of state and church, which, partly because of ignorance, and partly because of the selfishness of rulers and priests, have temporarily obstructed the fulfillment of nature's benign aims. The *laissez-faire* theory and its extreme typical expression, anarchism, did not originate in the accidents of commercial life, much less in the selfish designs of the trading class to increase its wares at the expense of other sections of society. Whether right or wrong, whether for good or for evil, it took its origin from profound philosophical conceptions; the belief in nature as a mighty force, and in reason as having only to cooperate with nature, instead of thwarting it with its own petty, voluntary devices, in order to usher in the era of unhindered progress. Spencer's insistent and persistent opposition to the extension of the sphere of governmental action beyond that of police duty, preventing the encroachment of one individual upon another, goes back to this same sublime faith in nature. The goal of evolution of Spencer's ethics, the perfect individual adapted to the perfect state of society, is but the enlarged projection of the ideal of a fraternal society, which made its way into the *Social Statics* from the same creed of revolutionary liberalism. His "Absolute Ethics," deductively derived from a first law of life, has in its origin nothing to do with science, but everything to do with the reason and nature of the Enlightenment. It has, of course, been often enough pointed out that the main features of Spencer's later ethics were already well along before he came to that conception of evolution upon which his sociology and ethics are professedly based. This point has, however, generally been employed as a mode of casting suspicion upon the content of his moral system, suggesting that after all it has no very intimate connection with the theory of evolution as such. But I am not aware that attention has been called to this converse fact of greater moment: that Spencer's entire evolutionary conception and scheme is but the projection upon the cosmic screen of the spectrum of the buoyant *a priori* ideals of the later eighteenth century liberalism.

Certain essays, now mostly reprinted in three volumes, entitled *Essays Scientific, Political, and Speculative*, put before our eyes the links of the transformation, the instruments of the projection. We may refer particularly to the essays on "Progress: Its Law and Cause," "Transcendental Physiology" (both dated 1857); "The Genesis of Science" (1854), and "The Nebular Hypothesis" (1858), together with "The Social Organism" (1860). What we find exposed in these essays is the increasingly definite and solid body of scientific particulars and generalizations, getting themselves read into the political and social formula, and thereby effecting transformation into the system outlined by the prospectus of 1860. This fusion is, indeed, already foreshadowed in the *Social Statics* itself.

This is not the time or place to go into detail, but I think I am well within the bonds of verifiable statement when I say that Spencer's final system of philosophy took shape through his bringing into intimate connection with each other the dominating conception of social progress, inherited from the Enlightenment, certain larger generalizations of physiology (particularly that of growth as change from homogeneity to heterogeneity, and of "physiological division of labor" with accompanying interdependence of parts) and the idea of cosmic change derived from astronomy and geology,—particularly as formulated under the name of the nebular hypothesis. Social philosophy furnished the fundamental ideals and ideas; biological statements provided the defining and formulating elements necessary to put these vague and pervasive ideals into something like scientific shape; while the physical-astronomic speculations furnished the causal, efficient machinery requisite for getting the scheme under way, and supplied still more of the appearance of scientific definiteness and accuracy. Such, at least, is my schematic formula of the origin of the Spencerian system.[3]

3. If our main interest here were in the history of thought, it would be interesting to note the dependence of the development of Spencer's thought, as respects the second of the above factors, upon factors due to the post-Kantian philosophy of Germany. I can only refer in passing to some pages of the *Social Statics* (255 to 261), in which, after making the significant statement that "morality is essentially one with physical truth—is, in fact, a species of transcendental physiology," he refers in support of his doctrine to "a theory of life developed by Coleridge." This theory is that of tendency towards individuation, conjoined with increase of mutual dependence,—a fundamental notion, of course, of Schelling. An equally significant foot-note (page 256) tells us that it was in 1864, while writing "The Classification of the Sciences," that Spencer himself realized that this truth has to do with "a trait of all evolving things, inorganic as well as organic." In his essay on "Transcendental Physiology," Spencer refers to the importance of carrying over distinctions first observed in society into physiological terms, so that they become points of view for interpretation and explanation there. The

We are now, I think, in a position not only to understand the independence of Spencer's and Darwin's work in
relation to each other, but the significance of this independence. Because Spencer's thought descended from the
social and political philosophy of the eighteenth century
(which in turn was a rendering of a still more technical
philosophy), and employed the conceptions thus derived to

conception also dominates the essay on "The Social Organism."
In fact, he makes use of the idea of division of labor, originally
worked out in political economy, in his biological speculations,
and then in his cosmological, in very much the same way in
which Darwin borrowed the Malthusian doctrine of population.
The social idea first found biological form for itself, and then
was projected into cosmological terms. I have no doubt that this
represents the general course of Spencer's ideas. In the essay on
"Progress," Spencer specifically refers to the law of the evolution
of the individual organism as established "by the Germans—
the investigations of Wolff, Goethe, and von Baer." The law
referred to here is that development consists in advance from
homogeneity to heterogeneity. He there transfers it from the
life-history of the individual organism to the record of all life;
while, in the same essay, he expressly states that, if the nebular
hypothesis could be established, then we should have a single
formula for the universe as a whole, inorganic as well as organic. And upon page 36 he speaks of that "which determines
progress of every kind—astronomic, geologic, organic, ethnologic,
social, economic, artistic."

One need only turn to some of the methodological writings
of Spencer to see how conscious he was of the method which I
have attributed to him. The little essay entitled "An Element in
Method," and certain portions of his essay entitled, "Prof. Tait
on the Formula of Evolution," are particularly significant. The
latter indicates the necessity of making a synthesis of deductive
reasoning, as exhibited in mathematical physics, with the inductive empiricism characteristic of the biological sciences; and
charges both physicist and zoologist with one-sidedness. The
former essay indicates that, in forming any generalization which
is to be used for deductive purposes, we ought to take independent groups of phenomena which appear unallied, and which
certainly are very remote from each other. I am inclined to think
that Spencer's method of taking groups of facts, apparently
wholly unlike each other, such as those of the formation of solar
systems, on one side, and facts of present social life, on the
other, with a view to discovering what he calls "some common
trait," has, indeed, more value for philosophic method than is
generally recognized. In a way, he has himself justified the
method, since his Synthetic Philosophy is, speaking from the
side of method, precisely this sort of thing, astronomy and
sociology forming the extremes, and biology the mean term. But,
of course, Spencer's erection of the "common trait" into a force,
or law, or cause, which can immediately be used deductively to
explain other things, is quite another matter from this heuristic
or methodological value. But this note has already spun itself
out too long.

assimilate and organize the generalized conceptions of geology and biology, it needed no particular aid from the specialized order of scientific methods and considerations which control the work of Darwin. But it was a tremendous piece of luck for both the Darwinian and Spencerian theories that they happened so nearly to coincide in the time of their promulgation. Each got the benefit not merely of the disturbance and agitation aroused by the other, but of psychological and logical reinforcement, as each blended into and fused with the other in the minds of readers and students. It is an interesting though hopeless speculation to wonder what the particular fate of either would have been, if it had lacked this backing up at its own weak point, a support all the more effective because it was so surprisingly unplanned,—because each in itself sprang out of, and applied to, such different orders of thought and fact.

This explains, in turn, the identification of the very idea of "evolution," with the name of Spencer. The days are gone by when it was necessary to iterate that the conception of evolution is no new thing. We know that upon the side of the larger philosophic generalizations, as well as upon that of definite and detailed scientific considerations, evolution has an ancient ancestry. From the time of the Greeks, when philosophy and science were one, to the days of Kant, Goethe, and Hegel, on one side, and of Lamarck and the author of the *Vestiges of Creation*, on the other, the idea of evolution has never been without its own vogue and career. The idea is too closely akin both to the processes of human thinking and to the obvious facts of life not to have always some representative in man's schemes of the Universe. How, then, are we to account for the peculiar, the unique position occupied by Spencer? Is this thoroughgoing identification in the popular mind of Spencer's system with the very idea and name of evolution an illusion of ignorance? I think not. So massive and pervasive an imposition of itself is accountable for only in positive terms. The genesis of Spencer's system in fusion of scientific notions and philosophic considerations gives the system its actual hold, and also legitimates it.

Spencer's work is rightfully entitled to the place it occupies in the popular imagination. Philosophy is naturally and properly technical and remote to the mass of mankind, save as it takes shape in social and political philosophy,—in a theory of conduct which, being more than individual, serves as a principle of criticism and reform in corporate affairs and community welfare. But even social and political philosophy remain more or less speculative, romantic, Utopian, or "ideal," when couched merely in terms of a program of criticism and reconstruction; only "science" can give it body. Again, the specializations of science are naturally and properly remote and technical to the interests of the mass of mankind. When we have said they are specialized, we have described them. But to employ the mass of scientific material, the received code of scientific formulations, to give weight and substance to philosophical ideas which are already operative, is an achievement of the very first order. Spencer took two sets of ideas, in themselves abstract and isolated, and by their fusion put them in a shape where their net result became available for the common consciousness. By such a fusion Spencer provided a language, a formulation, an imagery, of a reasonable and familiar kind to the masses of mankind for ideas of the utmost importance, and for ideas which, without such amalgamation, must have remained out of reach.

Even they who—like myself—are so impressed with the work of the philosophers of Germany in the first half of the nineteenth century as to believe that they have furnished ideas which in the long run are more luminous, more fruitful, possessed of more organizing power, than those which Spencer has made current, must yet remember that the work of German philosophy is done in an outlandish and alien vocabulary. Now, this is not a mere incident of the use of language,—as if a man happened to choose to speak in Greek rather than in French. The very technicality of the vocabulary means that the ideas used are not as yet naturalized in the common consciousness of man. The "transcendental" character of such philosophy is not an inherent, eternal characteristic of its subject-matter, but is a sign and exponent that the values dealt in are not yet thoroughly at home in human experience, have not yet found themselves in ordinary social life and popular science, are not yet working terms justifying themselves by daily applications.

Spencer furnished the common consciousness of his

day with terms and images so that it could appropriate to its ordinary use in matters of "life, mind, and society," the most fundamental generalizations which had been worked out in the abstract regions of *both* philosophy and science. He did *this* even though he failed to deduce "life, mind, and society" from a single formula regarding "force." This is a work great enough for any man,—even though we are compelled to add that the gross obviousness with which it was done shows that Spencer after all measured up to the level of the intellectual life of his time rather than, through sympathy with more individualized and germinal forces, initiated a new movement. Here, again, Spencer's own aloofness, his own deliberate self-seclusion counts. Spencer is a monument, but, like all monuments, he commemorates the past. He presents the achieved culmination of ideas already in overt and external operation. He winds up an old dispensation. Here is the secret of his astounding success, of the way in which he has so thoroughly imposed his idea that even non-Spencerians must talk in his terms and adjust their problems to his statements. And here also is his inevitable weakness. Only a system which formulates the accomplished can possibly be conceived and announced in advance.

Any deductive system means by the necessity of the case the organization of a vast amount of material in such a way as to dispose of it. The system *seems* to fix the limits of all further effort, to define its aims and to assign its methods. But this is an illusion of the moment. In reality this wholesale disposal of material clears the ground for new, untried initiatives. It furnishes capital for hitherto unthought of speculations. Its deductive finalities turn out but ships of adventure to voyage on undiscovered seas.

To speak less metaphorically, Spencer's conception of evolution was always a confined and bounded one. Since his "environment" was but the translation of the "nature" of the metaphysicians, its workings had a fixed origin, a fixed quality, and a fixed goal. Evolution still tends in the minds of Spencer's contemporaries to "a single, far-off, divine event,"—to a finality, a fixity. Somehow, there are fixed laws and forces (summed up under the name "environment") which control the movement, which keep it pushing on in a definite fashion to a certain end. Backwards, there is found a picture of the time when all this was set agoing, when the homogeneous began to differentiate. If evolution is conceived of as in and of itself *constant*, it is yet evolution by cycles,—a never-ending series of departures from, and returns to, a fixed point. I doubt not the time is coming when it will be seen that whatever all this is, it is *not* evolution. A thoroughgoing evolution must by the nature of the case abolish all fixed limits, beginnings, origins, forces, laws, goals. If there be evolution, then all these also evolve, and are what they are as points of origin and of destination relative to some special portion of evolution. They are to be defined in terms of the process, the process that now and always is, not the process in terms of them. But the transfer from the world of set external facts and of fixed ideal values to the world of free, mobile, self-developing, and self-organizing reality would be unthinkable and impossible were it not for the work of Spencer, which, shot all through as it is with contradictions, thereby all the more effectually served the purpose of a medium of transition from the fixed to the moving. A fixed world, a world of movement between fixed limits, a moving world, such is the order.

RELIGIOUS EDUCATION AS CONDITIONED BY MODERN PSYCHOLOGY AND PEDAGOGY

So far as I see, psychological theory at present simply emphasizes and reinforces some general principles which accompany a practical movement that is already going on, deriving its main motives from general considerations. Psychology has no peculiar gospel or revelation of its own to deliver. It may, however, serve to interpret and illuminate some aspects of what is already going on, and thereby assist it in directing itself.

I shall endeavor to present simply one principle which seems to me of help in this interpretation: the stress laid in modern psychological theory upon the principle of growth and of consequent successive expansions of experience on different levels. Since the mind is a growth, it passes through a series of stages, and only gradually attains to its majority. That the mind of the child is not identical with the mind of the adult is, of course, no new discovery. After a fashion, everybody has always known it; but for a long, long time the child was treated as if he were only an abbreviated adult, a little man or a little woman. His purposes, interests, and concerns were taken to be about those of the grown-up person, unlikenesses being emphasized only on the side of strength and power.

But the differences are in fact those of mental and emotional standpoint, and outlook, rather than of degree. If we assume that the quality of child and adult is the same, and that the only difference is in quantity of capacity, it follows at once that the child is to be taught down to, or talked down to, from the standpoint of the adult. This has fixed the standard from which altogether too much of education and instruction has been carried on, in spiritual as well as in other matters.

[First published in *Proceedings of the Religious Education Association*, 1903, pp. 60–66.]

But if the differences are those of quality, the whole problem is transfigured. It is no longer a question of fixing over ideas and beliefs of the grown person, until these are reduced to the lower level of childish apprehension in thought. It is a question of surrounding the child with such conditions of growth that he may be led to appreciate and to grasp the full significance of his own round of experience, as that develops in living his own life. When the child is so regarded, his capacities in reference to his own peculiar needs and aims are found to be quite parallel to those of the adult, if the needs and aims of the latter are measured by similar reference to adult concerns and responsibilities.

Unless the world is out of gear, the child must have the same kind of power to do what, as a child, he really needs to do, that the mature person has in his sphere of life. In a word, it is a question of bringing the child to appreciate the truly religious aspects of his own growing life, not one of inoculating him externally with beliefs and emotions which adults happen to have found serviceable to themselves.

It cannot be denied that the platform of the views, ideas, and emotions of the grown person has been frequently assumed to supply the standard of the religious nature of the child. The habit of basing religious instruction upon a formulated statement of the doctrines and beliefs of the church is a typical instance. Once admit the rightfulness of the standard, and it follows without argument that, since a catechism represents the wisdom and truth of the adult mind, the proper course is to give to the child at once the benefit of such adult experience. The only logical change is a possible reduction in size—a shorter catechism, and some concessions—not a great many—in the language used.

While this illustration is one of the most obvious, it hardly indicates the most serious aspect of the matter. This is found in assuming that the spiritual and emotional experiences of the adult are the proper measures of all religious life; so that, if the child is to have any religious life at all, he must have it in terms of the same consciousness of sin, repentance, redemption, etc., which are familiar to the adult. So far as the profound significance of the idea of growth is ignored, there are foisted, or at least urged, upon the child copies of the spiritual relationships of the soul to God, modeled after adult thought and emotion. Yet the depth and validity of the consciousness of these realities frequently depend upon aspirations, struggles, and failures which, by the nature of the case, can come only to those who have entered upon the responsibilities of mature life.

To realize that the child reaches adequacy of religious experience only through a succession of expressions which parallel his own growth, is a return to the ideas of the New Testament: "When I was a child I spoke as a child; I understood—or looked at things—as a child; I thought—or reasoned about things—as a child." It is to return to the idea of Jesus, of the successive stages through which the seed passes into the blade and then into the ripening grain. Such differences are distinctions of kind or quality, not simply differences of capacity. Germinating seed, growing leaf, budding flower, are not miniature fruits reduced in bulk and size. The attaining of perfect fruitage depends upon not only allowing, but encouraging, the expanding life to pass through stages which are natural and necessary for it.

To attempt to force prematurely upon the child either the mature ideas or the spiritual emotions of the adult is to run the risk of a fundamental danger, that of forestalling future deeper experiences which might otherwise in their season become personal realities to him. We may make the child familiar with the form of the soul's great experiences of sin and of reconciliation and peace, of discord and harmony of the individual with the deepest forces of the universe, before there is anything in his own needs or relationships in life which makes it possible for him to interpret or to realize them.

So far as this happens, certain further defects or perversions are almost sure to follow. First, the child may become, as it were, vulgarly *blasé*. The very familiarity with the outward form of these things may induce a certain distaste for further contact with them. The mind is exhausted by an excessive early familiarity, and does not feel the need and possibility of further growth which always implies novelty and freshness—some experience which is uniquely new, and hitherto untraversed by the soul. Second, this excessive familiarity may breed, if not contempt, at least flippancy and irreverence. Third, this premature acquaintance with matters which are not really understood or vitally experienced is not without effect in promoting scepticism and crises of frightful doubt. It is a serious moment when an earnest soul wakes up to the fact that it has been passively accepting and reproducing ideas and feelings which it now recognizes are not a vital part of its own being. Losing its hold on the form in which the spiritual truths have been embodied, their very substance seems also to be slipping away. The person is plunged into doubt and bitterness regarding the reality of all things which lie beyond his senses, or regarding the very worth of life itself.

Doubtless the more sincere and serious persons find their way through, and come to some readjustment of the fundamental conditions of life by which they re-attain a working spiritual faith. But even such persons are likely to carry with them scars from the struggles through which they have passed. They have undergone a shock and upheaval from which every youth ought, if possible, to be spared, and which the due observance of the conditions of growth would avoid. There is some danger that we shall come to regard as perfectly normal phenomena of adolescent life certain experiences which are in truth only symptoms of maladjustment resulting from the premature fixation of intellectual and emotional habits in the earlier years of childhood. Youth, as distinct from childhood, is doubtless the critical time in spiritual experience; but it would be a calamity to exaggerate the differences, and to fail to insist upon the more fundamental principle of continuity of development.

In other cases there does not seem to be enough fundamental seriousness; or else the youth lives in more distracting circumstances. So, after a brief period of doubt, he turns away, somewhat calloused, to live on the plane of superficial interests and excitements of the world about him. When none of these extreme evils result, yet something of the bloom of later experience is rubbed off; something of its richness is missed because the individual has been introduced to its form before he can possibly grasp its deeper significance. Many persons whose religious development has been comparatively uninterrupted, find themselves in the habit of taking for granted their own spiritual life. They are so thoroughly accustomed to certain forms, emotions, and even terms of expression, that their experience becomes conventionalized. Religion is a part of the ordinances and routine of the day rather than a source of inspiration and renewing of power. It becomes a matter of conformation rather than of transformation.

Accepting the principle of gradual development of religious knowledge and experience, I pass on to mention one practical conclusion: the necessity of studying carefully the whole record of the growth, in individual children during their youth, of instincts, wants, and interests from the religious point of view. If we are to adapt successfully our methods of dealing with the child to his current life experience, we have first to discover the facts relating to normal development. The problem is a complicated one. Child-study has made a beginning, but only a beginning. Its successful prosecution requires a prolonged and cooperative study. There are needed both a large inductive basis in facts, and the best working tools and methods of psychological theory. Child-psychology in the religious as in other aspects of experience will suffer a setback if it becomes separated from the control of the general psychology of which it is a part. It will also suffer a setback if there is too great haste in trying to draw at once some conclusion as to practice from every new set of facts discovered. For instance, while many of the data that have been secured regarding the phenomena of adolescence are very important in laying down base lines for further study, it would be a mistake to try immediately to extract from these facts a series of general principles regarding either the instruction or education of youth from the religious point of view. The material is still too scanty. It has not as yet been checked up by an extensive study of youth under all kinds of social and religious environments. The negative and varying instances have been excluded rather than utilized. In many cases we do not know whether our facts are to be interpreted as causes or effects; or, if they are effects, we do not know how far they are normal ac-

companiments of psychical growth, or more or less pathological results of external social conditions.

This word of caution, however, is not directed against
the child-study in itself. Its purport is exactly the opposite:
to indicate the necessity of more, and much more, of it. It
will be necessary to carry on the investigation in a cooperative way. Only a large number of inquirers working at the
same general question, under different circumstances, and
from different points of view, can reach satisfactory results.
If a Convention like this were to take steps to initiate and
organize a movement for this sort of study, it would mark
the dawn of a new day in religious education. Such a movement could provide the facts necessary for a positive basis
of a constructive movement; and would at the same time
obviate the danger of a one-sided, premature generalization
from crude and uncertain facts.

I make no apology for concluding with a practical suggestion of this sort. The title of my address, "The Relation
of Modern Psychology to Religious Education," conveys in
and of itself a greater truth than can be expressed in any
remarks that I might make. The title indicates that it is
possible to approach the subject of religious instruction in
the reverent spirit of science, making the same sort of study
of this problem that is made of any other educational problem. If methods of teaching, principles of selecting and using
subject-matter, in all supposedly secular branches of education, are being subjected to careful and systematic scientific study, how can those interested in religion—and who is
not?—justify neglect of the most fundamental of all educational questions, the moral and religious?

THE PSYCHOLOGICAL AND THE LOGICAL IN TEACHING GEOMETRY[1]

As one interested from the general educational side rather than from the technical mathematical side in the improved teaching of geometry, I venture to present an uncertainty which lurks in my mind after reading Professor Halsted's able and suggestive article in the December number of the *Educational Review*.

The field in which the uncertainty lies is the matter of the relation of the preliminary more intuitive and sensuous geometry to the later rational and rigorous geometry.

It is a question how far it is possible to separate the intuitive and applied geometry from the logical and scientific geometry, simply in terms of an earlier and a later, so that the former is done with once for all by the time the latter begins. The question in my mind is whether, until the student has reached the distinct plane of mathematical scholarship (and probably even then in the case of discovery as distinct from proof) there is not recurrent demand for a return to considerations and data which do not possess strict demonstrative quality. Are we to have a purely elementary geometry, which is wholly intuitive, finish it up at once for all, and then pass at a bound to rational geometry? Or is the real problem of teaching geometry one of *continuous* modulation and gradation from one to the other?

There is no question that Professor Halsted makes specific allowance for a preliminary geometry which does not strive to be rigidly demonstrative. As he says: "The field in

1. Since this article was written there has appeared in print (*Science*, March 13, 1903) the identical address of Professor E. H. Moore, entitled "On the Foundations of Mathematics," which dwells upon the evolutionary character of all mathematics as a reason for not making too fixed separation between various branches of mathematics or between pure and applied mathematics. I wish to record my indebtedness to Professor Moore for various suggestions.

[First published in *Educational Review* 25 (1903): 387–99.]

education is a proper one, and has come to stay" (*Educational Review*, Vol. 24, p. 457). And at the close of his article he makes specific provision for modification "designed to facilitate class teaching and acquirement by immature minds" (p. 470). At the same time he insists very properly that such modifications and sensuous elements be a kind which will not arrest the movement toward a more adequate scientific method; or, as he puts it, "The preliminary must fit the rational geometry" (p. 457).

These two limits give us a perfectly determinate problem. On the one side we have this consideration: What factors not valid in a strictly demonstrative sense are needed in order to assist the mind, which is only in process of becoming logical in general and of becoming geometrically logical in particular, in securing its introduction into, and vital familiarity with, geometrical subject-matter? On the other hand, we have this consideration: How shall the extralogical factor be so introduced as not to leave mental habits and preconceptions which have later on to be bodily displaced or rooted up in order to secure a proper comprehension of the subject? This way of stating the question certainly involves no controversy as to principle and so affords a platform upon which mathematician and educationalist may alike stand. This leaves teaching, as Professor Halsted says (p. 470), "a matter for the genius, the insight, the tact" of the individual author or teacher. Such an one must constantly consider from two standpoints what adaptations to the existing state of experience and of mental power are advisable: That of immediate efficiency of teaching, and that of relationship to the rigorous logical formulation which is the ultimate mathematical goal. Not every concession is to be accepted, even if it does seem to facilitate easier and quicker immediate apprehension, for this may be at the expense of continuous increase of comprehension, and hence not really learning at all. It is quite conceivable even to a layman's mind that supposed necessary adaptations are sometimes made which are not necessary and which obstruct later study. On the other hand no departure from absolutely logical methods is to be condemned simply because it is a departure. If such deviation be necessary to bring the subject within the range of the workings of the pupil's power, it is not in truth a deviation: The longest way around is indeed at times the shortest way home. Recognizing the two limits, the problem is not whether or no concession and adaptation to present visual and motor experience shall be made, but what particular adaptations are advisable and necessary.

So far it is clear sailing. There is no uncertainty. But I am disturbed by reading upon page 457 that it does not suffice "to start with inaccurate statements and, as we advance, to modify them so as to bring them into accord with wider vision and more stringent requirements. We must from the beginning bring up ourselves and our pupils on not only the truth, but the whole truth." This leaves quite the opposite impression, viz., that no adaptations or concessions whatever are to be made. This impression is strengthened from the fact that Professor Halsted at once proceeds to criticise a number of specific statements even in geometries of the professedly preliminary type, on the ground of failure to conform with the present status of advanced geometric science.

For example, in the discussion of the conception of the straight line as the most direct path of motion there is no hint of use of the test of adaptation or availability to conditions of growth reached. No other criterion of condemnation is used save scientific invalidity. Such invalidity certainly is conclusive as to the inadmissibility in the geometry of the mathematical science; that is, of the student who has reached a certain stage. But the question remains: Just when and where is this stage reached? Is it found in the mind of the first year high-school pupil? Of the average college sophomore? Or where? If Professor Halsted's article were simply on geometry and upon the errors of the professed geometrician, such questions would be quite irrelevant, but he writes upon the Teaching of Geometry. A logical hiatus appears in the condemnation of a given definition of a straight line (and of course the same holds in principle of any other procedure he condemns), unless it is also shown that definition is quite unnecessary from the standpoint of effective growth *into* mathematics. This gap may indeed be

quite coverable; it may be quite possible to show how a
logically adequate conception of the straight line can be
brought within range of apprehension from the very start.
But until this possibility has been demonstrated it is logically
insufficient to condemn any given method merely because it
does not square up with the requirements of rigorous demonstrative science.

To put the matter more positively, I should say that to
bring up the pupil from the beginning on the whole truth is
simply impossible. There are psychological as well as physical impossibilities, and the statement indicates one of them.
To try to put into practice such a method is to develop impossible text-books and train impossible teachers. *Towards*
the whole truth with all our heart; *on* it, no, because it is a
meaningless requirement. The need and demand for teaching arise from the fact that the whole truth is not there to
build upon. For a mind to build upon the very thing which
it is the goal of its endeavor to obtain is surely the Irish bull
of pedagogy.

The question of the correct definition of the straight
line is a matter of mathematics alone. A psychologist encroaches on such a field only at his deadly peril. But there is
need for making clear the fact that the content of a given
book or lesson for a given grade of pupils is not a matter of
mathematics alone. It is a psychological matter as well,
and upon such points educationalists who work upon a
sound psychological basis do not transgress in expressing a
judgment. The psychological questions involved may be
reduced to two:

1. What organs of apprehension and interpretation does
the student bring at a given time to the mastery of a particular topic? 2. What further mental modifications are induced and what reactions set up by the process of learning
which the student employs?

1. What the student actually learns is not what is in
the mind of the author or teacher who propounds the definition: What the student learns is what the proposition means
to him. This is certainly a truism. But it becomes a vital
statement when we recall that what a given statement means
to a pupil depends absolutely upon the interaction set up

between the topic presented and the habits which the pupil brings with him to it. It is a question of interaction, and the content of the final mental state is a net resultant of both factors. Because the conception that two points determine a straight line satisfies the logical conditions of the mathematical mind, it does not inevitably follow that it satisfies the psychological condition of a sixteen-year-old boy or girl, even with the maximum of explanation which the intelligent and clear teacher may give. The formal and verbal definition is the same to the expert and to the pupil; the mental definition (the measure of the actual learning) may be very different. It is even possible that the only meaning which the statement has to an intelligent beginner, working under the most favorable conditions, is suggested by Professor Halsted's statement that the assumption that two points determine a straight line "may be taken as authorizing the *graphic* designation of points and the *graphic operation to join* two designated points by a straight" (p. 468; italics mine). It may be the operation of drawing the line, and seeing it as it is drawn, which affords the actual mental content, or definition psychologically considered. In this case the student nominally employs the same definition that the scientist uses; but none the less he conceives the straight in terms of motion (symbolized by the drawing of the line) and of directness of course (symbolized by the track which marks the path of the moving point). If such be the case then the student is utilizing exactly the notion which Professor Halsted condemns, and nothing has been gained by a mere shift of terminology. If this notion is so abhorrent to mathematical logic that it must be avoided at all costs, then the problem is to secure such conditions of teaching as will prevent the student from employing terms of movement, and of course or track traversed, in realizing for himself the notion under consideration.

It is barely possible that even the advanced mathematician gets along without the addendum of reference to motion just because he has so thoroughly defined its conditions that the reference no longer affects or modifies any particular operation or result. Accordingly it is more economical to exclude it deliberately in a uniform way or by principle;

that is, by methods which finally define the possibility of motion itself in terms of other definitions and axioms. Putting the point in a less paradoxical way, it is conceivable that the advanced mathematician gets on logically without any reference to motion, just because his abstraction from the original concrete conditions of reality has been so perfected that all the terms he now consciously uses are those which are exclusively determined and constructed by means of his own previous abstractions. This certainly represents the logical ideal, complete control, no data, elements, or conditions operating excepting those which have been intentionally introduced and formulated. For this very reason it would be equally legitimate, I suppose, to begin with definitions and axioms of motion and arrive at conclusions in a reverse way. All that remains is for the scientist to play his own game according to the rules and conditions which he has himself determined. All this, of course, implies an original abstraction from, and *hence conscious reference* to, the complex conditions of reality, and demands a series of intervening similar abstractions of constantly increasing remoteness. The learner, of course, is at the other end of the series. *His* problem is not that of conforming a new construction to conditions created by previous abstractions, but that of overcoming the difficulty of making any abstraction of the sort desired. In all further steps as a learner he has to look both ways. On one hand, in order to abstract successfully from reality he has consciously to present that concrete reality to himself; he has, if you please, to be sensuous and intuitive and applied (that is to say, psychological) rather than abstract, demonstrative, and rigorous (that is, logical). But he also has to direct his further procedure in conformity with abstractions previously made and their resulting conditions. He has to abide by them and to harmonize his further endeavor with them. In so far he is logical. Anyone who gets hold of learning as a continuous process or movement of this kind will, I am sure, have with respect to principle no difficulty in reconciling the psychological or pedagogical statement with the scientific and logical; his difficulties may be numerous enough, but they will be in the region of detail, of practice, not of theory.

To return to our example: It is conceivable that the conscious recognition of a path of motion affords just the sort of combination of reference to concrete experience and to logical abstract as fits it to be a working tool for effecting transition from the unanalyzed complexity of present experience toward the defined control of greater abstractness. Relative to the pupil's *previous* experience, the conception of a path of motion is an abstraction; one, indeed, which offers considerable difficulty. The student has had plenty of experience of moving bodies, but may never have had occasion to discriminate between the moving body and the course it takes, the path it traverses and describes. Quite likely, too, he has had no occasion to conceive of motion reduced to lower terms, and defined as the track of a point rather than as that of a solid.

The point under consideration comes out clearly in the quotation from Laisant (p. 446) to the effect that the definition of a straight line as the shortest distance between points is *incomprehensible* to the beginner. The context clearly shows that this incomprehensibility is logical, not psychological. The idea of shortest distance certainly involves another idea, the length of the curve; and this in turn is capable of definition only as the limit of the sum of rectilinear length. These two considerations are certainly conclusive from the logical standpoint as to the impossibility of final comprehension. Logic, one may say, *is* comprehension; and what is il-logical is *ipso facto* in-comprehensible. But there still remains the psychological question: At what stage of development of an individual mind can logical comprehension of this type be secured? The problem of the beginner is not that of comprehension so much as that of apprehension—that is, of vital introduction to and assimilation of a new fact or idea. Taken on this score, it is possible that the notion of a straight line as the track, or course, or path of a point in most direct motion is not only comprehensible, but offers the maximum of comprehensibility. Speaking from the standpoint of an individual mind, such a notion may involve more actual abstraction and generalization than would for him the definition that satisfies the accomplished student. In previous experience the conception of a line has been bound up with a large number of other considerations which are irrelevant from the standpoint of geometry, and which accordingly must be deliberately excluded. If the conception of a straight line which is so unsatisfactory to the one who has surveyed the field, who has compared straight line and curve, is the most effective tool to effect this abstraction, then, in teaching it cannot be dismissed simply by reference to the logic of the mind that adequately realizes all the conditions which determine the outcome.

2. I mentioned a second test on the psychological side: that of the mental disposition, of habit-tendency, created in and through the act of learning. We have to consider the whole mental attitude set up by reaction to a given mode of presentation. Some minds are probably well adapted to consider strict mathematical relations, on their own ground, at quite an early age. It would be strange if there were not some to whom the strict scientific treatment appeals in some or in many topics at the age of sixteen, or even of twelve. The mathematical diathesis is doubtless as real as any other. It is certainly a mistake to keep such pupils on a less strong diet than they are able to digest and grow upon. But what of the others? What of those whose interest in this mode of instruction is restricted? Those to whom the game of absolute logic does not appeal, those who are not called to ascend to the higher levels of science, or ever perhaps to reach much control of geometry as a pure tool? Mathematicians as mathematicians are not called on to reckon with this class; but those who are concerned with teaching must take them into account. In the case of such minds a premature introduction to logical niceties and scientific accuracies simply increases intellectual and emotional repugnancy, and tends to induce habits of resort to mere memorizing, to tricks of recitation, to all kinds of evasion, mental and practical, or even to downright cheating; and finally to aversion to all further pursuit of subjects that even suggest the disagreeable experiences associated with mathematical learning. In other words, a method which is somewhat loose from the logical side (and this once more means simply the standpoint of the matured mind, surveying the whole field as a single

inter-related whole,) may be strict from the standpoint of present possibilities and also of impetus to further growth. There may be students who can secure from resort to algebra, to arithmetic, to mechanics, to graphic device, and to scores of resources that are not vigorous, mental discipline, mental activity and a growth in mental power not otherwise to be secured. There may even be pupils for whom to stretch a string, to drop a plumb line, has more *ultimate* logical worth than would be got by the original definition of a straight line as determined by two points, apart from reference to motor and visual experience.

If such things be true (and the emphasis is upon *such*) a further question arises: Whether the supposedly logical element of formal definitions, etc., may not be overdone in geometries of the prevailing type, so that (while improvement is to be expected in one direction by resort to stricter methods) reform may come from dropping some of the present show of scientific vigorousness. A psychological apprehension as distinct from a logical comprehension is valuable when it marks an advance over more imperfect intellectual attitudes and when it gives impetus to some further intellectual control. Why not, then, deal frankly with teaching on this basis? The definitions in the average text-book now used, whether or not they measure up to a strict standard, at least usually claim to present the matter in rational form. Might not better results be reached in many cases if notions were proffered not as making any such profession, but simply as statements of the point of view already reached and as leading on to a working method for future use? This standpoint would not, of course, exclude specific verbal formulation. On the contrary, a proposition would naturally come in to summarize the result reached,— though even here due opportunity should be provided for pupils to try their own hands at making the summary statements. But the formulae should be given in such a way that the student would recognize that they are provisional résumés and working hypotheses, not definitions purporting to possess finished logical worth.

Even here, in frankness, I must express my doubt whether the definition of even the competent mathematician

is absolutely logical in any other sense than answering to
the status of mental growth, mastery of methods and problems reached by him, in the same sort of way that the
relatively rough and ready notion of the beginner answers
to the growth and needs of the latter. I would suggest that
the distinction of psychological and logical is after all only
one of historical periods in a process of growth, and is a
distinction having meaning when periods taken in their
sequence may be contrasted, but not when taken barely in
themselves.

This, perhaps, is introducing a topic of possible controversy; if so, it is unfortunate. For in the former considerations I see the possibility of an *eirenicon* between the scientific mathematician and the educationalist, so far as relates
to practical matters of teaching. The former, as I understand
it, quarrels with many of the definitions and methods of
current text-books and teachers because they are illogical,
some of them almost to the point of self-contradiction. Very
well. The educationalist also quarrels (and in the main at
much the same points) because the definitions and methods
are not well contrived and selected from the standpoint of
psychological adaptation. There is some truth in the belief
that a current text-book is neither one thing nor the other.
Trusting to Professor Halsted's authority, it lacks much of
true geometric character; trusting to the belief of many
educators, its *profession* of scientific rigidity, its claim to use
absolute logical methods, prevents a free use on the part of
the pupil of his own experience and its flexible employ in
apprehending the matter presented and in getting a tool for
further effective control. Surely, when we claim to have the
scientific standpoint, that of rational statement and development, then we should have it in its purity and absoluteness.
But in the degree which this is impossible, we should not
allow pseudo-science or any inheritance from the past history
of mathematics, or any imitation at several removes of
present mathematical concepts, to come between the teacher
and the freest possible use of all matters and methods that
will facilitate learning, and that will stimulate the growth
of power of mathematical abstraction and generalization.

It is the halfway state, the compromise in present methods, that makes much of our difficulty. To the educator's eye, these are largely unpedagogical; to the mathematician's they are, it would seem, more or less unscientific. Wherever possible let geometry become more rigorous; wherever this is not possible, let us drop a pretense of logical quality which only loads us down with an outward and cumbrous apparatus, and content ourselves with doing whatever under the circumstances can be best done from the standpoint of teaching. A state of things which is neither rigorously logical nor yet justifiable psychologically, should not be permitted, with high-school pupils any more than with elementary, to prevent personal acquaintance with experiences which call for the use of geometric statement, nor familiarity with concrete applications of geometric principles. When the pupil is not capable of grasping the axiom or definition in the form logically required, it would appear to be better not to hamper him with a formulation which seems to be scientific but is not really so. Permit all such matters to remain more or less fluid, taken for granted practically rather than stated as logical assumptions, and there may be both an increase of present interest and of adequacy of apprehension, and also less obstacle to further developments of a more rigorously demonstrative sort.

It does not seem possible to draw a fixed line between the primary- and the grammar-school pupil; between the grammar- and the high-school pupil. At each point the pupil needs whatever of formulation and definition he is capable of really grasping, and whatever introduction into strict deductive reasoning he is capable of. But he also needs the habit of looking at definitions and propositions with reference to the real experiences which they express. He needs to see in them a sort of language in which the various symbols have meaning, not only in relation to each other, but also as expressing the experiences of life. More than any other one thing it would seem as if the high-school pupil, in particular, were at the point where his greatest need is neither merely intuitive nor strictly demonstrative geometry, but rather skill in moving back and forth from the concrete situations of experience to their abstracts in geometric statement. If the teacher be sufficiently imbued with the standpoint and methods of rational geometry, and yet remember that he is a teacher and not merely a mathematician, there is little ground for fear that progress in demonstration will not be as steady and rapid as circumstances really permit.

Not the least value, then, of Professor Halsted's article, to my mind, is that it condemns those books and teachers that profess logical rigidity and yet come short of it. Thus it should allow free scope to the principle of adaptation to conditions of need and growth. The point that I would urge as supplementary is the need of modulation in transition from the more intuitive to the more demonstrative phases of the subject. It is difficult to see how, short of having already become a mathematical specialist, some recourse to illustration and application in experience can be eliminated. Indeed, I am told that even in the very highest phases of mathematical inquiry there are still some matters in which even the trained mathematician finds it advisable to resort to intuitive constructions.

If this problem of modulation had been borne in mind more definitely, I do not think the "Perry Movement" would have come in for such apparently unreserved condemnation. It is the *teaching* of mathematics that the Perry Movement is particularly concerned with. To criticise that movement as to certain possible shortcomings from the standpoint of perfected mathematics is not entirely to the point. Improvement in the teaching of geometry is certainly dependent upon those who concern themselves with its more rational formulation and rigorous sequence. But it is also dependent upon those who look at it from the standpoint of common sense or ordinary experience; from its various practical applications in everyday life to technology and utilitarian ends; and upon those who ask for elements in the experience and intelligence of the pupil which may make his mathematics more vital to him. These two groups should cooperate with each other; not line up as hostile camps.

The serious problem of instruction in any branch is to acquire the habit of viewing in a twofold way the subject-matter which is to be taught day by day. It needs to be viewed as a development *out* of the present habits and experiences of emotion, thought, and action; it needs to be viewed also as a development *into* the most orderly intellectual system possible. These two sides, which I venture to term the psychological and the logical, are limits of a continuous movement rather than opposite forces or even independent elements. First and last of all, moreover, we need to recognize that while this is a movement which mind in general passes through, it is a movement which the minds of individual pupils are concerned with in very different degrees. Some minds are so framed to take an interest in method as method. Such pupils should have every opportunity to carry the interest with a purely logical statement and deduction to its *Ultima Thule*. But there are many other individuals (probably a considerable majority of mankind taken in gross) to whom considerations of method will always remain valuable chiefly because of their instrumental significance—because they are tools in the region of application, invention, construction, and for interpretation and further use of what has already been invented and constructed. It is a social wrong under the name of pure science to force such minds into paths having next to no meaning for them, and which consequently lead next to nowhere.

DEMOCRACY IN EDUCATION

Modern life means democracy, democracy means freeing intelligence for independent effectiveness—the emancipation of mind as an individual organ to do its own work. We naturally associate democracy, to be sure, with freedom of action, but freedom of action without freed capacity of thought behind it is only chaos. If external authority in action is given up, it must be because internal authority of truth, discovered and known to reason, is substituted.

How does the school stand with reference to this matter? Does the school as an accredited representative exhibit this trait of democracy as a spiritual force? Does it lead and direct the movement? Does it lag behind and work at cross-purpose? I find the fundamental need of the school today dependent upon its limited recognition of the principle of freedom of intelligence. This limitation appears to me to affect both of the elements of school life: teacher and pupil. As to both, the school has lagged behind the general contemporary social movement; and much that is unsatisfactory, much of conflict and of defect, comes from the discrepancy between the relatively undemocratic organization of the school, as it affects the mind of both teacher and pupil, and the growth and extension of the democratic principle in life beyond school doors.

The effort of the last two-thirds of a century has been successful in building up the machinery of a democracy of mind. It has provided the ways and means for housing and equipping intelligence. What remains is that the thought-activity of the individual, whether teacher or student, be permitted and encouraged to take working possession of this machinery: to substitute its rightful lordship for an inherited servility. In truth, our public-school system is but two-thirds

[First published in *Elementary School Teacher* 4 (1903): 193–204.]

of a century old. It dates, so far as such matters can be
dated at all, from 1837, the year that Horace Mann became
secretary of the state board of Massachusetts; and from
1843, when Henry Barnard began a similar work in Con-
necticut. At this time began that growing and finally successful warfare against all the influences, social and sectarian,
which would prevent or mitigate the sway of public influence over private ecclesiastical and class interests. Between 1837 and 1850 grew up all the most characteristic
features of the American public-school system: from this
time date state normal schools, city training schools, county
and state institutes, teachers' associations, teachers' journals,
the institution of city superintendencies, supervisory officers,
and the development of state universities as the crown of the
public-school system of the commonwealth. From this time
date the striving for better schoolhouses and grounds, improved text-books, adequate material equipment in maps,
globes, scientific apparatus, etc. As an outcome of the forces
thus set in motion, democracy has in principle, subject to
relative local restrictions, developed an organized machinery
of public education. But when we turn to the aim and
method which this magnificent institution serves, we find
that our democracy is not yet conscious of the ethical
principle upon which it rests—the responsibility and freedom
of mind in discovery and proof—and consequently we find
confusion where there should be order, darkness where there
should be light. The teacher has not the power of initiation
and constructive endeavor which is necessary to the fulfilment of the function of teaching. The learner finds conditions antagonistic (or at least lacking) to the development
of individual mental power and to adequate responsibility
for its use.

  1. *As to the teacher.*—If there is a single public-school
system in the United States where there is official and constitutional provision made for submitting questions of methods of discipline and teaching, and the questions of the
curriculum, text-books, etc., to the discussion and decision
of those actually engaged in the work of teaching, that fact
has escaped my notice. Indeed, the opposite situation is so
common that it seems, as a rule, to be absolutely taken for

granted as the normal and final condition of affairs. The number of persons to whom any other course has occurred as desirable, or even possible—to say nothing of necessary —is apparently very limited. But until the public-school system is organized in such a way that every teacher has some regular and representative way in which he or she can register judgment upon matters of educational importance, with the assurance that this judgment will somehow affect the school system, the assertion that the present system is not, from the internal standpoint, democratic seems to be justified. Either we come here upon some fixed and inherent limitation of the democratic principle, or else we find in this fact an obvious discrepancy between the conduct of the school and the conduct of social life—a discrepancy so great as to demand immediate and persistent effort at reform.

The more enlightened portions of the public have, indeed, become aware of one aspect of this discrepancy. Many reformers are contending against the conditions which place the direction of school affairs, including the selection of text-books, etc., in the hands of a body of men who are outside the school system itself, who have not necessarily any expert knowledge of education and who are moved by non-educational motives. Unfortunately, those who have noted this undemocratic condition of affairs, and who have striven to change it, have, as a rule, conceived of but one remedy, namely, the transfer of authority to the school superintendent. In their zeal to place the centre of gravity inside the school system, in their zeal to decrease the prerogatives of a non-expert school board, and to lessen the opportunities for corruption and private pull which go with that, they have tried to remedy one of the evils of democracy by adopting the principle of autocracy. For no matter how wise, expert, or benevolent the head of the school system, the one-man principle is autocracy.

The logic of the argument goes farther, very much farther, than the reformer of this type sees. The logic which commits him to the idea that the management of the school system must be in the hands of an expert commits him also to the idea that every member of the school system, from the first-grade teacher to the principal of the high school, must have some share in the exercise of educational power. The remedy is not to have one expert dictating educational methods and subject-matter to a body of passive, recipient teachers, but the adoption of intellectual initiative, discussion, and decision throughout the entire school corps. The remedy of the partial evils of democracy, the implication of the school system in municipal politics, is in appeal to a more thoroughgoing democracy.

The dictation, in theory at least, of the subject-matter to be taught, to the teacher who is to engage in the actual work of instruction, and frequently, under the name of close supervision, the attempt to determine the methods which are to be used in teaching, mean nothing more or less than the deliberate restriction of intelligence, the imprisoning of the spirit. Every well-graded system of schools in this country rejoices in a course of study. It is no uncommon thing to find methods of teaching such subjects as reading, writing, spelling, and arithmetic officially laid down; outline topics in history and geography are provided ready-made for the teacher; gems of literature are fitted to the successive ages of boys and girls. Even the domain of art, songs and methods of singing, subject-matter and technique of drawing and painting, come within the region on which an outside authority lays its sacrilegious hands.

I have stated the theory, which is also true of the practice to a certain extent and in certain places. We may thank our heavens, however, that the practice is rarely as bad as the theory would require. Superintendents and principals often encourage individuality and thoughtfulness in the invention and adoption of methods of teaching; and they wink at departures from the printed manual of study. It remains true, however, that this great advance is personal and informal. It depends upon the wisdom and tact of the individual supervisory official; he may withdraw his concession at any moment; or it may be ruthlessly thrown aside by his successor who has formed a high ideal of "system."

I know it will be said that this state of things, while an evil, is a necessary one; that without it confusion and chaos would reign; that such regulations are the inevitable accompaniments of any graded system. It is said that the average teacher is incompetent to take any part in laying out the course of study or in initiating methods of instruction or discipline. Is not this the type of argument which has been used from time immemorial, and in every department of life, against the advance of democracy? What does democracy mean save that the individual is to have a share in determining the conditions and the aims of his own work; and that, upon the whole, through the free and mutual harmonizing of different individuals, the work of the world is better done than when planned, arranged, and directed by a few, no matter how wise or of how good intent that few? How can we justify our belief in the democratic principle elsewhere, and then go back entirely upon it when we come to education?

Moreover, the argument proves too much. The more it is asserted that the existing corps of teachers is unfit to have voice in the settlement of important educational matters, and their unfitness to exercise intellectual initiative and to assume the responsibility for constructive work is emphasized, the more their unfitness to attempt the much more difficult and delicate task of guiding souls appears. If this body is so unfit, how can it be trusted to carry out the recommendations or the dictations of the wisest body of experts? If teachers are incapable of the intellectual responsibility which goes with the determination of the methods they are to use in teaching, how can they employ methods when dictated by others, in other than a mechanical, capricious, and clumsy manner? The argument, I say, proves too much.

Moreover, if the teaching force is as inept and unintelligent and irresponsible as the argument assumes, surely the primary problem is that of their improvement. Only by sharing in some responsible task does there come a fitness to share in it. The argument that we must wait until men and women are fully ready to assume intellectual and social responsibilities would have defeated every step in the democratic direction that has ever been taken. The prevalence of methods of authority and of external dictation and direction tends automatically to perpetuate the very conditions of inefficiency, lack of interest, inability to assume positions of self-determination, which constitute the reasons that are depended upon to justify the régime of authority.

The system which makes no great demands upon originality, upon invention, upon the continuous expression of individuality, works automatically to put and to keep the more incompetent teachers in the school. It puts them there because, by a natural law of spiritual gravitation, the best minds are drawn to the places where they can work most effectively. The best minds are not especially likely to be drawn where there is danger that they may have to submit to conditions which no self-respecting intelligence likes to put up with; and where their time and energy are likely to be so occupied with details of external conformity that they have no opportunity for free and full play of their own vigor.

I have dwelt at length upon the problem of the recognition of the intellectual and spiritual individuality of the teacher. I have but one excuse. All other reforms are conditioned upon reform in the quality and character of those who engage in the teaching profession. The doctrine of the man behind the gun has become familiar enough, in recent discussion, in every sphere of life. Just because education is the most personal, the most intimate, of all human affairs, there, more than anywhere else, the sole ultimate reliance and final source of power are in the training, character, and intelligence of the individual. If any scheme could be devised which would draw to the calling of teaching persons of force of character, of sympathy with children, and consequent interest in the problems of teaching and of scholarship, no one need be troubled for a moment about other educational reforms, or the solution of other educational problems. But as long as a school organization which is undemocratic in principle tends to repel from all but the higher portions of the school system those of independent force, of intellectual initiative, and of inventive ability, or tends to hamper them in their work after they find their way into the schoolroom, so long all other reforms are compromised at their source and postponed indefinitely for fruition.

2. *As to the learner.*—The undemocratic suppression of the individuality of the teacher goes naturally with the im-

proper restriction of the intelligence of the mind of the child. The mind, to be sure, is that of a child, and yet, after all, it is mind. To subject mind to an outside and ready-made material is a denial of the ideal of democracy, which roots itself ultimately in the principle of moral, self-directing individuality. Misunderstanding regarding the nature of the freedom that is demanded for the child is so common that it may be necessary to emphasize the fact that it is primarily intellectual freedom, free play of mental attitude, and operation which are sought. If individuality were simply a matter of feelings, impulses, and outward acts independent of intelligence, it would be more than a dubious matter to urge a greater degree of freedom for the child in the school. In that case much, and almost exclusive, force would attach to the objections that the principle of individuality is realized in the more exaggerated parts of Rousseau's doctrines: sentimental idealization of the child's immaturity, irrational denial of superior worth in the knowledge and mature experience of the adult, deliberate denial of the worth of the ends and instruments embodied in social organization. Deification of childish whim, unripened fancy, and arbitrary emotion is certainly a piece of pure romanticism. The would-be reformers who emphasize out of due proportion and perspective these aspects of the principle of individualism betray their own cause. But the heart of the matter lies not there. Reform of education in the direction of greater play for the individuality of the child means the securing of conditions which will give outlet, and hence direction, to a growing intelligence. It is true that this freed power of mind with reference to its own further growth cannot be obtained without a certain leeway, a certain flexibility, in the expression of even immature feelings and fancies. But it is equally true that it is not a riotous loosening of these traits which is needed, but just that kind and degree of freedom from repression which are found to be necessary to secure the full operation of intelligence.

Now, no one need doubt as to what mental activity or the freed expression of intelligence means. No one need doubt as to the conditions which are conducive to it. We do not have to fall back upon what some regard as the uncertain, distracting, and even distressing voice of psychology. Scientific methods, the methods pursued by the scientific inquirer, give us an exact and concrete exhibition of the path which intelligence takes when working most efficiently, under most favorable conditions.

What is primarily required for that direct inquiry which constitutes the essence of science is first-hand experience; an active and vital participation through the medium of all the bodily organs with the means and materials of building up first-hand experience. Contrast this first and most fundamental of all the demands for an effective use of mind with what we find in so many of our elementary and high schools. There first-hand experience is at a discount; in its stead are summaries and formulas of the results of other people. Only very recently has any positive provision been made within the schoolroom for any of the modes of activity and for any of the equipment and arrangement which permit and require the extension of original experiences on the part of the child. The school has literally been dressed out with hand-me-down garments—with intellectual suits which other people have worn.

Secondly, in that freed activity of mind which we term "science" there is always a certain problem which focuses effort, which controls the collecting of facts that bear upon the question, the use of observation to get further data, the employing of memory to supply relevant facts, the calling into play of imagination, to yield fertile suggestion and construct possible solutions of the difficulty.

Turning to the school, we find too largely no counterpart to this mental activity. Just because a second-handed material has been supplied wholesale and retail, but anyway ready-made, the tendency is to reduce the activity of mind to a docile or passive taking in of the material presented—in short, to memorizing, with simply incidental use of judgment and of active research. As is frequently stated, acquiring takes the place of inquiring. It is hardly an exaggeration to say that the sort of mind-activity which is encouraged in the school is a survival from the days in which science had not made much headway; when education was mainly concerned with learning, that is to say, the preservation and handing down of the acquisitions of the past. It is true that more and more appeal is made every day in schools to judgment, reasoning, personal efficiency, and the calling up of personal, as distinct from merely book, experiences. But we have not yet got to the point of reversing the total method. The burden and the stress still fall upon learning in the sense of becoming possessed of the second-hand and ready-made material referred to. As Mrs. Young has recently said, the prevailing ideal is a perfect recitation, an exhibition without mistake, of a lesson learned. Until the emphasis changes to the conditions which make it necessary for the child to take an active share in the personal building up of his own problems and to participate in methods of solving them (even at the expense of experimentation and error), mind is not really freed.

In our schools we have freed individuality in many modes of outer expression without freeing intelligence, which is the vital spring and guarantee of all of these expressions. Consequently we give opportunity to the unconverted to point the finger of scorn, and to clamor for a return to the good old days when the teacher, the representative of social and moral authority, was securely seated in the high places of the school. But the remedy here, as in other phases of our social democracy, is not to turn back, but to go farther—to carry the evolution of the school to a point where it becomes a place for getting and testing experience, as real and adequate to the child upon his existing level as all the resources of laboratory and library afford to the scientific man upon his level. What is needed is not any radical revolution, but rather an organization of agencies already found in the schools. It is hardly too much to say that not a single subject or instrumentality is required which is not already found in many schools of the country. All that is required is to gather these materials and forces together and unify their operation. Too often they are used for a multitude of diverse and often conflicting aims. If a single purpose is provided, that of freeing the processes of mental growth, these agencies will at once fall into their proper classes and reinforce each other.

A catalogue of the agencies already available would include at least all of the following: Taking the child out of doors, widening and organizing his experience with reference to the world in which he lives; nature study when pursued as a vital observation of forces working under their natural conditions, plants and animals growing in their own homes, instead of mere discussion of dead specimens. We have also school gardens, the introduction of elementary agriculture, and more especially of horticulture—a movement that is already making great headway in many of the western states. We have also means for the sake of studying physiographic conditions, such as may be found by rivers, ponds or lakes, beaches, quarries, gulleys, hills, etc.

As similar agencies within the school walls, we find a very great variety of instruments for constructive work, or, as it is frequently, but somewhat unfortunately termed, "manual training." Under this head come cooking, which can be begun in its simpler form in the kindergarten; sewing, and what is of even greater educational value, weaving, including designing and the construction of simple apparatus for carrying on various processes of spinning, etc. Then there are also the various forms of tool-work directed upon cardboard, wood, and iron; in addition there are clay-modeling and a variety of ways of manipulating plastic material to gain power and larger experience.

Such matters pass readily over into the simpler forms of scientific experimentation. Every schoolroom from the lowest primary grade up should be supplied with gas, water, certain chemical substances and reagents. To experiment in the sense of trying things or to see what will happen is the most natural business of the child; it is, indeed, his chief concern. It is one which the school has largely either ignored or actually suppressed, so that it has been forced to find outlet in mischief or even in actually destructive ways. This tendency could find outlet in the construction of simple apparatus and the making of simple tests, leading constantly into more and more controlled experimentation, with greater insistence upon definiteness of intellectual result and control of logical process.

Add to these three typical modes of active experimenting, various forms of art expression, beginning with music, clay-modeling, and story-telling as foundation elements, and passing on to drawing, painting, designing in various mediums, we have a range of forces and materials which connect at every point with the child's natural needs and powers, and which supply the requisites for building up his experience upon all sides. As fast as these various agencies find their way into the schools, the centre of gravity shifts, the régime changes from one of subjection of mind to an external and ready-made material, into the activity of mind directed upon the control of the subject-matter and thereby its own upbuilding.

Politically we have found that this country could not endure half free and half slave. We shall find equally great difficulty in encouraging freedom, independence, and initiative in every sphere of social life, while perpetuating in the school dependence upon external authority. The forces of social life are already encroaching upon the school institutions which we have inherited from the past, so that many of its main stays are crumbling. Unless the outcome is to be chaotic, we must take hold of the organic, positive principle involved in democracy, and put that in entire possession of the spirit and work of the school.

In education meet the three most powerful motives of human activity. Here are found sympathy and affection, the going out of the emotions to the most appealing and the most rewarding object of love—a little child. Here is found also the flowering of the social and institutional motive, interest in the welfare of society and in its progress and reform by the surest and shortest means. Here, too, is found the intellectual and scientific motive, the interest in knowledge, in scholarship, in truth for its own sake, unhampered and unmixed with any alien ideal. Copartnership of these three motives—of affection, of social growth, and of scientific inquiry—must prove as nearly irresistible as anything human when they are once united. And, above all else, recognition of the spiritual basis of democracy, the efficacy and responsibility of freed intelligence, is necessary to secure this union.

EDUCATION, DIRECT AND INDIRECT

The other day a parent of a little boy who recently entered our elementary school, after having been in a public school, told me that her son came to her and said, "I think we learn almost as much at that school as we did at the John Smith school—I believe, maybe, we learn more, only we have such a good time that we do not stop to think that we are learning anything." This story I tell to help illustrate the meaning of the term "indirect education." We have our choice between two methods. We may shape the conditions and direct the influences of school work so that pupils are forever reminded that they are pupils—that they are there to study lessons and do tasks. We may make the child conscious at every point that he is going to school, and that he goes to school to do something quite different from what he does anywhere else—namely, to learn. This is "direct education." Put in this bald way, however, the idea may well arouse some mental searchings of heart. Are we really willing to admit that the child does not learn anything outside of school—that he is not getting his education all the time by what he is thinking and feeling and doing, and in spite of the fact that his consciousness is not upon the fact that he is learning? This, then, is the other alternative—the child may be given something fixed up for purposes of learning it, and we may trust to the learning, instruction and training which results out of and along with this doing and inquiring for its own sake. This is "indirect education."

Having got thus far, we are ready to ask the question as to whether and how this indirect education has a place inside the school walls. Shall we show the door of the school as that kind of development which comes with doing things

[Address at the Francis W. Parker School, Chicago, January 1904. Published in *Progressive Journal of Education* 2 (1909): 31–38.]

that are worth doing for their own sake, the growth that comes with contact with the realities of the physical and social world, which is had for the sake of the fullness and reality of the contact? Shall we frame our school in such a way that the child is perpetually and insistently reminded that here is the place where he comes to learn things, to study, to get and recite lessons?

Before trying to answer this question, let us ask some of the ways in which we succeed in making so prominent, so overpowering in the consciousness of the child, the fact that in school he is undergoing education. I begin with one of the most obvious aspects of the matter, not because it is so very important in itself, but because it is such an admirable symbol and index of what lies back. I refer to all of the school machinery that hinges around the giving of marks—the eternal presence of the record book, the never-absent consciousness on the part of the child that he is to be marked for the poorness or goodness of his lesson, the sending home of graded reports upon purely conventional, mathematical or alphabetical schemes, the comparing by the children of their respective grades and all the scheming (sometimes cheating) thereby called forth.

That acute humorist who wrote under the name of John Phoenix tells a story of how he became disgusted with the inaccuracy of our descriptive language, having in mind such terms as little, remarkably, exceedingly, etc., etc., and evolved a scheme, which he thought would meet the whole difficulty, of substituting a decimal system of notation. The idea was that instead of saying that it was a moderately fine day, one would say that the weather was about 53 per cent good, while a particularly fine sunset might be described as a 95 per cent sunset. He goes on to say that, much elated with his project, he submitted it to his wife, who replied that she thought it was a fine scheme, and that she would put it in operation by telling him that he was a 99 per cent idiot.

I do not know whether this was intended as a caricature of the methods of our schools or not, but it may stand as a parody. Suppose we were to watch the child at his sports and games, and not having any confidence in an inherent development of power and knowledge through the very experience, thought it necessary to accentuate in his mind the fact that he had something to learn by giving him a mark of 60 per cent upon his game of marbles, and marking him "A" for his excellence in baseball. Suppose we tried to apply the same scheme to what the child gets from his daily conversation with older people; to the results accruing from the necessity he is under of adapting his modes of behavior to the demands of the social circle in which he lives and moves and has his being; suppose when our boy comes home fresh and elated from what he has seen in the park, or from a trip to the country, that after seeing his interest expressed by his telling, in his animated way, of his experiences, we were under obligation to decide that he was entitled to 82 per cent upon his accuracy of observation, while we should be compelled to give him not above 60 per cent upon his grammatical accuracy—all this so that he might be tested upon his growth or stimulated to further learning!

This is so clearly ridiculous that it may seem extremely unfair to the marking system in the schools. But what I want to point out is that the marking system implies as a fundamental and unquestionable axiom that the actual subject-matter with which the child is engaged, and the responsive play of his own emotional and mental activities upon it, do not suffice to supply educative motive and material—that over and above them some further stimulus in the way of an externally imposed conventional scheme of rating is required to keep attention fixed upon the importance of learning.

Now this assumption that education is not natural and attractive—inherently so—reacts most disastrously upon the responsibility of both the teacher and the child. Human nature being what it is, any teacher who works under the conditions imposed by considering the school just as a place to learn lessons, comes to feel that he has done his whole duty by the individual (so far as judging and estimating the work and worth of that individual is concerned) when he has, after full and impartial investigation as possible, given that student his mark—i.e., determined his success in learning lessons. If some scheme had been intentionally devised in order to prevent the teacher from assuming the full responsibility he ought to feel for keeping constant watch and ward over the life of the child, for relating the child's work to his temperament, capacities, and to totality of influences operating him—if the scheme, I say, had been intentionally devised for relieving the teacher of the necessity of the most intimate and unremitting acquaintance with the child, nothing better could have been found.

I should not have the slightest hesitation in making the statement that, given two schools of otherwise equal conditions, in one of which the marking system prevailed, and in the other did not, the latter would in time possess the teachers who had the most thorough and sympathetic knowledge of all the children, both as to their weak points and their strong points. All the influences at work, unconscious as well as conscious, compel the teachers to know the individuals with whom they are dealing, and to judge not merely their external work, to consider fairly how it should rank between the letters A and E, or zero and 100, but to judge the individual himself as a living, struggling, failing and succeeding individual. In one case, the individual has to be known and judged in terms of his own unique self, unrepeatable in any other self; and in the last analysis, incomparable with any other self just because he is his own self. The other scheme permits and encourages the teacher to escape with the feeling that he has done his whole duty when he has impartially graded the external and dead product of such a personality.

The same tendency to lack of full responsibility imposes itself upon the children and spreads among them. I have seen a powerful indictment against the marking and examination system, as ordinarily conducted, to the effect that it sets up a false and demoralizing standard by which the students come to judge their own work. Instead of each one considering himself responsible for the highest excellency to which he can possibly attain, the tendency is to suppose that one is doing well enough if he comes up to the average expectation; and that, indeed, everything above the required pass mark is so much to the student's credit—representing a sort of accumulation of merit, which in case of an emergency justifies a falling off. The point here is a far-reaching one. I have sometimes heard arguments which imply that there is something particularly strenuous in the disciplinary ideals of rigid tests and marks, and that their surrender means the substitution of a less severe and exacting standard—that it is a part of what is sometimes called "soft pedagogy." As I see it, the exact contrary holds. Where there is a system which fastens upon learning set lessons, the student cannot be reasonably held up to the best of which he himself is capable. All but the obvious failures can point in justification of themselves to the fact that they have come up to the standard which the school itself has officially set. If the student has done what the school proclaims it exacts of him, what further right to blame him? The "average" is a false and demoralizing standard.

Please do not think I am over-concerned about marks. They are indeed an evil, yet not in themselves of supreme importance. But they externally symbolize what I have said about the situation in the schools where the learning of lessons is made the measure of education. Any standard which can be stated, which can be put in external form, is by the necessity of the case a mechanical and quantitative thing. It points out to students certain particular things which are to be done and certain particular things which are to be avoided. And it not only permits but encourages them to believe that the whole duty of man is done when just these special things have been performed, and just these special things avoided. Neither the intellectual nor moral standard of life is capable of any such restriction. What the laws of life demand of everyone is that he always do absolutely the best that he can under all circumstances. The only reasonable, and, in the long run, the only effective standard by which students should learn to judge their own work is whether they have developed the subject that is given them to the utmost; whether they have seen all in the subject of study that it is possible for them to see; and whether by engaging it with their full attention may have got out of it all gain or power which is possible. To let the student substitute the standard of "passing," of coming up to a certain external limit, is to let him off altogether too easily; and the worst of it is that this easy-going standard tends to become habitual—it radiates to other spheres of life and makes itself at home in them.

The marking system in itself is a minor matter. It is an effect rather than a cause; a symptom rather than an underlying disease. The root of the evil lies much deeper. The artificial division of subject-matter, and the assignment of particular chopped-off sections of it as tasks to be accomplished in the form of lessons, lies much nearer the centre of the evils of this "direct education." Subjects are first rigidly marked off from each other, and then this arbitrarily selected subject-matter is arranged so as to provide the material which will make the student most conscious that he has before him just and only something which is to be learned by him. The reality of experience, the substance of truth or beauty that may be involved, becomes a wholly secondary matter. The main thing is that so many lines or pages have been assigned for the next lesson, and that the educational work is judged not by the refinement and growth of the organ of vision which it brings, not by the strengthening of the hunger and thirst after what is fine and true, but by exhibition of the mastery of specific tasks assigned.

It ought not to be necessary to point to the crippling and paralysis that result. There is, after all, a presumption that there are certain great currents of truth and rightness flowing through all subject-matter which has any right to occupy a place in the school curriculum. It is true, is it not, that the universe is really a wonderful place, and that history is a record of all the absorbing struggles, failures and successes of human aspiration and endeavor? If this be true, are we doing quite the fair thing by either the world of nature or of history, or the child, the newcomer into this wonderful world, when we manage to present all this to him as if it constituted just so many lessons which for no very obvious and vital reason have to be learned? If it were not pathetic, it would make one smile to hear the argument used sometimes against having eager and alert interest play a part in the school room. The argument rests on supposing that interest is something which simply attaches to the child's side of the educational problem—as if the things in themselves, the realities of nature and human life and art through which the child receives his education, were themselves quite uninteresting or even repulsive! The purpose of the newer movement in education is not to make things interesting to the child by environing him with a sort of vaudeville divertisement, with all sorts of spectacular accompaniménts. The aim is to permit the intrinsic wonder and value which attach to all the realities which lie behind the school curriculum to come home to the child, and to take him up and carry him on in their own onward sweep. It is true that we adults get too easily blasé, overcome by the mere routine of living, and somehow constitutionally distrustful of the surprising values that reside in the bare facts of living. But it requires, I think, an unusually hardened pessimism to assume that the universe of nature and society, which, after all, is the only thing which can form the material of studies and lessons, is without inherent inspiration and appeal to the child, or that the child, of all beings, is so made as to be dull and slow in responding to this appeal. Yet this is the assumption which underlies the treatment of the material of education as if it were something only fit to be given out in lessons and tasks—the assumption which underlies the notion that education is a purely and direct conscious process—conscious to him who receives as well as to him who gives. The simile of a friend who was herself a teacher always occurs to my mind. Education, she said, reminded her of nothing so much as a corpse. It was all so silent, composed and laid out, and so dead.

Here also I should resent the interpretation that that idea of education which believes in educating by bringing boy and girl into proper relations of contact and responsiveness to the things in experience which are best worth seeing and doing, represents a lowering of standards, a decrease of severity intellectually or morally. It is the converse which is true. The standard which the truth and order of the universe set up when they are given a fair chance, an open and free field, when they secure adequate access to the individual, is infinitely more exacting than the conventions which textbook and school teacher can manage to agree upon and to set up. The responsibility of responding to what is right and worthy is a much more significant thing than the responsibility for reciting a given lesson. And the influence of the teacher becomes much more real and lively when it takes the form of cooperating with the influences that proceed from occupations and subject-matter than when it is felt purely as an independent and direct source.

More particularly, "direct education" involves a low standard because it fixes the attention of pupils upon the demands which teacher and text-book make, instead of the demands of the subject-matter, moving in the medium of individual thought and endeavor. It substitutes the standard, "Have I got this well enough to recite today? What are the chances of my being called upon to recite today, anyway, since I recited yesterday?" for the standard of "What is there in this that is so real as to make it imperative that I rise to it and move along with it?" There is one inevitable tendency of treating subject-matter simply as lessons or tasks: the desires, wishes or real expectations of the teacher, the teacher's own peculiar interests, tastes and standards become the controlling element. For moral purposes it makes comparatively little difference whether the pupils look at these expectations and demands from the standpoint of seeing in how many cases and by what ingenious methods they may evade them and still go through the show of conformity, or whether (because of greater skill of the teacher, or what is called tact) the children devote themselves to measuring up in the most amiable way possible—and children rightly approached are amiable to the level of the teacher's methods and ideals. In either case, the children are getting set in external habits of morality, and are learning to find their centre of intellectual gravity outside their own selves.

I know by experience that even after we come to believe in certain modes of educational practice, because we find that in spite of our theories they actually work well with our own children, we are yet somewhat "hard of heart and slow to believe" in their underlying theory and ideals. I am reminded of a gentleman who used periodically to insist that his children be taken out of the school where the method that I have called indirect education was in vogue, and be sent to a school where they would really have to learn lessons (to work, as he called it), but who, after he had won his wife's assent, always ended by stating that although the theory of the thing was absurd and demoralizing, at just that time it seemed to be working so well that he thought they had better leave the children where they were a little longer. Indeed, the point of view is so relatively recent in educational practice that I think that even the most ardent believers in it need to at times remind themselves of its fundamental reasonableness, and of the basic realities upon which it rests. We need to remind ourselves that the newer types of study, the various forms of social occupations, the cooking, the shop work, weaving, music, painting and clay modeling, are not merely devices for making old studies more pleasing, nor for disguising the inherent disagreeableness they have for boys and girls, that they are not simply effective methods for getting children to study more and learn their lessons easier and better than they used to, but that they stand for something which is fundamentally moral. They stand for the belief that the only final educative force in the world is participation in the realities of life, and that these realities are inherently moral in effect. It is because the various studies and occupations, which play so prominent a part in what is called the new education, are just modes of participating in the moving forces of truth and rightness that they insist upon being made central in everything that has a right to be termed a school. When this centre is the heart of school life, I have no fears as to the quality of education that is the outcome.

THE RELATION OF THEORY TO PRACTICE IN EDUCATION[1]

It is difficult, if not impossible, to define the proper relationship of theory and practice without a preliminary discussion, respectively, (1) of the nature and aim of theory; (2) of practice.

A. I shall assume without argument that adequate professional instruction of teachers is not exclusively theoretical, but involves a certain amount of practical work. The primary question as to the latter is the aim with which it shall be conducted. Two controlling purposes may be entertained so different from each other as radically to alter the amount, conditions, and method of practice work. On one hand, we may carry on the practical work with the object of giving teachers in training working command of the necessary tools of their profession; control of the technique of class instruction and management; skill and proficiency in the work of teaching. With this aim in view, practice work is, as far as it goes, of the nature of apprenticeship. On the other hand, we may propose to use practice work as an instrument in making real and vital theoretical instruction; the knowledge of subject-matter and of principles of education. This is the laboratory point of view.

The contrast between the two points of view is obvious; and the two aims together give the limiting terms within which all practice work falls. From one point of view, the aim is to form and equip the actual teacher; the aim is immediately as well as ultimately practical. From the other point of view, the *immediate* aim, the way of getting at the ulti-

---

1. This paper is to be taken as representing the views of the writer, rather than those of any particular institution in an official way; for the writer thought it better to discuss certain principles that seem to him fundamental, rather than to define a system of procedure.

[First published in *Third Yearbook* of the National Society for the Scientific Study of Education, 1904, Part I, pp. 9–30.]

mate aim, is to supply the intellectual method and material of good workmanship, instead of making on the spot, as it were, an efficient workman. Practice work thus considered is administered primarily with reference to the intellectual reactions it incites, giving the student a better hold upon the educational significance of the subject-matter he is acquiring, and of the science, philosophy, and history of education. Of course, the *results* are not exclusive. It would be very strange if practice work in doing what the laboratory does for a student of physics or chemistry in way of securing a more vital understanding of its principles, should not at the same time insure some skill in the instruction and management of a class. It would also be peculiar if the process of acquiring such skill should not also incidentally serve to enlighten and enrich instruction in subject-matter and the theory of education. None the less, there is a fundamental difference in the conception and conduct of the practice work according as one idea or the other is dominant and the other subordinate. If the primary object of practice is acquiring skill in performing the duties of a teacher, then the amount of time given to practice work, the place at which it is introduced, the method of conducting it, of supervising, criticising, and correlating it, will differ widely from the method where the laboratory ideal prevails; and *vice versa*.

In discussing this matter, I shall try to present what I have termed the laboratory, as distinct from the apprentice idea. While I speak primarily from the standpoint of the college, I should not be frank if I did not say that I believe what I am going to say holds, *mutatis mutandis*, for the normal school as well.

I. I first adduce the example of other professional schools. I doubt whether we, as educators, keep in mind with sufficient constancy the fact that the problem of training teachers is one species of a more generic affair—that of training for professions. Our problem is akin to that of training architects, engineers, doctors, lawyers, etc. Moreover, since (shameful and incredible as it seems) the vocation of teaching is practically the last to recognize the need of specific professional preparation, there is all the more reason for teachers to try to find what they may learn from the more extensive and matured experience of other callings. If now we turn to what has happened in the history of training for other professions, we find the following marked tendencies:

1. The demand for an increased amount of scholastic attainments as a prerequisite for entering upon professional work.

2. Development of certain lines of work in the applied sciences and arts, as centres of professional work; compare, for example, the place occupied by chemistry and physiology in medical training at present, with that occupied by chairs of "practice" and of "*materia medica*" a generation ago.

3. Arrangement of the practical and quasi-professional work upon the assumption that (limits of time, etc., being taken into account) the professional school does its best for its students when it gives them typical and intensive, rather than extensive and detailed, practice. It aims, in a word, at *control of the intellectual methods* required for personal and independent mastery of practical skill, rather than at turning out at once masters of the craft. This arrangement necessarily involves considerable postponement of skill in the routine and technique of the profession, until the student, after graduation, enters upon the pursuit of his calling.

These results are all the more important to us because other professional schools mostly started from the same position which training schools for teachers have occupied. Their history shows a period in which the idea was that students ought from the start to be made as proficient as possible in practical skill. In seeking for the motive forces which have caused professional schools to travel so steadily away from this position and toward the idea that practical work should be conducted for the sake of vitalizing and illuminating *intellectual* methods two reasons may be singled out:

a) First, the limited time at the disposal of the schools, and the consequent need of economy in its employ. It is not necessary to assume that apprenticeship is of itself a bad thing. On the contrary, it may be admitted to be a good thing; but the time which a student spends in the training school is short at the best. Since short, it is an urgent matter that it be put to its most effective use; and, relatively speaking, the wise employ of this short time is in laying scientific foundations. These cannot be adequately secured when one is doing the actual work of the profession, while professional life does afford time for acquiring and perfecting skill of the more technical sort.

b) In the second place, there is inability to furnish in the school adequate conditions for the best acquiring and using of skill. As compared with actual practice, the best that the school of law or medicine can do is to provide a somewhat remote and simulated copy of the real thing. For such schools to attempt to give the skill which comes to those adequately prepared, insensibly and unavoidably in actual work, is the same sort of thing as for grammar schools to spend months upon months in trying to convey (usually quite unsuccessfully) that skill in commercial arithmetic which comes, under penalty of practical failure, in a few weeks in the bank or counting-house.

It may be said that the analogy does not hold good for teachers' training schools, because such institutions have model or practice departments, supplying conditions which are identical with those which the teacher has to meet in the actual pursuit of his calling. But this is true at most only in such normal schools as are organized after the Oswego pattern—schools, that is to say, where the pupil-teacher is given for a considerable period of time the entire charge of instruction and discipline in the class-room, and does not come under a room critic-teacher. In all other cases, some of the most fundamentally significant features of the real school are reduced or eliminated. Most "practice schools" are a compromise. In theory they approximate ordinary conditions. As matter of fact, the "best interests of the children" are so safeguarded and supervised that the situation approaches learning to swim without going *too* near the water.

There are many ways that do not strike one at first glance, for removing the conditions of "practice work" from those of actual teaching. Deprivation of responsibility for the discipline of the room; the continued presence of an expert ready to suggest, to take matters into his own hands; close supervision; reduction of size of group taught; etc., etc., are some of these ways. The topic of "lesson plans" will be later referred to in connection with another topic. Here they may be alluded to as constituting one of the modes in which the conditions of the practice-teacher are made unreal. The student who prepares a number of more or less set lessons; who then has those lesson plans criticised; who then has his actual teaching criticised from the standpoint of success in carrying out the prearranged plans, is in a totally different attitude from the teacher who has to build up and modify his teaching plans as he goes along from experience gained in contact with pupils.

It would be difficult to find two things more remote from each other than the development of subject-matter under such control as is supplied from actual teaching, taking effect through the teacher's own initiative and reflective criticism, and its development with an eye fixed upon the judgment, presumed and actual, of a superior supervisory officer. Those phases of the problem of practice teaching which relate more distinctly to responsibility for the discipline of the room, or of the class, have received considerable attention in the past; but the more delicate and far-reaching matter of intellectual responsibility is too frequently ignored. Here centres the problem of securing conditions which will make practice work a genuine apprenticeship.

II. To place the emphasis upon the securing of proficiency in teaching and discipline *puts the attention of the student-teacher in the wrong place, and tends to fix it in the wrong direction*—not wrong absolutely, but relatively as regards perspective of needs and opportunities. The would-be teacher has some time or other to face and solve two problems, each extensive and serious enough by itself to demand absorbing and undivided attention. These two problems are:

1. Mastery of subject-matter from the standpoint of its educational value and use; or, what is the same thing, the mastery of educational principles in their application to that subject-matter which is at once the material of instruction and the basis of discipline and control;

2. The mastery of the technique of class management.

This does not mean that the two problems are in any way isolated or independent. On the contrary, they are strictly correlative. *But the mind of a student cannot give equal attention to both at the same time.*

The difficulties which face a beginning teacher, who is set down for the first time before a class of from thirty to sixty children, in the responsibilities not only of instruction, but of maintaining the required order in the room as a whole, are most trying. It is almost impossible for an old teacher who has acquired the requisite skill of doing two or three distinct things simultaneously—skill to see the room as a whole while hearing one individual in one class recite, of keeping the program of the day and, yes, of the week and of the month in the fringe of consciousness while the work of the hour is in its centre—it is almost impossible for such a teacher to realize all the difficulties that confront the average beginner.

There is a technique of teaching, just as there is a technique of piano-playing. The technique, if it is to be educationally effective, is dependent upon principles. But it is possible for a student to acquire outward form of method without capacity to put it to genuinely educative use. As every teacher knows, children have an inner and an outer attention. The inner attention is the giving of the mind without reserve or qualification to the subject in hand. It is the first-hand and personal play of mental powers. As such, it is a fundamental condition of mental growth. To be able to keep track of this mental play, to recognize the signs of its presence or absence, to know how it is initiated and maintained, how to test it by results attained, and to test *apparent* results by it, is the supreme mark and criterion of a teacher. It means insight into soul-action, ability to discriminate the genuine from the sham, and capacity to further one and discourage the other.

External attention, on the other hand, is that given to the book or teacher as an independent object. It is manifested in certain conventional postures and physical attitudes rather than in the movement of thought. Children acquire great dexterity in exhibiting in conventional and expected ways the *form* of attention to school work, while reserving the inner play of their own thoughts, images, and emotions for subjects that are more important to them, but quite irrelevant.

Now, the teacher who is plunged prematurely into the pressing and practical problem of keeping order in the schoolroom has almost of necessity to make supreme the matter of external attention. The teacher has not yet had the training which affords psychological insight—which enables him to judge promptly (and therefore almost automatically) the kind and mode of subject-matter which the pupil needs at a given moment to keep his attention moving forward effectively and healthfully. He does know, however, that he must maintain order; that he must keep the attention of the pupils fixed upon his own questions, suggestions, instructions, and remarks, and upon their "lessons." The inherent tendency of the situation therefore is for him to acquire his technique in relation to the outward rather than the inner mode of attention.

III. Along with this fixation of attention upon the secondary at the expense of the primary problem, *there goes the formation of habits of work which have an empirical, rather than a scientific, sanction.* The student adjusts his actual methods of teaching, not to the principles which he is acquiring, but to what he sees succeed and fail in an empirical way from moment to moment: to what he sees other teachers doing who are more experienced and successful in keeping order than he is; and to the injunctions and directions given him by others. In this way the controlling habits of the teacher finally get fixed with comparatively little reference to principles in the psychology, logic, and history of education. In theory, these latter are dominant; in practice, the moving forces are the devices and methods which are picked up through blind experimentation; through examples which are not rationalized; through precepts which are more or less arbitrary and mechanical; through advice based upon the experience of others. Here we have the explanation, in considerable part at least, of the dualism, the unconscious duplicity, which is one of the chief evils of the teaching profession. There is an enthusiastic devotion to certain principles of lofty theory in the abstract—principles of self-activity, self-control, intellectual and moral—and there is a school practice taking little heed of the official pedagogic creed. Theory and practice do not grow together out of and into the teacher's personal experience.

Ultimately there are two bases upon which the habits of a teacher as a teacher may be built up. They may be formed under the inspiration and constant criticism of intelligence, applying the best that is available. This is possible only where the would-be teacher has become fairly saturated with his subject-matter, and with his psychological and ethical philosophy of education. Only when such things have become incorporated in mental habit, have become part of the working tendencies of observation, insight, and reflection, will these principles work automatically, unconsciously, and hence promptly and effectively. And this means that practical work should be pursued primarily with reference to its reaction upon the professional pupil in making him a thoughtful and alert student of education, rather than to help him get immediate proficiency.

For immediate skill may be got at the cost of power to go on growing. The teacher who leaves the professional school with power in managing a class of children may appear to superior advantage the first day, the first week, the first month, or even the first year, as compared with some other teacher who has a much more vital command of the psychology, logic, and ethics of development. But later "progress" may with such consist only in perfecting and refining skill already possessed. Such persons seem to know how to teach, but they are not students of teaching. Even though they go on studying books of pedagogy, reading teachers' journals, attending teachers' institutes, etc., yet the root of the matter is not in them, unless they continue to be students of subject-matter, and students of mind-activity. Unless a teacher is such a student, he may continue to improve in the mechanics of school management, but he can not grow as a teacher, an inspirer and director of soul-life. How often do candid instructors in training schools for teachers acknowledge disappointment in the later career of even their more promising candidates! They seem to strike twelve at the start. There is an unexpected and seemingly unaccountable failure to maintain steady growth. Is this in some part due to the undue premature stress laid in early practice work upon securing immediate capability in teaching?

I might go on to mention other evils which seem to me to be more or less the effect of this same cause. Among them are the lack of intellectual independence among teachers, their tendency to intellectual subserviency. The "model lesson" of the teachers' institute and of the educational journal is a monument, on the one hand, of the eagerness of those in authority to secure immediate practical results at any cost; and, upon the other, of the willingness of our teaching corps to accept without inquiry or criticism any method or device which seems to promise good results. Teachers, actual and intending, flock to those persons who give them clear-cut and definite instructions as to just how to teach this or that.

The tendency of educational development to proceed by reaction from one thing to another, to adopt for one year, or for a term of seven years, this or that new study or method of teaching, and then as abruptly to swing over to some new educational gospel, is a result which would be impossible if teachers were adequately moved by their own independent intelligence. The willingness of teachers, especially of those occupying administrative positions, to become submerged in the routine detail of their callings, to expend the bulk of their energy upon forms and rules and regulations, and reports and percentages, is another evidence of the absence of intellectual vitality. If teachers were possessed by the spirit of an abiding student of education, this spirit would find some way of breaking through the mesh and coil of circumstance and would find expression for itself.

B. Let us turn from the practical side to the theoretical. What must be the aim and spirit of theory in order that practice work may really serve the purpose of an educational laboratory? We are met here with the belief that instruction in theory is merely theoretical, abstruse, remote, and therefore relatively useless to the teacher as a teacher, unless the student is at once set upon the work of teaching; that only "practice" can give a motive to a professional learning, and supply material for educational courses. It is not infrequently claimed (or at least unconsciously assumed) that students will not have a professional stimulus for their work in subject-matter and in educational psychology and history, will not have any outlook upon their relation to education, unless these things are immediately and simultaneously reinforced by setting the student upon the work of teaching. But is this the case? Or are there practical elements and bearings already contained in theoretical instruction of the proper sort?

I. Since it is impossible to cover in this paper all phases of the philosophy and science of education, I shall speak from the standpoint of psychology, believing that this may be taken as typical of the whole range of instruction in educational theory as such.

In the first place, beginning students have without any reference to immediate teaching a very large capital of an exceedingly practical sort in their own experience. The argument that theoretical instruction is merely abstract and in the air unless students are set at once to test and illustrate it by practice teaching of their own, *overlooks the continuity of the class-room mental activity with that of other normal experience.* It ignores the tremendous importance for educational purposes of this continuity. Those who employ this argument seem to isolate the psychology of learning that goes on in the schoolroom from the psychology of learning found elsewhere.

This isolation is both unnecessary and harmful. It is unnecessary, tending to futility, because it throws away or makes light of the greatest asset in the student's possession —the greatest, moreover, that ever will be in his possession— his own direct and personal experience. There is every presumption (since the student is not an imbecile) that he has been learning all the days of his life, and that he is still learning from day to day. He must accordingly have in his own experience plenty of practical material by which to illustrate and vitalize theoretical principles and laws of mental growth in the process of learning. Moreover, since none of us is brought up under ideal conditions, each beginning student has plenty of practical experience by which to illustrate cases of arrested development—instances of failure and maladaptation and retrogression, or even degeneration. The material at hand is pathological as well as healthy. It serves to embody and illustrate both achievement and failure, in the problem of learning.

But it is more than a serious mistake (violating the principle of proceeding from the known to the unknown) to fail to take account of this body of practical experience. Such ignoring tends also to perpetuate some of the greatest evils of current school methods. Just because the student's attention is not brought to the point of recognizing that *his own* past and present growth is proceeding in accordance with the very laws that control growth in the school, and that there is no psychology of the schoolroom different from that of the nursery, the playground, the street, and the parlor, he comes unconsciously to assume that education in the class-room is a sort of unique thing, having its own laws.[2] Unconsciously, but none the less surely, the student comes to believe in certain "methods" of learning, and hence of teaching which are somehow especially appropriate to the school—which somehow have their particular residence and application there. Hence he comes to believe in the potency for schoolroom purposes of materials, methods, and devices which it never occurs to him to trust to in his experience outside of school.

I know a teacher of teachers who is accustomed to say that when she fails to make clear to a class of teachers some point relative to children, she asks these teachers to stop thinking of their own pupils and to think of some nephew, niece, cousin, some child of whom they have acquaintance in the unformalities of home life. I do not suppose any great argument is needed to prove that breach of continuity between learning within and without the school is the great cause in education of wasted power and misdirected effort. I wish rather to take advantage of this assumption (which I think will be generally accepted) to emphasize the danger of bringing the would-be teacher into an abrupt and dislocated contact with the psychology of the schoolroom—abrupt and dislocated because not prepared for by prior practice in selecting and organizing the relevant principles and data contained within the experience best known to him, his own.[3]

From this basis, a transition to educational psychology may be made in observation of the teaching of others—visiting classes. I should wish to note here, however, the same

2. There is where the plea for "adult" psychology has force. The person who does not know himself is not likely to know others. The adult psychology ought, however, to be just as genetic as that of childhood.

3. It may avoid misapprehension if I repeat the word *experience*. It is not a *metaphysical* introspection that I have in mind, but the process of turning back upon one's own experiences, and turning them over to see how they were developed, what helped and hindered, the stimuli and the inhibitions both within and without the organism.

principle that I have mentioned as regards practice work,
specifically so termed. The first observation of instruction
given by model- or critic-teachers should not be too definitely
practical in aim. The student should not be observing to find
out how the good teacher does it, in order to accumulate a
store of methods by which he also may teach successfully. He
should rather observe with reference to seeing the interaction
of mind, to see how teacher and pupils react upon each other
—how mind answers to mind. Observation should at first be
conducted from the psychological rather than from the "practical" standpoint. If the latter is emphasized before the student has an independent command of the former, the principle of imitation is almost sure to play an exaggerated part
in the observer's future teaching, and hence at the expense of
personal insight and initiative. What the student needs most
at this stage of growth is ability to see what is going on in
the minds of a group of persons who are in intellectual contact with one another. He needs to learn to observe psychologically—a very different thing from simply observing how a
teacher gets "good results" in presenting any particular subject.

It should go without saying that the student who has
acquired power in psychological observation and interpretation may finally go on to observe more technical aspects of
instruction, namely, the various methods and instrumentalities used by a good teacher in giving instruction in any
subject. If properly prepared for, this need not tend to produce copiers, followers of tradition and example. Such students will be able to translate the practical devices which are
such an important part of the equipment of a good teacher
over into their psychological equivalents; to know not merely
as a matter of brute fact that they do work, but to know how
and why they work. Thus he will be an independent judge
and critic of their proper use and adaptation.

In the foregoing I have assumed that educational psychology is marked off from general psychology simply by the
emphasis which it puts upon two factors. The first is the
stress laid upon a certain end, namely, growth or development—with its counterparts, arrest and adaptation. The
second is the importance attached to the social factor—to

the mutual interaction of different minds with each other. It is, I think, strictly true that no educational procedure nor pedagogical maxim can be derived directly from pure psychological data. The psychological data taken without qualification (which is what I mean by their being pure) cover everything and anything that may take place in a mind. Mental arrest and decay occur according to psychological laws, just as surely as do development and progress.

We do not make practical maxims out of physics by telling persons to move according to laws of gravitation. If people move at all, they *must* move in accordance with the conditions stated by this law. Similarly, if mental operations take place at all, they *must* take place in accordance with the principles stated in correct psychological generalizations. It is superfluous and meaningless to attempt to turn these psychological principles directly into rules of teaching. But the person who knows the laws of mechanics knows the conditions of which he must take account when he wishes to reach a certain end. He knows that *if* he aims to build a bridge, he must build it in a certain way and of certain materials, or else he will not have a bridge, but a heap of rubbish. So in psychology. Given an end, say promotion of healthy growth, psychological observations and reflection put us in control of the conditions concerned in that growth. We know that if we are to get that *end*, we must do it in a certain way. It is the subordination of the psychological material to the problem of effecting growth and avoiding arrest and waste which constitutes a distinguishing mark of educational psychology.

I have spoken of the importance of the social factor as the other mark. I do not mean, of course, that general theoretical psychology ignores the existence and significance of the reaction of mind to mind—though it would be within bounds to say that till recently the social side was an unwritten chapter of psychology. I mean that considerations of the ways in which one mind responds to the stimuli which another mind is consciously or unconsciously furnishing possess a relative importance for the educator which they have not for the psychologist as such. From the teacher's standpoint, it is not too much to say that every habit which a pupil exhibits is to be regarded as a reaction to stimuli which some persons or group of persons have presented to the child. It is not too much to say that the most important thing for the teacher to consider, as regards his present relations to his pupils, is the attitudes and habits which his own modes of being, saying, and doing are fostering or discouraging in them.

Now, if these two assumptions regarding educational psychology be granted, I think it will follow as a matter of course, that only by beginning with the values and laws contained in the student's own experience of his own mental growth, and by proceeding gradually to facts connected with other persons of whom he can know little; and by proceeding still more gradually to the attempt actually to influence the mental operations of others, can educational theory be made most effective. Only in this way can the most essential trait of the mental habit of the teacher be secured—that habit which looks upon the internal, not upon the external; which sees that the important function of the teacher is direction of the mental movement of the student, and that the mental movement must be known before it can be directed.

II. I turn now to the side of subject-matter, or scholarship, with the hope of showing that here too the material, when properly presented, is not so *merely* theoretical, remote from the practical problems of teaching, as is sometimes supposed. I recall that once a graduate student in a university made inquiries among all the leading teachers in the institution with which he was connected as to whether they had received any professional training, whether they had taken courses in pedagogy. The inquirer threw the results, which were mostly negative, into the camp of the local pedagogical club. Some may say that this proves nothing, because college teaching is proverbially poor, considered simply as teaching. Yet no one can deny that there is *some* good teaching, and some teaching of the very first order, done in colleges, and done by persons who have never had any instruction in either the theory or the practice of teaching.

This fact cannot be ignored any more than can the fact that there were good teachers before there was any such thing as pedagogy. Now, I am not arguing for not having pedagogical training—that is the last thing I want. But I claim the facts mentioned prove that scholarship *per se* may itself be a most effective tool for training and turning out good teachers. If it has accomplished so much when working unconsciously and without set intention, have we not good reason to believe that, when acquired in a training school for teachers—with the end of making teachers held definitely in view and with conscious reference to its relation to mental activity—it may prove a much more valuable pedagogical asset than we commonly consider it?

Scholastic knowledge is sometimes regarded as if it were something quite irrelevant to method. When this attitude is even unconsciously assumed, method becomes an external attachment to knowledge of subject-matter. It has to be elaborated and acquired in relative independence from subject-matter, and *then* applied.

Now the body of knowledge which constitutes the subject-matter of the student-teacher must, by the nature of the case, be organized subject-matter. It is not a miscellaneous heap of separate scraps. Even if (as in the case of history and literature), it be not technically termed "science," it is none the less material which has been subjected to method—has been selected and arranged with reference to controlling intellectual principles. There is, therefore, method in subject-matter itself—method indeed of the highest order which the human mind has yet evolved, scientific method.

It cannot be too strongly emphasized that this scientific method is the method of mind itself.[4] The classifications, interpretations, explanations, and generalizations which make subject-matter a branch of study do not lie externally in facts apart from mind. They reflect the attitudes and workings of mind in its endeavor to bring raw material of experience to a point where it at once satisfies and stimulates the needs of active thought. Such being the case, there is something wrong in the "academic" side of professional training, if by means of it the student does not constantly get object-lessons of the finest type in the kind of mental activity which characterizes mental growth and, hence, the educative process.

It is necessary to recognize the importance for the

---

4. Professor Ella F. Young's *Scientific Method in Education* (University of Chicago Decennial Publications) is a noteworthy development of this conception, to which I am much indebted.

teacher's equipment of his own habituation to superior types of method of mental operation. The more a teacher in the future is likely to have to do with elementary teaching, the more, rather than the less, necessary is such exercise. Otherwise, the current traditions of elementary work with their tendency to talk and write down to the supposed intellectual level of children, will be likely to continue. Only a teacher thoroughly trained in the higher levels of intellectual method and who thus has constantly in his own mind a sense of what adequate and genuine intellectual activity means, will be likely, in deed, not in mere word, to respect the mental integrity and force of children.

Of course, this conception will be met by the argument that the scientific organization of subject-matter, which constitutes the academic studies of the student-teacher is upon such a radically different basis from that adapted to less mature students that too much preoccupation with scholarship of an advanced order is likely actually to get in the way of the teacher of children and youth. I do not suppose anybody would contend that teachers really can know more than is good for them, but it may reasonably be argued that continuous study of a specialized sort forms mental habits likely to throw the older student out of sympathy with the type of mental impulses and habits which are found in younger persons.

Right here, however, I think normal schools and teachers' colleges have one of their greatest opportunities—an opportunity not merely as to teachers in training, but also for reforming methods of education in colleges and higher schools having nothing to do with the training of teachers. It is the business of normal schools and collegiate schools of education to present subject-matter in science, in language, in literature and the arts, in such a way that the student both sees and feels that these studies *are* significant embodiments of mental operations. He should be led to realize that they are not products of technical methods, which have been developed for the sake of the specialized branches of knowledge in which they are used, but represent fundamental mental attitudes and operations—that, indeed, particular scientific methods and classifications simply express and illustrate in their most concrete form that of which simple and common modes of thought-activity are capable when they work under satisfactory conditions.

In a word, it is the business of the "academic" instruction of future teachers to carry back subject-matter to its common psychical roots.[5] In so far as this is accomplished, the gap between the higher and the lower treatment of subject-matter, upon which the argument of the supposed objector depends, ceases to have the force which that argument assigns to it. This does not mean, of course, that exactly the same subject-matter, in the same mode of presentation, is suitable to a student in the elementary or high schools that is appropriate to the normal student. But it does mean that a mind which is habituated to viewing subject-matter from the standpoint of the function of that subject-matter in connection with *mental* responses, attitudes, and methods will be sensitive to *signs of intellectual activity* when exhibited in the child of four, or the youth of sixteen, and will be trained to a spontaneous and unconscious appreciation of the subject-matter which is fit to call out and direct mental activity.

We have here, I think, the explanation of the success of some teachers who violate every law known to and laid down by pedagogical science. They are themselves so full of the spirit of inquiry, so sensitive to every sign of its presence and absence, that no matter what they do, nor how they do it, they succeed in awakening and inspiring like alert and intense mental activity in those with whom they come in contact.

This is not a plea for the prevalence of these irregular, inchoate methods. But I feel that I may recur to my former remark: if some teachers, by sheer plentitude of knowledge, keep by instinct in touch with the mental activity of their pupils, and accomplish so much without, and even in spite of, principles which are theoretically sound, then there must be in this same scholarship a tremendous resource when it is more consciously used—that is, employed in clear connection with psychological principles.

5. It is hardly necessary to refer to Dr. Harris's continued contention that normal training should give a higher view or synthesis of even the most elementary subjects.

When I said above that schools for training teachers have here an opportunity to react favorably upon general education, I meant that no instruction in subject-matter (wherever it is given) is adequate if it leaves the student with just acquisition of certain information about external facts and laws, or even a certain facility in the intellectual manipulation of this material. It is the business of our higher schools in all lines, and not simply of our normal schools, to furnish the student with the realization that, after all, it is the human mind, trained to effective control of its natural attitudes, impulses, and responses, that is the significant thing in all science and history and art so far as these are formulated for purposes of study.

The present divorce between scholarship and method is as harmful upon one side as upon the other—as detrimental to the best interests of higher academic instruction as it is to the training of teachers. But the only way in which this divorce can be broken down is by so presenting all subject-matter, for whatever ultimate, practical, or professional purpose, that it shall be apprehended as an objective embodiment of methods of mind in its search for, and transactions with, the truth of things.

Upon the more practical side, this principle requires that, so far as students appropriate new subject-matter (thereby improving their own scholarship and realizing more consciously the nature of method), they should finally proceed to organize this same subject-matter with reference to its use in teaching others. The curriculum of the elementary and the high school constituting the "practice" or "model" school ought to stand in the closest and most organic relation to the instruction in subject-matter which is given by the teachers of the professional school. If in any given school this is not the case, it is either because in the *training class* subject-matter is presented in an isolated way, instead of as a concrete expression of methods of mind, or else because the *practice school* is dominated by certain conventions and traditions regarding material and the methods of teaching it, and hence is not engaged in work of an adequate educational type.

As a matter of fact, as everybody knows, both of these

causes contribute to the present state of things. On the one hand, inherited conditions impel the elementary school to a certain triviality and poverty of subject-matter, calling for mechanical drill, rather than for thought-activity, and the high school to a certain technical mastery of certain conventional culture subjects, taught as independent branches of the same tree of knowledge! On the other hand traditions of the different branches of science (the academic side of subject-matter) tend to subordinate the teaching in the normal school to the attainment of certain facilities, and the acquirement of certain information, both in greater or less isolation from their value as exciting and directing mental power.

The great need is convergence, concentration. Every step taken in the elementary and the high school toward intelligent introduction of more worthy and significant subject-matter, one requiring consequently for its assimilation thinking rather than "drill," must be met by a like advance step in which the mere isolated specialization of collegiate subject-matter is surrendered, and in which there is brought to conscious and interested attention its significance in expression of fundamental modes of mental activity—so fundamental as to be common to both the play of the mind upon the ordinary material of everyday experience and to the systematized material of the sciences.

III. As already suggested, this point requires that training students be exercised in making the connections between the course of study of the practice or model school, and the wider horizons of learning coming within their ken. But it is consecutive and systematic exercise in the consideration of the subject-matter of the elementary and high schools that is needed. The habit of making isolated and independent lesson plans for a few days' or weeks' instruction in a separate grade here or there not only does not answer this purpose, but is likely to be distinctly detrimental. Everything should be discouraged which tends to put the student in the attitude of snatching at the subject-matter which he is acquiring in order to see if by some hook or crook it may be made immediately available for a lesson in this or that grade. What is needed is the habit of viewing the entire curriculum as a continuous growth, reflecting the growth of mind itself. This in turn demands, so far as I can see, consecutive and longitudinal consideration of the curriculum of the elementary and high school rather than a cross-sectional view of it. The student should be led to see that the same subject-matter in geography, nature-study, or art develops not merely day to day in a given grade, but from year to year throughout the entire movement of the school; and he should realize this before he gets much encouragement in trying to adapt subject-matter in lesson plans for this or that isolated grade.

C. If we attempt to gather together the points which have been brought out, we should have a view of practice work something like the following—though I am afraid even this formulates a scheme with more appearance of rigidity than is desirable:

At first, the practice school would be used mainly for purposes of observation. This observation, moreover, would not be for the sake of seeing how good teachers teach, or for getting "points" which may be employed in one's own teaching, but to get material for psychological observation and reflection, and some conception of the educational movement of the school as a whole.

Secondly, there would then be more intimate introduction to the lives of the children and the work of the school through the use as assistants of such students as had already got psychological insight and a good working acquaintance with educational problems. Students at this stage would not undertake much direct teaching, but would make themselves useful in helping the regular class instructor. There are multitudes of ways in which such help can be given and be of real help—that is, of use to the school, to the children, and not merely of putative value to the training student.[6] Special attention to backward children, to children who have been out of school, assisting in the care of material, in forms of hand-work, suggest some of the avenues of approach.

This kind of practical experience enables, in the third place, the future teacher to make the transition from his

6. This question of some real need in the practice school itself for the work done is very important in its moral influence and in assimilating the conditions of "practice work" to those of real teaching.

more psychological and theoretical insight to the observation of the more technical points of class teaching and management. The informality, gradualness, and familiarity of the earlier contact tend to store the mind with material which is unconsciously assimilated and organized, and thus supplies a background for work involving greater responsibility.

As a counterpart of this work in assisting, such students might well at the same time be employed in the selection and arrangement of subject-matter, as indicated in the previous discussion. Such organization would at the outset have reference to at least a group of grades, emphasizing continuous and consecutive growth. Later it might, without danger of undue narrowness, concern itself with finding supplementary materials and problems bearing upon the work in which the student is giving assistance; might elaborate material which could be used to carry the work still farther, if it were desirable; or, in case of the more advanced students, to build up a scheme of possible alternative subjects for lessons and studies.

Fourthly, as fast as students are prepared through their work of assisting for more responsible work, they could be given actual teaching to do. Upon the basis that the previous preparation has been adequate in subject-matter, in educational theory, and in the kind of observation and practice already discussed, such practice-teachers should be given the maximum amount of liberty possible. They should not be too closely supervised, nor too minutely and immediately criticised upon either the matter or the method of their teaching. Students should be given to understand that they not only are *permitted* to act upon their own intellectual initiative, but that they are *expected* to do so, and that their ability to take hold of situations for themselves would be a more important factor in judging them than their following any particular set method or scheme.

Of course, there should be critical discussion with persons more expert of the work done, and of the educational results obtained. But sufficient time should be permitted to allow the practice-teacher to recover from the shocks incident to the newness of the situation, and also to get enough experience to make him capable of seeing the *fundamental* bearings of criticism upon work done. Moreover, the work of the expert or supervisor should be directed to getting the student to judge his own work critically, to find out for himself in what respects he has succeeded and in what failed, and to find the probable reasons for both failure and success, rather than to criticising him too definitely and specifically upon special features of his work.

It ought to go without saying (unfortunately, it does not in all cases) that criticism should be directed to making the professional student thoughtful about his work in the light of principles, rather than to induce in him a recognition that certain special methods are good, and certain other special methods bad. At all events, no greater travesty of real intellectual criticism can be given than to set a student to teaching a brief number of lessons, have him under inspection in practically all the time of every lesson, and then criticise him almost, if not quite, at the very end of each lesson, upon the particular way in which that particular lesson has been taught, pointing out elements of failure and of success. Such methods of criticism may be adapted to giving a training-teacher command of some of the knacks and tools of the trade, but are not calculated to develop a thoughtful and independent teacher.

Moreover, while such teaching (as already indicated) should be extensive or continuous enough to give the student time to become at home and to get a body of funded experience, it ought to be intensive in purpose rather than spread out miscellaneously. It is much more important for the teacher to assume responsibility for the consecutive development of some one topic, to get a feeling for the movement of that subject, than it is to teach a certain number (necessarily smaller in range) of lessons in a larger number of subjects. What we want, in other words, is not so much technical skill, as a realizing sense in the teacher of what the educational development of a subject means, and, in some typical case, command of a method of control, which will then serve as a standard for self-judgment in other cases.

Fifthly, if the practical conditions permit—if, that is to say, the time of the training course is sufficiently long, if the practice schools are sufficiently large to furnish the required number of children, and to afford actual demand for the work to be done—students who have gone through the stages already referred to should be ready for work of the distinctly apprenticeship type.

Nothing that I have said heretofore is to be understood as ruling out practice teaching which is designed to give an individual mastery of the actual technique of teaching and management, provided school conditions permit it in reality and not merely in external form—provided, that is, the student has gone through a training in educational theory and history, in subject-matter, in observation, and in practice work of the laboratory type, before entering upon the latter. The teacher must acquire his technique some time or other; and if conditions are favorable, there are some advantages in having this acquisition take place in cadetting or in something of that kind. By means of this probation, persons who are unfit for teaching may be detected and eliminated more quickly than might otherwise be the case and before their cases have become institutionalized.

Even in this distinctly apprenticeship stage, however, it is still important that the student should be given as much responsibility and initiative as he is capable of taking, and hence that supervision should not be too unremitting and intimate, and criticism not at too short range or too detailed. The advantage of this intermediate probationary period does not reside in the fact that thereby supervisory officers may turn out teachers who will perpetuate their own notions and methods, but in the inspiration and enlightenment that come through prolonged contact with mature and sympathetic persons. If the conditions in the public schools were just what they ought to be, if all superintendents and principals had the knowledge and the wisdom which they should have, and if they had time and opportunity to utilize their knowledge and their wisdom in connection with the development of the younger teachers who come to them, the value of this apprenticeship period would be reduced, I think, very largely to its serving to catch in time and to exclude persons unfitted for teaching.

In conclusion, I may say that I do not believe that the principles presented in this paper call for anything utopian. The present movement in normal schools for improvement of range and quality of subject-matter is steady and irresistible. All the better classes of normal schools are already, in effect, what are termed "junior colleges." That is, they give two years' work which is almost, and in many cases quite, of regular college grade. More and more, their instructors are persons who have had the same kind of scholarly training that is expected of teachers in colleges. Many of these institutions are already of higher grade than this; and the next decade will certainly see a marked tendency on the part of many normal schools to claim the right to give regular collegiate bachelor degrees.

The type of scholarship contemplated in this paper is thus practically assured for the near future. If two other factors cooperate with this, there is no reason why the conception of relation of theory and practice here presented should not be carried out. The second necessary factor is that the elementary and high schools, which serve as schools of observation and practice, should represent an advanced type of education properly corresponding to the instruction in academic subject-matter and in educational theory given to the training classes. The third necessity is that work in psychology and educational theory make concrete and vital the connection between the normal instruction in subject-matter and the work of the elementary and high schools.

If it should prove impracticable to realize the conception herein set forth, it will not be, I think, because of any impossibility resident in the outward conditions, but because those in authority, both within and without the schools, believe that the true function of training schools is just to meet the needs of which people are already conscious. In this case, of course, training schools will be conducted simply with reference to perpetuating current types of educational practice, with simply incidental improvement in details.

The underlying assumption of this paper is, accordingly, that training schools for teachers do not perform their full duty in accepting and conforming to present educational standards, but that educational leadership is an indispensable part of their office. The thing needful is improvement of education, not simply by turning out teachers who can do better the things that are now necessary to do, but rather by changing the conception of what constitutes education.

SIGNIFICANCE OF THE SCHOOL
OF EDUCATION[1]

The topic at once arouses the query: Has it any—any, that is to say, different from that possessed by any school as a place in which children and youth receive instruction? Well, let us see. I am a great believer in the sanctions and sanctities of history. What light does history throw on the significance of the School of Education?

It may be a cause of surprise to say that the School of Education is just coming of age—that it is now just twenty-one years old. You may, some of you, have thought of it as coming into existence as we took possession of these buildings; while others would think themselves certainly justified by the facts in saying that it is now in its third year of existence. But I date its origin from the year 1883. It was in that year, by a coincidence which I think also is an omen of good, that Colonel Parker came to the Cook County Normal School, and that the Chicago Manual Training School was opened under the direction of Mr. Belfield. It is pleasing to recall that Colonel Jacobson and Mr. Ham, who took so active a part in promoting the Chicago Manual Training School, also encouraged and assisted in every way in their power Colonel Parker in introducing manual-training work into the Cook County Normal School, where it was found from the very opening of Colonel Parker's work.

Since the School of Education in its present form is the direct outcome of the foundation and endowment of the Chicago Institute by the magnificent gift of Mrs. Emmons Blaine, and since this gift was the happy fruit of the inspiration proceeding from Colonel Parker's work at the Cook County Normal School (was intended, indeed, to consum-

1. A paper read before the School of Education Parents' Association, Chicago, January 28, 1904.

[First published in *Elementary School Teacher* 4 (1904): 441–53.]

mate that work, to bring to fuller realization the possibilities
it had made evident), no apology is needed for beginning
my talk with this factor in the constitution of the significance
of the School of Education.

The fact which this portion of our history—for I shall
always claim that we are entitled to call it *our* history—puts
before us is the meaning of the training of teachers in any
educational project. Colonel Parker was sufficiently well
known as a warrior and prophet in the cause of educational
progress before he came to Chicago; but the storm centre of
educational reform was transferred from Quincy to Chicago
in 1883, because Colonel Parker was enough of a prophet
to foresee that the important thing, the controlling thing, in
any educational movement is the personality and training
of those who are to carry it on. It is to persons that everything in life at last comes back; and it is to teachers that
everything in school life comes back. Moreover, Colonel
Parker was enough of a warrior to see that the training of
teachers is the strategic point in the educational campaign.
Only from such a fortress can the battle economically and
effectively be carried on. It goes without saying, however,
that with the Normal School there was connected, as an
organic part of the work of training teachers, an elementary
school, and in idea, if not always in fact, a high school.
Colonel Parker was the reformer that he was just because
he saw that the cause of the child and the cause of the
teacher are one. It is through the improvement of the
standards, ideals, and working equipment of the teacher that
the cause of education is to be advanced. But it is only in
the enrichment, direction, and freedom of the life of children
that this progress takes effect and has reality. The better
training of teachers and the providing of a better school life,
in which the children may find themselves, are Siamese
twins of educational reform.

If we turn to history, we learn at least this: one fundamental and striking element in the significance of the
School of Education is the desire and resolute purpose to
promote the cause of education, not only here, but everywhere, through inspiring teachers with more vital and adequate conceptions of the nature of their work, and through

furnishing them with the intellectual equipment necessary
to make them effective and apt in carrying out such broad-
ened and deepened ideals.

But, as I have already reminded you, this same year,
the year 1883, was the year of the birth of another integral
portion of our School of Education—the Chicago Manual
Training School. This, too, had its origin in discontent with
then prevailing methods and aims of education, particularly
in high-school work. It was to some extent, I take it, like
the movement which Colonel Parker represented, a protest
against a one-sided education—an education which took account of the employment of the senses upon the symbols of
things, but not sufficiently of the use of touch and sight and
muscular sense upon things themselves; a protest against
an ideal of education which identified instruction with training of powers of intellectual assimilation and accumulation
at the expense of the training of the executive organs; a
protest against an education which prepared for the more
bookish and conventional professions of life at the expense
of commerce, business, and those modes of productive creation which lie near the foundations of our social life. The
Chicago Manual Training School, in other words, stood for a
hitherto neglected factor and function in the educational
field. It also, like the work of Colonel Parker in the Cook
County Normal School, was a pioneer work. It was original
and creative in its own department. We have a right to recall
with pride, that in tracing the origins of two factors of our
present school, we are also dealing with the origins of two
movements of national significance—movements whose influence never was shut up within their own walls, or even
within the city of Chicago, but which became models and
inspirations of similar work all over the country.

So far at least we have no mean and insignificant ancestry. But the School of Education is the School of Education
of the University of Chicago, and that reminds us that there
are other historical forces which have to be taken into account in reckoning up the significance of the School of
Education. From this point of view, two other schools—the
old University Elementary School, afterward called the Laboratory School, and the South Side Academy—demand recog-

nition. Younger in years, they form the immediate ties which bind the School of Education to the university work as such.

The Laboratory School, as the name implies, was founded expressly for the purpose of scientific investigation and research into problems connected with the psychology and sociology of education. Its aim was to further the application of scientific conceptions and methods to the conduct of school work. The application of science to the physical departments of life is a fact so familiar that it hardly arouses much attention, even for a moment, excepting in its more unusual and extraordinary manifestations. But the conception that the methods of inquiry which prevail in science can be brought to bear in any useful way upon practical school problems is a very recent notion. Its recentness may, indeed, be judged from the fact that the Laboratory School was, like the two other factors which we have considered, a pioneer. With the exception of a kindergarten maintained for a short time under the auspices of a department of education at Leland Stanford University, the school had no predecessor. Taken as forming a factor, then, in the significance of the School of Education, the incorporation of the Laboratory School marks the necessity of training teachers, not only by giving them inspiration, practical insight, and skill, but by giving them command of the most fundamental intellectual tools of the work which they are called to do. Over and above this, it stands for necessity of making the body of thought upon which education depends something more than, upon one side, a set of abstract and general theories, reinforced by a large amount of routine and empirical devices, upon the other. It commits the School of Education to the significant task of continuous research into the principles underlying educational practice, and to continual criticism of methods that are in practical use, with a view to influencing intelligent thought and practice all over the country—a function which the Laboratory School had already fulfilled to a surprising extent, considering its short history and modest equipment.

Speaking in terms of relationship to the University, the incorporation of the Laboratory School signifies bringing to bear of the intellectual methods of which the modern university is the appropriate home and embodiment, upon all the questions of education, both elementary and secondary. To infuse lower education with the intellectual ideals which inspire university work, to show how the methods and operations of mind which are so fruitful for discovery and application in the highest flights of the mind can be made effective and operative from the very beginning of the school training of the child, is surely a fact of considerable significance. All of that significance is now embodied in the life of the School of Education.

The South Side Academy was founded in the year 1892 especially as a preparatory school for the University. This institution thus completes the circuit of connections with the University. To have represented here simply the training of teachers, simply the modern, more practical and applied, aspects of education, or even simply inquiry and application of scientific method, would still leave a gap. An educational institution which contains and represents all possibilities of the educational situation must surely include the important work of giving the information, discipline, and culture which are necessary for entering upon university work. At times, many of us become impatient with the seeming slow advance of educational ideals in our colleges, and revert more or less jocosely to the mediaeval origin of such institutions; but in our sober and serious hours we all know that the college is a noble exponent and organ of all the things that are necessary to our higher life; and that any abating of its interest in that vague and somewhat intangible thing we call culture, would bring about a permanent loss in what is most worth while in our life. If the university is of such importance, then of equal importance are the institutions which devote themselves to preparation for it. "The College Preparatory School" is a phrase sometimes used as a term of reproach. Sometimes college preparation does mean a narrowing of the kind of work done, a restriction upon preparation for full participation in all the ranges of social life, and then the term rightly carries some depreciatory coloring with it. But this is unnecessary, and, indeed, a perversion. As long as colleges exist, and adequately perform their social service, so long will college preparatory work also be an honor and not a reproach. If the cultural work of schools became too remote and abstract and dead, because of isolation from the more immediately practical, moving force of society, so also manual and commercial education easily becomes cramped, servile, and hard when apart from the illuminating and expanding elements of a cultural education.

This, then, is the answer of history to our question as to the significance of the School of Education. Put in terms of its origin, the School of Education signifies a bringing together of all factors of the educational problem. Upon the personal side it cherishes and maintains continuity with the past. While the great leader, Colonel Parker, has gone, a large part of the faculty trained by him is today a part of the School of Education. The original director of the Chicago Manual Training School, and a staff some parts of which have been connected with the same work almost from the beginning, participate in our present work. We have also those who have been connected from their inception with the Laboratory School and the South Side Academy. The roster would not be complete if I did not include one who, through connection with the Department of Education and the Laboratory School, also brings the School of Education into the most intimate contact with the Chicago schools, thus enabling the School of Education to embody as a living part of its own work the fruits of a career of labor and honor in our public-school system. There is a piety of history as well as a natural piety, and I am proud to have the honor of reminding all present that the School of Education, instead of abruptly and violently severing it from the past, has at all points, so far as possible, gathered up into itself the wisdom and the experience that accrue with the growing years. I am glad also to be able to say that, while the School of Education is an endowed, and in that sense a private, school, its whole past history commits it to the idea that as it grows out of, so it is to grow into public-school work, to be a help and encouragement in its growth.

But what does all this signify as to the future? The story indicates that the School of Education is not a *parvenu*. It has earned the right to its position through years of toil and struggle and conflict. Yet all this does not answer the question as to what it is to signify for the future of education.

I suppose all concerned with the School are met from time to time with the remark that it must be a work of very great difficulty to weld or fuse into one whole so many different elements. But this remark applies only to the mechanical side of the school situation. It is true, just a question of mechanics. But higher and deeper lie what may be termed the *organics* of the School. The fact is that here a number of living organisms, each doing well its own work, but each doing a limited work, have been brought into such living relation with one another as to enable each to receive and to get reinforcement. The problem is not one of mechanical adjustment, but of living multiplication and reproduction. Each element brings to the whole School of Education a factor without which there could not be an educational whole, and hence a factor which reacts upon every other so as to increase its efficiency and multiply its power.

It is especially significant to note that the School of Education now incarnates in itself all the elements which constitute the theoretical educational problem of the present. I mean we have right here in concrete, actual institutional form all the factors which any writer on education of the present day would lay down as involved in the problem of education. Thus we have the so-called practical and utilitarian element. This comes not merely from the Chicago Manual Training School, but from the stress laid from the first in the Cook County Normal School upon manual training, and the important place given in the Laboratory School to social occupations. Thus the motor, the executive side of the individual is appealed to. The School of Education recognizes that an "all-around-education" is a mere name if it leaves out of account direct interest in seeing things and in doing things. The so-called practical and utilitarian factor is thus here not an isolated and independent thing, but the utilization of an otherwise wasted (and hence perverted) source of energy. But the School also stands for the most thoroughgoing recognition of the importance of scientific and cultural elements in education. Moreover, the School stands for these things, not merely within its own structure, but (through the training of teachers and the promulgation of sound educational theory) for educational progress and reform far beyond itself. I can imagine no greater catastrophe than that an institution which embodies within itself three distinct lines of pioneer work should become so institutionalized, or so content to rest upon its past, as not to recognize that there is still pioneer work to do, and that there always will be as long as the horizon of life recedes with every step we take. To have initiated these distinct and independent portions of an educational system represented here, was a great achievement. To stop here, not to recognize the growth that may come from their fusing into a vital whole, would be a calamity all the greater because of what has been achieved in the past.

I should not be surprised to know that some of the parents who hear me have been asking themselves, as I have been speaking, why these matters are put before them rather than before the teachers in the various schools which have come together. The answer is simple and direct. It is because the teachers coming from these various institutions, and elsewhere, and who now constitute the teaching staff of the School of Education, cannot do the work which they have to do without a cooperation which depends upon your sympathy. And by "sympathy" I do not mean either a mild and courteous toleration, or a willingness to excuse and palliate our various mistakes, but a sympathy which *understands* what it is that we are trying to do, and which cooperates and criticises because it understands and thus wants to help us better perform our own task. There is one kind of coeducation to which no one takes objections—one which is absolutely indispensable if the future of the School is to be as significant as its own past exacts of it. This is coeducation of teachers, children, and parents by one another. I say *by* one another rather than *with* one another, for I think coeducation is not the passive reception of the same instruction side by side, but the active participation in the education of one by others. If the School is to move along steadily and as a whole within itself, it must be because it moves along with the body of parents who have entrusted their children to it, and because in turn the parents move along sympathetically with the endeavors and experiments and changes of the School itself.

Hence I have not hesitated to put before you the past of the School as indicating the problems which it has to meet in the future. I am sure that, if you will but bear in mind this past and consider the particular portion of the School in which you individually are most interested—elementary, high school, academic, or manual training—from the standpoint of the complex whole into which each such part enters and in which it must function, you will understand the work of that particular part much better, and be able to extend a more effective sympathy to us in the way both of encouragement or of criticism.

To make this very general talk somewhat more concrete, let me close by mentioning a particular point in which we shall especially and increasingly need your cooperation. In spite of all the advances that have been made throughout the country, there is still one unsolved problem in elementary and secondary education. That is the question of duly adapting to each other the practical and the utilitarian, the executive and the abstract, the tool and the book, the head and the hand. This is a problem of such vast scope that any systematic attempt to deal with it must have great influence upon the whole course of education everywhere. The School of Education, both in its elementary and secondary departments, is trying to make its contribution to this vexed question. Utility and culture, absorption and expression, theory and practice, are indispensable elements in any educational scheme. But, as a rule, they are pursued apart. As already indicated, the different schools which have entered into combination here make it necessary for the School of Education to fuse hitherto separated factors. In this attempt we shall need your sympathetic intelligence. The fusion cannot be carried on without some modification, some transformation upon each side. It will be necessary to introduce more of the physical and manual element, more of expression in art, and of construction in the shop into the academic curriculum. On the other hand, without attacking or weakening the integrity of technical and technological preparation, it will doubtless be found necessary to infuse the more direct industrial and practical education with things derived from the larger outlook of history, science, and all we mean by general culture. Just because the isolation of these things in the past has told so heavily against the best interests of education, it is all the more necessary for an institution like the School of Education not to perpetuate this divorce, but to take earnest, constant, and progressive steps toward developing a balanced educational system in which each element shall have its proportionate place, at the same time enabling students to emphasize whatever side their own tastes and interests most definitely demand.

In the second place, I wish to enlist your sympathy with the social ideals and spirit which must prevail in the School of Education, if it is to be true to its own past. We trust, and shall continue to trust, to the social spirit as the ultimate and controlling motive in discipline. We believe, and we believe that our past experience warrants us in the belief, that a higher, more effective, more truly severe type of personal discipline and government may be secured through appeal to the social motives and interests of children and youth, than through an appeal to their anti-social ones. We have confidence in their responses to the normal demands of an orderly social life, rather than in their reactions against exactions which seem to them personal and arbitrary. The growth of this social spirit in an institution the size of this School must, indeed, be slow, but there is absolutely no reason why it should not be steady and irresistible—no reason, at least, if the parents understand the methods that are operating, and in all their conversations and intercourse with their own children, and with the teachers of the School, co-operate to this end.

There are, of course, very different methods of conducting a school, so far as what is ordinarily termed order and government are concerned. Doubtless part of the most important and influential result of the work of Colonel Parker was due to the constant warfare that he waged against appeal to purely extraneous and external motives in education—the use of bribes and threats as means of keeping students at their work and "in order." No experienced and successful teacher has any doubt that right *instruction* is the primary means of maintaining discipline. Students who are interested in their work and in doing their work well are not students who are a menace to the well-being of the school. Wherever there are boys and girls there will be a certain amount of mischief and carelessness. Such things are easily enough taken care of as they show themselves. The only serious threat to a school's "order" is found in a class of students who decline more or less deliberately to accept responsibility for their own conduct; and who consequently throw it back upon the teachers to see to it that they behave themselves properly. Under this system more or less constant espionage, a system of definite and detailed rules, appeal to purely competitive motives, reports, comparative standings, become inevitable parts of the school system.

The School of Education feels, however, that it is offering facilities which ought to appeal to a class of both parents and teachers who want a different kind of a school. There certainly is within the area which the School of Education can draw upon a sufficiently large number of parents and students who are interested in education for the sake of education, and in the school for the sake of what can be got from it worth having to justify an attempt to reduce to a minimum all of these mechanical and unworthy devices for keeping school order. It must be possible on some other basis to secure and maintain a wholesome social and moral spirit in the school. It cannot be too definitely stated that it is only to this class that the School of Education wants to appeal for material for its student body. It does not anticipate nor demand an unreasonable, much less a priggish, perfection from its students. But it does want and expect those who come to it to be sufficiently aware of and interested in the educational privileges which are extended to them to take some initiative in developing that tone and atmosphere which will make unnecessary a servile dependence upon the ordinary machinery of petty rules, constant markings, reports, etc. The moral and social influence which the members of the student body exert upon each other is far more potent for good in the long run than any devices which teachers can set up and keep going; and the presence or absence of this influence must go back largely to home influences and surroundings.

The School of Education wishes particularly, then, the cooperation of parents in creating the healthy moral tone

which will render quite unnecessary resort to lower and
more unworthy motives for regulating conduct. We also ask
the cooperation of the parents to help make the school in
some sense an organizing centre for the general social interests of the children, so far as these are carried on outside
of their own homes. We do not wish the School to take the
place of the home in furnishing children and youth with
natural social recreation and modes of intercourse, but it is
desirable that the interests, in the way of diversion and
recreation, of children out of school be at least in general
harmony with the pursuits of the children in school. Such
matters as simplicity in dress, to the extent at least of fitness
of dress for the school work which is to be done, and of lack
of ostentation and display, are not to be despised. The culti-
vation of a democratic tone, an *esprit de corps* which attaches
itself to the social life of the school as a whole, and not to
that of some clique or set in it, requires no apology for mention. Indeed, an indefinite number of things might be
specified. But time does not permit this, and so I must confine myself to the general statement that we hope that you
will not look at either the Elementary or the High School
as a place to which your children go just for the sake of
receiving instruction. We hope you will remember that a
school has a corporate life of its own; that, whether for good
or for bad, it is itself a genuine social institution—a community. The influences which centre in and radiate from this
corporate social life are indefinitely more important with
respect to the moral development of your children than is
simply class-room instruction in the abstract; and with reference to development of an all-around intellectual efficiency is
at least a matter of equal importance.

Without, then, any further attempt to specify details of
matters in which we shall need your cooperation, I may
close with an exhortation to bear in mind the fundamental
importance to yourselves and to your own children, as well
as to the School, of the maintenance of the right sort of
social aims and spirit throughout the School as a whole.

CULTURE AND INDUSTRY IN EDUCATION

There may have been a time when the problem of the relation of industry and education had to be read in this way: what shall the school do for industry? But now the question has to be read the other way about: what is industry to do for the school? or, rather what is it to do *with* the school? Business is the dominating force in modern life. It underlies and it shapes the activities and enjoyments, the possibilities and the achievements, of even those who have least to do with it—who perhaps pride themselves on having nothing to do with it.

In politics, recent revelations have brought it to the minds of the American people that our public life is in the dominion of business methods and aims. The political amateur may have whiled away his time discussing what the government should or should not do for business and commerce. The average voter imagined himself voting in accordance with principles which regulated the activities of political parties. But today the average man has a suspicion that political parties, their leaders and platforms, are agencies administered by commercial forces. The serious question is not what politics is to do for business, but what business is to do with our politics.

In like way, the academician within the walls of his own study, dreaming that he is a spiritual leader of the forces of which he is in fact a tamed parasite, may conceive modern business and education as two independent institutions; and may consider whether the ties between them should be loosened here or tightened there. Meantime unconsciously if not consciously, by force of conditions if not by intention, the ideals and methods that control business take possession of the spirit and machinery of our educational system.

[First published in *Proceedings of the Joint Convention of the Eastern Art Teachers Association and the Eastern Manual Training Association*, 1906, pp. 21–30.]

If there is to be any result save blind conformity, passive reproduction, it must proceed from facing the overlordship of industry in modern life, with all that it imports. The question as respects education is how the school is to secure the good and avoid the ill of this sovereignty; how it may select and perpetuate what in it is significant and worthy, and may reject and expel what is degrading and enslaving.

This problem is the more urgent because the notions of both education and industry which exist in the minds of the cultivated classes of the community, the ideas that are the signboards of the traditional path of culture in Europe and America, are survivals of a belief in the separation, even opposition, of education and industry. Pardon me if I take you to the fountain head of these ideas—to Aristotle, who formulated them. He, speaking not for himself, but for the marvelous life of Greece, saw life divided into two parts, one the superior, the intrinsically valuable realm—that of ends, goods in themselves; the other, secondary, necessary, yet base because not valuable intrinsically—the region of means. The aim is to live a life of cultivated leisure in the possession of the final goods; to exercise reason, to enjoy knowledge, to share in the results of the arts, to take some part in the formation of the ideas that regulate public life, to engage, that is, in the communication, the exchange of thought.

Such a life must be underpinned and buttressed with the needful means. It exists only when based upon command of the necessities of life; food, clothing, shelter, enough, in short, of economic wealth to safeguard and to adorn life. The life of cultured leisure which alone is worthy in itself, the life of the spirit, requires the substructure of the economic, the material life. Work exists for the sake of leisure, industry for the sake of culture, as war exists for the sake of peace, but one and the same person cannot have both. Work is needful for the existence of the higher life, which is the aim of education, and yet it is incompatible with it.

Separation of classes was the source and the outcome of this scheme. Artisans, craftsmen, mechanics, handworkers of all sorts, since engaged in activities which have their worth beyond themselves, are menial, servile. Their occupations disfigure and degrade the body as they distort and harden the soul. They fill the mind with utilitarian and mercenary interests. They make such demands on time and energy as to leave no leisure for culture and participation in the public life of ideas. It is impossible, so Aristotle sums up the matter, to live the life of a laborer and devote one's self to the pursuit and exercise of excellence. No one except base in soul or compelled by hard necessity will consent to such a life.

A true education is a liberal education: that is an education designed to prepare one to share in the free life of leisure; designed to form the habits that have to do with the practice of things excellent in themselves. Its aim is not preparation for living, but for noble living, for enjoying, without engaging in industrial production, science, art and the direction of public affairs. Such an education keeps itself as far as may be from everything industrial, utilitarian, professional. The functions of an artisan are not such, says Aristotle, as should be learned by any good man, except occasionally for the satisfaction of his own wants. To labor for others is slavish. Nor was a distinction put between the artist and the artisan. Pupils are to be educated in the performance of the arts only so far as is necessary to secure ability to appreciate the results of the performances of others. Anything else is professional, that is, servile. The fact that stands out here, a fact as obvious as a pyramid on a plain, is that the separation in education between culture and labor, between a liberal and a professional training, is the reflex of a more fundamental social difference between a working class and a leisure class.[1] Educational division lines grew out of social stratifications just as they perpetuate them. It is not that Aristotle created these distinctions. But he honestly looked the social facts of his times in the face, and translated what he saw into their intellectual equivalents. This report was the differentiation of workers and thinkers, the busy and the leisured, those occupied with material and with ideal things, and the corresponding division of educa-

---

1. This did not mean necessarily a separation between the rich and the poor. In fact, Aristotle speaks of the industrial class as likely to be rich. The fact that they continue at business in spite of their being well-to-do is only another proof of the debased character of their minds.

tion into that which was for use and that which was for culture.

So far as the social differentiation still persists, so far it still fixes the fundamental cleavage in educational theory and practice. It cannot be denied that the social separation continues. In many respects the objectionable qualities which led Aristotle to condemn the life of labor and commerce have increased. Physical constraint with its evil mental results, division of labor, with accompanying lack of initiative and lack of knowledge of the basis and aim of the activity in which one is engaged, fierceness of competition and desire to exploit others, the importance attached to sheer money possession—these things have increased, not decreased since Aristotle's time.

For some years, I preserved a little piece of cast iron taken from a typical American factory, one of our large agricultural machinery works. I preserved it as a sort of Exhibit A of our social and educational status. The iron came out of the casting with a little roughness upon it which had to be smoothed off before it could become a part of the belt for which it was designed. A boy of fifteen or sixteen spent his working day in grinding off this slight roughness —grinding at the rate of over one a minute for every minute of his day. When we consider the stupefying monotony of such activity, its total lack of intellectual and imaginative content, its absolutely routine character, one can conceive how far the present day is justified in throwing stones at Aristotle for his frank description and appreciation of the industrial situation.

Practically we have established a universal system of schooling at the public expense. In theory this extends from kindergarten to or even through college. But we know that the vast majority of boys and girls leave at the end of their fourth or fifth grade. And why? To go to work, and in the cities, for the most part, to go to work at relatively unskilled forms of labor. We know that our present scheme of industry requires at hand a large supply of cheap, unskilled labor. We know that this precludes special training; that the education which should develop initiative, thoughtfulness and executive force would not turn out recruits for our present system.

And, if we are honest, we know that it is not intended that these shall be turned out in numbers except such as may be required to take charge of running the machinery to which the masses are subordinate.

In short, we are engaged in training a comparatively small number for an academic life of leisure and culture; we are engaged in failing to train the great number so that anything but somewhat passive and dulled participation in unidealized labor is possible to them; we are permitting a few to train themselves so as to control the labor of these masses to their own ends. It is this which makes me say that the question is not so much what the schools are to do for industry, as what our industrial system is to do with the schools.

There are, after all, fundamental differences of a more favorable sort between the Greek situation and ours. In the first place, the ideal of an interdependent life has taken the place of that of an independent life. The world market, the world commerce, the system of production for wide distribution with its vast mechanism of exchange, has bound us closely together in one whole. The idea of a self-contained, self-sufficing life in economic isolation has become impossible. As Carlyle grimly remarked when a contagious disease starting in slum sweatshops had found its way to the homes of the well-to-do to whom the poor laborers purveyed, industry has made all the world one, if not for good, then for evil.

In the second place, ancient industry rested on routine and custom, as ancient commerce, carried on almost solely for objects of luxury, rested on adventure and semi-piracy. Modern industry and modern exchange rest on science—on the application of ideas to the management of nature's energies. The individual workman may have but little cognizance of this intellectual foundation and outlook, but it is there and controls the whole process.

In the third place, the laboring classes are no longer excluded from participation in the management of public affairs. In principle, and increasingly in fact, the division into fixed social classes, one superior the other inferior, has given way. These are conditions making for fluidity, transfer and circulation.

Each one of these changes means something typically important for education. With the substitution of interdependence for independence goes the idealization of work, of labor. The merely leisure life appears to our present conscience as a vain, an idle life. To render service to others is not now the badge of servility, but the insignia of moral nobility. The dependence upon applied science of modern methods of production and distribution renders impossible a fixed separation of theory and practice with exaltation of the former and contempt for the latter, inevitable enough where industry meant blind routine and commerce blind adventure. Industry has henceforth inherent backing in intelligence, inherent outlook upon the things of the spirit. It is elevated to the plane of reason, of truth; and speculative or theoretic intelligence is found to be crippled and halting until securing its outlet and test in the fuller reality of action.

The third change noted, the extension of suffrage and of public power to the masses, is equally fraught with educational import. When laboring people are excluded from political activities, it is possible to maintain a double system of education, one sort for cultured leisure called liberal, the other sort for work, called professional, mechanical, utilitarian. But now that our final political destinies have been put in the charge of those who labor, it is foolish to imagine either a conserved or a progressing society without that free and large education which should give them a maximum of insight and appreciation. To borrow a phrase from English political history: "We must educate our masters," and unless we wish to be badly mastered we must educate them well.

Such are some of the motives which are back of the persistent effort, along the whole line of educational activity, to break down inherited traditions as to what constitutes a liberal education, to fill the gulf between vocation and culture. Quite apart from the truth of the generalizations which I have permitted myself, one has only to look at the present educational situation from the kindergarten to the university, to see that, whatever be the theoretical explanation, the most interesting and vital problems in educational practice today are such as concern the connexion of play and work, of the intellectual and informational and the dynamic and motor factor; of instruction from books and teachers and from self-guided productive activities; such as concern in short the development of a type of education which shall make at once a man or a woman and a worker.

Our higher education is hastening to introduce schools of commerce as well as schools of technology; our secondary education is transforming itself through schools or courses for the manual arts and for commerce; the effort is put forth not merely to enrich but to reconstruct elementary education by the introduction of constructive and productive activities —and these not as frills but as fundamentals. There is an agitation for trade schools, or for the development of industry in education till it becomes a more serious factor in preparation for the realities of economic life; or at least for some educational method which shall do the work of the dying, or dead, apprentice system.

I have spoken of industry in relation to our traditional ideas of a cultural education. It would not be seemly to speak to a joint meeting of art and manual training teachers without also a few words regarding art in education. Fortunately for me those few words are just those necessary to the integrity of my argument. The instinct of the Greek in classifying together artist and artisan, was, I think, correct and prophetic: Not that the artist is to be pushed down to the plane assigned by the Greek to the craftsman, but that the laborer is to be brought up to the level assigned by us to the creative artist. For after all, is there any way in which the life of industry can avoid the ethical taint of servility save through informing itself with the spirit of art? On the educational, as on the social side, this is perhaps our supreme, our test question.

Recent educational theory has tended increasingly to centralize itself about the idea of the fundamental importance of the prolongation of infancy; the period of relief, of leisure, from the stresses and strains of independent economic activity. Childhood is, we have learned to say, preeminently the play time; education, the play time and freedom from direct economic pursuits are all synonymous terms. There is, then, something almost ludicrous, something at least paradoxical in our situation. We proclaim the growing importance of industry as an educational factor at the very time when we have discovered that play is the key to education. We are fighting, on one hand, child labor in the factory, while we are urging child industry in the school.

In truth this situation would present an insoluble contradiction were it not for the intervention of art. Art is always the mean term, the connecting link, of play and work, of leisure and industry. Even Aristotle admitted that it was not so much what was done as it was the spirit in which it was done that made it free or servile. The very freedom of childhood from direct economic responsibility gives all the more opportunity for reproduction and mastery of the typical industries which maintain and forward social life, freed from mercenary and competitive associations and saturated with human and scientific significance. To accomplish this is to raise the industrial factor in education to the artistic plane, and thereby to cover the distance between work and culture.

Play is not amusement; the play of childhood is not recreation. Amusement and recreation are ideas which require a background of monotony, or enforced toil, to give them meaning. Play as work, as freely productive activity, industry as leisure, that is as occupation which fills the imagination and the emotions as well as the hands, is the essence of art. Art is not an outer product nor an outer behavior. It is an attitude of spirit, a state of mind—one which demands for its satisfaction and fulfilling a shaping of matter to new and more significant form. To feel the meaning of what one is doing and to rejoice in that meaning, to unite in one concurrent fact the unfolding of the inner life and the ordered development of material conditions —that is art. The external signs—rhythm, symmetry, arrangement of values, what you please—these things *are* signs of art in the degree in which they exhibit the union of inner joyful thought and outward control of nature's forces. Otherwise they are dead and mechanical.

Art in a word is industry unusually conscious of its own meaning—adequately conscious, emotionally and intellectually. In the impact of economic life under present conditions, there is slender opportunity for such consciousness—hence our art itself is corrupt with the separation of beauty from use, of leisure from work. But the period of education is just the period in which the play of productive and manipulating activities may become surcharged in their performance with such fulness of social and scientific meaning that the association, once established, shall never be lost. There is always danger that an educational preparation for industry shall become over-technical and utilitarian, carrying back into the school the most undesirable features of the present industrial régime. Our protection lies in making the industrial activities in the school artistic. Or there is danger that the harshly utilitarian be escaped only at the risk of an obviously amateurish fooling with occupations—a reduction of the play idea to make-believe and idle pretense. The remedy once more is to make the play of childhood productive, efficient of results; to make it art. This alone refines and idealizes the harsher and duller features of labor while it directs and articulates the play spirit, which, pursued apart from productive control of physical materials, becomes weak and sentimental. Art is like industry in that it must achieve visible and tangible embodiment ministering to human use —a result so visible and tangible as to involve judgment by palpable standards, while so ministering to the human spirit as to carry its own standard with it in the joy of thought it expresses and feeds. Like industry, it needs definite tools, accurate processes, an exact technique. But in elevating the materials, the technique, the outward means and ends, into the region of personal imagination, it gives an education which educates not alone to specific utilities and commodities, but to the widest of all uses: to the just apprehension of values wherever and whenever presented. So I end as I began. Let us cease asking ourselves what the school can do for industry, and let us begin asking ourselves what industry, conceived in the spirit of art, may do for the school.

[Remarks on "Shortening the Years of Elementary Schooling" by Frank Louis Soldan]

I find myself in such accord with the proposition that I shall not take your time in making any arguments against it. The reasons for it have been so fully presented that I do not see my way to add anything in that line. So I shall confine my remarks to raising two questions which come to the minds of all of us, and making some statements suggested by these questions.

1. Will the reduction of the elementary period to six years tend to restrict the movement now making to enrich the curriculum; by which I understand the movement to introduce more worthy objects of study and important modes of activity? Will it promote a reaction to the more formal and mechanical course which we are just now at great cost escaping?

2. Will the beginning of more specialized and professional work at the very outset of the university period tend to exclude important facts of general culture from the education of those going into professions?

I put the question in this way because, if these results were to follow, I suppose we would all condemn the propositions before us; because they suggest real dangers, and yet suggest their own adequate answer. If the proposition were carried out in a purely mechanical way—simply lopping of a year here and transferring it bodily from this year to that—then the scheme would undoubtedly have these undesirable results. But this quantitative and external re-arrangement is only, I take it, for the purpose of securing administrative conditions of an internal and qualitative readjustment. The real value of the scheme is in the opportunity it affords and the demand it makes for a more efficient division of labor between the elementary, secondary, and collegiate members of the educational organism.

[First published in *School Review* 11 (1903): 17–20.]

While there is altogether too much separation between the grades and the high school and the high school and the college, there is not enough distinction. The separation is in the outward forms; too many barriers; too many encouragements to dropping out at the various transitions; too many discouragers from continuity. But at the same time there is too little recognition, practical and theoretical, of the definite kind of work most profitably to be undertaken by each.

The elementary school has too long a period to be occupied advantageously with its own particular task; it is induced and even compelled to assume aims outside of its own proper function, to the confusion of its own work, and to the detriment of the service it might render other parts of the system. The high school, on the contrary, has too little time to perform its own work, and consequently it is cramped and irritated and hurried in its operations.

1. *The elementary period.*—It would seem as if the length of time allowed would enable the elementary school to accomplish its own work and do something besides. But the length of time allotted represents a misconception of the aim of this period, and so tends to a misdirection of energy. The aim, as ordinarily considered, is to cover a certain amount of ground in studies and thus acquire a certain amount of knowledge. Since this represents all the information the mass of future citizens will get in any scholastic way, there has been a constant tendency to increase the term of time so as to cover more ground.

When I say that the acquiring of knowledge is not the proper end of elementary education, and to make that the aim is to encroach upon secondary instruction, I do not mean that children at present are getting too much knowledge. Of course, they get too little, and less, in my judgment, than they would get if the focus of effort was somewhere else. I mean the aim is placed wrong. The proper aim of elementary tuition, I should say, is to organize the instincts and impulses of children into working interests and tools. The stress should be upon method, not upon result; not that we do not want results, but that we get better results, when we transfer the emphasis of attention to the problem of mental attitude and operation. We need to develop a certain active interest in truth and its allies, a certain disposition of inquiry together with command of the tools that make it effective; and to organize certain modes of activity in observation, construction, expression and reflection.

Six years ought to be enough to accomplish this task. And the limiting of the period to that time would, in my judgment, tend in the long run to make clear what is the real issue of elementary education. Such an outcome in the minds of the general public and of teachers would free energy from devotion to false aims and irrelevant tasks. The elementary school would be relieved of its two chief time-wasting factors: on one side, daily repetition of drill in rudiments which have been previously mastered; and, upon the other, anticipations of advanced subject-matter so difficult that it can be pursued intelligently only at a later period. The present elementary-school child spends too much time in oscillation between doing over again what has already been done, and reaching out in a blind way to do the things belonging to the future. He vibrates too much between marking time, and rushing forward, grasping and uncertain, to come abruptly and violently up against matters for which he has no adequate organs of apprehension. A reduction of time, and an accompanying definition of the real problem and function of the elementary school would have a tendency to remedy both of these evils. In other words, I am unable to find myself in agreement with the distinguished authority who said that the elementary school is all right except in its later years—the grammar-school period. The waste of time in these years appears to my mind only as one aspect of a larger question. The main object in laying hands upon the seventh and eighth grades is to encourage the movement for reconstruction all along the line.

2. *The secondary period.*—As to the fact that the high school has not enough time to do its own work properly, the case is so much clearer that I need not detain you with a detailed discussion. The high school at present has no definite task of its own, and no specific aim. It begins at no definite point and it ends at none. It stops, as President Harper has just told us, in the middle of a situation. It carries nothing to completion, but spends its energy in preparation for a work finished elsewhere. It makes beginnings, of the issue

of which it has no vision, and over the consequences of which it has no supervision. Hence the waste that results from confusion and continual distraction of energy. A six-year period would enable the high school to face its own peculiar problem: That of opening to the mind avenues of approach to all the typical phases of nature and society, and acquiring a sympathetic knowledge of these areas of life—culture, in a word. Facing its own problem without distortion from outside pressure, it would have free space and leisure in which to work out that knowledge of the universe of nature and of humanity that is worth while; and that would enable its graduates to undertake later specialization in professional and research lines in an intelligent way—intelligent both as to consciousness of their own capacities, tastes, and needs, and as to the knowledge of the relations of the particular province to which they are to devote themselves to the whole federated field of life. If I were to take enough of your time, I think I could show the bearings of this proposition upon the conflict in the high school of the scientific, social, historical and linguistic groups of studies. This conflict is now so serious that the average student is either compelled to narrow his sphere of study and thus to narrow himself; or, if he tries to broaden out, to lose himself in a footless marsh.

I am not specially optimistic as to the immediate outcome in this matter. I do not anticipate that a change of time-periods will make an immediate solution along the lines indicated. I have no doubt that the change would be at first of a somewhat mechanical nature. The eighth grade would be transferred to the high school without much re-qualification; some of the preceding work in the elementary grades would be cut off. At first, the high schools in their fifth and sixth years would largely duplicate the present work of the first and second years of college. But this would not last long. There would be a demand for a new adjustment and sequence of work—the broadening of the horizon would suggest new arrangements. The economics of the situation would gradually compel a more internal reorganization. Upon the whole, it is certain that the conditions under which work is done and the aims of that work must fit together.

If we change the conditions, there will be a general,

even if largely unintentional, modification of purposes and consequently of the methods and materials employed. In the due course of time there will be a real system—a unity of aim with the distinction of functions best fitted to realize it in a continuous cooperative way.

INTRODUCTION [to *The Psychology of Child Development* by Irving W. King]

Mr. King has attempted in the following pages to bring out the practical or working value of a certain standpoint and method in psychology. The attempt is made in connection with the mass of material, accumulated in the past generation, having to do with the development of the human individual between infancy and adolescence—for we all need to remember that "the child" is not a distinct genus or species, but is the human being himself in a certain characteristic stage of development. That the development is more rapid, its necessity more imperative, its outward results more obviously striking at this period of the life of an individual than at other times goes without saying. But I believe there is some need for saying what Mr. King has so clearly brought out: that the real interest, both scientific and educational (or moral), in the material of child-study lies precisely in its relation to the general question of development —throwing light upon processes and functions of growth, wherever growth is going on, and by contrast upon arrest of growth and how that is effected. The accumulation of material, the making of generalizations, the collecting of statistical averages, of stories relating to a particular kind of being called "the child," are subordinated to this one end.

There has been much promulgation of the gospel of the "genetic," where in truth only the material, not the method nor the final interpretation, is genetic. As Mr. King has shown, Preyer, the founder of the scientific psychology of childhood, frequently uses pre-existing classifications of psychology upon which evolutionary and genetic ideas (ideas centering in the fact of growth) have taken no effect. He employed them as Procrustean beds by which to measure the

[First published in *The Psychology of Child Development* by Irving W. King (Chicago: University of Chicago Press, 1903), xi–xx.]

meaning of the facts dealt with. The *data* were genetic, but not the method of treating them, nor the conclusions finally reached. The same sort of thing happens in much that is covered by the current term "child-study." Even though the familiar classifications and "powers" of the faculty-psychology are dropped and despised, we may get in their place only discussions of isolated "interests" whether individual or statistically grouped accumulations of incidents and anecdotes, descriptions of the more sensational and quasi-pathological phenomena of childhood and youth. The *material* is genetic, but because it is not considered in relation to problems of *growth*, of development, the final effect and value, both psychological and pedagogic, are not genetic.

When the material, but not the method, is genetic, we are likely to take the observed fact as an isolated thing, complete in itself, needing only to be compiled, compared, or averaged with other like facts, to entitle it to figure in a generalization, or, even worse, in a rule for the proper treatment of "the child" at such a period—as if, it having been shown that 73 per cent of children of a given age take interest in a blood-and-thunder story, it were then urged, as a pedagogical precept, that there is a presumption in favor of children of this age being fed on such stories. The illustration is a purely imaginary one, but not so the state of things of which it is too accurate a symbol. The method, as well as the material, is genetic when the effort is made to see just *why and how* the fact shows itself, what is the state out of which it naturally proceeds, what the *conditions* of its manifestation, how it came to be there anyway, and what other changes it arouses or checks after it comes to be there. Knowledge that 73 per cent of eight-year-old boys and girls have a predilection for stories of the "nickel-novel" order would not be a fact to be despised, but it would be only preliminary to the real scientific problem, and the really practical, or educational, conclusion. We should want to know the *conditions*, the context, social and personal, in which the fact showed itself; we should want to see it, not as an independent fact, but as a fact of developing life, in the history of a mind. We should not know how to explain it scientifically, to tell what its meaning was, until we knew the circumstances which provoked it, which called it forth. We should want to know how largely these conditions were themselves in turn the product of previous conditions, of earlier environing influences, of previous modes of treating and indulging children. We should want to know certain negative or restrictive conditions so as to be able to form a judgment as to how largely this "interest" is a reaction against certain arbitrary and unnecessary limitations which children felt, or how largely it is a wild effort to compensate for certain unnecessary lacks in the surroundings, so that, if these were made good, the real *psychological* interest and attitude at the bottom of the fact would seek and find a radically different expression. And we should hardly be able to know such things until we knew something about the other 27 per cent.

Having placed the fact with reference to its generating and stimulating conditions, we might be able to pass a scientific judgment upon it. But we should not be able to form a practical or educational conclusion—that is, a conception of what mode of action to base upon the fact as thus observed and explained—until we knew something about its *after-history* as well as its prior history. We should want to know how it reacted; how it operated as a condition provoking further changes, or preventing certain lines of growth, and thus tending to arrest retrogression. For in a truly genetic method, the idea of genesis looks both ways; this fact is itself generated out of certain conditions, and in turn tends to generate something else. This latter way of looking at it—the *functional*, as Mr. King has stated and explained it—is necessary to complete the genetic, and it is particularly indispensable when we try to base any practical conclusions, whether moral or instructional, upon the simple psychological facts of the case.

The problem of interpreting children's acts is thus a complex and difficult one in any case. But it is much simplified if we begin with larger and more typical facts, instead of with such definite and specialized instances as that of our imaginary, yet too true, illustration. Mr. King has well brought out the inadequacy of some of the existing material dealing with "interests" of children between, say, six or seven and adolescence. And the reason, I think, is that the forms taken have frequently been so specialized that they are products of social and domestic conditions, of prior modes of education and habituation, too complicated to permit of unraveling in the present state of inquiry. In such cases we get the appearance without the reality of a scientific result. But this complexity should not discourage us from attacking cases of greater generality; an interest in *a* game is likely to be a result of special circumstances; interests relating to a class of games (such as shooting) are more general, while the interest in games as such presents us with a fact of almost uniform generality. We can study, to be sure, only particular games, but the more we keep in mind the features which give them generic meaning, the more we are on the lookout for the conditions that provoke and satisfy the game-interest as such, the more we strive to see what *sort* of a result children get from playing the game, the more likely are we to be on a hopeful trail. Certainly one of the reasons for emphasizing, as Mr. King has done, the importance of a knowledge of the psychology of infancy is that here conditions and results, by the nature of the case, are less highly specialized, less dependent upon local differences in the environments and upon previously formed habits, upon ways in which the child has previously been dealt with by others—a matter even more important than the ways in which he has been consciously instructed.

I come back to my original proposition: the true value, scientific and practical, of child-psychology is not that we may know this or that fact about children, or even know this or that about the constitution of that plenary being, "the child," but that we may know how the growth of a human being proceeds, what helps and hinders, what furthers and what arrests it, and how these results are brought about. When genetic psychology is conceived in this spirit, the quarrel about the practical and moral worth of scientific psychology to the parent and teacher will cease from lack of material to feed upon—but not till then.

This leads me to say that the genetic-functional standpoint, as that is expounded and illustrated by Mr. King, also gives a solution for the controversy about the relationship of child and of adult psychology. We are told that it is only ourselves we know; that it is only ourselves we can directly get at; that our knowledge of the mental and emotional states of children, even when we bring the most sympathetic insight and recollection to bear, must after all be based upon our knowledge of ourselves and be a projection out of our own conscious lives. And this is true. We are also told that in the adult we are dealing with complicated results, with habits of perceiving, feeling, and thinking, which got formed and set and almost automatic in the dim and forgotten past, and that we cannot really analyze or interpret these fixed effects save by reference to children in whom we find the causal conditions still operating. And this is true. Mr. King has sufficiently warned his readers against carrying over bodily, as it were, the events and contents which characterize the adult consciousness into the child's. But the moment we take as our problem the matter of growth (or arrest) we find that the true psychology of adult experience becomes infinitely more available and more indispensable for dealing with and interpreting what the child does and says than was the old rigid classification-psychology. The *kind of situation* that arouses hope, anger, affection, alertness, concentration, comparing, fallacious inference in the adult is that and only that which arouses it in the child. It is only by intimate and thorough acquaintance with the conditions that provoke such responses in *our* lives that we can get a vital understanding of what goes on in children. It is only as we see how our reactions in such matters modify our own further behavior, our ways of thinking and feeling, how they promote growth or tend to arrest us, that we can really judge of influences and effects in children. To fix attention upon the genetic-functional aspect is just the way to enable us to get the full benefit of our study of our own selves, and to make us aware of the reciprocal necessity of knowledge of self in understanding another—be he child or man—and of another in understanding the self.

What we need, in short, for both scientific and educational purposes, is to get rid of *externality* in psychology. Scientific inquirers have largely got rid of the externality of the fixed classifications and definitions of the faculty-psychology, though the latter still hold too firmly in thrall the popular mind. But it is quite possible to substitute an externality of "elements" and "combinations" which have a technical but not a real existence, since they are cut loose from the vital situations in which they originate and function, and are thus petrified into things by themselves. Or it is quite possible to get lost in an externality of brain centres, nerve-cells and fibres. Or again we may leave the externality of rigid classifications only to find ourselves in the externality of the ways and thoughts of children. We cannot have too many experimental facts, nor too many physiological facts, nor too many facts of child-psychology, any more than we can have too much of the *reality* of logical inquiry and organization. But none of these, and no aggregation of them, is psychology, either for the scientific inquirer or for the educator. They are psychology only when they are seen and used in relation to problems of the changes of conscious experience —how they come about and what they do. It is the clearness with which Mr. King has grasped this idea, and the thoroughness with which he has applied it to the material of "child-study" that promises to make his book most helpful not only to professed psychologists but to all who are interested —and who is not?—in attaining a better understanding of children.

Reviews

The Place of Industries in Elementary Education
By Katharine Elizabeth Dopp. Chicago:
The University of Chicago Press, 1903.

The culture-epoch theory in education, like the recapitulation theory in biology is undergoing a promising transformation. The conception no longer is that the individual is
compelled to pass through certain periods of development
simply because his animal or human progenitors passed
through like states. The emphasis has shifted to the common
forces and elements in the life and social process. We now
believe that the human organism goes through a series of
states approximating in some respects those of his animal
ancestors, just because the same life-causes, acting under
similar conditions, bring about like results. Upon the social
and educational side we turn to history, not for light upon
what the child *must* go through, or must be made to go
through, but for help in interpreting the development which
he is actually going through, and for light in guiding that
growth.

This means that the historical method is invading the
business of education, and is likely to be one of the most
fundamental forces in directing its immediate future. In
some sense, every advance in civilization makes the problem of education more and more difficult. It widens the distance between the immaturity of the child (which remains,
so far as we know, practically unchanged upon the physical
or heredity side) and the comprehensive, complex, remote,
and subtle conditions which he needs to master. The new-
comers into civilization find themselves face to face with
technical, mechanical, and intellectual devices and resources
in the development of which they have had no share or lot;
and which are so far beyond them that they have no instinctive or natural means of understanding them. The problem
of education—the problem of establishing vital connections

[First published in *Elementary School Teacher* 3 (1903): 727–
28.]

between the immature child and the cultural and technical achievements of adult life—thus continually increases in difficulty. It is coming to be recognized that the historical method, more than any one thing, is the key which unlocks difficulties. By knowing the social and intellectual conditions under which arose a given industrial device, plan of government, or type of scientific interest and theory, and by presenting that to the child in connection with its social and human context, we put him in the simplest and freest attitude toward it. In my judgment, Dr. Dopp's book is the most helpful thing that has yet been published in the way of giving to teachers this point of view, and of putting them into scholarly and sane relations to the material involved in working it out on its educational side.

The various stages of social development are briefly and yet scientifically described from the hunting, fishing, pastoral, and agricultural stages, the age of metals, travel, trade, and transportation, the city-state, the feudal system, the handicraft system, or period of town economy, up to the industrial system of today, or period of national economy. The special value for the teacher of this summary is that it not merely gives the external facts in a clear way, but also sets forth the mental attitudes and atmosphere that cluster about and are promoted by each period. This last point is brought out with special force in the third chapter, "Origins of Attitudes that Underlie Industry," in which a lucid and straightforward psychological interpretation is given of the evolution of the race-interest in various forms of work and play. For example, it is shown how the pastoral stage is closely related to the evolution of art and of games, especially various forms of athletic tests. The growth of interest in animals and animal activities, and of their imitative dramatic reproduction, is suggested. The relation of the industrial activities of spinning, weaving, etc., to the evolution of conscious interest in rhythm is brought out, etc.

In the fourth chapter the development of interest in various forms of work and play is taken up as that shows itself in the child. Points of similarity in the interests of the child with those of various periods in the race are indicated, not on the ground that the child is predestined to recapitulate the cultural development of the race, but because, having the same career to achieve, there is a present organic necessity for the genesis and growth of similar typical attitudes. With sure, clear touch the drama of psychic evolution in the child is delineated. Practical suggestions are made as to ways in which the teacher can seek and find in the records of the corresponding development of the race, methods and materials with which, not to humor the child, but to assist him in more complete and effective reattainment of the splendid achievements of the race.

The book concludes with a reinterpretation of the educational significance of various occupations and industries in the school. It would be difficult to find a more luminous statement of the educational import of all that goes by the name of manual training, constructive, and occupational work than is presented in this chapter. Many readers will, I am sure, agree with the reviewer in satisfaction at the hint given in one passage that there are other volumes in preparation which will put under the working command of teachers some of the wealth of material which is now locked up in the reports and museums of ethnologists and sociologists. We are emerging from a time in which manual training and constructive work are regarded, in the lower grades, as a form of "busy-work" or a concession to the desire of the child for amusement, and in the upper grades, as having a distinctively technical, or even utilitarian and professional, aim. I know nothing in recent literature more likely to be effective in promoting this educational change and in bringing to light its significant possibilities than the volume now under review.

In conclusion, one ought to recognize the simplicity and clearness of the style of the volume. Because of the ease with which the material is handled and presented, it is likely that only the expert will adequately recognize the amount of actual scholarship and research packed into this little volume of two hundred pages. As a combination of fidelity to fact and truly popular presentation, it may well serve as a model for like attempts in the future.

World Views and Their Ethical Implications
A Syllabus of Lectures in Advanced Ethics.
By W. R. Benedict, Professor of Philosophy
in the University of Cincinnati.
Cincinnati University Press, 1902.

I am glad to have an opportunity of calling attention to this little volume of a hundred pages, prepared as a syllabus accompanying collegiate lectures. No one would doubt for a moment that all systems of philosophy, or World Views, carry with them implications of the utmost significance for conduct; few would deny that one of the main *motifs* in the generation of philosophic systems has been the consciousness of certain ultimate issues as to morality, the possibility of rationally valuing life as worthy or unworthy. Such being the case, it is a striking fact that there is almost a total lack of literature upon the inherent bearings of philosophic standpoints and outlooks upon the moral problems of life. The great writers, Plato, Spinoza, Kant, Hegel, turn up, of course, both in histories of metaphysics as such, and in histories of ethics as such; but rarely do we have a consideration of what the metaphysical view means, *per se*, when translated into ethical equivalents. Professor Benedict's book is worthy of recognition as a sincere and rational attempt at just this translation.

Moreover, the way the test is undertaken is worthy of note. Self-imposed limitations practically exclude periods before Kant—an outcome specially to be deplored, I think, in the case of Spinoza, who is an unapproachable instance of an organic union of a typical World View with a typical theory of life; one which, while analogous in some regards to the Idealistic Monism, finally adopted and expounded by Professor Benedict, has its distinctive points. There is an account of the ethical implications of the systems of Kant, Fichte, Schelling, Hegel and Schopenhauer, occupying about half the volume, while the remainder discusses the ethical implications of systems as such: Dualism, and, under Monism, Materialism and Idealism. The historical account might

[First published in *International Journal of Ethics* 14 (1904): 389–90.]

perhaps be criticized on the ground that in the case of Fichte the treatment falls short of the ideal held in view in the book, and also of the possibilities of the case. It is brief and there is little rendering of Fichte's theory of knowledge and being into their ethical evaluations; Fichte's system might be made very fruitful as a type-case of an effort to construe the whole universe in terms of the moral standpoint as such.

Dualism is rejected on the ground that its ethical correlates are an unsolvable antagonism of good and bad, animal and spiritual, principles in man's life, whose logical outcome is asceticism, and an assumption of an arbitrary struggle of external forces. Materialism is welcomed in so far as it represents a movement toward unity; but is criticized on the ground that it attempts to define existence apart from existence-for-consciousness, which is impossible. Moreover, it is contended that science itself in its apparently most materialistic conquest, physiological psychology, really transcends materialism. "Matter has drawn very close to consciousness. Here, in the consciousness which brain makes possible, is the explanation of matter, the reason for matter, and the reason in matter" (p. 72).

It is impossible to summarize the idealistic Monism set forth by Professor Benedict, because the account is itself but the summary appropriate to a syllabus. It is in line with certain recent renditions of Hegel, notably Bradley's and Royce's, but is truer to Hegel, in the reviewer's mind, as well as more satisfactory in itself, in laying greater stress upon the *positive* significance of conflict and the suffering that attends it, in the constitution of an active and worthful universe, instead of tending to give a negative interpretation of conflict as due to the "finite" over against the complete, or to "appearance" over against Reality. It is to be hoped that Professor Benedict will give in ample form what he has set forth here in outline. Especially noteworthy is the temper in which Professor Benedict holds to the irrationality of a demand for finality—for absolute explanation—upon one side, while, upon the other, he insists upon the moral duty of adopting as a hypothesis that world-view which, all things taken into account, seems to serve relatively best the purpose of rationalizing existence and life.

Humanism: Philosophical Essays
By F. C. S. Schiller. London: Macmillan and Co., 1903.

A reviewer of *Humanism* has an unusually hard task set him and one whose accomplishment he is bound to view with dissatisfaction. For he must either sacrifice its rich variety of concrete content to a statement of a few generalized features; or he must, in behalf of a scheduling and summarizing of detached essays on a multitude of different subjects—as different as "Mephistopheles," "Non-Euclidean Geometry," "Darwinism and Design," "Lotze's Monism," etc.—forego a consideration of what gives the book a claim to be a representative of a single philosophic point of view, the herald of a philosophic system which, if not so new nor yet so unformed in the ages from Plato to Hegel as Mr. Schiller seems to suppose, yet issues in fresh, clarion tones from his trumpet. And in this dilemma the present reviewer elects to stand with the Schiller of the title-page and the preface rather than with the Schiller who in the dozen years between 1892 and 1902 wrote fifteen interesting and most suggestive, but somewhat detached, essays. In a word, it is the general tone and temper of the book that seem to me significant, and to which I shall devote myself, even at the expense of inevitable passing over of pages of fresh and pregnant philosophic construction and criticism—even at the cost (to which it is somewhat harder to reconcile myself) of not recording my almost total dissent from the positions taken in the essays entitled "Activity and Substance" and "Philosophy and the Scientific Investigation of a Future Life."

First, then, as to Humanism itself—not the name, but the fact. What is that attitude which as Mr. Schiller naïvely says—for as even Homer nods, so a sense of humor occasionally fails even Mr. Schiller—he "knows to be habitual in William James and in myself, and which seems to be sporadic and inchoate in many others"? The answer is that as

[First published in *Psychological Bulletin* 1 (1904): 335–40.]

a philosophic standpoint and method it "takes Man for granted as he stands and the world of man's experience as it has come to seem to him. This is only the starting point, from which we can proceed in every direction, and to which we must return, enriched and with enhanced powers over our experiences from all the journeyings of Science" (pp. xvii–xviii). Or again, Humanism is "content to take human experience as the clue to the world of human experience, content to take Man on his own merits. . . . To remember that Man is the measure of all things, *i.e.*, of his whole experience world, and that if our standard measure be proved false all our measurements are vitiated; to remember that Man is the maker of the sciences which subserve his human purposes; to remember that an ultimate philosophy which analyzes us away is thereby merely exhibiting its failure to achieve its purpose, . . . is the real root of Humanism" (pp. xix and xx).

Humanism thus conceived seems to me a method not only sane and sensible, but inevitable almost to the point of the truistic, and it required the chorus of objections in which a dozen critics have joined in the last few months to persuade me that there was, as a standpoint, as a method, anything particularly novel, not to say revolutionary, involved. But the critics with one voice have acclaimed this point of view as subjective, irretrievably so, as individualistic, as solipsistic. When Mr. Schiller remarks that if Man as the standard measure be proved false all further measurements are thereby vitiated, he has, to my mind, answered the critics by anticipation. The standpoint cannot fairly be labelled as per the above, unless the human nature which is taken as furnishing the key and clue to human experience be purely subjective, be enclosed within an exclusively psychical individuality. And if such be the case, it is clearly impossible for this individual to transcend these limits in his philosophizing any more than in any other of his industries or pursuits. The critic has indeed, in such case, the right to condemn "Humanism" as sceptical and solipsistic in tendency; but his right is earned and maintained only at the cost of putting his own critique and his own philosophizing in the same boat. He has pursued the expensive process of fatally disparaging the organ and medium of all science and philosophy in order to put in an unfavorable light a particular method which he does not like.

But surely a thinker may freely avow that he is going to take Man as he finds him, rather than as he might fix him up to be, and is going frankly to recognize that Man so taken is the measure of experience, without thereby having committed himself to "finding" Man made of stubble blown together on a quicksand. Even the Scriptures give us the right to think of Man as composed of a substance as tough, even if as plastic, as clay. It is not clear to me why it is not as open to Schiller, to James, to myself (it is the critics who embolden me to this temerity), as to others to make use of whatever universal and objective factors enter into the human make-up. But as for building upon a hypothetic universality which exists not in everyday concrete human nature, as observation and description, history and analysis reveal that human nature; which exists only in projections which are the special monopoly of philosophy, and which turn out to be projected by a humanity which in its immediately present constitution is only subjective and individualistic—that is a flight which I am willing to deny myself. Meantime there are those who do not share in these pessimistic views of human nature, even "as it is," those who take a more generous view not merely of its possibilities, but of its actualities; who, indeed, are loath to speak of its possibilities save as there is found for them a basis in the actualities.

Humanism necessarily assumes a sympathetic, not an antagonistic attitude towards all the natural sciences. This is not because it reduces philosophy to naturalism, but because it finds it can draw freely upon the methods and results of the sciences in forming its conception of Man as the Measure, or in applying this measure to this or that realm of experience. It is no surprise accordingly to find where Professor Schiller stands as regards the contemporary *crux*: the relation of philosophy to psychology. At many points, most notably throughout the important essay on Truth, he shows himself a thorough disbeliever in that modern revival of the old time heresy of two-fold truth, which holds that something may be true for psychology, and false or else meaningless for logic (and *vice versa*); while he insists upon the renascence of logic which is bound to come when thinking, when truth seeking and testing, is considered in its concrete implications with the emotive and voluntary life. And when the critics object that we have here confusion of merely descriptive science with normative and evaluative science, they make their point (as in the case already noticed) by first ignoring the real position of those whom they criticize, and then by attributing to them the critic's own beliefs.

For the contention of the humanist is precisely the unreality of the separation from each other of describable facts and normative values. The humanist really believes that values *are* normal, even to the extent of being current in life itself. Hence, aims, ideals, standards, are a part of the facts which psychology itself has to reckon with. The factual continuity of biological function and psychological operation with logical norm is one of the most significant things to be noted and described. Similarly the humanist, while feeling the social sciences to be especially near to him, will not balk at any method or datum of the physical sciences, because the physical sciences help one in forming a right conception of what Man the Measure is, and, as Mr. Schiller puts it, of how Man measures, and by what devices one may make concordant his measures with those of his fellow-man. The humanist is thus able to transfer the conception of the unity of all knowledge, which to the epistemological idealist is a barren postulate of an ultimate but unrealizable achievement, into a working postulate of present method. It becomes the idea of the *continuity* of experience; the only idea, so far as I can see, which saves us from the mutually sterilized, and hence sterile, nothing of the natural and the ideal in which the transcendentalist indulges, and from the wholesale merging of the spiritual in the natural which is the materialist's objective.

In the second place, characteristic of Mr. Schiller's work is a worthy and adequate recognition of the significance of experience in its *immediate* aspect. Were not the term sure to be misconstrued as one of denial (that is, of the mediate as real), humanism as expounded by Mr. Schiller might almost be termed *Immediatism*. This phase of his thought is so well wrought out in what seems to me the ablest essay in his volume, that "On Preserving Appearances," that I need hardly do more than refer to it. "The only reality we can start with is our own personal, immediate experience. We may lay it down therefore that *all immediate experience is as such real, and that no ultimate reality can be reached except from this basis, and upon the stimulation of such immediate experience.* . . . The distinction of 'appearance and reality' is *not* one which transcends our experience, but one which arises in it. It does *not* constitute a relation between our world and another, nor tempt us to an impossible excursion into a realm inexorably reserved for the supreme delectation of the Absolute" (p. 192). And the same may be said of course of the distinction between the absolute and the relative, the finite and the infinite, the real and the ideal, subject and object, and all the other antitheses which are dear to philosophy's heart. They all arise *within* immediate experience. And to quote further from Mr. Schiller: "The process of reaching them is everywhere the same; we experiment with notions which are suggested to our intelligence by our immediate experience, until we hit upon one which seems to be serviceable for some purpose which engrosses us. . . . They remain on the same plane of interpretation, and all alike are attempts, more or less successful, to supplement some unsatisfactory feature or other in our primary experience" (pp. 193–94). Here I shall simply add what indeed Mr. Schiller does not deny, but hardly seems to realize the full force of: the necessity of the *genetic* method to put before us (1) the *meaning* of philosophic categories and philosophic antitheses, in terms of their *origin* in typical crises or junctures of immediate experience, and (2) the *validity* of such conceptions in terms of their relative success witnessed in their further career in "supplementing the unsatisfactory features" which called them out. It is this methodological feature which, so far as I understand the matter, specially characterizes the recent *Studies in Logical Theory*, rather than a broader Humanism on one side, or a narrower Pragmatism on the other.

In the third place, a feature which used to be called

Voluntarism, which is now termed Pragmatism, and which personally I should, for reasons which I shall not go into, prefer to call Instrumentalism, is characteristic of Mr. Schiller's thought. In his own words: It is the "thorough recognition that the purposive character of mental life generally must influence and pervade also our most remotely cognitive activities. . . . It is a systematic protest against the practice of ignoring in our theories of Thought and Reality the purposiveness of all our actual thinking, and the relation of all our actual realities to the ends of our practical life. It is an assertion of the sway of human valuations over every region of our experience, and a denial that such valuation can validly be eliminated from the contemplation of any reality that we know" (p. 8). Or, as he develops one phase of it in a footnote which contains some of the most pregnant thinking of the entire volume (pp. 11 and 12), it is the recognition that knowing is itself a kind of action, which like any mode of action modifies the world of reality in which it occurs, the objects at which it is directed. In my judgment the volume would be noteworthy if it advanced only this one idea: that it is sheer superstition, crude survival, that knowing simply reveals a nature which Reality already has, not affecting or transforming or farther determining it in any way. "The determinate nature of reality does *not* subsist 'outside' or 'beyond' the process of knowing it," and all our knowing is a mode of action in which the known reality gains more specifically determined character—this is an Idealism which is experimental, not merely epistemological, and which is ethical, not merely intellectualistic, and which, so far as I can see, alone makes possible a metaphysic which in truth and not merely in word acknowledges Evolution.

This is little enough to say of Mr. Schiller's Pragmatism. But it ought to be enough to suggest, (1) that it is *one* feature of Mr. Schiller's thought, not the "whole thing." It is an important feature, indeed; but it gains its especial prominence just now because of the persistent ignoring in current epistemology of psychological, biological and sociological teachings as to the intimate connections of thought processes with larger emotive and volitional issues. I confess to surprise that its critics have not recognized that if this phase of the new philosophic movement is at times exaggerated beyond its due import, this exaggeration is simply a natural reflex of the prevalent minimizing of it. In any case, there is no excuse for the view which identifies this philosophic movement, in head and in members, with just and only pragmatism. Mr. James, who surely ought to know since he gave the term its present currency, has used it only to express a certain method of testing and evaluating philosophic conceptions. He has never designated the *substance* of his philosophy (as distinct from one aspect of its method) anything but Radical, or Pluralistic, Empiricism. The category of purpose is *a* category, not the only one, and it is a category which, like any other, has its own specific conditions and function within experience; it is not *a priori*, and externally determinative.

(2) There is nothing in pragmatism which commits it to a narrow or offensively practical conception of "Practice." I would not say that there are no serious problems involved in getting a sufficiently broad and comprehensive conception of Practice, of conduct: to define Practice is no easy matter. I would not say that Mr. Schiller, in particular, has not moments in which he gives coloring to the claims of the critics that knowledge is relegated to a mere utilitarian device. But how unnecessary this is appears from the scope of his own definition: "The purposive character of mental character must influence and pervade also our most remotely cognitive activities."

(3) And the sapient remark of almost all the critics that theory is itself a form of action, that knowing too is a mode of practice, instead of standing as a charge or accusation, only repeats one of the most cherished convictions of pragmatism. The only difference is that pragmatism in holding to knowledge, to intellectual operations as a mode of activity, does not believe in the reality of an activity which is confined merely to mirroring, to re-presenting, a preexisting reality. It believes that activity really effects, really counts, really constructs; and that in so doing, it actually modifies Reality, entering into its own inherent evolution. And this by its inherent and primary, not by a derived and accidental law.

The Life of Reason, or the Phases of Human Progress
By George Santayana. First volume, "Introduction and
Reason in Common Sense"; second volume, "Reason in
Society." New York: Charles Scribner's Sons, 1905.

These two volumes, to be followed by three others upon
"Reason in Art, in Religion and in Science,"[1] afford more
than the promise, they afford the potency, of the most significant contribution, made in this generation, to philosophic revision. The volumes evade labeling by any of the nicknames
of philosophic schools. Since probably they do this of conscious choice, it is discourteous to attempt a labeling. In calling the view set forth *naturalistic idealism*, I shall, accordingly, be understood to wish to phrase the impression left
upon my own mind, and to suggest that impression to the
reader, rather than to classify the author. That reason is real,
that it is a life, that its life is the significant and animating
principle of all distinctively human activity, that is, of commerce, government and social intercourse; of religion, art and
science as well as of philosophy; that the life of reason so
expressed is one with the reflective principle in its simplest,
most direct expressions in common sense, that is, in the perception of objects, the acknowledgment of persons, and the
entertaining of ideas—this may well be called idealism, in
the classic, if not in the modern epistemologic, sense. But
equally marked is Dr. Santayana's insistence that reason is
natural and empirical; that it is a direct outgrowth of natural conditions, and that it refines and perfects the nature it
expresses; it is not transcendental either in its origin, its objects—the material with which it occupies itself—or in purpose.

Nature shows itself in a life of sentiency and of impulse.
But some sentient moments mean more, satisfy more, and
are at a deeper level, than others. The significance of such
moments, persistently entertained, constitutes reason. For so

1. The first two of these are now (Jan., 1906) published.

[First published in *Science*, n.s. 23 (1906): 223–25.]

entertained, they afford standards of estimation, of criticism, of construction; they become the starting-points of sustained effort to bring all experiences into harmony with themselves. Vital impulse gives moments of excellence; these excellences, grasped and held, modify vital impulse which now veers in sympathy with the judgments of past and the anticipations of future thus instituted—just because reflection is a consciousness of relative worth, it perforce is a new attitude of will. These better moments, while they satisfy, or are agreeable, are not just pleasures; for "a betterment in sentience would not be progress unless it were a progress in reason, and the increasing pleasure revealed some object which could please" (p. 4). Neither, of course, is reason the abstract formula of the intellectualist. It is the value of feeling consciously operative in the judging and reconstructing of experiences. In reason, the pleasures of sense are included in so far as they can be intelligently enjoyed and pursued.

In the Life of Reason, if it were brought to perfection, intelligence would be at once the universal method of practice and its continual reward (p. 5).

Again,

The Life of Reason is simply the unity given to all existence by a mind *in love with the good*.[2] In the higher reaches of human nature, as much as in the lower, rationality depends on distinguishing the excellent; and that distinction can be made, in the last analysis, only by an irrational impulse. As life is a better form given to force by which the universal flux is subdued to create and serve a somewhat permanent interest, so reason is a better form given to interest itself, by which it is fortified and propagated, and ultimately, perhaps, assured of satisfaction. . . . Rationality . . . requires a natural being to possess or to impute it. When definite interests are recognised and the values of things are estimated by that standard, action at the same time veering in harmony with that estimation, then reason has been born and a moral world has arisen (pp. 46–47).

This conception is made the basis of an appreciation of Greek philosophy, the wisest and most suggestive, though one of the briefest, known to the present writer; and of a

2. The context shows that "the good" is interpreted naturalistically and empirically. It is the persistent consciousness of one's most excellent experiences as these are standards of appraisal and of action.

criticism of liberalism (that is, of conventional naturalism—
always a contradiction), for failing to see that meanings,
values, ideas, are supremely real, are quintessentially, natural; and of transcendentalism, for hypostatizing ideals into
causes and substrates of the universe; for introducing my-
thology by translating meanings into underlying substances
and efficient causes, and thus into physical, instead of moral
realities, which have their energy and career in the aspiring
and volitional life of thought which effects, and which is, human progress.

The working of this discriminative sense of excellence,
and its increasing control of vital impulse, through union
with it, is then traced through "the discovery of natural objects," "the discovery of fellow-minds," the development of
ideas, or of universals as themselves concretions, the relationship of things and ideas, and the sense in which (although consciousness is inefficient) thought practically operates, thus making a transition to the discussion of the
ordinary practical life in which ends, purposes, are pursued.
It is impossible to do justice to the volume, delicacy and
justice of the observations herein contained, or to the pellu-
cid, informed and pregnant style in which these observations
have found their natural expression. A superficial reader,
even the philosophic reader who does not think what he
reads, may infer that there is a lack of system; the ordinary
logical machinery is kept out of sight. But Dr. Santayana has
not only swallowed logical formulae; he has digested them.
There are many books with much pretense of system and
coherent argumentation that have not a fraction of the in-
evitableness and coherency of these chapters. In the main,
Emerson's demand for a logic, so long that it may remain
unspoken, is fulfilled.

Of course, disagreements, divergencies of estimation will
arise. To me, for example, it seems that Dr. Santayana does
scant justice to modern philosophy, to the Lockeian-Kantian
movement; and that, in spite of his sympathy with and appropriation of Greek thought, Dr. Santayana's own position
would be inconceivable, without this movement. One may
believe (as the present writer is inclined to), that Dr. Santayana forces too far the doctrine of the inherently chaotic

or maniacal character of consciousness by itself, suggestive as is that idea, and ignored as has been the element of truth in it. One may also think that in failing to see *how* brute conflict naturally evokes thought, he underestimates the part played in the progress of mankind by the ventures and insistencies of just brute vital impulse, however uninformed; and that accordingly, at times, the pale cast of thought is too emphasized and the fear of individualistic assertion too acute. Again, it seems to me that he gives the indifferency of facts to ideas, to purposes, too absolute a character, failing to see the full strength of the pragmatic doctrine that in a universe in which ends are developed in conception and insisted upon in action, thought must, as a part of the inherent machinery of such conception and realization, attribute indifferency and disregard to the "world of facts"—in order, that is, to free and multiply ends, and to liberate and vary the selection and use of means.

But, with whatever of criticism and qualification, those who think, as does the present writer, that the really vital problem of present philosophy is the union of naturalism and idealism, must gratefully acknowledge the extraordinary force and simplicity with which Dr. Santayana has grasped this problem, and the rich and sure way in which he has interpreted, in its light, the intricacies and depths of our common experiences. It is a work nobly conceived and adequately executed.

Miscellany

INTRODUCTION OF THE ORATOR

It is with a sense of especial appropriateness and of unusual honor that I undertake the fulfilment of the duty assigned to me in this day's auspicious ceremonies—the introduction of Mr. Nicholas Murray Butler, the President of Columbia University and the Orator of the Day.

President Butler ranks among the oldest and firmest friends of that educational work whose successful and beautiful culmination we are here and now celebrating. His interest and support go back to the early days of the struggles and triumphs of the Cook County Normal School under the direction of Colonel Francis Wayland Parker—the true spiritual father of this institution. Those were days when many educational ideas that are now almost commonplace were regarded as strange and almost revolutionary, and when friendship meant a degree of educational independence and courage all too rare. The attachment then formed was strengthened through the later days of the Chicago Normal School and of the Chicago Institute. And so, when the magnificent generosity of Mrs. Emmons Blaine made possible the work whose formal opening we are today signalizing, it is not strange that the Faculty of the School of Education turned with unanimous acclaim to him whose voice we are now to hear.

Moreover, this historic friendship is so helpful and precious, because, while personal to Colonel Parker and his loyal staff, it was also more than personal. It grew up and was fostered because of personal interest in, and devotion to, the highest educational aims and ideals connected with the training of teachers for their calling. When the educational history of the last quarter of the nineteenth century

[First published in *University* (of Chicago) *Record* 9 (1904): 12–13.]

comes to be written, and its significance appreciated to the full, all will realize the importance of the work accomplished by Mr. Butler in the founding and nurturing of what is now the Teachers College of Columbia University. It is not too much to say that the endeavors then put forth represent both the first organized movement in this country to put manual training in its proper place in elementary schools—upon, that is, a strictly educational, not merely utilitarian, basis—and also the first organized movement to put the training of teachers upon the soundest and firmest basis by associating it with university ideals and methods. The Teachers College of Columbia University, of which Mr. Butler was practically the founder as well as the present official head, was the first institution for the training of teachers undertaken in this country under university auspices. As the School of Education is the second institution of this type, we may safely regard the remarkable success attendant upon its prototype as the happiest of omens for the realization of the possibilities inherent in the great institution we are dedicating today.

Finally, we greet President Butler as a distinguished educational leader—a distinction won not merely through apprenticeship in the affairs of practical administration, but pre-eminently through the knowledge and power gained in the constant professional study of educational philosophy and educational principles.

Finally, then, we congratulate ourselves upon the honor of having these noble buildings dedicated to the sublime and spiritual cause of education through the kindly offices of one who, by his own training, study, and writings, has evidenced his right to be an exponent of that cause.

I have the honor of introducing President Nicholas Murray Butler, of Columbia University, who will deliver the address incident to the formal dedication of Emmons Blaine Hall to the work of the training of teachers.

THE ORGANIZATION AND CURRICULA OF THE [UNIVERSITY OF CHICAGO] COLLEGE OF EDUCATION

I. PREREQUISITE FOR ADMISSION TO PROFESSIONAL WORK

Students are admitted as classified and unclassified students.

1. Candidates are admitted as classified students upon the basis of two years' scholastic work over and above a high-school course of at least four years. These two years' work may be done either in colleges or training schools for teachers. It is recommended that the latter be inspected, graded, and accredited through the same University machinery, and upon the same basis, as that now used in analogous cases. This implies that certain students may be admitted to partial standing in the School of Education with the right to transfer to complete standing as soon as certain deficiencies have been completed. (See 2 and II, a.)

2. Candidates are admitted as unclassified students who are graduated from an approved high school; who have had two years' experience in teaching, and have reached twenty-one years of age; and who show themselves prepared to take up study with advantage to themselves; (a) such unclassified students shall be admitted to take at one time not more than two studies in the regular courses; and shall take at least one course in fulfilment of prerequisites for admission as a classified student; (b) but if, in addition to the above requirement, such unclassified students show that they have fulfilled all the requirements for some one line of work, show good reason for not taking a regular course, and also receive the formal recommendation of the instructor in charge of the line of work in which they wish to specialize, they may be permitted to specialize in one line of study.

[First published in *Elementary School Teacher* 3 (1903): 553–62.]

II. GRADUATION

The curriculum is to be so arranged that, taken in connection with the fulfilment of entrance requirements, it may lead to the degree of A.B., Ph.B., or S.B., and also to a Bachelor's diploma in education.

a) It is recommended that statements be prepared showing the amount of work, including both prerequisites for admission and work in the School of Education, required for graduation in each of the courses under III, and that, so far as possible, a system of compensations and transfers be established—similar to the existing statements regarding the "Preparatory and Junior College Schedule Combined," such as is found upon p. 71 of the *Annual Register* for 1901–2. It is expected that in this way both the Bachelor's degree and the diploma in Education may be secured in from two to three years' residence, according to previous attainments.

b) It is recommended that the curriculum leading to one of these degrees be so constituted as not to include an ancient language, excepting as an elective.

III. NOMENCLATURE

The committee recommends the following names for the constituent parts of the School of Education:

1. The College of Education, for the professional work.

2. The University High School, for the combined secondary schools—it being understood that the Chicago Manual Training School constitutes the technological course of the University High School, and as such has its own Dean, Course of Study, Circulars, etc.

3. The Schools, with such distinguishing prefixes as may be determined, for the present University Elementary School, the Laboratory School, and other such schools as may be added from time to time.

The Curricula

Three classes of curricula have been arranged in the College of Education:

I. Courses in Arts and Technology.

II. A General Course for kindergartners, elementary-school teachers, critic teachers, departmental supervisors in elementary schools, etc.

III. Courses for students preparing to teach in secondary schools.

I. COURSES IN ARTS AND TECHNOLOGY

Work in these courses will not lead to a degree. The prerequisites (academic, technological, and as regards experience) will be determined by a committee of the College on Arts and Technology. All persons thinking of entering upon work in any of the following courses should therefore enter into correspondence with the authorities of the College of Education as soon as possible. It will be noted that the following courses are all arranged on the same general plan, viz., 5 Majors in educational theory, 7 Majors in the technical aspects of the subject specialized in, and 6 Majors of elective work. These 18 Majors constitute a course of two years. A Major is regularly 5 hours of work per week. All technological and hand-work is upon the basis of University laboratory courses, viz., 2 hours of such work are the equivalent of 1 hour of a regular recitation or lecture.

1. *Music.*
2. *Speech, Oral Reading, and Dramatic Art.*
3. *Drawing and Painting.*
4. *Modeling.*
5. *Textiles.*
6. *Household Arts.*
7. *Woodworking.*
8. *Metal-Work.*

II. THE GENERAL COURSE

1. *General prerequisites for admission.*—These include:

a) Graduation from a high school or academy accredited by the University of Chicago, or from a school of like standing.

The work of such secondary school must cover the same amount of work required for admission into the Junior Colleges of the University, viz., 15 units. It must also include the units prescribed for admission to all courses, excepting the two units of Latin, for which language work, other than English, may be substituted. The prescribed units are:

History: 1 unit.
English: 2 units.
Mathematics: 2½ units.
Physics: 1 unit.
Foreign Language: 2 units.

The remaining 6½ units may be selected from the official list already provided with reference to admission to a Junior College.

b) Two years' work of a college grade over and above the high-school work already described. This may be done either in a college, or in a normal, or in a training school for teachers.

When the work of such schools has been accredited by the University authorities, it will count in the fulfilment of the specified requirements (given below) for admission to the College of Education. Students graduating from schools whose work has not been so accredited will be admitted on probation, with the understanding that the work they have done will be compared with the list of requirements for admission; and that deficiencies are to be made up either in a Junior College of the University or in the School of Education.

2. *Specific requirements (beyond admission to college) for admission to the General Course in the School of Education.*

Philosophy (including Psychology and
    Ethics) and Educational Theory and
    Practice .... 2 Mjs.
English .... 2 Mjs.
History .... 2 Mjs.
Modern Language, other than English .. 2 Mjs.

NOTE.—In case these 2 Majors, taken in connection with previous work in Modern Language in the high-school course, do not give the student a reading knowledge of at least one Modern Language other than English, additional Majors will be required.

Mathematics .... 2 Mjs.
Science .... 4 Mjs.

NOTE.—Of these four, 1 should be in Botany, 1 in Physiography, and the other 2 in Chemistry or Geology, or in the Biological group.

An Art .... 1 Mj.

NOTE.—This may be Drawing, Shopwork, etc. If not presented for admission, it becomes a condition and is to be taken in the College of Education.

Electives .... 3 Mjs.

NOTE.—These Majors may be selected from any of the subjects named in the above list, or from an Ancient Language.

3. *Curricula of the General Course.*—The General Course includes 18 Majors, or two years' work, and, based upon the fulfilment of the preceding requirements *a*) and *b*), is of the grade of a Senior College in the University. The course is as follows:

Education .... 3 Mjs.
History, English, and Oral Reading ..... 3 Mjs.
Arts .... 2 Mjs.
Mathematics .... 1 Mj.
Science, including Geography .... 3 Mjs.

NOTE.—The work in Arts is upon the basis of laboratory courses in the University, 2 hours being the equivalent of 1 hour in lecture or recitation.

Electives .... 6 Mjs.

NOTE.—These electives may be selected from any of the subjects mentioned in the above list. The student may either distribute these electives with a view to general teaching, or may concentrate them to specialize for kindergarten teaching, critic teaching, departmental teaching, etc.

4. *Graduation from the General Course.*—Completion of the entrance requirements *a*) and *b*) and of the necessary 18 Majors of the curriculum of the College of Education will

entitle a student to receive a special diploma in Education, and also an appropriate Bachelor's degree. The work represents four years over and above graduation from a high school of recognized grade.

III. COURSES PREPARATORY TO TEACHING IN SECONDARY SCHOOLS

These courses have the following features in common:

1. They presuppose the completion of the course of one of the Junior Colleges, or of its equivalent, under present University regulations.

2. They require a certain amount of work in educational theory after the completion of the Junior College work. The amount varies from 4 to 5 Majors in different courses.

3. They require completion of a certain amount of work in the particular subject which the person intends to teach in a secondary school. This varies from 6 to 8 Majors in the different subjects.[1]

These subjects are classified as follows, and constitute the various courses in which an intending high-school teacher may specialize:

History and Civics.	Physics.
Greek.	Chemistry.
Latin.	Geography, Physiography, and Geology.
French.	
German.	Biology (including Zoology and Botany).
English Language and Literature.	
Mathematics.	Home Economics.

4. They require the completion of a sufficient amount of elective work to make up the 18 Majors required for graduation from a Senior College.

NOTE.—In case the student enters upon a course looking toward teaching in a secondary school without having completed certain subjects in the Junior College, these subjects will have to be taken from the elective work of the Sen-

---

1. See also note under III, 4.

ior College. Psychology and Ethics are required for graduation and do not count in fulfilment of the 4 or 5 specified Majors in Education. Each one of the subjects listed also demands completion of certain courses in the Junior Colleges which may, in certain cases, exceed the amount necessary to fulfil the requirements of a Junior College course. In such cases the deficiency must be made up in the Senior College.

Graduation from courses preparatory to teaching in secondary schools.—The courses as outlined above are based upon the present provisions for receiving the degree of either A.B., Ph.B., or S.B. in the University, according to the character of the student's work. In addition, the completion of any one of the courses specified will entitle the student to a professional diploma in Education from the College of Education.

The Senior College Curricula are as follows:

History and Civics.

Education:

General	3 Mjs.	
Special	1 Mj.	4 Mjs.
Political Science: Civil Government of the United States		1 Mj.
History		6 Mjs.
Teachers' Training Course in History ..		1 Mj.
Sociology: Social Origins		1 Mj.
Geography		1 Mj.
Electives[2]		4 Mjs.
Total		18 Mjs.

Greek.

Education:

General	3 Mjs.	
Special	1 Mj.	4 Mjs.
History: Greek History		1 Mj.
Classical Archaeology		1 Mj.

2. In case the student is preparing to teach Civics as well as History, most of these electives should be taken in Political Science.

Greek	6 Mjs.
Electives	6 Mjs.
Total	18 Mjs.

Latin.

Education:
General	3 Mjs.	
Special	1 Mj.	
		4 Mjs.
History: Roman History		1 Mj.
Classical Archaeology		1 Mj.

Latin:
Tacitus' *Germania* and *Agricola*	1 Mj.	
Cicero's *Letters*	1 Mj.	
Latin Writing	1 Mj.	
Ovid	1 Mj.	
Teachers' Courses: General, 2 Mjs.[3]	1 Mj.	
Caesar	1 Mj.	
Cicero and Virgil	1 Mj.	
		7 Mjs.
Electives		5 Mjs.
Total		18 Mjs.

French.

Education:
General	3 Mjs.	
Special	1 Mj.	
		4 Mjs.
History		1 Mj.
French[4]		5 Mjs.
English Literature		2 Mjs.
Electives[5]		6 Mjs.
Total		18 Mjs.

3. One of the teachers' courses counts as the fourth course in Education, specified above, and accordingly is not included in this total.
4. The requirement in French may be reduced if the student presents advanced work in French on admission.
5. A reading knowledge of one modern language besides English and French is desirable.

German.

Education:
  General .... 3 Mjs.
  Special .... 1 Mj.
                                         4 Mjs.

History .... 1 Mj.
German[6] .... 5 Mjs.
English Literature .... 2 Mjs.
Electives[7] .... 6 Mjs.
  Total .... 18 Mjs.

English Language and Literature.

Education:
  General .... 3 Mjs.
  Special .... 1 Mj.
                                         4 Mjs.

History .... 2 Mjs.
English Language and Literature ..... 6 Mjs.
Electives .... 6 Mjs.
  Total .... 18 Mjs.

Mathematics.

Education:
  General .... 3 Mjs.
  Special .... 1 Mj.
                                         4 Mjs.

Mathematics:[8]
  College Algebra or Surveying 1 Mj.
  Analytics .... 1 Mj.
  Calculus .... 1 Mj.
  Theory of Equations ..... ⎫
  Analytical Mechanics .... ⎪
  Calculus .... ⎬ 3 Mjs.
  Modern Synthetic   ⎪
    Geometry .... ⎪
  Teachers' Courses .... ⎪
  History of Mathematics .. ⎭
                                         6 Mjs.

6. The requirement in German may be reduced if the student presents advanced work in German on admission.
7. A reading knowledge of one modern language besides English and German is desirable.
8. Pedagogy of Mathematics included under Education.

Physics:
    General Physics .... 3 Mjs.
    Mechanical Drawing ...... 1 Mj.
                                 4 Mjs.
Astronomy .... 1 Mj.
Electives, enough to make 18 Majors .. 3–12[9]
    Total .... 18 Mjs.

Physics.

Education:
    General .... 3 Mjs.
    Special .... 1 Mj.
                                 4 Mjs.
Mathematics:
    Analytics .... 1 Mj.
    Calculus .... 1 Mj.
                                 2 Mjs.
Physics:
    General Physics .... 3 Mjs.
    Senior-College Physics .... 3 Mjs.
                                 6 Mjs.
Geography: Meteorology .... 1 Mj.
Electives enough to make 18 .... 5–14[10]
    Total .... 18 Mjs.

Chemistry.

Education:
    General .... 3 Mjs.
    Special .... 1 Mj.
                                 4 Mjs.
Mathematics: Analytics .... 1 Mj.
Physics: General Physics .... 2 Mjs.
Chemistry:
    General Chemistry ...... 3 Mjs.

9. Within these limits, 3 to 12 Majors, the number depends on the work done previous to admission to the School of Education. (See "Pre-Pedagogical Courses," p. 339.)
10. Within these limits, 5 to 14 Majors, the number depends on the work done previous to admission to the School of Education. (See "Pre-Pedagogical Courses," p. 339.)

Qualitative Analysis ...... 2 Mjs.
Quantitative Analysis ..... 2 Mjs.
General Organic Chemistry . 1 Mj.
                                        8 Mjs.
Electives, enough to make 18 .... 3–12[11]
      Total .... 18 Mjs.

Geography, Physiography and Geology.

Education:
  General .... 3 Mjs.
  Special .... 1 Mj.
                                     4 Mjs.
Astronomy: General Astronomy ...... 1 Mj.
Geology:
  Physiography .... 1 Mj.
  Elementary Mineralogy and
    Petrology .... ½ Mj.
  Field and Laboratory Work . ½ Mj.
  General Geology .... 1 Mj.
  Geographic Geology ...... 1 Mj.
  Additional Geology
    (or Geography) .... 1 Mj.
                                     5 Mjs.[12]
Zoology: Zoogeography .... 1 Mj.
Botany .... 1 Mj.
Geography:
  Meteorology .... 1 Mj.
  Geography of Continents ... 2 Mjs.
                                     3 Mjs.[13]
Electives, enough to make 18 .... 3–13[14]
      Total .... 18 Mjs.

11. Within the limits, 3 to 12 Majors, the number depends on the work done previous to admission to the School of Education. (See "Pre-Pedagogical Courses," p. 339.)
12. The student preparing to teach Geology should take at least two additional Majors of Geology.
13. The student preparing to teach Geography should take at least two additional Majors in Geography.
14. Within the limits, 3 to 13 Majors, the number depends on the work done previous to admission to the School of Education. (See "Pre-Pedagogical Courses," p. 339.)

Biology (including Zoology and Botany).
Education:
    General .... 3 Mjs.
    Special .... 1 Mj.
                                                   4 Mjs.
Chemistry: General Chemistry .... 2 Mjs.
Geology: Physiography .... 1 Mj.
Zoology:
    General Zoology .... 1 Mj.
    Field Course .... 1 Mj.
    Invertebrate Zoology ...... 2 Mjs.
    Zoogeography .... 1 Mj.
                                                   5 Mjs.[15]
Physiology: General Physiology ...... 1 Mj.
Botany:
    Morphology .... 1 Mj.
    Physiology .... 1 Mj.
    Ecology .... 1 Mj.
    Physiographic Botany ..... 1 Mj.
                                                   4 Mjs.[16]
Electives, enough to make 18 .... 1–12[17]
     Total .... 18 Mjs.

Home Economics.
Education .... 4 Mjs.
Sociology:
    House Sanitation (Depart-
    ment of Sociology, Course
    52) .... 1 Mj.
    Sanitary Aspect of Food and
    Water (Department of
    Sociology, Course 43) ... 1 Mj.
    Food and Dietetics (School
    of Education) .... 1 Mj.

15. The student preparing to teach Zoology, especially, should take at least two additional Majors of Zoology. In this case, one of the two may be substituted for the fourth Major of Botany.
16. If the student is preparing to teach Botany, especially, three additional Majors of Botany are recommended. In this case one of the above Majors in Zoology may be omitted.
17. Within these limits, 1–12 Majors, the number depends on the work done previous to admission to the School of Education. (See "Pre-Pedagogical Courses," p. 339.)

Evolution of the House
  (School of Education) ...   1 Mj.
                          —————— 3 of the 4.

Chemistry:[18]
  Analytical Chemistry (De-
  partment of Chemistry,
  Courses 6, 7, and 8) ....   3 Mjs.
  Elementary Organic
  Chemistry ....   1 Mj.
                                 4 Mjs.
Physiological Chemistry .... 1 Mj.
Bacteriology .... 1 Mj.
Electives .... 5 Mjs.
    Total .... 18 Mjs.

In each case it is understood that the special subjects mentioned in the special course are subject to modification, when other courses will, in the judgment of the head of a University department and with the approval of a Director of the School of Education, better meet the needs of the intending teacher.

IV. PROPOSED PRE-PEDAGOGICAL COURSES IN THE JUNIOR COLLEGES

The foregoing points give the essentials of the arrangements of Senior-College work with reference to preparation for teaching in secondary schools. The Faculty of the School of Education recommends to the other faculties concerned the following permissive modifications of the existing work of the Junior Colleges:

1. For Teachers of History and Civics

Philosophy:
  Psychology ....   1 Mj.
  Ethics ....   1 Mj.
                              2 Mjs.
History .... 3 Mjs.
Language (other than English) .... 4 Mjs.
English Composition .... 2 Mjs.

18. General Chemistry is presupposed.

Mathematics:
   Trigonometry .... 1 Mj.
   College Algebra or Surveying 1 Mj.

                                                2 Mjs.

Science:
   Physiography .... 1 Mj.
   General Zoology,
   Zoogeography, or   } ...... 1 Mj.
   Elementary Botany   2 Mjs.

Electives .... 3 Mjs.
     Total .... 18 Mjs.

2. For Teachers of Greek and Latin

Same as now in the College of Arts.

3. For Teachers of French

Philosophy .... 2 Mjs.
History .... 2 Mjs.
French .... 5 Mjs.
English Composition .... 2 Mjs.
Mathematics .... 2 Mjs.
Science .... 2 Mjs.
Electives .... 3 Mjs.
     Total .... 18 Mjs.

4. For Teachers of German

Philosophy .... 2 Mjs.
History .... 2 Mjs.
German .... 5 Mjs.
English Composition .... 2 Mjs.
Mathematics .... 2 Mjs.
Science .... 2 Mjs.
Electives .... 3 Mjs.
     Total .... 18 Mjs.

5. For Teachers of English

Philosophy .... 2 Mjs.
History .... 2 Mjs.
Modern Language (other than English) 3 Mjs.[19]

19. The requirement in Language shall not extend beyond a reading knowledge of two languages other than English. A reading knowledge of two languages other than English will be required,

English .... 4 Mjs.

Mathematics .... 2 Mjs.

Science .... 2 Mjs.

Electives .... 3 Mjs.

Total .... 18 Mjs.

6. *For Teachers of Science and of Home Economics*

Philosophy:

Psychology .... 1 Mj.

Ethics .... 1 Mj.

2 Mjs.

History:

Modern Europe .... 1 Mj.

United States .... 1 Mj.

2 Mjs.

Language[20] (not English) .... 4 Mjs.[21]

English Composition .... 2 Mjs.

Mathematics:

Trigonometry .... 1 Mj.

College Algebra⎱ .... 1 Mj.

or Surveying ⎰

2 Mjs.

Electives: Within Science[22] (including

Mathematics) .... 6 Mjs.

Total .... 18 Mjs.

---

even though more than three Majors are necessary to secure this result.

20. The requirement in Language shall not extend beyond a reading knowledge of two languages other than English.

21. In case the student does not present Latin or Greek, a reading knowledge of two Modern Languages other than English will be required, even though more than four Majors are necessary to this end.

22. Two majors in each of the following subjects in which University credit was not given on admission: (1) Chemistry, (2) Physiography and Geology, (3) Biology (Zoology, Botany, Physiology).

THE SCHOOL OF EDUCATION

The Building

The permanent building for the School of Education is nearing completion and will be ready for occupancy October 1, 1903. It is situated on Scammon Court, between Kimbark and Monroe Avenues, and faces the Midway Plaisance. The building is of stone, with tile roof to correspond with the other buildings of the University, although the actual details of the style are somewhat different. It has a frontage of 350 feet, and a depth, through its two wings, of 162 feet. It is four stories high, but passenger and freight elevators give easy access to the upper floors. An attractive feature of the plan is the large open court, the quadrangle, which is now accepted as the best arrangement for a university building. The court will offer great possibilities for landscape effects, and in the final plan will be symmetrical and surrounded with buildings. The wings on the east and west sides are low to insure a circulation of air in the court, and also to take advantage of the prevailing western winds in summer. To increase the effect of the whole, and to insure a certain privacy, the building is set upon a terrace.

The west half of the building is assigned mainly to the College of Education, and the first two floors in the east wing to the University Elementary School.

In the basement of the east wing is the casting and kiln room. The department of home economics is on the third floor. There are two rooms for kitchens—one for elementary and one for advanced work—and ample space for laboratory and other purposes. In addition there are three rooms for psychology and two class-rooms. On the fourth floor liberal

[First published in *University of Chicago Bulletin of Information* 3 (May 1903): 5–6.]

space is devoted to domestic arts. It will include a dyeing room and allotments of space for the various branches of textile work, and for clay-modelling. On the same floor, near the middle, a large lunch-room has been provided, with its own complete kitchen equipment.

The kindergarten and the first, second, third, and fourth grades are on the first floor in the east half of the building. The kindergarten is placed in the north end of the east wing; the room over it is designed for a playroom. The fifth, sixth, seventh, and eighth grades are on the second floor. Connecting with each grade-room, there is a smaller room, half the size of the grade-room, to be used for purposes of group-work.

The first floor in the west wing will be devoted to lecture-rooms and to recitation-rooms in mathematics and astronomy. The larger part of this wing will be equipped as a physical laboratory, which will be used by the pupils of both the elementary and the pedagogical department. The laboratory equipment will be ample and modern.

The large area on the second floor, in the central part of the building, is intended to accommodate the library. Next to this, on the west, are the rooms for history and literature. The west wing will be equipped for the study of geography and geology, with a third room for blackboard drawing. In the north end, over the faculty-room, is the room for speech, oral reading, and dramatic art. This will be provided with a fine stage and the necessary accessories for the presentation of dramatic work.

The space on the third floor immediately over the library has been assigned to the museum. The museum will be furnished with gas and water. It is intended that the museum shall be used largely for practical work in connection with all the departments of the school. Adjoining the museum on the west are two rooms for biology, one for elementary, the other for advanced pupils. The room for the latter occupies the south end of the wing, thus receiving light from south and west. The north end of the wing will be devoted to work in chemistry. In connection with this department are a weighing-room and a photography-room.

The space in the centre of the building on the fourth

floor, immediately over the museum, has been assigned to art—drawing and painting. It will be lighted in part from the ceiling. The remainder of this floor will be used by various handicrafts—wood work, bookbinding, and printing. One room is assigned to music.

Two large suites, including offices, vaults and work-rooms for administrative purposes, and reception-rooms, have been located on the first floor, one on either side of the main entrance and adjoining the spacious lobby. Near one of them is the passenger elevator.

The general arrangement is such as to insure plenty of light for each of the rooms and for all of the corridors. From this fact it is believed that the building will lend itself easily to the decorative effects which can be planned with a view to an appropriate treatment of the building as a whole. The corridors are lined with brick of a soft gray color, and the floor is of cement, in a shade of red harmonizing with the walls. The finish overhead is in rough plaster to add life to the color effects. The interior woodwork is of dark-stained birch. Birch has been selected rather than oak or other woods of a more porous nature, because of the ease with which it may be kept clean. With the exception of the kiln-room and the casting-room, there are no work-rooms in the basement. The building will be equipped with a complete interior telephone system. The heating and ventilation will be of the Plenum system, the same as in our public schools, except that the amount of air furnished each person per hour will be greater, and the velocity of the air entering the room not so great. In addition, the laboratories are equipped with an exhaust system.

General Information

THE COLLEGE OF EDUCATION

The University of Chicago School of Education was formed by the consolidation with the University of Chicago of the Chicago Institute founded by Mrs. Emmons McCormick Blaine.

The College of Education offers courses which deal,

from the point of view of pedagogy, with the problems arising in elementary and secondary education. The courses are
designed for the training of teachers and supervisors in elementary, secondary, and normal schools, for the preparation
of kindergartners, and other specialists in educational work.
Each member of the Faculty, being familiar with the plan
and work of the entire School, is able to present his courses
so that the relationship of his subject to the other subjects
in the curriculum clearly appears.

It is the aim to develop educational theory, and to illustrate, in practice, educational principles with special reference to the needs of those who are already engaged in
teaching, or who are desirous of fitting themselves for such
professional work.

The curriculum in the College of Education embraces
the pedagogical presentation of all subjects taught in the elementary, secondary, and normal schools, and it also includes
psychology and history of education.

PREREQUISITES FOR ADMISSION

Candidates are admitted as classified and unclassified
students.

1. Candidates are admitted as classified students upon
the basis of two years' scholastic work over and above a
high-school course of at least four years. This two years' work
may be done either in colleges or training schools for teachers.

2. Candidates are admitted as unclassified students who
are graduated from an approved high school; who have had
two years' experience in teaching, and have reached twenty-
one years of age, and who show themselves prepared to take
up study with advantage to themselves; (a) such unclassified students shall be admitted to take at one time not more
than two studies in the regular courses; and shall take at
least one course in fulfilment of prerequisites for admission
as a classified student; (b) but if, in addition to the above
requirement, such unclassified students show that they have
fulfilled all the requirements for some one line of work,
show good reason for not taking a regular course, and also
receive the formal recommendation of the instructor in

charge of the line of work in which they wish to specialize, they may be permitted to specialize in one line of study.

GRADUATION

The curriculum is so arranged that, taken in connection with the fulfilment of entrance requirements, it may lead to the degree of A.B., Ph.B., S.B., or Ed.B. (Bachelor of Education), according to the course pursued, and also to a Bachelor's diploma in Education.

METHOD OF THE RECITATION

The course will include a discussion of the function of recitation in the process of education. This will be taken up from both the social and the intellectual sides. Upon the social side the problem of individual and class teaching will be briefly discussed. Some use will be made of recent discussions in social psychology in indicating some of the ways in which social conditions modify the development of the individual. The main emphasis of the course, however, will be upon the intellectual side of the recitation. Upon this side the recitation will be discussed as furnishing the medium through which intellectual control or direction of mental processes is secured. Since the problem of intellectual control is that with which logic is concerned, the discussion will be carried on chiefly in terms of logical method. From this point of view the formal steps of the Herbartian school will be set forth and criticised. There will then be a brief discussion of the nature and value of experimentation of abstraction, symbols, comparison, induction, deduction, classification, and generalization, with special reference to the materials and methods available in class-work which represent these various logical functions.

Students who have not had a course in elementary logic should, if possible, familiarize themselves with Jevons, Fowler, Welton, Creighton, or some other elementary textbook in logic before taking the course. McMurry's *Method of the Recitation* gives a convenient summary of the Herbartian formal steps of instruction, and will be useful for reference during the course.

[First published in *Elementary School Teacher* 3 (1903): 563.]

Appendixes

Appendix 1

THE PSYCHOLOGY OF JUDGMENT
by John Dewey

The paper called attention to the fact that from the standpoint of consciousness as a stream in which there are both continuity and change, the distinctions of the subject, predicate and copula do not appear with the same definiteness as they do from either the logical or the linguistic standpoint. As a contribution, toward the statement of their psychical equivalents there was suggested a certain interpretation of James' well known distinction of the relatively substantive and transitive of the focal and marginal aspects of the stream. From this standpoint, the subject is those phases which are moving from the fringe into the focus, while the predicate is those phases of the fringe which anticipate what the stream is moving toward, and thus stand for the direction of interest and attention. The "local sign" of the subject, on this basis, seems to be feelings of resistance and tension; that of the predicate feelings of relief and resolution.

[Abstract of a paper read at the Twelfth Annual Meeting of the American Psychological Association at St. Louis, Mo., December 1903. Published in *Psychological Bulletin* 1 (1904): 44–45.]

Appendix 2

THE ST. LOUIS CONGRESS OF ARTS AND SCIENCES
by Hugo Münsterberg

The Universal Exposition at St. Louis constitutes, in the expansion of the grounds, in the plans of the buildings, in the stage of the preparation, in the eagerness of all countries to participate, and, above all, in the inner scope of the undertaking, a gigantic work of immeasurable value for the Southwest and of high importance for national and international progress. In the face of this broad development it was a most natural wish that where commerce and industry, art and education, the products of all lands and callings, are exhibited, the work of the scientist should come also to a full presentation. To be sure, just as modern art will reign over every hall and beautify every corner in the mimic city, so science will penetrate the educational and hygienic exhibitions, will swing the wheels in the industrial halls, and will show its inventions under every roof. And yet, just as art demands its own unfolding in the gallery of paintings and sculptures, so science seeks to concentrate all its energies on one spot, and show the cross-section of human knowledge in our days. That, however, cannot be done for the eyes. The great work which grows day by day in quiet libraries and laboratories, and on a thousand university platforms, can be exhibited only by words. Every visible expression, like that of heaped-up printed volumes, would be dead to the World's Fair spectator. How to make such words living, how to make them helpful to the thinkers and scholars themselves, and, at the same time, to human progress,—this was the problem which burdened the responsible authorities of the Exposition.

The official history of the steps which followed is easily told. The directors of the Exposition appointed an Administrative Board to supervise the arrangements for a representa-

[First published in *Atlantic Monthly* 91 (1903): 671–84. See Dewey's article, this volume, pp. 145–50.]

tive gathering of scholars. The chairman of that board is the president of Columbia University, Nicholas Murray Butler; Boston is represented by the president of the Massachusetts Institute of Technology, Henry S. Pritchett; Washington, by the librarian of Congress, Herbert Putnam; Chicago, by the president of the University of Chicago, William R. Harper; the welcoming state of Missouri, by the president of its State University, Richard H. Jesse; the legal aspect is represented by Frederick William Holls, the member of the International Court of Arbitration at The Hague; and the World's Fair itself, by F. J. V. Skiff, director of the exhibits. Finally Mr. Howard J. Rogers, as chief of the department of education, took charge of the technical supervision of all the congresses held in connection with the World's Fair. The Administrative Board, immediately after its organization, appointed a scientific board of scholars to work as the Committee on Plan and Scope. Of this America's most famous scientist, Professor Simon Newcomb of Washington, was chairman. In this committee Newcomb himself represented the exact sciences; W. H. Welch of Johns Hopkins, medicine; George F. Moore of Harvard, theology; Albion Small of Chicago, the social sciences; John B. Moore of Columbia, jurisprudence; Elihu Thompson, the technical sciences; and the writer, the philosophical sciences. This committee met several times in New York, discussed several plans, and finally accepted one, recommended it to the Administrative Board, and then stepped out of existence. The Administrative Board approved the plan and recommended its realization to the directors of the World's Fair. The decisive step quickly followed. The World's Fair authorities accepted the plan, voted the necessary large sum of money, appointed Professor Newcomb as president, Professor Small and myself as vice presidents of the whole congress, and made us at the same time an organizing committee with power to prepare the whole undertaking, with the technical supervision of the Administrative Board. Since that time—that is, since February—the organizing committee has been steadily at work; and while its work must still be for a time a quiet one, it may lie not outside of the line of this work if one of its members steps up to the honored platform in Park Street and tells a wider circle what those plans are, and why they ask for interest and favor.

The whole plan has been controlled by one single definite purpose, and this purpose itself has been marked out by the convergence of many reasons. I might approach the point best if I quote extensively at first from a letter which I wrote last fall, in reply to a private inquiry, to the World's Fair authorities, long before the official congress boards were appointed. I said there: —

"The traditional scheme of World's Fair congresses consists in a long list of unconnected meetings with a long programme of unconnected papers. I realize fully that such a routine scheme offers to the management the fewest possible difficulties: it needs hardly any preparation. But already at the last Paris Exposition, there was a general feeling that such an arrangement was on the whole useless, without any important value for science, and without any reason for being. And while the city of Paris, with its large body of scholars of first rank and its old traditions, and especially its convenient location, prevented the internal shortcomings of the congresses from being manifest, nothing of that kind holds for St. Louis. No scholar would feel attracted by a repetition of such meetings there; every one would feel that a World's Fair was the worst possible place for such an undertaking, and that there was no reason to do in St. Louis what each science is doing much more comfortably every year in quiet places of its own selection. In the meantime the aversion to international congresses, with their confusion of languages, has grown on all sides. On the other hand, the idea of overcoming this aversion of Europeans by paying them richly for coming would be most dangerous to the reputation of scholarly life in America. Real scholars are not used to being paid for attending the usual congresses and for reading papers in them. The Europeans would interpret such offers as a symptom of American inability to prepare good papers, and they would thus come in a missionary spirit; they would come to speak down to Americans, and the result would be a serious blow to the reputation of American intellectual life. Add to this all the growing feeling of a surfeit of over-specialization in the sciences of to-day, a feeling which would be forced on every one who should see such a list of a hundred congresses no one of which knows what its neighbors are doing; the American nation, with its instinctive desire for organization and unity in work, would especially dislike such disconnection.

"In my opinion, the St. Louis plan can be a success only if a way is found to do in every one of these respects exactly the opposite thing. Instead of heaping up once more the scattered specialistic researches, we must strive toward unity of thought; instead of artificially creating the missionary spirit in Europe, we must secure a plan of complete coöperation among the scholars of the world; and instead of arranging the usual programme with its traditional lack of purpose and lack of relation to the occasion, we must create something which has a clear, definite, and new purpose, something which has a mission, and which can fulfill its mission only by calling together the whole world.

"All these demands can be fulfilled by one change: instead of a hundred unconnected congresses, let us have *one* congress,—one congress with a hundred sections, to be sure, but one congress; and let us give to this one congress the definite purpose of working toward the unity of human knowledge. Let us give to it the mission, in this time of scattered specialized work, of bringing to the consciousness of the world the too much neglected idea of the unity of truth. Let the rush of the world's work stop for one moment for us to consider what are the underlying principles, what are their relations to one another and to the whole, what are their values and purposes; in short, let us for once give to the world's sciences a holiday. The workaday functions are much better fulfilled in separation, when each science meets at its own place and time, or still better, when each scholar works in his own library or in his laboratory; but this holiday task to bring out the underlying unity, this synthetic work, —this demands really the coöperation of all, this demands that once at least all sciences come together in one place, at one time. Such an achievement and its printed record would make an epoch for our time, and would be welcomed by the best scholars of the whole world, making it a duty for them to do their share.

"The necessary condition would be a plan in which

every possible striving for truth, every theoretical and practical science would find its exact place; as a matter of course, such a plan would have no similarity with chance combinations of the university catalogue. It must be really a plan which brings the inner relations of all branches of knowledge to light. The very existence of such a ground plan which would give to every section its definite position in the whole system would bring the unity of knowledge strongly to consciousness. Then a programme would have to be worked out for each of these sections, in which the chief papers would deal with the relations of each section to its neighbors and with its leading problems; then programmes for groups of sections, for departments, to consider their common fundamental methods and problems; then such for groups of departments, for divisions, till finally crowned by a reunion of all the divisions. The papers would thus form a network of intellectual relations in which every subject would be interrelated with every other.

"All this can be done only by the first men of the sciences, by men who have a view beyond the narrow limits of their special problems, and who have the authority to express the principles, to lay down the methods, to judge fairly of the fundamental problems of their sciences. But it will be easy to get the assistance of first-class men of all nations for such an end, because the scholars who are tired of the routine congresses, the papers of which do not offer more than any magazine issue, will be ready to work for such an unique undertaking, with an original and important task. And this scheme would also allow of attracting the Europeans over the ocean by a fair honorarium, because— while it would be unbecoming to pay for attendance on a regular congress where they would talk on their own special researches—it would be quite correct to offer full compensation if the speaker were invited to prepare a definite piece of work in the service of a complete plan; Europeans and Americans would in this case stand on the same level, receiving the same honorarium for the papers and differing sums merely for traveling expenses. If thus some hundred leading Europeans and some hundred leading Americans took part, there is no doubt that many hundred less known men would come over the ocean to the congress without any compensation, and that thousands of Americans would join. On the other hand, those interrelated addresses printed with a short abstract of the discussions would be a gigantic monument of the intellectual work of the St. Louis Exposition; it would be a lasting work which no private association could perform. The libraries of our specialistic work to-day form one big encyclopaedia where one thing stands beside the other. This record would become at last a real system; the whole would be a real 'Congress of the United Sciences.' Such a congress might meet in the second half of September, thus being completed before our universities opened. It would be easy to arrange for hospitality in connection with a visit to Chicago, Niagara, Boston, New York, Philadelphia, Baltimore, Washington, for the foreign guests, giving them a chance to see in October the large universities at work, and allowing them to reach home at the end of October, when the European universities open."

Enough of my letter, which was quickly followed by the administrative development that I have sketched step by step, and now, since the whole machinery of boards and committees has worked through a season, the tentative idea has grown into a full-fledged plan, the classifications are completed, the programmes of the meetings are worked out, the honorary list of speakers is sketched, the coöperation of all countries is invited, and it can be foreseen that before the year comes to an end many hundred scholars all over the world will be at work in their libraries to prepare their part in an undertaking which seemed a vague dream so few months ago. We may consider at first the internal plan, the classification of human knowledge, the principles of grouping and differentiating the sciences; and then the external plan, the technique of the congress, the outer devices for the realization of unity within the chaos. And finally, a word of the obstacles and difficulties, of our fears, which are not small, and of our hopes, which are greater.

We have divided human knowledge into two parts; into seven divisions; into twenty-five departments; into one hundred and thirty sections, with the possibility of an unlimited number of sub-sections; and the preliminary list of

the sections has come in printed form, probably, already
into many a scholar's hand. But such a mere list is not an
argument for its principles of classification. An alphabetical
programme which runs from Anthropology to Zoölogy may
have no smaller number of parts. The real interest lies in the
logic of the arrangement. The logical problem how to bring
order into the wilderness of scientific efforts has fascinated
the philosophers from Aristotle and Bacon to Comte and
Spencer. The way in which a special time groups its efforts
toward truth becomes therefore also a most significant expression of the deeper energies of its civilization, and not the
least claim which our coming congress will make is that the
programme of its work stands out as a realization of principles which characterize the deepest strivings and the in-
most energies of our own time as over against the popular
classifications of the nineteenth century.

The positivism which controlled human thought at the
height of the naturalistic thinking of the nineteenth century
settled the problems in a simple manner. All mental and
moral sciences, history and philology, jurisprudence and
theology, ethics and aesthetics, economics and politics, deal
clearly with human phenomena, with functions of men; but
man is a living organism, biology is the science of living organisms: all those branches of knowledge, from history to
ethics, from jurisprudence to aesthetics, are thus ramifications of biology. The living organism, on the other hand, is
merely one type of physical bodies on earth, and the science
of these physical bodies is physics. Biology is thus itself
merely a department of physics. But the earthly bodies are
merely a part of the cosmic totality; the science of the universe is astronomy; physics is thus merely a part of astronomy. And the whole universe is controlled by mathematical
laws; astronomy is thus again subordinated to mathematics.
This Comtian speculation was a conscious or subconscious
fundamental thought for the anti-philosophic period that
lies behind us.

Then came a time which knew better, and which over-
came this thinly disguised example of materialism. It was a
time when the categories of the physiologist lost slightly in
credit, and the categories of the psychologist won repute.

This newer time held that it is artificial to consider ethical and logical life, historic and legal action, literary and religious emotion, merely as a physiological function of the living organism; the mental life, however necessarily connected with brain processes, has a positive reality for itself. The psychical facts represent a world of phenomena which in its nature is absolutely different from that of material phenomena, and, while it is true that every ethical action and every logical thought can, from the standpoint of the biologist, be considered as a property of matter, it is not less true that the sciences of mental phenomena, considered impartially, form a sphere of knowledge closed in itself, and thus coördinated, not subordinated, to the knowledge of the physical world. We would say thus: all knowledge belongs to two classes, the physical sciences and the mental sciences. In the circle of physical sciences we have the general sciences, like physics and chemistry, the particular sciences of special objects, like astronomy, geology, mineralogy, biology, and the formal sciences, like mathematics. In the circle of mental sciences we have correspondingly, as a general science, psychology, and as the particular sciences all those special mental and moral sciences in which man's inner life is dealt with, like history or jurisprudence, logic or ethics, and all the rest. Such classification, which had its philosophical backing about twenty years ago, penetrated the popular thought as fully as the positivism of the foregoing generation, and it was certainly superior to its materialistic forerunner.

Of course it was not the first time in the history of civilization that materialism was replaced by dualism, that biologism was replaced by psychologism; and it was also not the first time that the natural development of civilization led again beyond this point: that is, led beyond the psychologizing period. There is no doubt that our time presses on, with all its powerful internal energies, away from this world's view of yesterday. The materialism was anti-philosophic, the psychological dualism was unphilosophic. To-day the philosophical movement has set in. The one-sidedness of the nineteenth-century creed is felt in the deeper thought all over the world; the popular movements and scholarly efforts alike show the signs of a coming idealism, which has something better and deeper to say than merely that our life is a series of causal phenomena. Our time longs for a new interpretation of reality; from the midst of every science wherein for decades philosophizing was despised, the best scholars turn again to a discussion of fundamental conceptions and general principles. Historical thinking begins to take again the leadership which for half a century belonged to naturalistic thinking; specialistic research demands increasingly from day to day the readjustment toward higher unities, and the technical progress which fascinated the world becomes more and more simply a factor in an ideal progress. The appearance of this unifying congress itself is merely one of the thousand symptoms appearing in our public life, and if the scientific philosophy produces to-day suddenly books upon books to prove that the world of phenomena must be supplemented by the world of values, that description must yield to interpretation, and that explanation must be harmonized with appreciation; they echo in technical terms the one great emotion of our time.

This certainly does not mean that any step of the gigantic materialistic, technical, and psychological development will be reversed, or that progress in any of these directions ought to cease; on the contrary, no time was ever more ready to put its immense energies into the service of naturalistic work; but it does mean that our time recognizes the one-sidedness of these movements, recognizes that they belong only to one aspect of reality, and that another aspect is possible; yes, that the other aspect is the one of our immediate life with its purposes and its ideals, its historical relations and its logical aims. The claim of materialism, that all psychical facts are merely functions of the organism, was no argument against psychology, because the biological aspect was possible, and yet the other aspect is certainly a necessary supplement; in the same way it is no argument against the newer view that all purposes and ideals, all historical actions and logical thoughts, can be considered as psychological phenomena. Of course we can consider it as such, and we must go on to do so in the service of the psychological and sociological sciences; but we ought not to imagine that we have expressed and understood the real character of our historical or moral, our logical or religious life when we have described and explained it as a series of phenomena. Its immediate reality expresses itself above all in the fact that it has a meaning, that it is a purpose which we want to understand, not by considering its causes and effects, but by interpreting its aims and appreciating its ideals. We should say therefore to-day that it is most interesting and important for the scientist to consider human life with all its strivings and creations from a biological, psychological, sociological point of view; that is, to consider it as a system of causal phenomena; and many problems worthy of the highest energies have still to be solved in these sciences. But that which the jurist or the theologian, the student of art or of history, of literature or of politics, of education or of morality, is dealing with refers to the other aspect in which inner life is not a phenomenon but a system of purposes, not to be explained but to be interpreted, not to be approached by causal but by teleological methods. In this case the historical sciences are no longer sub-sections of psychological or of sociological sciences; the conception of science is no longer identical with the conception of the science of phenomena; there exist sciences which do not deal with the description or explanation of phenomena at all, but with the internal relation and connection, the interpretation and appreciation of purpose. In this way the modern thought demands that sciences of purposes become coördinated to sciences of phenomena.

But at the very threshold it is clear that purposes and phenomena alike can be of two kinds. We have physical phenomena and we have mental phenomena. Their only difference is that the mental phenomena with which psychology deals are individual phenomena given to one subject only, while the physical phenomena are objects for every possible subject. In the same way there are purposes that are individual purposes, and other purposes which have a more than individual meaning, which are intended as purposes valuable for every one whom we acknowledge as a subject: the logical, the ethical, the aesthetic purposes. These purposes of more than individual value are called our norms; the sciences which deal with them are thus the normative sciences, which interpret our absolute intentions. On the other side stand the sciences of the individual intentions; their totality represents the system of historical purposes in its endless ramifications of political, legal, educational, literary, and religious activities. They form the historical sciences, and we come thus necessarily to a fourfold division of all theoretical knowledge: we have the normative sciences, the historical sciences, the physical sciences, and the mental sciences. That is indeed the chief grouping of theoretical knowledge which our International Congress has definitely accepted, thus leaving far behind it the one-sidedness of materialism and of phenomenalism.

But we are fully aware of another one-sidedness of which we should be guilty if these four divisions of knowledge should be declared as the only ones. That would mean that science is considered to be identical with theoretical science. Positivism takes that for granted too. The conception of practical science was not seldom declared to be a contradiction in itself, and all the technical sciences, for instance, were considered as a mixture of theoretical science and art. But as soon as we understand that the different sciences do not mean different material only, but first of all different aspects, then we must see also that a really new science enters into existence when the task is to understand the relations between physical or mental, normative or historical facts on the one side, and practical ends of ours on the other. The study of these relations between the facts and our ends constitutes indeed a whole group, which as practical sciences must be coördinated to the theoretical sciences. But there arises at once another interesting problem of classification. If the practical sciences link facts and ends, we can group them either with reference to the facts which we want to apply or with reference to the ends which we want to reach. Both ways are logically correct. Every one of the normative or historical, physical or mental, sciences can have, according to the first scheme, its practical counterpart. The engineer applies physical or chemical knowledge, the physician biological knowledge, and in the same way the jurist applies the knowledge of the legal purposes as they have formed themselves in historical development, and so on. But if we enter into the details of the applied sciences, we notice soon that most of them are not confined in their real work to the application of one special theoretical science. Most of them bring about a synthesis of various theoretical sciences for a certain end. Not seldom do we see that normative and historical, physical and psychical sciences converge and become united in one practical discipline, and for this reason it is clearly the simplest scheme to group them not with reference to the applied facts, but with reference to the ends which they are serving. Three large divisions separate themselves in this way. Practical sciences may work toward the material welfare, or they may work toward a harmonization of human interests, or, finally, they may work toward the ideal development of man. It is difficult to select words which express exactly the characteristics of these three groups. For our purpose it may be sufficient to call those sciences which serve material welfare, the utilitarian sciences; those which harmonize the interests of man, regulative sciences; and those which work toward his perfection, cultural sciences. And we have now reached the first level of our classification; we have divided human knowledge into theoretical knowledge and practical knowledge; the theoretical knowledge into the four divisions of normative, historical, physical, and mental sciences; the practical into the three divisions of utilitarian, regulative, and cultural sciences. The question of the logical principle of classification is settled by this determination. The further branching of these seven divisions into departments, and that of the departments into sections, offers much less difficulty and fewer reasons for disagreement.

Nevertheless, even the departmental sub-division may involve at once logical disputes. Our first division was the normative sciences, and the congress proposes to divide this division into two departments, the philosophical sciences and the mathematical sciences. That the philosophical sciences, like logic, ethics, aesthetics, with all their affiliations, belong here no one will doubt, and no serious student of the profounder problems of philosophy will hesitate to acknowledge finally, perhaps after some initial resistance, that all metaphysics is at bottom the general theory of the ultimate values of our logical, ethical, and aesthetic purposes, and thus belongs too under the normative sciences. But it may be different with our second department, mathematics. Many mathematicians would say that the mathematical objects are independent realities whose properties we study like those of nature, whose relations we "observe," whose existence we "discover," and in which we are interested because they belong to the real world. All that is true, and yet the objects of the mathematician are objects made by the will, created in the service of logical purposes, and thus different from all phenomena into which sensation enters. The mathematician of course does not reflect upon the purely logical origin of the objects which he studies, but the system of knowledge must give to the study of the mathematical object its place in that group where the more than individual—that is, the normative—purposes are classified. No doubt the purpose of the mathematical object is the application of the arithmetical or geometrical creation in the world of phenomena, and the mathematical concept must thus fit the world so absolutely that it can be conceived as a description of the world after abstracting from the content; mathematics would then be the phenomenalistic science of the form and order of the world. In this way mathematics has a claim to a place in both fields: among the sciences of phenomena, if we emphasize its applicability to the world; and among the teleological sciences of purposes, if we emphasize the free creation of its objects by the logical normative will. It was clearly more in harmony with the whole plan of the congress to prefer the latter emphasis, as it brings out more clearly the real roots of the sciences. Mathematics thus stands as a second department beside philosophy, in the normative division.

No other department offers similar difficulties. We have sub-divided the division of historical sciences into the departments of political sciences, economic sciences, legal sciences, educational sciences, philologic sciences, aesthetic sciences, and religious sciences; the division of physical sciences into the departments of general physical sciences, astronomical sciences, geological sciences, biological sciences, and anthropological sciences; and the division of mental sciences into the departments of psychological sciences and sociological sciences. We have thus sixteen departments in the theoretical work. The division of utilitarian sciences was carried out into medical sciences, practical economic sciences, and technological sciences; the division of regulative sciences into practical political sciences, practical legal sciences, and practical social sciences; and, finally, the division of cultural sciences into practical educational sciences, practical aesthetic sciences, and practical religious sciences; making thus nine departments in the practical field. These twenty-five departments have been divided further into one hundred and thirty sections. Questions of logical principle were to a less degree involved here, and it was not seldom merely a problem of practical fitness, whether a special branch of knowledge ought to be instituted as an independent section or to be considered as a sub-section only, which joins fellow sciences to form a whole section. As we divided the department of astronomy into astrometry and astrophysics, the department of psychology into the sections of general psychology, experimental psychology, child psychology, comparative psychology, and abnormal psychology; the department of medicine into the sections of hygiene, sanitation, contagious diseases, internal medicine, psychiatry, surgery, gynaecology, ophthalmology, otology, dentistry, therapeutics; the department of practical and social sciences into the sections of treatment of the poor, treatment of the defective, treatment of the dependent, prevention of vice and crime, problems of labor, problems of the family, and so on, seventy-one in the theoretical departments and fifty-nine in the practical ones, it is evident that a certain arbitrariness of the separation lines was unavoidable, and that many a compromise and adjustment to wider interests must come into play. Many of the sections may appear inexcusably large, as, for instance, the section on the history of modern languages, or on the history of the common law, or on the history of modern Europe, and it would certainly have been easier to provide from the first for three times the number of sections; but on the one side the plan gives full opportunity for the forming of smaller sub-sections, and, above all, the chief accent has to lie on the coöperation of those whose special fields lie by principle near together.

We have as yet merely the plan of sciences before us, not the plan of the congress, an empty outline which must be filled with a programme for real work. To fulfill our purpose the dry logical scheme must transform itself into a dramatic action, and only star players will be able to do justice to its meaning. The first procedure necessary to translate our classification into life will be the transformation of the logical order into a temporal order, while the methodological branching out of the sciences must appear in a corresponding differentiation and succession of meetings. The congress must thus open with an assemblage of all its members, must then divide itself into its divisions; after that, into its departments; then into its sections; and finally, into its last ramifications. The concrete plan is this: We begin on Monday, the 19th of September, 1904, late enough to avoid the tropical summer heat of St. Louis, and early enough still to make use of the university vacations. On Monday morning the subject for the whole congress is knowledge as a whole, and its marking off into theoretical and practical knowledge. Monday afternoon the seven divisions meet in seven different halls; Tuesday the seven divisional groups divide themselves into the twenty-five departments, of which the sixteen theoretical ones meet in sixteen different halls on Tuesday morning, and the nine practical, on Tuesday afternoon. In the following four days the departments are split up into the sections; the seventy-one theoretical sections meeting on Wednesday, Thursday, Friday, Saturday, about eighteen each morning in eighteen halls, and the fifty-nine practical sections on the same days in the afternoons, the arrangement being so made that sections of the same department meet as far as possible on different days, every one thus being able to attend in the last four days of the first week the meetings of eight different sections, four theoretical and four practical ones, in the narrower circle of his interests. In the second week a free sub-division of the sections is expected, and, moreover, a number of important independent congresses, as, for instance, an international medical congress, an international legal congress, and others, are foreseen for the following days. These independent congresses will highly profit from the presence of all the leading

American and foreign scholars, whose coming to St. Louis will be secured by the liberal arrangements of the official congress in the first week; on the other hand, these free congresses represent indeed the logical continuation of the set work of the first seven days, as they most clearly indicate the further branching out of our official sections, leading over to the specialized work of the individual scholars. And yet this second week's work must be, as viewed from the standpoint of our official congress, an external addition, inasmuch as its papers and discussions will be free independent contributions not included in the one complete plan of the first week, in which every paper will correspond to a definite request. The official congress will thus come to an end with the first week, and we shall indicate it by putting the last section of the last department, a section on religious influence in civilization, on Sunday morning, when it will not be, like all the others on the foregoing days, in competition with fifteen other sections, and may thus again combine the widest interests. In this section there will be room also for the closing exercises of the official occasion.

The arrangement of the sciences in days and halls is however merely an external aspect. We must finally ask for the definite content. Our purpose was to bring out the unity of all this scattered scientific work of our time, to make living in the world the consciousness of inner unity in the specialized work of the millions spread over the globe. The purpose was not to do over again what is daily done in the regular work at home. We desired an hour of repose, an introspective thought, a holiday sentiment, to give new strength and courage, and, above all, new dignity to the plodding toil of the scientist. Superficial repetitions for popular information in the Chautauqua style and specialistic contributions like the papers in the issues of the latest scientific magazines would be thus alike unfit for our task. The topics which we need must be those which bring out the interrelation of the sciences as parts of the whole; the organic development out of the past; the necessary tendencies of to-day; the different aspects of the common conceptions; and the result is the following plan: —

We start with the three introductory addresses on Scientific Work, on the Unity of Theoretical Knowledge, and on the Unity of Practical Knowledge, delivered by the president and the two vice presidents. After that the real work of the congress begins with a branching out of the seven divisions. In each one of them the topic is fundamental conceptions. Then we resolve ourselves into the twenty-five departments, and in each one the same two leading addresses will be delivered; one on the development of the department during the last hundred years, and one on its methods. From here the twenty-five departments pass to their sectional work, and in each of the one hundred and thirty sections again two set addresses will be provided; one on the relations of the section to the other sciences, one on the problems of to-day; and only from here does the work move during the second week into the usual channels of special discussions. We have thus during the first week a system of two hundred and sixty sectional, fifty departmental, seven divisional, three congressional addresses which belong internally together, and are merely parts of the one great thought which the world needs, the unity of knowledge.

One thing is clear from the beginning,—that there is no place in this plan for second-rate men with second-hand knowledge. We need the men who stand high enough to see the whole field. That must not be misunderstood. We do not need and we do not want there philosophers who enter into metaphysical speculations, and still less do we want vague spirits which generalize about facts of which they have no concrete substantial knowledge. No; the first-class man in every science is to-day a specialist, but the time is gone by when it was the pride of the specialist to lack the wider view and the understanding of the relations of his specialty to his neighbor's work. We want the men who combine the concentration on productive specialized work with the inspiration that comes from looking over wide regions. We are seeking them in all countries. Only the first two days' work will be essentially the welcome gift of the hosts, the contribution of American scholarship. In every one of the hundred and thirty sections, however, at least one of the leading addresses will be offered by a leading foreign scholar, and all countries will be represented. Every address will be followed by a discussion, but our work will not be really completed when the president delivers on Sunday his closing address on the Harmonization of Practical Sciences. The spoken word is then still to be transformed into its lasting expression. The Exposition has voted the funds not only to remunerate liberally all those who take their share in the work, but also to print and publish in a dignified form those three hundred and twenty addresses as a gigantic monument of modern thought, a work which might set the standard for a period, and will do by the unique combination of contributors, by its plan and its topics, by its completeness and its depth, what in no private way could be accomplished. Hundreds of colleagues are helping us to select those men for the departments whose word may be most helpful to the whole. Thousands will listen to the word when it is spoken, and the printed proceedings will, we hope, reach the widest circles, and become a new force in civilization, a real victory of science.

We know very well that there will be some, and there may be many, who will not care, and who will make a demonstration of their disapproval. They boast of their contempt for "generalities," and are convinced that "methodology" is the unpardonable sin of the scientist. Those scholars, they say, who are worth hearing have authority through their specialistic work; you would do better to give them a chance to speak on a special point of their latest research rather than about unproductive commonplaces. And if the scholars are willing to indulge in such fancies, nobody, they add, will care to make a journey to listen to them. Of course no one is in doubt that such arguments will flourish. To rebut them, we may at first recall the most external, the most trivial side of the matter. It can be taken almost for granted that hardly any foreign scholar of repute would care to cross the ocean for the purpose of reading a paper at the St. Louis Exposition if his expenses were not paid; and yet it would give a pitiable impression of American scholarship if, contrary to all usage, honorariums were offered for attending a regulation congress with arbitrarily chosen communications. Payments which cover the whole expedition from England or France or Germany are certainly admis-

sible only when every one is requested to do a definite piece
of work as part of a systematic whole comparable to a contribution for a cyclopaedia. But moreover, would it really be
so much more worth while to invite the speakers for the
freeing of their minds from their latest discovery? Would it
be really more attractive to the hearers, would it be more
productive 'for human knowledge in every direction? The
contrary seems true. Such an invitation to the leading
scholars would remain without profit for their own work,
because it would not stimulate them to do anything that they
would not be doing just as well without the external occasion
of the congress. In the best case they would read a paper
which would have appeared a few weeks later in their professional archives in any case; and a greater probability
even than this is that it has appeared in some archive in a
similar form weeks or years before. But the address which
the congress will request will be something which probably
would have remained unwritten without this fortunate
stimulus, because the holiday hours for reposeful considerations of principles do not come to the busy scholar if they
are not almost forced upon him. Therefore the congress will
be able to become a positive gain to human knowledge and
not a mere recapitulation. It will be more than an echo.

And is it really more attractive to listen to a contribution
of special research? It is just the true productive scholar
who will shake his head here. He knows too well that the
detailed new discovery needs that careful examination which
is possible only by reading and re-reading a scientific paper
in the seclusion of one's own library. To hear a paper by a
great man is valuable: it may become an inspiration for our
whole life, if he has the genius of the true thinker, if he
opens before us the wide stretch of land to a far horizon, but
not when he comes with a bit of detailed information for
which we might much better wait for the next number of
the scientific magazine. And only through such wide-reaching
outlook can he really hold the attention of a large number
of scholarly minds. As soon as he enters into a special
problem, he will too easily either popularize it, and thus
remove it from the higher interests of scientific thinkers, or
demand such an amount of special knowledge that the circle
of attentive listeners is narrowed down to a round-table

colloquium. This the experiences of a hundred previous congresses, national and international, have proved beyond doubt. Scholars attend them to meet their colleagues personally, but not to listen to papers, and seldom does one hear a paper for which it is worth while to make a journey. And is it really necessary to eliminate in the least the personal differences and personal interests of our speakers? Does not the character of our topics give fullest freedom to the personal preferences and specialistic achievements of every scholar? If we demand in every section one leading address on the relation of that science to other sciences, we do not prescribe beforehand what relations ought to be emphasized; we leave that fully to the choice of the speaker. If in the section on American political history the relations to other sciences are to be sketched, we leave it to our scholar whether he wants to emphasize more the relation of American politics to European politics, or to economic life, or to legal life, or to American physiography; or in the section of electricity, we leave it to the scholar to emphasize its relations to optics, or to chemistry, or to the theory of nature, if he but points to the totality of possible relations, and determines thus the exact geographical position of his science on the intellectual globe, and thus helps by his address to weave the network of scientific interrelations. In a still higher degree is all this true for those who speak on the problems of to-day. Certainly we do not want an address on the problems of a whole science to become merely an account of the one problem to which our speaker has devoted his last pamphlet; but we surely do not mean that he must first forget his own writings and neutralize his mind till every specific interest is lost. He ought to see the whole, but he ought to see it from his particular standpoint. If finally the value of such general addresses is looked upon with a skeptical eye, because it seems a waste to spend energy on such general problems when so many special problems are still unsolved, the complainants do not understand the real meaning of their own work, and do not learn from the history of scholarship, which shows that just such generalities have made the world. It is quite true that too many by their long training instinctively shrink away from every comprehensive abstraction; but the immense educational value of a great unifying undertaking like ours lies just in the opportunity to overcome such latent resistance. If we did not want to offer anything but that which those specialists, who wish to be specialists only, do every day in the year, and if we were thus willing merely to follow the path of least resistance, then it would be certainly a wasted effort to attempt anything beyond an imitation of earlier congresses, which few scientific participants consider models for imitation.

Nearly connected with all this is a misunderstanding which seems easily to arise even among those who are in sympathy with our plan. They have the instinctive feeling that the whole undertaking is after all one of logic and methodology, and thus the immediate concern of the philosopher. It seems to them as if philosophy had here swallowed the totality of special sciences. There would be some who might answer that even if this were true, the misfortune would not be great, inasmuch as the desire for philosophical foundation awakens in our day everywhere in the midst of the work of research. But it is not true; it is the part of logic to map out the classification of sciences; but as soon as they are classified it is no longer the province of logic to discuss the logically arranged scientific problems and methods and conceptions. It belongs to methodology, and thus to philosophy, to determine the topics whose discussion is profitable for the interrelation of sciences; but the discussion of these problems concerns no more the philosopher but the special scientist. With the exception of those few most general addresses, which might be said to belong to the philosophical theory of knowledge, the philosopher has no greater share in it than the physician or the jurist, the historian or the theologian, the astronomer or the sociologist. A discussion on logically grouped subjects is decidedly not a discussion from the standpoint of logic.

And finally, there are some who would say that it is not the philosopher who oversteps his rights here, but the scientist in general. The whole plan which puts science at the head, and makes all those hundreds of human functions which constitute human progress only sections and sub-sections thereof, stands out as mere arrogance of self-adoring scholasticism. Inflated science once again wants to be bigger than the totality of civilization, instead of seeing that all this scientific thinking and discovery is only one of the many functions in which the progress of mankind realizes itself. The time has passed when a Hegelian construction could assert that the world is the product of logical thought; for us to-day progress is the widest conception, and thought and science only the special case; let us not fall back to the overestimation of academical work in proclaiming a scheme which makes knowledge the ruler of all. The fallacy of this fear is evident. Let us concede that human progress is the wide conception, and scientific thought the narrow, included in the wider; but can it be the purpose of a congress to exhibit progress? Whatever may be done in such a congress in addresses or in discussions, it must go on in words, in sentences, in judgments, and is therefore a part of science. Progress itself is exhibited in all those noble buildings for commerce and industry, for art and education. It is a function of our congress to exhibit that one feature of progress which needs the spoken form,—scientific thought. As soon as that is granted it is evident that the totality of scientific thoughts must be grouped according to their own inherent characteristics. Scientific thought concerning human progress is then merely one of many parts in the scientific whole; coördinated perhaps with the scientific thought concerning the stars, or the chemicals, or the mathematical forms, or God. While science in general is thus subordinated to progress, the science of progress is subordinated to science in general, and it is thus really not academic lack of modesty if the congress considers the conception of knowledge as the widest possible of all conceptions in its realm. The congress does not, cannot, seek to maintain that knowledge as such embraces the totality of human functions; it knows very well that it will be lodged only in a corner of the immense exhibition grounds, where many other functions of human progress will show their vigorous life in more imposing palaces. Its only ambition is that its systematic exhibition of scholarship may become worthy of its fellow exhibitions all over the ground, and at the same time really helpful to the serious thought of the twentieth century.

Appendix 3

THE INTERNATIONAL CONGRESS OF ARTS AND SCIENCE
by Hugo Münsterberg

To the Editor of Science: I returned only a few days ago from Europe and, therefore, have not seen until now the letter of Professor Dewey in *Science* of August 28 and that of Professor Woodward in *Science* of September 4, both of which deal with the International Congress of Arts and Science and especially with my essay on that congress, published in the May number of the *Atlantic Monthly*.

Professor Woodward's document gives me hardly a chance for a reply, since I can not see that it contains an argument. It is only a general expression of his contempt, on principle, for every effort to classify sciences from a logical point of view. "While we may not go out of our way," he says, "to oppose philosophers and literary folk who indulge in such extravagances, it is our duty to repudiate them when they appear in the public press in the guise of science; for they tend only to make science and scientific men ridiculous." It may appear surprising if my chief aim was to make science ridiculous for the amusement of literary folk, that I took my medical degrees and have since been conducting scientific laboratories. But the worst of it is that those 'philosophers and literary folk' who have indulged in the acceptance of a program 'which bordered on absurdity' are the president of the congress, Professor Simon Newcomb, Mr. Pritchett, the president of the Massachusetts Institute of Technology, and others who were up to this time believed to have a certain interest in 'science'—for Professor Woodward is mistaken if he doubts that the program and classification which he saw has the endorsement of the entire committee. But the kind criticism of Professor Woodward requires the less discussion as he is also mistaken in his second presupposition.

[First published in *Science*, n.s. 18 (1903): 559–63. See Dewey's rejoinder, pp. 151–52, this volume.]

He thinks that the classification of sciences which has been accepted for the International Congress was sketched in my article for the purpose of inviting criticism of the scheme. That was not the case. It was merely a communication concerning a settled arrangement, fully discussed and definitely voted by the proper authorities. If I had been longing for criticism, I should hardly have published it in a form which offers merely results and not reasons; and however 'absurd and ridiculous' my system may be, I have at least never evaded the duty to give the reasons and arguments for my positions. A 'scientific man' can not of course read what philosophers and literary folk are writing; otherwise, I might refer him to the first volume of my 'Grundzuege der Psychologie,' in which about 500 pages are devoted to just this discussion; perhaps also to a short essay in the first volume of the 'Harvard Psychological Studies' (Macmillan's), where he might find a large map with a tabular view of such classification. There is no doubt that it is more comfortable to 'repudiate' such 'extravagances' than to argue about them; but is it really more 'scientific'?

It is quite different with the very interesting letter from Professor Dewey of Chicago. His letter is full of important arguments worthy of serious consideration. He points clearly to certain dangers in the scheme, and the question is only whether those disadvantages ought not to be accepted in order to gain certain advantages which strongly outweigh them. Every one of the points he raises has been indeed matter for long discussion in the committees, and only after conscientious deliberation have we come to the decisions which he regrets.

As I tried to bring out in my *Atlantic Monthly* article, our real aim is to have a congress which has a definite task and which does not simply do the same kind of work that men of science are attempting every day and everywhere. We do not want, therefore, a bunch of disconnected congresses and in each one a bundle of disconnected papers which could just as well have appeared in the next number of the scientific magazines. We want to use this one great opportunity to work, in a time of scattered specialization, towards the unity of thought. We want to bring out the interrelations of all knowledge and to consider the fundamental principles which bind the sciences together. We want to create thus a holiday hour for science, with a purpose different from that of its workaday functions, an hour of reposeful self-reflection. Therefore, not everybody who would like to be heard could be admitted to the platform, but only those who are leaders in their field, and even these may not speak on their chance researches of the last week, but on definite subjects which all together form one systematic whole. Such a monumental work could be created only under the exceptional conditions of a congress embracing all sciences and all countries, and important enough to attract those who are masters in their work with a wide perspective. This was our aim and this alone our chief claim, as I tried to bring out in my essay, and I see with great satisfaction that Professor Dewey feels in full harmony with this essential part of the undertaking.

The aspect which he dislikes is this: If we are to invite the leaders of all special sciences, each to consider the relations of his science to the other departments of knowledge, then we must clearly chop the one totality of knowledge into many special parts. That involves at once certain principles of division about which different opinions may exist. We have agreed to recognize 25 different departments with 134 sections, and such decision involves, of course, at once a certain grouping. The sections of the same department stand nearer together than the sections of different departments, and some of those departments again stand in close relations and thus form larger units. We grouped our 25 departments into 7 such chief divisions. Now Professor Dewey says we had no right to do all this, because our classification partly anticipates the work which is to be done by those who are to give the addresses. If each department has from the beginning a definite place on the program, its relations to all other sciences are determined beforehand and it has become superfluous to call in the scholars of the world simply to concur in the committee's ideas concerning the system of knowledge.

But I might ask, what else ought we to have done? I know very well that instead of the 134 sections, we might have been satisfied with half that number or might have indulged in double that number. But whatever number we might have agreed on, it would have remained open to the reproach that our decision was arbitrary, and yet we did not see a plan which allowed us to invite the speakers without defining beforehand the sectional field which each was to represent. A certain courage of opinion was then necessary and a certain adjustment to external conditions was unavoidable; in every case we consulted a large number of specialists. Quite similar is the question of classification. Just as we had to take the responsibility for the staking out of every section, we had also to decide in favor of a certain grouping if we desired to organize the congress and not simply to bring out a helter-skelter performance. Professor Dewey says: "The essential trait of the scientific life of to-day is its live-and-let-live character." I agree with that fully. In the regular work in our libraries and laboratories the year round everything depends upon this democratic freedom in which every one goes his own way, never asking what his neighbor is doing. It is that which has made the specialistic sciences of our day as strong as they are. But it has brought about at the same time this extreme tendency to disconnected specialization with its discouraging lack of unity; this heaping up of information without an ordered and harmonious view of the world; and if we are going to do what we aim at, if we want really to satisfy, at least once, the desire for unity, the longing for coordinations, then the hour has come in which we must not yield to this live-and-let-live tendency. It would mean to give up this ideal if we were to start at once without any principle of organization, ordering the sciences according to the alphabet, perhaps, instead of according to logic. The principles which are sufficient for a directory would undermine from the first the monument of scientific thought which we hope to see erected through the cooperation of the leaders of science. Therefore, some principle had to be accepted. And just as with number of sections, it may be said here too, that whatever principle could have been chosen would probably have had its defects and would certainly have been open to the criticism that it was a product of individual arbitrary decision.

A classification which in itself expresses all the practical relations in which sciences stand to each other is of course absolutely impossible. Professor Dewey's own science, psychology, has relations to philosophy, relations to physiology, and thus to medicine, relations to education and sociology, relations to history and language, relations to religion and law. A program which should try to arrange the place of psychology in the classified list in a way that psychology should become the neighbor of all these other sciences is unthinkable. On the other hand, only if we had tried to construct a scheme of such exaggerated ambitions, should we have been really guilty of anticipating a part of that which our speakers are to tell us. We leave it to the invited scholar to discuss the totality of relations which practically must exist between psychology and other departments of knowledge. We confine ourselves to that minimum of classification which indicates the pure logical relation of the science in the sense of subordination and coordination, that minimum which every editor of an encyclopaedic work would be asked to indicate without awakening suspicion of interference with the ideas of his contributors.

The only justified demand which could be made was that we choose a system of division and classification which should give fair play to every existing scientific tendency. And here alone came in the claim which I made for that scheme which has been accepted for the congress. I believed that our classification, more fully than any other, would leave room for every wholesome tendency of our times. I showed that a materialistic system would give fair opportunity to the natural sciences but not to the mental sciences; that a positivistic system would offer room for both mental and natural sciences; but that only an idealistic system has room for all; for the naturalistic and mental sciences, and also for those tendencies which are aiming at an interpretative as well as a descriptive account of civilization. And while we are trying to get, as I said, an organization with a minimum of classification, we were thus trying to provide at the same time for a maximum of freedom. Whatever other principles of classification we might have chosen would have led to an arbitrary suppression of some existing tendencies in modern thought. To use Professor Dewey's illustration: Those students of art, history, politics and education who treat them as systems of phenomena and those who treat them as systems of purposes, alike find in different sections their full opportunity. I have a slight impression that Professor Dewey would have preferred a classification which would have room only for one of the two groups. Our congress will be less partial than our critics. We shall have place and freedom for all.

But there is no reason to speak to-day, as I had to do in May, of a plan for the future. Our undertaking has already a little history. The program has been tried. Then was the moment for the appearance of those destructive effects which Professor Dewey feared. Professor Newcomb, Professor Small and I, who have been honored by the invitation to work as an organizing committee, have just returned from Europe, where we were to bring personal invitations to those who had been selected for the chief addresses. Professors Newcomb and Small visited France, England, Austria, Italy and Russia. I had to see the scholars of Germany and Switzerland. As the Germans have the reputation of being the most obstinate in their scientific ideas, their attitude towards the presented program may be considered as the severest test of it. I had to approach 98 scholars in Germany. Every one saw the full program with the ominous classification of science before he made his decision. Only one third of those whom I invited felt obliged to decline, and among them was not a single one who refused to come on account of the objections foreshadowed by Professor Dewey. Some can not come because of ill health, some because of public engagements, some on account of the expense, and some because they are afraid of sea-sickness, but not a single one gave the slightest hint that he was disturbed by the limitations which the program might put on him. On the other hand, among those two thirds whom we hope to see here next September, very many expressed their deep sympathy with the plans and the program, and not a few insisted that it was just this which tempted them to risk the cumbersome voyage, while they would have disliked to participate in a routine congress without connected plan and program.

Of course that would not count for much in the minds

of my critics, if those who have promised to come and deliver addresses under the conditions of our program were merely 'literary folk who indulge in such extravagances.' I may pick out some of the German names. For human anatomy there comes Waldeyer of Berlin; for comparative anatomy, Fuerbringer of Heidelberg; for embryology, Hertwig of Berlin; for physiology, Engelmann of Berlin; for neurology, Erb of Heidelberg; for pathology, Marchand of Leipzig; for pathological anatomy, Orth of Berlin; for biology, Weismann of Freiburg; for botany, Goebel of Munich; for mineralogy, Zirkel of Leipzig; for geography, Gerland of Strassburg; for physical chemistry, Van't Hoff of Berlin; for physiological chemistry, Kossel of Heidelberg; for geophysics, Weichert of Göttingen; for mechanical engineering, Riedler of Berlin; for chemical technology, Witt of Berlin, and so on. Or to turn to the department of Professor Dewey: For history of philosophy, Windelband of Heidelberg; for logic, Riehl of Halle; for philosophy of nature, Ostwald of Leipzig; for methodology of science, Erdmann of Bonn; for aesthetics, Lipps of Munich; for psychology, Ebbinghaus of Breslau; for sociology, Toennies of Kiel; for social psychology, Simmel of Berlin; for ethnology, von den Steinen of Berlin; for pedagogy, Ziegler of Strassburg. Or to mention some other departments: Among the philologists I notice Brugman of Leipzig, Paul of Munich, Delitzsch of Berlin; Sievers of Leipzig, Kluge of Freiburg, Muncker of Munich; Oldenberg of Kiel and others. Among the economists, Schmoller of Berlin, Weber of Heidelberg, Stieda of Leipzig, Conrad of Halle, Sombart of Breslau, Wagner of Berlin. Among the jurists, Binding of Leipzig, Zorn of Bonn, Jellineck of Heidelberg, von Lizst of Berlin, Wach of Leipzig, von Bar of Göttingen, Kahl of Berlin, Zitelmann of Bonn, and so on. Among the theologians, Harnack of Berlin, Budde of Marburg, Pfleiderer of Berlin. For classical art, Furtwaengler of Munich; for modern art, Muther of Breslau; for mediaeval history, Lamprecht of Leipzig. Enough of the enumeration. The list from England and from France is on the same level, and I anticipate that when we soon shall send out invitations to several hundred Americans for definite addresses, their response will not be less general, their list not less noble. But American participation is a question of the future. The list of acceptances which I have given here stands as a matter of fact beyond discussion. Is there really any doubt still possible that we have secured on the basis of that disastrous program the greatest combination of leaders of thought which has ever been brought together? When we three came home from our European mission after four months of hard labor to secure this result surpassing our own expectations, we might have felt justified in the hope that scientific men of this country would welcome us otherwise than with the cry that we, under the guise of science, have made science ridiculous.

Appendix 4

IS SUBJECTIVE IDEALISM A NECESSARY POINT OF VIEW FOR PSYCHOLOGY?[1]
by Stephen Sheldon Colvin

'The world is my idea.' These words, which form the opening sentence to Schopenhauer's 'World as Will and Idea,' may be taken to express with literal exactness the speculative attitude of the psychology of to-day towards reality. This attitude of subjective idealism has been inherited through a long and highly reputable line of philosophic descent. It meets us at the beginning of modern philosophy in Descartes's famous *cogito ergo sum*; it finds a more complete expression in Berkeley's dictum that all *esse* is *percipi*, but attains its most suitable formulation for the purposes of psychology in the sceptical analysis of David Hume, who, discarding as fictions the *res extensae* and *res cogitantes* of his predecessors, declared the mind, and the known universe as a whole, to be merely a 'bundle of perceptions.'

It is safe to say that the psychology of to-day has not gone much beyond this standpoint of the great English empiricist. Rejecting the soul as a metaphysical superstition, and affirming the knowledge of an extra-mental world to be mediate, and hence uncertain, it rests content to remain within the circle of its own ideas, except perchance when it now and then strays into the realm of physiology, or is lured away into the attractive but uncertain domain of the unconscious. In general, however, it asserts that the limits of the ego can not be transcended; that reality is what the subject makes it, and that without this making the external is, for all we know, non-existent.

It is an extremely fascinating doctrine, this radical sub-

---

1. This paper was read before the North Central Section of the American Psychological Association, at Chicago, November 26, 1904.

[First published in *Journal of Philosophy, Psychology and Scientific Methods* 2 (1905): 225–31. See Dewey's reply, pp. 153–57, this volume.]

jectivism, which becomes solipsism when interpreted in terms of the intellect, and pragmatism when formulated in the categories of the will. The doctrine seems so self-evident, it is so clear and convincing, that it is apt to be accepted without question. Therefore, even to hint at the possibility of its untruth may appear rash. The present discussion, however, ventures to raise the question as to whether its validity may not legitimately be doubted, and whether modern empirical psychology is obliged to assume this point of view as the only possible theoretical interpretation of reality.

We can best answer this query by reviewing the chief arguments that have induced psychology to accept as certain the theory that known reality is purely subjective. These arguments fall under the general head of the relativity of sensation, and rest on the assumption that the only certain knowledge is that which is direct and immediate. The ancients were impressed with this thought, and from the days of Protagoras and Aristippus down to those of Aenesidemus and Sextus Empiricus felt the force of the doctrine of *homo mensura*. The senses constantly deceive us, and do not certainly point to a stable externality; hence only of the subjective states can reality be unreservedly affirmed. To this argument modern psychology has added another, which rests on the hypothesis that all our conscious states are physiologically conditioned. There is no psychosis without a neurosis. The external stimulus (standing for the extra-mental object) becomes a conscious fact only by exciting the end organs of sensation, traversing the afferent nerves, and producing a change in the cerebral cortex. To suppose that a process so mediated can reveal to us an independent reality, we are told, is sheer nonsense. We must reject the world of the naïve realist, and admit that all we can know are elements of our own consciousness.

The physiological argument is excellently and briefly stated by Professor Strong as follows: "The physiological argument takes its departure from the fact that every perception is correlated with a perceptional brain event, which latter is a fairly remote effect of the action of the perceived object on the senses; and argues from this that it is impossible the knowledge of the extra-bodily object should be immediate. It points, moreover, to the account of the constitution of the object given by physical science, according to which color and other secondary qualities are in the object something entirely different from what they are in the mind."

This is the argument, and in effect the only one by which subjective idealism attempts to set forth and coordinate its facts. I say that it is the only argument, because other reasons given to substantiate the view-point of solipsism are in the nature merely of supposedly self-evident postulates, not in any sense demonstration or proof. On the other hand, the arguments from the relativity and mediate nature of sensation are not adequate to reach the conclusions which they aim to establish, for they are incapable of proving positively their thesis. All they accomplish is to discredit the view of naïve, uncritical realism, but to show that this view is unsatisfactory is by no means to prove that subjective idealism is true. As a positive proof, the entire argument is a failure, for the simple reason that it can establish the relativity of our perceptions only by holding that among these there are certain factors that are not relative. At every step it assumes in some instances to be true that which in general it is trying to prove false. The fallacy here contained I have endeavored elsewhere[2] at some length to point out, and shall not attempt within the limits of this paper to review it. I will simply repeat that the argument from the relativity of perception to subjective idealism fails as a positive proof, because it assumes that we possess an absolute knowledge, immediate and direct, of certain experiences in order to prove that other, and indeed all, experiences of exactly the same nature are relative, mediate, and subjective. So it happens that if the premise be true the conclusion must of necessity be false, while the truth of the conclusion establishes the falsity of the premises by which the very conclusion is reached.

This, then, is where the argument from relativity leaves us. We find it sufficient to discredit the assumptions of the plain man, but insufficient to construct for itself a view. Sub-

2. *Philosophical Review*, March, 1902, in an article on 'The Common-Sense View of Reality.'

jective idealism, if it hopes to establish its contention, must do so on grounds other than negative. This it attempts to do by the assertion that we can know only ideas. Translated into terms of solipsism this statement reads, I can know only my own conscious states. This is the very citadel of the idealistic faith, and is generally considered impregnable. In regard to it Schopenhauer has remarked that solipsism can not be proved false, but that the practical man who seriously holds to such an hypothesis is a fit subject for the madhouse. The correct position, however, I believe to be the opposite. I can see no madness in a person holding theoretically, or even practically, the position of solipsism. It means a radical but consistent interpretation of experience in terms of the new idea, and conduct for this reason should be no different from the point of view of the subjective idealist than from that of the uncritical realist. The former would recognize among his ideas certain mental states that were relatively unstable and subject to his voluntary control, while there would be others unyielding and beyond his power to change or direct. The approaching train, although merely his idea, would still be a fact capable of causing destruction to another idea, or set of ideas, his physical body. In this purely mental world would be subjective and objective elements. The solipsist would find it necessary to relate these elements in a proper coordination and subordination, and he thus would act with a due regard for himself and others. It seems to me that the objection of practicability urged against subjective idealism is based upon a misunderstanding of the scope and meaning of the doctrine. It is not for this reason that it must be set aside, but rather because when rigidly interpreted it leads to a self-contradiction far more fatal than that which confronts the realist. This statement to be justified must be examined further.

The assertion that I can know only my ideas may mean one or both of two things, namely: I can have as an object of direct, intuitive knowledge only my past conscious states; or that, in any mental state I may possess, my knowledge is limited to a content which is itself a part of that mental state. Let us look at the latter consideration first. For example, suppose I make the explicit or implicit judgment, this object is a book; the subjective idealist would assert without hesitation that the book of my experience is a purely subjective affair, an ideal element in the sum total of the conscious moment. There may be an external reality corresponding to my experience of book, but of that I can have no knowledge.

The first objection which I believe may be brought legitimately against this assertion is that the content of a total state of consciousness can not itself be ideal, paradoxical as this statement may seem. The content is not a part of the conscious state, as the branches are a part of the tree, or the sun a part of the universe. The content is of a different order and nature. If the content were in the ordinary sense ideal, mark what would follow. This content, as ideal, must likewise have an object, for we know of no consciousness devoid of content, nor can we imagine any. But carrying out our assertion, that we can know only ideas, we would be forced to admit that this content of the content would itself have a content, also ideal, and so on to infinity.

Let us look at the matter from a slightly different point of view. Every complex state of consciousness ordinarily is held to be made up of more simple psychic elements, namely, sensations and images. It is these, according to the doctrine of idealism, that the complex state of consciousness knows, and not an extra-mental reality corresponding to them. These are the objects of our immediate knowledge, which are present as elements in the complex noetic state. Should we say, to avoid the difficulty of the infinite regress pointed out above, that these elements do not know but are known, we plunge ourselves into another equally great difficulty; for how can we then explain the process by which a combination of non-noetic states form a complex conscious state capable of knowledge? So we are confronted with a dilemma in both cases. If we assert that the complex conscious state has simply conscious states as objects of knowledge, it would seem to follow that as conscious they must be conscious of something, and so on *ad infinitum*. If, however, we consider them non-noetic elements of consciousness, we are forced to raise the question as to how their combination can yield a complex noetic state.

But I am quite sure that this entire argument will appear to many as a quibble that can easily be set aside by the assertion that the noetic state has been illegitimately divided into subject and object, knower and known. Knowledge-of-book is one total complex in which the knowledge and the book are separated only by a false abstraction. And this I am quite willing to grant. The immediate state of consciousness is a complete unit and there can be no artificial separation between knowledge-of-book and book: there is no knowledge without book and equally there is no book without knowledge. Book in this sense is not something that I know, so much as a state of consciousness through which I know. If this is a true analysis, however, we can not say that we know ideas, but that we know by means of ideas, or that all knowledge is ideal, an assertion of a truism which no one can dispute. But in *this* state of knowledge there is an intention which ascribes an extra-mental reality to every noetic psychosis. It is that intention which sets up an object non-ideal, or at least extra-ideal. If the intention can not realize itself knowledge is false, for it does not reach its object. To assume that we really know we must believe the intention is capable of realizing itself. It is this intention that gives an object to our knowledge, and this very intention asserts the extra-ideal character of that which it intends. If there is nothing to which the intention can refer, then all knowledge is an illusion. We can not know that we have a mental state even; which seemingly subjective knowledge is, as will be shown later, in the moment of knowing a fact of extra-mental reference.

But the problem may be approached from still another standpoint. To do this we may again go back to our consciousness of book, concerning which, as has already been said, we are told by the idealist that the book, and hence all its qualities, are mere determinations of my present conscious state. I reply that if this is so, I can never know book; nay more, I can never know even its most subjective quality, color; for the color is not merely the determination of my present conscious state. It exists as color only because my present state of consciousness is linked with past experiences. Take away all reference to that which transcends the present moment (and all else in extra-mental), and the content of my experience vanishes. Doubtless something would remain, but what that something would be we can only surmise; it certainly would not be color; it clearly would not be a judgment in regard to an experience; no, not even a sensation, for a sensation is intellectual and demands more than the immediate experience for its reality. Even the animal so low down the scale of mental life that it possesses no more complex a conscious state than 'thing-a-me-bob-again,' to use an expression borrowed from James, has in that experience transcended the immediacy of the conscious now. And here we come again to the essence of the whole difficulty. Any intellectual state, whatever it may be, depends for its validity on a something which transcends itself. The very act of knowing affirms the extra-mental, and immediate knowledge does not exist, at least as far as human beings are concerned. If we possessed this immediate knowledge we should not know it. All our conscious processes must be mediate. To criticise knowledge because it is mediate is to deny the possibility of any certainty whatsoever. An immediate cognition is a contradiction. It can not even arrive at *cogito*. This was the great discovery of Descartes, hinted at before in Anselm's much-abused ontological argument, namely, that knowledge, to be certain, must transcend itself, and that intellectual certainty posits something beyond the state which expresses the certainty.

But some one may urge that this extra-mental reference that knowledge demands is a reference from one conscious experience to another, and therefore a reference which does not transcend the consciousness of the individual. This brings us back from the second meaning of the proposition to the first, namely, that we can know only our past mental states; an assertion which by implication is contained in that part of the proposition already discussed; for, as we have already seen, knowledge of the present state demands as its warrant a knowledge of past experiences. Thus these two meanings in the assertion of subjective idealism fall under one head in the last analysis. The first proposition, in the light of what has already been said, can be examined briefly.

It must be remembered that the past conscious experience as such no longer exists. Our knowledge of it is a mediate one, as indirect and remote in many ways as the knowledge of a physical fact, and it is as truly extra-mental as is the spatial universe. Any argument which may be applied to prove the unreality of the external world may be used to prove the unreality of past experience. It is the source of deception and illusion quite as much as is the world outside. The latter is external to us in space, the former, however, in time. If we doubt the existence of the one we can legitimately doubt the existence of the other as well, and the only reality of which we then can be certain in the sense that subjective idealism demands is a reality of the immediate moment. Regarding this, however, as has already been pointed out, no assertion can be made which does not transcend its immediacy; in other words, all knowledge, even of the most rudimentary type, must on this assertion cease. If subjective idealism were true, no one could make the assertion. Indeed, the mind would be that bundle of conscious elements that Hume conceived, but the bundle would have no bond of connection between its various parts, mental life would have neither continuity nor meaning; it would in fact be nothing at all that we can conceive, a point of consciousness without relation to past or future. To this psychic atomism does solipsism, when rigidly interpreted, inevitably lead. Such a doctrine can not be successfully refuted, for it offers no point of attack. Its mere statement is an absurdity.

If the above analysis be correct, we are forced to the conclusion that, while naïve realism contains contradictions, it can not so easily be set aside as ordinarily supposed. The plain man is often accused of views that he does not possess, and though his suppositions in regard to reality may be stated to his disadvantage, it does not follow that by plunging him into difficulties his critics have removed all difficulties from their path. Subjective idealism can not establish its position by negative criticism. Its positive assertions have been shown to be full of contradictions, and are untenable. But if both naïve realism and subjective idealism prove incapable of giving us a true knowledge, two roads to reality are left open: one by means of a critical realism, and the other by means of an absolute idealism. The merits of these two views it is not my purpose here to discuss. I will simply add in conclusion that many of the difficulties which subjective idealism encounters confront absolute idealism as well.

Appendix 5

AN OPEN LETTER TO PROFESSOR DEWEY CONCERNING IMMEDIATE EMPIRICISM
by Charles M. Bakewell

On first reading your article entitled '[The Postulate of] Immediate Empiricism' [see this volume pp. 158–67] it seemed to bear out the promise of its title and to give us a statement of an empiricism at once radical and thorough-going. But on carefully rereading it the impression forces itself upon me that you have made the empiricism so thorough that it has overleaped itself. My difficulty is so obvious a one that I dare say you have a ready answer. Probably I have missed part of your meaning. But as I think that others of your readers may share that difficulty, I venture to lay it before you in the hope of eliciting an explicit reply.

The name *immediate empiricism*, or *immediatism*, is intended, if I have caught your meaning, to emphasize two characteristics of the 'new philosophy' now generally called pragmatism: (1) 'Things are what they are experienced *as*,' —which gives us the one 'postulate' of immediate empiricism; and (2) Every experience is 'that experience which it is and no other,' or, in other words, every experience is a '*determinate* experience,'—which gives us the 'criterion' of immediate empiricism. "This determinateness," you write, "is the only, and is the adequate, principle of control or 'objectivity'" (p. 164). And, elsewhere, "If one wishes to describe anything truly, his task is to tell what it is experienced as being."

Now as you further explain the first of the above propositions you make it mean, sometimes, no more than this: every experience, as experience, is what it is experienced as. Or, again, you interpret it as meaning simply, that if one starts out to explain any fact of experience, he must stick 'in the most uncompromising fashion' to that definite initial

[First published in *Journal of Philosophy, Psychology and Scientific Methods* 2 (1905): 520–22. See Dewey's reply, "Immediate Empiricism," pp. 168–70, this volume.]

experience from which he sets out, as a real experience. With either interpretation the first proposition becomes as simple, elementary, 'tautologous' even, as the second; and both would be accepted at a glance, as a matter of course, precisely as one would assent without argument to the propositions, A is A, and A is not non-A.

The obviousness of these propositions gives your general position its plausibility. But to get out of them any 'criterion,' or "principle of 'objectivity,'" do you not then, and without giving any logical defense, substitute this highly questionable interpretation of your first proposition; everything experienced is, and is no more than, it is then and there experienced as? Is this what immediatism means? I gather that it is, not only from the general drift of your discussion, but in particular from such expressions as the following, which you use as equivalent in describing a typical case of a 'corrected experience': 'the experience has changed,' 'the thing experienced has changed,' 'the concrete reality experienced has changed' (p. 160). And, in speaking of the Zöllner lines, you write, "the lines of *that* experience (the initial 'uncorrected' experience) *are* divergent: not merely *seem* so" (p. 163).

I am aware that by a certain placing of the emphasis, and by introducing qualifying and explanatory phrases, all of these expressions could be reduced to the tautological form. But they suggest the interpretation that the real thing aimed at in the original experience is gone and that we are dealing with another, and maybe even a different kind of a real thing. And some such interpretation seems to be required if immediatism is to furnish a 'key to the question of the objectivity of experience.' In the 'corrected experience' of the Zöllner lines, you imply, the lines that then are at once *seen* as converging and *known* as parallel are the lines of that particular experience, and not the real and self-same lines of the initial experience. But why should there be any problems at all if each experience is a new and a different reality? Why must experience be 'corrected,' and how can we speak of *it* as being corrected if it is in fact simply superseded? You write: "It is in the concrete thing *as experienced* that all the grounds and clues to its own intellectual or logical rectification are contained." Here the phrase 'its own' seems to bring back the reference to a permanent objective reality that is carried through the process of correcting,—a view which immediatism aims to supplant. And when you speak of the initial experience, say of the Zöllner lines, as containing, *as experienced*, 'all the grounds and clues' to its correction, how can you make this out except by reading into that initial experience as part of *its* reality that fuller meaning and larger context which only a later knowledge (experience) brings to light? This would, however, give us, as far as it goes, an idealism,—and of a decidedly transcendental kind.

My difficulty, in short, is simply this: Either everything experienced is real exactly as, and no further than, it is then and there experienced,—and then there is no occasion to speak of correcting or rectifying experience; or, there is in every experience a self-transcendency which points beyond that thing *as experienced* for *its own* reality,—and then good-by to immediatism. Either atomism[1] or transcendentalism. And either view seems, in your article, to pass over very easily into its opposite, in good old Hegelian fashion.

Is there another alternative which I have overlooked?

---

1. Not, to be sure, the atomism of the earlier English psychology, to which you refer in a footnote. But immediatism seems to give us a kind of atomism differing from that only in greater complexity of the atoms. The reals are chopped off from one another. If, on the other hand, this consequence is avoided by making the earlier experience contain implicitly the later to which it leads, immediatism gives way to a doctrine of mediation.

Appendix 6

OF WHAT SORT IS COGNITIVE EXPERIENCE?
by Frederick J. E. Woodbridge

Professor Dewey's recent article in the *Journal of Philosophy, Psychology and Scientific Methods*[1] has definitely contributed to a clearer understanding of what the term 'real' means to many advocates of immediate empiricism and pragmatism. The real is simply *that* which is experienced and *as* it is experienced. It would seem that there could be little further misunderstanding on that point. The challenge to the pragmatist to tell what he means by reality appears, thus, to have been met successfully. If it were necessary to lend external authority to Professor Dewey's exposition, one might cite the ancient statement of Aristotle that reality is whatever can be the subject of investigation. From such a definition of reality it is evident that reals may differ from one another in any way in which they are found to differ; and that, consequently, there may be 'true' reals and 'false' reals if warrant can be found for such a distinction among the things which may be investigated.

There is no need of an elaborate proof to show that this definition, in spite of—rather, just because of—its simplicity and obviousness, is the only fruitful definition of reality. The history of thought is in evidence. To the metaphysician it is a real blessing, for it frees him from the trivial question whether there is anything real at all, and turns him to the more fruitful and important question, what is the nature of the real, when is it most fittingly and appropriately defined?

Now, it is just that question which seems to cause confusion and dilemma. And it is here that further clarification is needed. For the natural and obvious answer to the ques-

1. "The Postulate of Immediate Empiricism," Vol. II., No. 15, p. 393. [*Middle Works* 3:158–67.]

[First published in *Journal of Philosophy, Psychology and Scientific Methods* 2 (1905): 573–76. See Dewey's reply, "The Knowledge Experience and Its Relationships," pp. 171–77, this volume.]

tion when is reality most fittingly and appropriately defined, seems to be this: when it is *truly* defined. That this answer is the cause of the greater part of current controversies about pragmatism is obvious enough. It seems worth while, therefore, to say something about it, and elicit, possibly, further discussion from Professor Dewey and others.

The dilemma in question is apparent. If reality as true is but one sort of reality or one sort of experience, how can it possibly be affirmed that the nature of reality is most fittingly defined, when we have that sort, when, that is, reality is experienced as true? The answer occasionally given that it is thus most fittingly defined because defined in a way which most usefully meets the needs which raise the demand for definition, seems to many minds to be unsatisfactory. The reasons for dissatisfaction vary much, from quaking fear for the possible loss of an absolute to a genuine conviction that the whole knowing experience is a transcendent kind of experience, related to all other kinds in a way in which they are not related to it. I willingly leave the absolutist to his fears, but would say something in favor of the transcendence of knowledge.

As what I have to say has been definitely shaped in its formulation by Professor Dewey's article, I use some of his expressions to bring out the point I would raise for discussion:

"In each case," says Professor Dewey, "the nub of the question is, *what sort of experience* is meant or indicated: a concrete and determinate experience, varying, when it varies, in specific real elements, and agreeing, when it agrees, in specific real elements, so that we have a contrast, not between *a* Reality, and various approximations to, or phenomenal representations of, Reality, but between different reals of experience. And the reader is begged to bear in mind that from this standpoint, when 'an experience' or 'some sort of experience' is referred to, 'some thing' or 'some sort of thing' is always meant.

"Now, this statement that things are what they are experienced to be is usually translated into the statement that things (or, ultimately, Reality, Being) *are* only and just what they are *known* to be, or that things are, or Reality *is*, what it is for a conscious knower—whether the knower be conceived primarily as a perceiver or as a thinker being a further and secondary question. This is the root-paralogism of all idealisms, whether subjective or objective, psychological or epistemological. By our postulate, things are what they are experienced to be; and, unless knowing is the sole and only genuine mode of experiencing, it is fallacious to say that Reality is just and exclusively what it is or would be to an all-competent all-knower; or even that it *is*, relatively and piecemeal, what it is to a finite and partial knower. Or, put more positively, knowing is one mode of experiencing, and the primary philosophic demand (from the standpoint of immediatism) is to find out *what* sort of an experience knowing is—or, concretely how things are experienced when they are experienced *as* known things."

Again, Professor Dewey says in a foot-note, "The adequacy of any particular account [of the truth-experience] is not a matter to be settled by general reasoning, but by finding out what sort of an experience the truth-experience *actually* is." I have italicized the word 'actually.'

Now, my difficulty in getting a clear understanding of these and similar statements gets sharply pointed in the question: In what sort of experience do I find out what any sort of experience is, and is *actually* or otherwise? Is the answer to that question this: In the sort of experience you are having at the time? If so, I find out what sort of an experience a moral experience is by having it, and what sort a cognitive experience is by having it. But how shall I distinguish a moral experience from one that is cognitive? By having, I suppose the answer would run, a new experience in which the two are experienced as different.

Such an answer—and let it be kept in mind that I am not burdening anybody with such an answer, but am using it as one which seems to be implied in the statement under consideration—deserves to be pushed to its full limit in order to get a clear view of the sort of experience which it indicates. So pushed it appears to me to be this: If I am to find out what the different sorts of experience are, how they are related to one another, how they are distinguished, what sorts of objects constitute them, what has been their history, what their promise is, which of them may be called true, and which false, I must have an experience in which what I desire to find out is to some extent, at least, experienced. But this desired experience, which would contain within it all the possible riches of science and philosophy, is just the sort of experience which is generally called a cognitive experience. If, therefore, the suggested answer is the correct one, it appears to me clear that in cognitive experience all other sorts of experience may exist without alteration; for, otherwise, how could we find out what sort they are? How could they be identified as the concrete, particular sorts of experience indicated? In other words, in the cognitive sort of experience all other sorts appear to be transcended. The nub of the *question*, to use Professor Dewey's words once more, is, undoubtedly, what sort of experience is meant or indicated. But it would appear that this question can be *answered* only in a cognitive experience!

As I have said, I burden no one with the answer which appears inevitably to lead to this conclusion. Yet I willingly take the burden myself. While I do not like the word 'experience' as an ultimate term in metaphysics, I can find little objection to it when it is used as equivalent to 'some thing' or 'some sort of thing,' when 'thing' may be, apparently, any term or any relation. Thus using the word, I can readily assent to such expressions as this: There are many sorts of experience of which the cognitive sort is only one and one which can be confused with the others only to the detriment of all. But I must now add that the cognitive experience is of such a 'sort' that it enables us to tell what the others *actually* are when we ask the question about *their* sort. This question may not be asked and may not be answered. In that case no one sort of experience is identified or distinguished. And what sort of an experience would that be if not precisely what we should mean by an unconscious experience?[2]

I do not know whether those philosophers who bear by choice or by imputation the name of pragmatists deny, as a rule, the transcendence of the cognitive experience as here

2. That, I may remark, is why I dislike the word 'experience.' 'Unconscious experience' looks so like a contradiction.

defined. When it is denied, I see no alternative but to assert that in the cognitive experience all other experiences become altered. But if we must have cognitive experience in order to have science and philosophy, and cognitive experience alters things, why then it appears to me that science and philosophy will be hugged to the bosom of the absolute idealist as his legitimate offspring!

In the endeavor to escape from the barren consequences of the position that *all* experience is in its nature cognitive and cognitive only, or, in other words, that all *things* are 'states of consciousness,' there appears danger of running to the opposite extreme. That is why, as it seems to me, the revolt against absolutism fails to convince many who are by no means absolutists. We attempt to give an account of experience which will commend itself to thought. How can we succeed if we raise the suspicion that any account of experience for thought must necessarily be, not only partial and inadequate, but radically different from what experience is? Surely here is a point where discussion can not fail to be important and profitable.

COGNITIVE EXPERIENCE AND ITS OBJECT
by B. H. Bode

In a recent issue of the *Journal of Philosophy, Psychology and Scientific Methods*[1] Professor Dewey contributes an interesting discussion of the postulate which forms the basis of immediate empiricism. According to his presentation this postulate amounts to the statement that things are what they are experienced to be. One experience must be held to be as real, as ultimate, as any other, and so the usual distinction between appearance and reality is necessarily wrong in principle. That is to say, the standard according to which we condemn certain experiences as erroneous, while others are judged to be 'true,' is not some fact external to the experience itself to which the experience in question either does or does not manage to conform, but resides within the experience itself. This seems to mean that if the experience by inner motivation 'points' to some further experience in which the prior experience fulfills itself, then this later experience is true to the extent to which the transition to the later experience takes place without any fundamental change in the quality or characteristic which continuously fulfills the corresponding quality present in the initial stage. Truth, then, is simply a relation which obtains among experiences that are equally real, and does not imply that certain experiences are simply appearances, in contrast to others which are not.

That this postulate is actually involved in immediate empiricism appears to be beyond rational dispute. All experiences are equally real. At this point, however, Professor Woodbridge raises the doubt whether immediate empiricism

1. Vol. II., No. 15, pp. 393–99. [*Middle Works* 3:158–67.]

[First published in *Journal of Philosophy, Psychology and Scientific Methods* 2 (1905): 653–63. See Dewey's reply, "The Knowledge Experience Again," pp. 178–83, this volume.]

has been sufficiently mindful of the unique character of those experiences which are commonly called cognitive.[2] He expresses the fear that in their zeal to avoid the postulate of idealism the pragmatists have gone to the opposite extreme, and tend to dispose of all facts as 'experiences,' without much regard to the difference between the cognitive and the non-cognitive.

The point involved becomes apparent when, having accepted the empiricist's definition of reality, we take up the 'fruitful and important question, what is the nature of the real, when is it most fittingly and appropriately defined?' (p. 393). For in the face of this question another inevitably suggests itself: 'If reality as true is but one sort of reality, or one sort of experience, how can it possibly be affirmed that the nature of reality is most fittingly defined when . . . reality is experienced as true?' (p. 394).

All experiences, as has been said, are equally real, and, moreover, they alone are real, yet this discovery does not absolve us from the obligation to answer the question, 'In what sort of experience do I find out what any sort of experience is, and is *actually* or otherwise?' (p. 395). And the answer to this question, it is held, necessitates the conclusion that 'the whole knowing experience is a transcendent kind of experience, related to all other kinds in a way in which they are not related to it' (p. 394). That is to say, 'In the cognitive experience all other sorts of experience may exist without alteration,' or, 'In the cognitive sort of experience all other sorts appear to be transcended' (p. 396).

At first sight it may appear that whatever difficulty may be felt arises from the fact that too sharp a separation is made by the critic between the cognitive experience and 'other experiences.' Professor Dewey says, 'I should define a cognitive experience as one which has certain bearings or implications which induce and fulfill themselves in a subsequent experience in which the relevant thing is experienced *as* cognized, *as* a known object, and is thereby transformed or reorganized' (p. 162). And this definition seems to take

2. *Journal of Philosophy, Psychology and Scientific Methods*, Vol. II., No. 21, pp. 573–76.

in all kinds of experiences, so that no injustice can be charged with regard to a special class of experiences. Thus, in the illustration given by Professor Dewey, the first experience is a 'fearsome noise,' which by its own peculiar constitution induces an investigation or inquiry, and so leads on to the experience labeled, 'noise as a wind-curtain fact.' With regard to the latter two things may be noted: (a) Its character differs from that of the preceding experience only in the circumstance that it is *more predominantly* of the kind described by James as 'knowledge-about' or 'pointing,' rather than of the kind known as direct 'acquaintance-with'; and (b) It is 'a change of experienced reality effected through the medium of cognition' (p. 161). Considered as 'true' it is superior to the prior experience, because in it we find the fulfillment, the readjustment, the satisfaction of the preceding experience, which 'clamored for reform.' Considered as real, both experiences are simply instances of present functioning, and so stand on the same level.

This seems to dispose of the suggestion that the difference between the cognitive and the non-cognitive has been overlooked and that the transcendent nature of cognition has been treated with neglect. If all experiences are the same in kind, there need be no occasion to emphasize a difference of this sort, nor is it obvious that the transcendent character of cognition does not receive due consideration. While there is doubtless 'a change of experienced reality effected through the medium of cognition,' this does not preclude the possibility of satisfying the demand of the critic that 'in cognitive experience all other sorts of experience may exist without alteration.' (For 'other sorts' we must substitute 'other instances.') The other instances exist within it in the sense that they are continuous with it and are the objects to which the experience in question refers or 'points.' A difficulty can arise here, it would seem, only if we treat the former experiences as entities which are transferred bodily in order to be included as integral parts of the present experience.

Yet the point urged by Professor Woodbridge can not be set aside so easily. The explanation of the pragmatist gains whatever plausibility it may possess from the fact that the implications involved in the concept of an experience developing solely by inner motivation are not carried out to their logical conclusion. In a developing experience the later stage, as we have seen, is to be described as predominantly of the 'pointing' type, and this characteristic indicates that it is not a final stage. If the experience beginning with the 'fearsome noise' were permitted to run its full course, the experience of 'noise as a wind-curtain fact' would turn out to be simply a stage in a process, the goal of which would be another experience of the type of 'acquaintance-with,' differing, however, from the initial stage in the fact that it would be of this type, not merely predominantly, but completely or ideally. The complete 'truth' of any experience, it seems, must be sought in this final stage.

This final stage or term, however, can not, apparently, be considered as cognitive in the sense of answering a question regarding the nature of any other experience, nor can it be termed cognitive as this term is defined by Professor Dewey. I can not say, 'This is what that means,' for such affirmation implies pointing, and pointing is a characteristic that pertains solely to the stages which precede the final goal. The final stage, therefore, is neither true nor untrue, except for the onlooking psychologist. Though it be conceded that the progressive fulfillment of an experience brings out with increasing clearness the truth or meaning of the starting-point, the last stage is a bourne whence no traveler returns, even in retrospect. And the nature of this final stage is necessarily a question of supreme interest and importance.

I wish to repeat that the final stage is not one in which any questions are asked or answered. And, as Professor Woodbridge contends, if this be true, it follows that 'no one sort of experience is identified or distinguished. And what sort of an experience would that be if not precisely what we should mean by an unconscious experience?' (p. 396).

In a measure this sudden transition from a world which is synonymous with experience to a world which is most startlingly realistic is anticipated or at least suggested by statements such as the following, quoted from Professor Dewey: "The reader is begged to bear in mind that from this standpoint, when 'an experience' or 'some sort of experience' is referred to, 'some thing' or 'some sort of thing' is

always meant" (p. 159). If these final terms can be properly
characterized as unconscious experience, then conscious experience is a phrase which must be confined to relations between such final terms, and it seems to follow at once that
'consciousness may be defined, therefore, as a kind of continuum of objects.'[3]

It may, perhaps, be objected that Professor Woodbridge
passes too hastily from an experience in which 'no one sort
of experience is identified or distinguished' to the conclusion
that such an experience or reality can be properly termed an
unconscious experience. It takes too much for granted. The
opponent may point out that identifying and distinguishing
are lacking only in the sense which presupposes comparison
with other experiences.

Nevertheless, this inference that the final experience
may properly be termed unconscious seems capable of sufficient justification. In other words, it appears that, as the
doctrine is stated, the element of 'knowledge-about' or 'pointing' is a constitutive and essential part of any experience of
which we can form any respectable conception. While in the
presentation of this doctrine it is usually made to appear
that the first and the last stages of the continuous development through which experience becomes differentiated both
belong to the same general type of 'acquaintance-with,' there
is a difference which seems essential. This difference has
been indicated already by the statement that the first stage
is only predominantly of this type, while the last is completely or ideally so. If the first stage were ever complete in
this sense the inner motivation by which it leads on to further experience could not be present, for the complete stage
is a cave where all tracks lead inward. It would be a sort of
island in an ocean of 'pointing' experiences. In the actual
experience the feature which we discriminate is the one
which forms the point of departure, which prompts investigation and further observation. Such a feature is necessary
in order that this particular bit of experience may form organic connections with other experiences. And if we attempt

3. F. J. E. Woodbridge, "The Nature of Consciousness," *Journal of
Philosophy, Psychology and Scientific Methods*, Vol. II., No. 5,
pp. 119–25.

the task of trimming away, mentally, from this experience all such features as would lead beyond themselves, we seem in the end to have nothing left but a mass of undifferentiated 'material' for which the epithet 'unconscious' seems entirely appropriate. And since the first stage can be made self-sufficient only by 'trimming,' it would appear that in the last stage also such sufficiency can be attained only at the cost of all inner differentiation. That is to say, pragmatism tacitly postulates an object of reference which lies beyond the experience of the individual.

To this conclusion it may perhaps be objected that the final stage or term is simply an abstraction or limiting term and not to be regarded as an experience anywhere realized or realizable. On the basis of this interpretation, however, it is difficult to see how solipsism is to be avoided. If we are to have a common world there must be numerically identical points which are common to the different systems of experience, and such identical points can be provided only by these final terms.

It appears, then, that the realistic conclusion follows from the premises laid down by the doctrine of pure experience. The distinction between the cognitive and the non-cognitive can not be evaded. And from the utter disparity between the two it seems necessary to conclude that 'consciousness and knowledge do actually disclose to us that which is in no way dependent on consciousness and knowledge for its existence or character. Knowledge is thus palpably realistic.'

Is a realistic view of knowledge, then, our final hope? The acceptableness of this conclusion must depend in part upon the account which is given of the nature of those objects which knowledge is said to reveal. It seems that consciousness is, in a sense, an accidental feature of reality, since objects are not particularly affected by the circumstance of being known. It is claimed that even in a world like this no limits can be set to knowledge, but it is not clear that any increase in knowledge would even approximate to the inner unity by virtue of which things are what they are. Knowledge reveals to us a set of qualities and relations, but the thing-hood of objects inevitably escapes us.

Or shall we say that this demand is a return to scholastic essences and that whatever characteristics or attributes an object may possess are of the sort that are revealed to us in all knowing? This also involves implications which it is not easy to accept. What shall we say to such experiences as sweetness, contrast effects and harmoniousness? They undoubtedly have a basis in fact, but what sort of a fact is it? To say that it is the same sort of fact as that which we know when we experience them is to me rather unintelligible. And if it is conceded to be a different sort of fact, we seem forced to fall back on the distinction between primary and secondary qualities, which is simply the entering wedge of idealism.

Considerations of the sort here presented make it impossible for me to convince myself that the time has come to abandon the conception of selfhood as the ultimate category in metaphysics for that of pure experience or of objects existing independently of consciousness. Professor Woodbridge rightly warns the pragmatists against the tendency to do violence to the character of transcendence pertaining to the cognitive experience. That this character is put in jeopardy by their procedure I am forced to believe. But, in order to be just to this character, is it necessary, or even defensible, to postulate objects which are not dependent upon consciousness for their existence and their nature? Idealism, whatever its form, has difficulties in plenty; yet, to my mind, it indicates the direction in which the solution of our problems is to be sought, if it is to be found at all.

TEXTUAL APPARATUS
INDEX

TEXTUAL COMMENTARY

Dewey's writings in the present volume were published during the four years 1903–6, a critical period in which he resigned from the University of Chicago and moved to Columbia University.

Details of the 1903–4 events leading to Dewey's decision to leave the University of Chicago have been fully discussed in Robert L. McCaul, "Dewey and the University of Chicago,"[1] and in George Dykhuizen, *The Life and Mind of John Dewey*.[2] But, even though Dykhuizen mentions that "when Dewey sent his letter of resignation to President Harper on 5 April 1904, he had no position elsewhere,"[3] no previous account of these years has recorded Dewey's difficulty in deciding whether he should even continue in teaching at all. When he wrote his friend James McKeen Cattell of Columbia University that he had submitted his resignation, Dewey said simply, "I have nothing in view and shall have to rely on my friends to let me know of things that might appropriately come within my scope."[4] He was genuinely surprised when Cattell answered two days later that, although no post was open at Columbia just then, he wanted to consult President Nicholas Murray Butler at once about the possibility of arranging a place for Dewey there.[5] Pleased by this evidence of Cattell's "friendship and esteem," Dewey nevertheless responded, "I am not in good shape to decide anything just now. I want a rest. . . . When I wrote you I had absolutely no idea of any immediate response anywhere . . . and consequently I can't gather myself together to make a prompt

1. *School and Society* 89 (1961): 152–57, 179–83, 202–6.
2. (Carbondale: Southern Illinois University Press, 1973), pp. 107–15.
3. *Life and Mind of John Dewey*, p. 116.
4. John Dewey to James McKeen Cattell, 12 April 1904, Manuscript Division, Library of Congress.
5. Cattell to Dewey, 14 April 1904, Library of Congress.

decision."[6] Even while Butler was trying to establish a special
chair in philosophy for Dewey, Dewey wrote to Cattell, "My
mind is about like this. I have to choose between (1) cutting
loose from institutional connections; (2) trying to get an
administrative position (the Univ. of Ill. will want a pres.
for example) & (3) teaching philosophy. . . . Having got
as far as believing that my future is largely a choice between
philosophy at Columbia & an administrative position (the
technique of which I have learned in the last few years), I
am interested in completing the Columbia picture as far as
may be—(I should say I haven't turned a finger about an
administrative position—nobody knows of my resignation
but you, outside my dept. here)."[7]

Butler succeeded quickly in setting up a chair for
Dewey, who formally accepted Columbia's offer 28 April
1904. That his decision had been difficult and that doubt
lingered in Dewey's mind can be seen in his letter of that
same day to W. T. Harris, where he says, "I am not still entirely sure that I wish to devote myself permanently to philosophical rather than to administrative work, and I may come
back to you some time with a request for advice."[8]

But once made, Dewey's decision to join the Columbia
University faculty (with seats in the Faculties of Philosophy,
Columbia College, and Teachers College) had a pervasive
influence on his writings throughout the remainder of his
career. In the present volume, the articles on philosophy and
psychology illustrate particularly well the effect on Dewey of
the stimulating interaction with his colleagues. Successive
volumes in the *Middle Works* show a gradual increase in the
proportion of social and political commentary, an increase
that also resulted in large part from his association with
colleagues in the social sciences.[9]

Leaving the like-minded group of pragmatists at the
University of Chicago and moving into "direct contact with

6. Dewey to Cattell, 16 April 1904, Library of Congress.
7. Dewey to Cattell, 7 April 1904, Library of Congress.
8. Dewey to William Torrey Harris, 28 April 1904, William Torrey
Harris Papers, Hoose Library, University of Southern California, Los Angeles.
9. For a concise description of these associations, see Dykhuizen,
Life and Mind of John Dewey, pp. 119–24.

the Aristotelian realism of [F. J. E.] Woodbridge and the monistic realism of [W. P.] Montague" provided, as Dewey said, "a new challenge and a new stimulus."[10] He was immediately immersed in philosophical polemic; "The Postulate of Immediate Empiricism" (1905), for instance, provoked three responses, and to these Dewey in turn replied with three additional articles that also appear in the present volume.

Dykhuizen has rightly noted that Dewey's "publications in education [outside those in *A Cyclopedia of Education*] during his first ten years at Columbia were not nearly as numerous as those in philosophy."[11] As an example, in the present volume, only the article "Culture and Industry in Education" came from the first two Columbia years (1905–6) represented here. Nevertheless, the interest was surely there, however fallow it may have lain for a time: Dewey never compartmentalized his philosophical and educational concerns. As he wrote later:

I have wondered whether . . . philosophers in general, although they are themselves usually teachers, have not taken education with sufficient seriousness. . . . Philosophizing should focus about education as the supreme human interest in which, moreover, other problems, cosmological, moral, logical, come to a head.[12]

Dewey's last two years at Chicago, 1903 and 1904, had produced numerous works specifically dealing with educational topics. The abrupt decline in publishing such articles thereafter can be attributed to his having severed ties with the Laboratory School that had provided him with unparalleled opportunities for observation and a constant flow of ideas.

Despite his heavy load of administrative work and teaching during 1903 and 1904, and despite the difficulties

---

10. "Experience, Knowledge, and Value: A Rejoinder," in *The Philosophy of John Dewey*, ed. Paul A. Schilpp (Evanston: Northwestern University, 1939), p. 522.
11. *Life and Mind of John Dewey*, p. 138.
12. "From Absolutism to Experimentalism," in *Contemporary American Philosophy: Personal Statements* (New York: Macmillan Co., 1930) 2:23.

occasioned by internal institutional controversies, Dewey had
maintained his usual high level of publication, as evidenced
by the twelve items of 1903 in this volume (including the
important "Logical Conditions of a Scientific Treatment of
Morality")—all published the same year that his pivotal
Studies in Logical Theory (*Middle Works*, Volume 2) appeared. When these 1903 writings in the present volume,
along with the *Studies* (six separate pieces), are added to
the ten items in this volume that appeared in 1904, Dewey's
output in two extremely strenuous years is seen to be twenty-
eight publications.

Of the total of thirty-six items in the present volume,
twenty-six were printed only one time during Dewey's lifetime and offer no problems of copy-text or editorial procedure. One article that appeared in print only one time requires further comment; that article and the remaining nine
items are discussed title by title in the sections that follow.[13]

"Logical Conditions of a Scientific Treatment of Morality"

The first impression of this article in Volume 3 of the
first series of the Decennial Publications of the University of
Chicago, entitled *Investigations Representing the Departments* (Chicago: University of Chicago Press, 1903), serves
as copy-text. The article was reprinted once the same year
as a pamphlet, probably from standing type, with separate
pagination added and with a new title-page. No other
changes were made for the separate reprinting.

When Dewey included this article in his collective volume *Problems of Men* (New York: Philosophical Library,
1946), he made a number of substantive changes as well as
some changes in accidentals. All those substantive changes,
made by Dewey some forty-two years after the article first
appeared, appear in the List of 1946 Variants in this volume.

13. For a full statement of the editorial framework within which
    texts of *The Middle Works of John Dewey, 1899–1924* have been
    developed, see Fredson Bowers, "Textual Principles and Pro-
    cedures," *Middle Works* 1:347–60.

"Ethics"

First published in Volume 7 of the *Encyclopedia Americana* (New York: Scientific American, © 1903), in 1904, this article has in the past been incorrectly identified as a 1903 publication because of the 1903 copyright date. The first edition had five impressions, in 1904, 1906, 1907, 1911, and 1912. In the 1906 and 1907 impressions, Dewey's article appeared in Volume 6 rather than Volume 7.

The second edition, published in 1918, had eleven impressions between 1918 and 1939; in the second and subsequent editions, "Ethics" appeared in Volume 10. Examination of editions printed during Dewey's lifetime show a third edition (1940), with ten printings, and a fourth (1950), of which impressions only through 1952 were collated.

According to Alan H. Smith, Executive Editor of *Encyclopedia Americana*:

Type is newly set for each edition for volumes that are being completely recast, for individual pages or clusters of them that are substantially recast, or for portions of articles into which "patch" updating or corrections are entered.

It is our standard procedure to furnish authors with proofs of articles going into the *Americana* for the first time. Subsequently, if major changes are required, we go back to the author for the revisions or for approval of proposed revisions. If only minor changes are made, such as updating an event or bibliography or correcting an error, these are not usually referred to the author, although they may be.[14]

Type was newly set for the four editions of the "Ethics" described above. Inasmuch as few substantive changes—and those minor—were made in the article throughout its publishing history, it seems likely that, following standard house procedure, these changes were made by the publisher rather than by Dewey. Machine collation of the 1952 third printing of the fourth edition against the 1950 first printing of that edition reveals no differences between them. Sight collation of the 1952 printing (University of Texas-Austin, 658412) against the copyright deposit copy (AE5E3, copy 2) shows four substantive variants and sixty-three accidental variants.

14. Alan H. Smith to Jo Ann Boydston, 21 May 1974.

Of this number, seven variants in the kind of type used for run-in headings are not discussed further here. The remaining fifty-six accidental changes were first introduced in the 1918 second edition, with the exception of a comma after "evolution" (56.40), which first appeared in the 1950 fourth edition.

Copy-text is the 1904 first impression. Two corrective changes in substantives from the 1918 edition have been accepted as emendations of the copy-text: addition of the word "century" (45.4), and deletion of "the" (47.34). A third substantive change that first appeared in 1918, the deletion of the final "s" from "considerations" (48.14), has been rejected as an undesirable alteration of Dewey's intended meaning.

Changes at the end of the article to delete text and to revise and expand the bibliography have been considered as a single substantive variant: in the 1918 resetting, three and one-half lines of Dewey's text were omitted and a bibliography added; in 1940, ten and one-half additional lines were omitted, and the bibliography revised and expanded for the last time in impressions collated. The present edition is a conflation of the 1904 and 1918 texts, adding the 1918 bibliography to Dewey's 1904 text. The 1940 revised and expanded bibliography is contained in the List of 1940 Variants.

From the accidental changes made in 1918, nine have been selected as emendations: addition of the date of death "1903" (55.15); change in spelling to Dewey's more usual "program" (46.38, 54.29); three corrections of the 1904 edition—supplying omitted punctuation (46.31, 53.39), changing a semicolon to a comma (40.25); and three punctuation changes necessary to clarify meaning (45.24, 49.11–12, and 53.6).

The Influence of Darwin on Philosophy and Other Essays in Contemporary Thought

In 1910, Dewey collected and revised a number of previously published articles in *The Influence of Darwin*

(New York: Henry Holt and Co., 1910). Four articles in the present volume, discussed separately in following sections— "Beliefs and Existences," "The Experimental Theory of Knowledge," "Experience and Objective Idealism," and "The Postulate of Immediate Empiricism"—were among those revised for publication in D: *The Influence of Darwin*.

The publishing history of each of these four articles is identical: one journal appearance before revision and publication in D. The same editorial procedures have been used for each in the present edition. Therefore, the usual chronological order of textual commentary has been reversed here. General comments about D, and comments that apply equally to all the articles as revised in D, are made before the first publication of each article is discussed separately.

The Influence of Darwin was registered for copyright upon publication 23 April 1910 with the number A261481. All copies located of the book have the notice "Published April, 1910" on the copyright page. Records of the Henry Holt Publishing Company in the Special Collections of Princeton University indicate a small second printing was made around 1917; collation of two copies of the book against the copyright deposit copy[15] reveals no variants in the texts of the four articles. Peter Smith, New York, issued a facsimile reprint of the book in 1951.

That most of the substantive changes made for D were authorial is beyond doubt: in notes at the beginning of each article in D, Dewey called attention to his revisions. One class of substantive changes, however, offers a problem of editorial treatment: the regular, frequent, and consistent substitution of "that" for "which" in restrictive clauses. In the order of their appearance listed above, the number of instances of such substitution in these articles is: 21; 11; 21; 9. In seven cases (90.15, 92.12, 92.24, 131.31, 135.3, 135.9, 139.9) such changes occur in sentences otherwise substantively revised by Dewey. Dewey was, however, far from consistent in this practice, whether in original composition

15. Library of Congress, copyright deposit A261481; Dewey Center (a) and (b). Both the copyright deposit copy and the Dewey Center (a) copy have the date 1910 on the title page; no date appears on the title page of the Dewey Center (b) copy, which is undoubtedly from the second printing.

or in revision, and no regular pattern of occurrence on which
editorial decision can be based exists. Thus, although it
seems probable that a number of these changes were instituted by an editor at Holt, it is now impossible to distinguish
the possible editorial regularization from Dewey's intended
revision, and these changes have therefore been accepted as
emendations of the copy-text in the present edition.

"Beliefs and Existences"
["Beliefs and Realities"]

First published as "Beliefs and Realities" in *Philosophical Review* 15 (1906): 113–19, this article was not reprinted
until Dewey revised and published it in D: *The Influence of
Darwin*, with the new title "Beliefs and Existences." The
first impression serves as copy-text for the present edition.

Dewey said his revisions of the article for D were
"verbal," chiefly to substitute "some more colorless word"
for the word "Reality" because "eulogistic historic associations" with that word had "infected the interpretation of the
paper itself."[16] He did, in fact, change "reality" to "existence"
sixteen times and to "business" once, eliminated it once, and
further, added quotation marks or capitalized "reality" fifteen
more times. But he also substantively revised the article
throughout, and his substantive changes have been incorporated in the present edition as emendations. The addition
of quotation marks to, and the capitalization of, "reality"
have been considered Dewey's own accidental changes with
substantive implications, and in each case, they have been
accepted as emendations.

Accidental changes occurring within substantive revisions have also been used as emendations of the copy-text
because they clearly reflect Dewey's intended changes.
Twenty additional instances of accidental revision, occasioned by or related to substantive change, have been used
for emendation: commas added (87.30; 90.3,15; 93.16[2];
94.37; 98.23; 99.13); commas deleted (87.31; 89.38; 90.4;
94.29,37,38; 97.32–33); comma changed to semicolon

16. *Middle Works* 3:83.

(89.37); colon substituted for comma (90.5–6); commas replaced by parentheses (89.36[2]). One other accidental emendation based on a change in D has been made as more nearly reflecting Dewey's characteristic practice—hyphenation of "all-absorbing" (90.33).

"The Experimental Theory of Knowledge"

The only appearance of this article before its revision for D: *The Influence of Darwin* was in the English journal *Mind*, n.s. 15 (1906): 293–307, which is copy-text for the present edition.

As Dewey pointed out in D, he made "considerable change in the arrangement and in the matter of the latter portion" in the revised version.[17] The following table shows the earlier order of the passages indicated; from this, the reader can reconstruct the *Mind* arrangement of material for comparison (*Mind* page numbers are from the copy-text printing).

Middle Works		*Mind*	
114.6–117.2	Both the thing meaning . . . occupied.	300.20–303.1	Both the thing meaning . . . occupied.
117.2–9	One may, that is, . . . in the future.	304.31–38	One might, that is, . . . in the future.
117.25–118.17	In the reflective determination . . . adverb "truly";	305.12–39	In this reflective determination . . . adverb 'truly'.
122.11–124.8	by reason of disappointment . . . preserved a secret.	303.1–304.27	By reason of disappointment . . . preserved a secret.
124.34–125.22	Subsequent meanings and subsequent fulfillments . . . cognitional object.	299.35–300.17	*Subsequent fulfilment* . . . cognitional object.

17. *Middle Works* 3:107.

Besides this shifting of passages, as Dewey noted, he also changed considerably "the matter" of the article for its new edition in D. His substantive alterations have been used here to emend the copy-text as he intended.

Following the procedure described in the "Textual Principles and Procedures,"[18] Dewey's typical spellings have been restored from their British forms in such words as "odor," "reflection," and "characterize," to the more authoritative American spellings of D. Twenty other accidental changes have been accepted as emendations from D; five of these are Dewey's addition of quotation marks to "consciousness" to call attention to his special use of the word. Fifteen other changes in accidentals for D, necessary for clarification of meaning or occurring in substantive revision, and judged to have been made by Dewey, have also been used to emend the *Mind* text: semicolon for colon (108.9); commas added (108.25, 111.9, 112.7, 114.14, 116.11, 116.15, 117n.2, 126.27, 126.35[2]); comma deleted (111.22); semicolon changed to comma to set off phrase rather than clause (116.16); and substitution of semicolons for periods to join two short sentences (113.6, 113.8), following Dewey's usual practice in revision.

Two corrections have also been adopted from D: "a non-mental object," for "an non-mental object" (123.21), and "is *ab origine*" for "is *aborigine*" (123.25).

"Experience and Objective Idealism"

Copy-text for this, the third article in the present volume that Dewey revised for inclusion in D: *The Influence of Darwin,* is its original publication in the *Philosophical Review* 15 (1906): 465–81.

Along with Dewey's substantive revisions, fifteen emendations of accidentals—all occurring in connection with substantive changes—have been made here: commas added (129.39, 131.12–13, 139.3, 141n.3, 142.22); commas deleted (130.2, 130.25, 131.13, 131.27, 137.2, and 137.23);

18. *Middle Works* 1:359.

semicolon changed to comma (129.30); comma changed to semicolon (134.21); comma moved from the end of quoted material to position following documentation at 131n.11; and parentheses added at 137.2. Two additional changes have been accepted as emendations: commas deleted at 143.40 and 144.1.

"The Postulate of Immediate Empiricism"

The first publication of this article in the *Journal of Philosophy, Psychology and Scientific Methods* 2 (1905): 393–99 is copy-text for the present edition. It was not reprinted until its revision for D: *The Influence of Darwin*, which has served as the basis for a number of substantive emendations, and for two emendations in accidentals, both representing the addition of commas needed to mark off words in a long series at 131n.2.

"Democracy in Education"

First published in *Elementary School Teacher* 4 (1903): 193–204, this article appeared three more times during Dewey's lifetime; each of the three subsequent editions, as described below, is derived and without authority. The EST impression serves as copy-text for the present volume.

The *Journal of the National Educational Association* impression of "Democracy and Education" (18 [1929]: 287–90), omitted the first twenty-four lines of the article. In the remaining portion, this impression made forty-nine unauthorized changes in accidentals, including eleven instances of added italics, twenty-three instances of closing up hyphenated words, fourteen spelling changes, and one correction—the spelling of "insistence" (238.35). Besides the initial omission of lines, six minor unauthoritative changes in substantives occurred in this impression; one of these was a necessary correction that would have been made editorially for the present edition: "likely" for "like" at 234.9.

The article appeared in *Progressive Education* 8

(1931): 216–18, with further excisions (229.28–231.4; 234.39–239.38) and the new title "Democracy for the Teacher."

The text of "Democracy in Education" that appeared in *Education Today*, ed. Joseph Ratner (New York: G. P. Putnam's Sons, 1940), pp. 62–73, follows the EST text closely in all respects, as well as making the two emendations adopted in the present edition.

"Education, Direct and Indirect"

Apparently the only extant version of this material is the printing in the *Progressive Journal of Education* 2 (1909): 31–38, which has served as copy-text. A note on the first page of that printing carries the following notice:

This exposition of the methods of the new education was given as an address at the Francis Parker School, Chicago, in January, 1904. This rescript has been arranged and italicized for the use of teachers by Louis W. Rapeer, professor of education, at the University of Washington. At the time the address was given Prof. Dewey was director of the school of education of the University of Chicago.

Although the language and phrasing of the article make it seem likely that instead of speaking spontaneously Dewey read from typescript or manuscript, no copy of either has been located. Professor Rapeer probably took stenographic notes at the time the address was given; his somewhat puzzling use of the word "rescript" may simply refer to his transcription of those notes. Whether he rearranged the material of the original address, as indicated by his use of the word "arranged," cannot now be determined, nor can we know whether his italics coincided at any point with Dewey's own. However, to restore, at least in large degree, Dewey's own probable intentions for the material, all italic passages have been changed here to roman type.

"The Relation of Theory to Practice in Education"

After its first impression as Part I in the *Third Yearbook* of the National Society for the Scientific Study of Education

(Chicago: University of Chicago Press, 1904), pp. 9–30, this article was reprinted, probably from plates, one time in 1912. Machine collation of two copies of the second impression (Yale, L 10/N28y/II.3; University of Southern California, 37053) against a copy of the first impression (Illinois State Library) reveals only the following changes: type reset to change date on title page; type reset on copyright page to note "Published February 1904 / Second Impression May, 1912"; and one line (257.12) reset to supply "f" in "of" omitted in the first impression.

"Culture and Industry in Education"

Dewey's address at the Horace Mann School, Teachers College, to art and manual training teachers, "Culture and Industry in Education," first appeared in ATA: *Proceedings of the Joint Convention of the Eastern Art Teachers Association and the Eastern Manual Training Association*, May 31, June 1, and June 2, 1906 (New York: n.p., 1906), pp. 21–30. A second edition of the article was published in EBM: *Educational Bi-Monthly* 1 (1906): 1–9, and a third in TC: *Teachers College Bulletin*, Ser. 10, No. 1 (1919): 10–18.

Sight collation of ATA and EBM shows that the EBM appearance of the article, published in October, 1906, was substantively revised; the amount and nature of these revisions leave no doubt that they were made by Dewey. ATA was probably printed in August, as indicated by a note in the bound volume of addresses to association members that the "membership list is updated and corrected to August 1, 1906." Dewey then provided copy for his former colleague at the University of Chicago, Ella Flagg Young, editor of EBM, probably by marking his changes in a printed copy of ATA, or possibly in a carbon copy of the article prepared at the time the ribbon copy was given to the editors of ATA.

The ATA edition of the article, which serves as copy-text for the present edition, varies from EBM at thirty-four points in accidentals. One of these is a typographical error introduced by EBM, "synonomous" (291.38) and one is the ambiguous line-end hyphenation of "pre-eminent" (291.36–37), which appears within a line in the copy-text. EBM corrected two typographical errors in ATA: "sovereinty" (286.5) and "butressed" (286.25). Along with these two corrections, the present edition has emended the copy-text accidentals at five places, according to what was judged to be Dewey's intention for the text: "signboards" (286.11), "pretense" (293.14), two commas setting off the added words "or dead" (291.15–16), and the addition of a comma at 293.18.

With one exception, Dewey's substantive revisions of the text have been accepted as emendations; that exception is the EBM change, probably through typographical error, of "objectionable" (288.6) to "objectional."

A note on the first page of the TC printing states that the text is based on ATA, which is verified by the agreement between ATA and TC in sixty substantive readings that Dewey revised for EBM.

LIST OF SYMBOLS

Page-line number at left is from present edition; all lines of print except running heads are counted.

The abbreviation *et seq.* following a page-line number means that all subsequent appearances of the reading in that section are identical with the one noted.

Reading before bracket is from present edition.

Square bracket signals end of reading from present edition, followed by the symbol identifying the first appearance of reading.

W means Works—the present edition—and is used for emendations made here for the first time.

The abbreviation [*om.*] means the reading before the bracket was omitted in the editions and impressions identified after the abbreviation; [*not present*] is used where appropriate to signal material not appearing in identified sources.

The abbreviation [*rom.*] means roman type and is used to signal the omission of italics.

Stet used with an edition or impression number indicates a substantive reading retained from an edition or impression subsequently revised; the rejected variant follows the semicolon.

The asterisk before an emendation page-line number indicates the reading is discussed in the Textual Notes.

The plus sign + means that the same reading appears in all collated printings and editions later than the one noted.

For emendations restricted to punctuation, the curved dash ∼ means the same word(s) as before the bracket, and the inferior caret ∧ indicates the absence of a punctuation mark.

EMENDATIONS LIST

All emendations in both substantives and accidentals introduced into the copy-texts are recorded in the list that follows, with the exception of certain regularizations described and listed in this introductory explanation. The reading to the left of the square bracket is from the present edition. The bracket is followed by the abbreviation for the source of the emendation's first appearance and by abbreviations for subsequent editions and printings collated that had the same reading. After the source abbreviations comes a semicolon, followed by the copy-text reading. Substantive variants in all texts collated are also recorded here; the list thus serves as a historical collation as well as a record of emendations.

The copy-text for each item is identified at the beginning of the list of emendations in that item; for items that had a single previous printing, no abbreviation for the copy-text appears in the list itself.

The following formal changes have been made throughout:

1. Book and journal titles are in italic type; articles and sections of books are in quotation marks. Book titles have been supplied and expanded where necessary.

2. Superior numbers have been assigned consecutively throughout an item to Dewey's footnotes; the asterisk is used only for editorial footnotes.

3. Single quotation marks have been changed to double when not inside quoted material; opening or closing quotation marks have been supplied where necessary.

The following spellings have been editorially regularized to conform to Dewey's usual practice as it appears in the word before the square bracket:

aesthetic] esthetic 148.25, 156.24, 160.6, 171.13, 172.38–39, 173.36, 179.18, 179.38, 180.29, 181.3, 181.14, 182.22

blasé] blase 246.8
centre] center 97.36, 130.19, 135.22, 136.36, 231.27, 239.7, 245.6,
    247.27, 248.22, 251.8, 253.21, 254.11, 274,10, 284.4,
    284.26, 304.7, 343.40
cooperate] coöperate 95.39, 203.5
entrusted] intrusted 280.38
fibres] fibers 304.8
focuses] focusses 236.23
preexisting] preëxisting 318.35
pretense] pretence 321.28
recognize] recognise 205n.39
régime] regime 293.10
résumé] resumé 224.36
scepticism] skepticism 213.4
self-enclosed] self-inclosed 123.4, 124.19
thoroughly] thoroly 220.37
though] tho 224.33
through] thro, thru 223.13, 228.7
Zoogeography] Zoögeography 337.23, 338.12, 340.8
zoologist, zoology] zoölogist, zoölogy 11.13, 205n.29, 332.25–26,
    337.23, 338.1, 338.8, 338.9, 338.11, 338n.1, 338n.2, 338n.6,
    340.7, 341n.11

The following instances of word division and hyphenation have been editorially altered to conform to Dewey's
known practice, which appears to the left of the bracket:

anyone] any one 81.29, 193.3
casting-room] casting room 344.23
coexistences] co-existences 6.30
common-sense (adj.)] common sense 132n.4
common sense (noun)] common-sense 49.1
cooperate] co-operate 214.20, 215.6–7, 227.34, 247.1, 272.13,
    280.22, 280.26, 281.14, 282.27–28, 283.40, 284.3, 284.33,
    298.5
coordinate] co-ordinate 31.36, 41.1
everyday] every-day 28.29
everyone] every one 67.11, 244.28
hand-work] handwork 329.20
high-school (adj.)] high school 218.31
kiln-room] kiln room 344.22
life-history] life history 68.15, 68.17, 71.21, 205n.14
lunch-room] lunch room 343.4
make-believe] make believe 293.14
practice-teachers] practice teachers 269.25
practice teaching] practice-teaching 258.12, 271.5
preoccupation] pre-occupation 264.17
pre-pedagogical] pre pedagogical 337n.3

quasi-] quasi 141.22–23, 141.23
reception-room] reception room 344.7
short-cut] short cut 71.33
someone] some one 93.33, 123.24, 149.40
subject-matter] subject matter 217.16, 227.37–38
thoroughgoing] thorough-going 200.35, 206.32
well-graded (adj.)] well graded 232.15
work-rooms] work rooms 344.6–7, 344.23

"Logical Conditions of a Scientific Treatment of Morality"

Copy-text is the first appearance of the article in *Investigations Representing the Departments, Part II: Philosophy, Education.* University of Chicago, The Decennial Publications, first series, 3: 115–39 (Chicago: University of Chicago Press, 1903).

11.7   unanalyzed] W;   analyzed
27.30   indeed∧] W;   ∼,

"Ethics"

Copy-text is the first impression of the article, Ao4: *Encyclopedia Americana* (New York: Americana Company, 1904). Some emendations made for the present edition have been based on changes made in the 1918 second edition, A18 (New York: Americana Corporation, 1918). Revisions made in the third edition appear in the List of 1940 Variants in "Ethics."

40.25   development,] A18;   ∼;
42.22   1901] W;   1902
44.39   defense,] W;   ∼∧
45.3–4   5th century] A18;   5th
45.24   strife,] A18;   ∼;
46.18   change),] W;   ∼)∧
46.31   pleasure),] W;   ∼);   A18;   ∼)∧
46.38; 54.29 program] A18;   programme
47.34   capacities] A18;   the capacities
48.14   considerations] *stet* Ao4;   consideration A18
49.11–12   positive∧] A18;   ∼,
51.18   Leibniz] W;   Leibnitz

52.9	Helvétius] W; Helvetius
52.10	1772] W; 1773
53.6	province‸] A18; ~,
53.8	1746] W; 1747
53.13	1631] W; 1632
53.39	prominent:] A18; ~‸
54.1	1832] W; 1842
55.15	44] W; 43
55.15	1818–1903] A18; 1818–
57.33–36	live, . . . those situations] stet Ao4; live. A18
57.37–58.8	Consult the . . . 1901).] A18; [not present]
58.5	Sorley] W; Sorly A18
58.7	Introduction to] W; 'Introduction to the Study of A18

"Notes upon Logical Topics"

61.4	career‸ enables] W; career, enable
63.31	diametrically] W; diammetrically
65.18	Benjamin] W; Benj.
67.7	language,] W; ~‸
69.14	Shakespeare] W; Skakespeare

"Philosophy and American National Life"

73.22	people,] W; ~;
77.31,32,32–33,36	university] W; University

"The Terms 'Conscious' and 'Consciousness' "

79.24	Ussher] W; Asher

"Beliefs and Existences"
["Beliefs and Realities"]

Copy-text is the first impression in *Philosophical Review* 15 (1906): 113–19, entitled "Beliefs and Realities." Emendations have been made from Dewey's revisions in D: *The Influence of Darwin on Philosophy and Other Essays in Contemporary Thought* (New York: Henry Holt and Co., 1910), pp. 169–97.

83.1   EXISTENCES] D;   Realities.
83.4–5   ways, towards. . . . They are] D; ways: they are
83.6   or judge] D;   and judge
83.6   justify] D;   either justify
83.7   who insist] D;   insist
83.8   meanings form their content] D;   meaning they supply
83.13   characters] D;   always characters
83.13   mere] D;   just
83.14; 84.38;   that] D;   which
86.3,14,20;
87.17; 88.1,7,31;
89.5; 93.38; 94.7,15,
27; 95.23; 96.6;
97.20,22
83.15   they help] D;   they are things which help
83.20   presence] D;   both presence
83.23–24   Such movement . . . working out] D;   For such im-
            mediate meanings are the bases, the 'predicaments' of
            human conduct. Conduct is the real, and thus the logi-
            cal, working out
83n.2–9   December 28, 1905, and reprinted . . . was desirable.]
            D;   December 28, 1905.
84.1   affirmed, acted] D;   affirmed, that is, acted
84.2   crucial fulfilment] D;   experience
84.8–11   terms of . . . characters, forms.] D;   terms of contact
            with objects.
84.12   the course of existence] D;   reality
84.13,14,19   existence] D;   reality
84.15   "Reality"] D;   ∧~∧
84.15   naturally instigates] D;   naturally—that is, metaphysi-
            cally—instigates
84.18   means ways] D;   is ways and ends
84.20   existence discerning, judging] D;   reality∧ judging
84.23   with beings] D;   of beings
84.24   its complication on the other,] D;   on the other, its
            complication
84.26–27   on the] D;   upon the
84.29   succeed in] D;   get anything but vanity by
84.30   "consciousness"] D;   ∧~∧
84.30   business] D;   reality
84.36–37   world is meant] D;   world it is
84.39   *for* life as well as *by* life.] D;   for production.
85.1   philosopher,] D;   philosopher,[1] . . . [¶] [1]I have found
            much instruction in Dr. Lloyd's article in the *Journal of
            Philosophy, Psychology, and Scientific Methods*, Vol. II,
            p. 337, on "The Personal and the Factional in the Life
            of Society."
85.1   occupied] D;   occupied of late

85.3–4   an ultimately valid principle] D;   a metaphysical prin-
            ciple
85.5   in natural existence] D;   in reality
85.7–8   just natural, empirical.] D;   just metaphysical.
85.11   Stoic] D;   the Stoic
85.14   Forswearing] D;   Foreswearing
85.15   affection] D;   affections
85.15   adventure, the genuineness] D;   adventure,
85.16   an oath] D;   the oath
85.17   Reality] D;   a reality
85.19   meanings] D;   ideas or meanings
85.19–20   everything] D;   all
85.20   of course] D;   then
85.27   other] D;   radically other
85.27–28   beliefs that shall develop] D;   beliefs, developing
85n.7   feeling] D;   feelings
86.1   to rectify] D;   rectifying
86.1   cultivate] D;   cultivating
86.2   heal] D;   healing
86.2   fortify] D;   fortifying
86.2–3   the dream of a knowledge] D;   of a knowledge
86.7; 87.20 "Reality"] D;   ∧reality∧
86.7   empirically unrealizable] D;   unrealizable
86.11   object] D;   universe
86.12   different] D;   differing
86.13   are] D;   have been
86.14   Reality] D;   reality
86.16   outlook.] D;   outlook, into pure cognitional objectivity,
            —mechanical, sensational, conceptual, as the case
            may be.
86.28   body in order expressly] D;   body expressly in order
86.31   because of] D;   because one is so sure of
86n.1   Hegel may be excepted] D;   Of course I except Hegel
86n.7–10   I wish to recognize . . . own intention.] D;   I wish
            to state the debt to Hegel of the view set forth in this
            paper.
87.3   succès] D;   succés
87.5   or the world empirically] W;   of the world empirical-
            ly D;   the world
87.7   "Reality,"] D;   ∧reality,∧
87.14   "absolute"] D;   ∧~∧
87.15   in terms] D;   and in terms
87.21   invoke a] D;   invoke the
87.26   by] D;   in
87.28   only] D;   [rom.]
87.30   in Reality,] D;   in metaphysical reality∧
87.31   things∧] D;   ~,
88.3   diagram] D;   to diagram

88.24   ultimate] D;   absolute
88.24   principle] D;   principle of conduct
88.25   the principle] D;   the supremely real
88.28   implied moral metaphysic] D;   metaphysic
88.29   this implication] D;   it
88.31–32   true existence] D;   reality
88.36–37   in its function of] D; as
89.1   all genuine things] D;   reality
89.7   effected] D;   affected
89.10   Because] D;   But just because
89.16   as] D;   to be
89.20   existence] D;   realities
89.22   complete] D;   effected
89.29–30   knowledge to be achieved only in] D;   knowledge in
89.36   man (since . . . desire)] D;   ∼, ∼,
89.37   phenomenal;] D;   ∼,
89.37   and has] D;   having
89.37–38   God, who as God is] D;   God as God, as
89.38–39   being∧—the term] D;   being,—a Being the term
89.40–90.1 it then had to be conceived] D;   it was then con-
           ceived
90.1   comes] D;   came
90.3   disciplines] D;   disciplined
90.3   till,] D;   ∼∧
90.4   world∧] D;   ∼,
90.4   may] D;   might
90.5   may yield] D;   yield
90.5–6   knowledge:] D;   ∼,
90.7   not] D;   not then
90.7–10   theory that since . . . or God.] D;   theory of knowl-
           edge and of its relation to man and to God—perfect
           content of perfect thought.
90.12   with] D;   in
90.15   that,] D;   which∧
90.20   is marked by] D;   marked
90.22   and by a] D;   and a
90.25   expresses] D;   expressed
90.31–32   his combination] D;   the combination
90.33   all-absorbing] D;   all∧absorbing
90.38   nature, science was] D;   nature, not only was science
90.38   and also] D;   but
91.5   the opportunity] D;   as the opportunity
91.6   being),] D;   ∼)∧
91.14   operated] D;   functioned
91.16   supernatural truths] D;   supernaturally realizable
           truths
91.18   charged] D;   surcharged
91.19–20   previously reserved] D;   reserved

91.37   to be as] D;   as
91.38   upon] D;   in upon
92.8   "phenomenal."] D;   ∧~·∧
92.12   that] D;   which may
92.15   limit] D;   arbitrarily limit
92.17   that] D;   how
92.18–19   knowledge that] D;   knowledge in its own aims, conditions, and tests which
92.20   that this] D;   how the
92.24   and tests that] D;   of procedure which
92.24   formulated] D;   generically formulated
92.26   existence] D;   both reality
92.32; 93.2,23; 96.35;   "reality"] D;   ∧~∧
97.19,22,34
93.1   its] D;   their
93.1–2   counterpart] D;   counterparts
93.3   already] D;   already given
93.5   human "mind"] D;   'mind'
93.6   "unreal."] D;   unreal∧ over against the objectively real.
93.10   an invidious sense,] D;   a sense metaphysically invidious,
93.12   bound] D;   bound in detail
93.13   sciences in detail] D;   sciences
93.14   in] D;   always in
93.16   activities,] D;   ~∧
93.16   since] D;   as
93.16   his,] D;   ~∧
93.16   genuinely] D;   metaphysically
93.19   being the] D;   since they are
93.24   never could be sure] D;   would never be aware
93.27   truth] D;   truth is
93.28   put] D;   it puts
93.34   or] D;   and
94.3   inquiry] D;   the inquiry activity
94.14   belief] D;   personal belief
94.16   in] D;   as
94.18   becomes a] D;   is the
94.21–22   unfavorable] D;   the unfavorable
94.22   securing] D;   of securing the
94.22   consequences. Observation] D;   consequences; observation
94.27–28   judging them from a new standpoint] D;   utilization as means
94.28–29   tests concepts by using them as] D;   fulfills the other by use as
94.29   methods∧] D;   ~,
94.29   active] D;   personally active
94.29–30   experience personally conducted] D;   immediate ex-

perience, personally initiated, personally conducted,
94.33   nothing] D; all that
94.33–34   admitting the genuineness both of thinking] D;   the
           giving of genuine metaphysical reality both to thinking
94.34   of their] D;   to their
94.35   except] D;   is
94.36   existence] D;   reality metaphysically taken
94.36   is not] D;   is
94.37   belief∧ which,] D;   ∼, ∼∧
94.38   man∧] D;   ∼,
94.39   demean itself so unworthily] D;   so unworthily demean
           itself
95.1   "real"] D;   metaphysically ∧real∧
95.2   world] D;   universe
95.5   an] D;   the
95.11   must be] D;   are at once
95.26   to belief] D;   of belief
95.39   information] D;   informations
95.39   instruction] D;   instructions
96.1   and that] D;   that
96.3   needs] D;   social needs
96.5   philosophy] D;   metaphysics
96.6   that are] D;   as such are
96.8   these facts] D;   they would
96.9   present traits] D;   offer facts
96.11   on] D;   in
96.21   "phenomenal"] D;   ∧∼∧
96.27   genuinely] D;   metaphysically
96.28   existences] D;   reality
96.35   "consciousness,"] D;   ∧∼,∧
96.39   reals] D;   metaphysical reals
97.2   intelligence] D;   consciousness
97.2–3   specific undertakings] D;   facts
97.3   not] D;   not seen
97.4   idealism] D;   current idealism as a knowledge theory
97.6   living beings] D;   lives
97.12   things, so that they] D;   real things; that in their real-
           ity they
97.14–15   things:—the   latter   thus   becoming]   D;   things,
           whereby the latter are made
97.17   they] D;   that they
97.19   a] D;   its
97.19   possession of pure intellect] D;   possession
97.31   "realities"] D;   ∧∼∧
97.31   philosophers] D;   philosophies
97.32–33   realities∧ and] D;   ∼, or
97.33   he is interested] D;   but
97.35   accredit] D;   authorize the accrediting

97.35   concrete] D;   of concrete
98.1   especially] D;   specially
98.2   knowledge] D;   consciousness
98.2–3   that because the] D;   because all the
98.4   we] D;   that we
98.5   extensive] D;   the most extensive
98.5   methods] D;   methods for testing the meaning and
           worths of beliefs
98.20   by] D;   into
98.21   convictions] D;   beliefs
98.23   are] D;   are rendered
98.23   less,] D;   ~∧
98.26   acknowledgment] D;   fullest acknowledgment
98.30–99.1 obscurantism] D;   sheer obscurantism
98n.13   genuinely] D;   really
99.2   moral] D;   spiritual
99.4   then the] D;   then there haunts us the
99.6   "spiritual values" haunts us] D;   ∧spiritual values∧
99.7–8   thereby weaken] D;   weaken
99.8–9   and in that sense, the] D;   the
99.9–10   and if knowledge] D;   if knowledge
99.13   freedom] D;   the freedom
99.13   ours,] D;   ~∧
99.14   the freer the thought] D;   and the freer it is
99.21   did he] D;   if he did
99.24   conscious] D;   more conscious
99.25   orderly] D;   more orderly
99.27   natural] D;   truly natural
99.27   then its] D;   then is its
99.28   is at one with] D;   at last one
99.28   human] D;   humane
99.32   kindle and engender new beliefs.] D;   enkindle burnt
           out forms of belief and engender new.
99.38   experience] D;   feel
99.39   that perhaps is agreement] D;   that is perhaps the
           only agreement possible on strictly intellectual matters
100.4   is to be thinking] D;   is thinking
100.7–9   of action:—and yet . . . and comparison.] D;   of ac-
           tion.

"The Experimental Theory of Knowledge"

The first impression in *Mind*, n.s. 15 (1906): 293–307
is copy-text. Emendations have been drawn from Dewey's
revisions of this article, pp. 77–111 in D: *The Influence of*

Darwin on Philosophy and Other Essays in Contemporary Thought (New York: Henry Holt and Co., 1910). Changes internal to passages that Dewey shifted in the process of revision appear in this list; the original order of those passages in the copy-text is discussed in the Textual Commentary.

107.1–2, 107n.1–3   THE EXPERIMENTAL THEORY OF
                     KNOWLEDGE[1] . . . [¶] [1]Reprinted, with . . . July,
                     1906.] D; I.—The Experimental Theory of Knowledge.
107.3   knowing] D;   knowledge
107.22   This case] D;   This
107.24   introduced. Let] D;   ~. [¶] ~
107.26; 109.15;   that] D;   which
110.19,n.6; 112.4;
113.29; 116.13(2);
123.3; 127.12
108.4(2)   there] D;   in consciousness
108.9   smell;] D;   ~:
108.10   "not experienced as" such] D;   'not experienced as';
              is not so directly in consciousness
108.18   exercise] D;   anywhere exercise
108.21; 109.19,25; 111.38–39   "consciousness"] D;   ∧~∧
108.23   present—present, at all events] D;   present—either in
              a world of things, or, at all events
108.24   a] D;   the
108.25   *that*,] D;   ~∧
108.31   context] D;   comprehension
108.33   honored] D;   honoured also
108.39   distance between] D;   immense distance of
109.2–3   finite knowledge,] D;   finite knowledge, of relative
              knowledge,
109.6   exists] D;   holds
109.9   things experienced] D;   experiences
109.16–17   this statement] D;   this
109.23–24   existence] D;   being, absolute,
109.25   *reflected*] D;   [*rom.*]
109n.12   already be] D;   be already
109n.19   mediacy] D;   Mediacy
109n.21   immediately present] D;   present
110.7   "consciousness,"] D;   ∧~,∧
110.7–8   the immediate is related] D;   to relate the immediate
110.12–13   forever] D;   for ever
110.18   a way] D;   way
110.21–23   to anticipate . . . prior experience.] D;   to some ex-
              tent, on the basis of prior experience, to anticipate.
110.32   over] D;   of
110n.1   the *flux*] D;   the mode and operation of the *flux*

110n.2   and in *habit* . . . of organization—] D;   (that he
           carelessly proclaimed and then abandoned as a merely
           negative thing, useful to drown dogmatists in),
111.8   For an observer the new quale might be] D;   The new
           quale might be for an observer
111.9   *K*,] D;   ∼ᴧ
111.9   *G*] *stet* EM;   [*rom.*] D
111.11   should] D;   would
111.15   pictures] D;   others
111.18–19 Gratification-terminating-movement-induced-by-smell]
           D;   ∼ᴧ∼ᴧ∼ᴧ∼ᴧ∼ᴧ∼
111.22   terminating] D;   terminated
111.22   career_ᴧ] D;   ∼,
112.7   thing,] D;   ∼ᴧ
112.23   assurance_ᴧ or] D;   assurance, in
113.3   present] D;   present to oneself
113.6   itself; it] D;   ∼. It
113.7   or cognitive] D;   the cognitive
113.8–9   fulfilment; or] D;   fulfilment. Or
113.10   hunting] D;   hunting consciousness
113.20–21 Before the . . . introduced,] D;   In other words, be-
           fore there can properly be use of the idea of confirma-
           tion or refutation,
113.27   *S'*] D;   *S*
113.30–31 operation incited by it] D;   operation which it in-
           cites
113.35   another at] D;   another or at
114.2   indicating] D;   intentionally indicating
114.5–6   meant to mean. Both the thing] D;   meant to mean.
           [¶] Let us return to the situation in which a smell is
           experienced to mean a certain fulfilment through an
           operation. Both the thing
114.13–14 that is,] D;   ∼ᴧ
114.31   are present,] D;   is presented,
114.31   they are] D;   it is
114.32   They are present] D;   It is presented
114.36   upon the adequacy] D;   the adequacy
115.6   *through the*] D;   *through an*
115.8   now] D;   shall now
115.23–24 already been] D;   been already
115n.1   *Studies in*] W;   Contributions to
115n.11   which meant] D;   which are meant
115n.12   they] D;   was
116.11   *detectable difference*,] D;   ∼ᴧ
116.15   which,] D;   ∼ᴧ
116.16   knowledge,] D;   ∼;
116.23   accidental] D;   *de facto*
116.29   that determines the success] D;   which determines
           control of intention as to its success

116.36   at least brings] D;   will at least bring
117.2   formerly occupied. One may, that is,] D;   formerly
            occupied. [¶] Observing the futility of such a method,
            one may turn scientist, and then epistemologist only as
            logician, only, that is, as reflecting upon the nature
            and implications of the scientific process. One might,
            that is,
117.3–4   may voluntarily] D;   might voluntarily
117.5   account] D;   come to account
117.6   discriminate] D;   to discriminate
117.8   safeguard] D;   to safeguard
117.8   employing] D;   employ
117.9–24   Superficially, it may . . . self-enclosed entities.] D;
            The presupposition here is clearly that odour, person
            and rose are elements in one and the same real world
            (or, what is the same thing, of the constitution of one
            object), and that accordingly specific and determinable
            relations exist among the elements. The smell will
            present itself indifferently as a condition of the organ-
            ism or as a trait of some other object, the rose; or, in
            exceptional cases, to be referred exclusively to the or-
            ganism, as initiator of the operations indicated by the
            odour and terminated in the rose, while as defining
            the goal of operations and fulfilment of meaning it is
            a property of the object. To smells as themselves ob-
            jects of cognition, many other traits and relations simi-
            larly attach themselves—all having reference, sooner
            or later, to the more effective and judicious use of
            odours as cognitionally significant of other things.
117.25   the] D;   this
117n.2   surplus,] D;   ~∧
118.10   things] D;   characteristic quality of things
118.11   relation,[9]] W;   ~,[1] D;   ~,∧
118.15   were] D;   would
118.15–16   to translate] D;   translate
118.17–122.11 "truly";∧ at least, if we . . . by reason of dis-
            appointment a person] D;   'truly'.[1] By reason of disap-
            pointment, the person
118n.2   thing] D;   cognitional thing
118n.4   the truth] D;   truth
121.38   about on] W;   about
122n.10   final] D;   absolute
123.3–5   attitude (the . . . "ideas") accuses] D;   attitude ac-
            cuses
123.19   function] D;   [rom.]
123.19   new property involves] D;   is
123.21   a non-mental] D;   an non-mental
123.22–24   office and use.[11] To be . . . concerned.[12] Will

not] W;   office and use.[1] To be . . . concerned.[2] Will
not D;   office and use.[1] Will not

123.25   is *ab origine*] D;   *is aborigine*

123.28   viewing] D;   this way of viewing

123.29   mental expresses only] D;   mental, does not express its
own experienced quality, but only

123n.4   necessary function] D;   function

123n.9–13   [11]Compare his essay . . . *Philosophy and Psychology.*] W;   [1]Compare his essay, "Does Consciousness
Exist?" in the *Journal of Philosophy, Psychology, and
Scientific Methods*, Vol. I., p. 480. [¶] [2]Compare the
essay on the "Problem of Consciousness," by Professor
Woodbridge, in the Garman Memorial Volume, entitled
"Studies in Philosophy and Psychology." D;   [1]"Does
'Consciousness' Exist?" *The Journal of Philosophy, Psychology and Scientific Methods*, vol. i., p. 480. The
whole article should be consulted. It has, of course,
attracted much attention; but its full logical bearing,
in cutting under the charge of psychologism as mere
subjectivism, does not seem to me to have been appreciated as yet.

124.7   assumes] D;   appears to assume

124.8–34   And as if to add to . . . a meaning in general.] D;
[¶] The spectator or critic may decide that the smell is
a feeling or state of consciousness or idea—but in this
case he is talking about smell in a different context,
another thing, having another meaning in another
situation—his own cognitive problem as psychologist
or whatever. But for itself the smell is a definite thing
or quale which identifies itself with its intention—
securing another thing as its own fulfilment. And the
enjoyed rose is not that of the artist or the botanist—
it is not the object of some other intention and problem,
but is precisely the qualities meant or intended by this
particular smell.

124.34–36 Subsequent meanings . . . the object] D;   *Subsequent* fulfilment may increase this content, so that the
object

124.36   may] D;   will

124.39   a knowledge] D;   knowledge

125.3   a merely] D;   the merely

125.13   the other] D;   other

125.23–31 IV [¶] From this excursion . . . claim to mean] D;
[¶] So far as this type of reflexion supervenes, we have
knowledge of the critical or scientific type. We have
things which claim to mean

126.27   execution,] D;   ~∧

126.30   and to their] D;   and their

126.33   denotes] D;   means
126.35   is, one may say,] D;   ~∧ ~∧
127.4   of] D;   to
127.9   generated] D;   confirmed
127.10–11 alert for them, . . . them anxiously,] D;   alert to
          note them, anxiously to search for them
127.12   rational] D;   all our rational
127.13   legitimate] D;   all legitimate
127.16–17 *significant*] D;   adequately *significant*
127.22–23 own sake over that of "mere" activity.] D;   own
          sake.
127.23   an order] D;   the order
127.24   the participation] D;   participation
127.26–27 to deprive] D;   deprive
127.27   ground] D;   reason

"Experience and Objective Idealism"

Copy-text is the first impression in *Philosophical Review*
15 (1906): 465–81; emendations have been made from
Dewey's revisions in the article, pp. 198–225 in D: *The Influence of Darwin on Philosophy and Other Essays in Contemporary Thought* (New York: Henry Holt and Co., 1910).

128.1, 128n.1–2 IDEALISM[1] . . . [¶] [1]Reprinted, with . . .
          (1906).] D;   IDEALISM.
128.2   I] D;   [*not present*]
128.8; 129.21,   that] D;   which
25; 131.1,
13,14; 132.15,17;
133.40; 134.32;
138.13; 139.18
(2); 142.5,13,
14,33
128.13   as this experience is] D;   as thought renders this ex-
          perience
128.17   with] D;   and
128.20   seems] D;   seem to me
128.23   its relation to] D;   of
128.26–27 a preservation that affords] D;   and in such a way
          as to afford
129.2   nature] D;   meaning
129.7–8   if true opinion be achieved, it is only] D;   if this be
          true opinion, it is such only
129.12   an] D;   its own
129.13   The regions] D;   This accounts for the regions

129.14   hold sway are thus explained.] D;   hold sway.
129.18   imitativeness; hence] D;   imitativeness, characteristic
           of reality subjected to conditions of change; hence
129.29   *embodiments*] D;   special *embodiments*
129.30   insecure, to reason] D;   insecure; and of reason
129.34   meaning in] D;   meaning as in
129.39   Experience presents] D;   It represents
129.39   good,] D;   ~∧
130.1   much] D;   much of
130.1   Neo-Kantian] W;   neo-Kantian
130.2   professedly] D;   logically
130.2   epistemological∧] D;   ~,
130.5   knowable∧] D;   knowable, or objective
130.6–7   may be, . . . an assurance] D;   may be anything you
           please, morally and spiritually), carries an assurance
130.8   reality] D;   reality of normative values,
130.10   epistemology] D;   it
130.11   Neo-Kantianism] W;   neo-Kantianism
130.17–18 expressed meaning.] D;   expressed meaning; ideal-
           ism as ideality against experience, as struggle and fail-
           ure to achieve meaning.
130.21–22 validation] D;   validity
130.23   obstacle which prevents] D;   obstacle preventing
130.24   making way] D;   making its way
130.25   responsible∧] D;   ~,
130.34   been] W;   taken
131.9   here bound up] D;   bound up here
131.12–13 universality,] D;   ~∧
131.13   necessity∧] D;   ~,
131.17   scientific] D;   scientific knowledge
131.21   episode] D;   typical episode
131.27   given and∧] D;   given to,
131.27   in∧] D;   ~,
131.31   a tossing that] D;   which
131n.2   Locke doubtless derived this notion from Bacon.] D;
           [*not present*]
131n.8   has] D;   is
131n.10   Memory∧"] D;   ~,"
131n.11   2),] D;   2)∧
131n.12   is opposed to] D;   opposed it to
132.2   both] D;   not merely
132.3   and also to confer] D;   but as a function constitutive
           of the
132.4   upon] D;   of
132.4   sensational] D;   the perceptual
132.7   that claims] D;   which has directly or indirectly
132.8   capacity.] D;   capacity, perceptual as well as scientific.
132.13   required] D;   requisite

132.16   sensory] D;   empirical
132.17   are] D;   would remain
132.18   II] D;   I.
132.21   of a] D;   as a
132n.15   "experimental testing,"] D;   ∧~,∧
132n.19   Baconian] D;   Lockeian
132n.23   ignorance of] D;   falsely supposed
132n.24   usage. [This pious . . . 1909.]] D;   usage.
133.7   an agency] D;   that
133.8–9   operative] D;   transcendent
133.9   constructive] D;   noumenal
133.11   idealism.] D;   idealism. The first sense, if validated,
           would leave us at most an empirical fact, whose im-
           portance would make it none the less empirical. The
           second sense, by itself, would be so thoroughly tran-
           scendental, that while it would exalt 'thought' in theory,
           it would deprive the categories of that constitutional
           position *within* experience which is the exact point of
           Kant's supposed answer to Hume. Hence, an oscillation
           to the first sense, so that thought is supposed to be at
           once a deliberate, reflective, corrective, reorganizing
           function with respect to the defects of experience,
           while to it is also attributed an absolute and uncon-
           scious function in the original constitution of experi-
           ence.
133.16   a regulative] D;   the regulative
133.16   sense, thought as] D;   sense, that of the importance of
           thought in
133.20   is *already*] D;   *already* is
133.22   any one] D;   this
133.22–23 compared with . . . of itself.] D;   discriminated
           from that.
133.23–24 The concept . . . that] D;   So the concept first is
           that
133.26   is treated as] D;   is
133.28   recognition] D;   consciousness
133.28   fallacy] D;   fatal fallacy
133.33–38 experienced object. . . . The concept] D;   experi-
           enced object. The concept
133.38   triangle,] D;   a triangle∧
133.38–39 means doubtless a] D;   for example, means a
133.39   of] D;   for
133.39–40 but to Kant it] D;   but it
134.1   that unconsciously] D;   unconsciously
134.3–4   space perception, even . . . be a triangle.] D;   space
           perception.
134.10   recognition] D;   consciousness
134.10–11 to logical function] D;   function

134.11   some prior] D;   some
134.12–15   seems clear. And it . . . various relationships.] D;
            seems clear.
134.19   this] D;   that this
134.21   identification;] D;   ~,
134.22   character] D;   and character
134.27   combines] D;   recombines
134.27   in] D;   into
134.29   is] D;   is also
135.1   application; it is another] D;   applications, and an-
            other
135.3   that functions] D;   which does function
135.9   thinking that secured] D;   thoughts which found ex-
            pression in
135.11   arrangements] D;   categorizations
135.15   prior] D;   a prior
135.15–16   organizations, biological and social in] D;   organiza-
            tion, which is biological in
135.20   a practical] D;   the practical
135.27   had] D;   has
135.29   natural] D;   biological
135.31   only supernaturally] D;   supernaturally
135.34   in thought as] D;   as
136.6   original] D;   *a priori*
136.7   and institutionalizations] D;   or institutionalizations
136.10   create mechanical] D;   mechanical
136.40   The categories] D;   Like God's rain, the categories
136.40–137.1   cover alike the] D;   fall alike upon the
137.2   (unlike God's rain$_\wedge$)] D; $_\wedge$~,$_\wedge$
137.21   by first accepting] D;   very largely by accepting as its
            own presupposition
137.23   *non-existence*$_\wedge$] D;   ~,
137.25   and to] D;   and
137.27   III] D;   II.
137.36   a factor] D;   as a factor
138.4   instinctive] D;   intrinsic
138.16   such] D;   this sense of
138.19   relevant] D;   the relevant
138.20   an appropriate] D;   the relevant
138.21–22   intellectual material depends upon] D;   thought ma-
            terial will depend simply upon
138.23–24   perception, moreover, is strictly teleological,] D;
            perception is strictly teleological, moreover,
138.26   by] D;   in this
138.26–27   contexts] D;   context
138n.3–4   controlling] D;   the controlling
138n.4   conditions] D;   condition
139.3   "neutral"] D;   the 'neutral'

139.3   emotion,] D;   ~∧
139.3   a purpose] D;   purpose
139.9   sense that] D;   logical sense in which
139.11   equaling] D;   equalling
139.12   the work of observation and description forms] D;
           such a logical function is
139.13   division] D;   intentional division
139.13   *within*] D;   [*rom.*]
139.14   registration] D;   registraton
139.28   time] D;   given time
139.36   measured] D;   ascertained
139.37   to logic∧] D;   as a branch of logic,
140.10   inferential] D;   mediate
140.15   a searched] D;   the searched
140.31   the empirical relevancy] D;   its empirical relevancy
140.31–32 the empirical worth of this contrast] D;   its em-
           pirical worth
140n.2   his own correction] D;   its own corrective
141.3   it] D;   that
141.5   IV] D;   III.
141.7   value] D;   values
141.16   bearing,] D;   ~∧
141.21   are now] D;   become
141.25   leaves] *stet* PR;   leave D
141n.3   identifying] D;   embodying
141n.3   distinction,] D;   ~∧
141n.4   logical control,] D;   the logical control of perceptive
           experience,
141n.4   all experience whatsoever.] D;   experience *qua* experi-
           ence.
142.10–11 instances, as distinct from] D;   instances, etc., the
           fact that it has an 'upon the whole' character, in-
           stead of
142.11   secures] D;   is also
142.18   exasperating] D;   almost exasperating
142.21   perfecting] D;   perfectng
142.22   object,] D;   ~∧
142.23   measure intelligence] D;   measure
142.30   reduction] D;   reflection
142.31   present,] D;   present into elements defined on the basis
           of the past,
142.31   and] *stet* PR;   [*om.*]
142.32   though] D;   yet
142.34   precedents∧] W;   ~,
143.2   are] W;   is
143.10   content and value] D;   meaning
143.33   transformed] D;   altered
143.34   they are called] D;   called

143.40   experimental$_\wedge$] D; ~,
144.1   idealism$_\wedge$] D; ~,
144.8   experience,] D; experience with the contrasts in value
           this transition brings,

"St. Louis Congress of the Arts and Sciences"

146.5   necessary] W; natural
146.20   *non sequitur*] W; *nonsequitur*
147.18 $_\wedge$are "not] W; '~ $_\wedge$~
148.36   Congress] W; congress

"The Realism of Pragmatism"

156.10   *Studies in*] W; *Contributions to*

"The Postulate of Immediate Empiricism"

Copy-text is the first impression of the article in *Journal of Philosophy, Psychology and Scientific Methods* 2 (1905): 393–99; emendations have been made from Dewey's revisions for the new edition, pp. 226–41 in D: *The Influence of Darwin on Philosophy and Other Essays in Contemporary Thought* (New York: Henry Holt and Co., 1910).

158.2, 158n.1–3 EMPIRICISM[1] . . . [¶] [1]Reprinted, . . . 1905.]
           D; EMPIRICISM
158.8,18,19; that] D; which
161.14; 162.15,
24; 164.27,32;
165.14
158n.12   *Philosophical Review*,] D; *Phil, Rev.*,
158n.17   *certainty*.] D; *certainty in* knowledge.
159.7   zoologist, and] D; zoologist, etc., and
159.14   denoted] D; meant
160.6–7   technologically.] D; ~, etc.
160.7   assume that, because] D; assume, because
160.7–8   *standpoint of the knowledge experience*] D; [*rom.*]
160.9   be, therefore] D; be, that, therefore
160.13–16 roots. . . . [¶] I start] D; roots. [¶] For example, I
           start

160n.14   means *his*] D;   means that *his*
161.1   existence] D;   reality
161.7   cases, only in retrospect is the] D;   cases, it is only in
           retrospect that the
161.8   cognitionally] D;   is cognitionally
161.9   content] D;   contents
161.9   a] D;   the
161.21   to the empiricist] D;   [*ital.*]
161.22   genuine] D;   real
161.29   of this sort] D;   of which this is true
162.1   (∧or] D;   (-∼
162.11   he] D;   which he
162n.3   holds] D;   hold
163.6   control. Suppose] D;   control, a principle of guidance
           and selection, the normative or standard element in
           experience. Suppose
163.10   can the] D;   can there be the
163.10   be drawn] D;   that we draw
163.35, 163n.1–6 is true or truer.⁹ . . . [¶] ⁹Perhaps the point
           . . . above paragraph.] D;   is experienced as true or
           as truer.
164.23   tension] D;   transcendence
165.6   reals∧] D;   ∼,
165.6–7   continuity,] D;   ∼∧
165.12   they lie] D;   it lies
166.1   quality] D;   quantity
166.2   the thing] D;   it
166.13–167.29 [NOTE: The reception . . . p. 174.]] D;   [*not
           present*]

"The Knowledge Experience and Its Relationships"

177.3   ∧the nature] W;   '∼
177.3   "when] W;   ∧∼

"Emerson–The Philosopher of Democracy"

185.16   natural] W;   right
185.31   gives] W;   give
187.8   Immanuel] W;   Imanuel
187.21   *n*th] W;   *nth*
187.27   manners] W;   manner
191.14–15 tenderly] W;   continually
191.16   home] W;   homes

"The Philosophical Work of Herbert Spencer"

194.29; 196.13; Universe] W; universe
198.11; 206.30
197.25–26 propositions] W; purposes
201.14   1851] W; 1850
202.25   millennium] W; millenium
205n.19 ethnologic] W; ethnological
205n.24 Prof.] W; Professor
206.26   the Vestiges] W; The Vestiges

"The Psychological and the Logical in Teaching Geometry"

217.4   acquirement] W; aquirement
220.3   is] W; in

"Democracy in Education"

Copy-text is *Elementary School Teacher* 4 (1903): 193–204. Another appearance of the article, JN: *Journal of the National Educational Association* 18 (1929): 287–90, is noted as the first appearance of the two emendations that would have been made editorially in the present edition.

234.9   likely] JN; like
238.36 insistence] JN; insistense

"Education, Direct and Indirect"

240.31 as that] W; that

"The Relation of Theory to Practice in Education"

Copy-text is the article's first impression, Part I, *Third Yearbook* of the National Society for the Scientific Study of Education (Chicago: University of Chicago Press, 1904). The 1912 second impression, Y12 is noted as the source of one emendation.

256.33   candidates] W;   condidates
257.12   of] Y12;   o

"Significance of the School of Education"

276.21–22; 278.21–22   Laboratory School] W;   laboratory school
278.21   Department of Education] W;   department of educa-
           tion

"Culture and Industry in Education"

Copy-text is the first publication of this article in *Proceedings of the Joint Convention of the Eastern Art Teachers
Association and the Eastern Manual Training Association*,
May 31, June 1, and June 2, 1906 (New York: n.p., 1906),
21–30. Emendations of the copy-text have been made from
Dewey's substantive revision of the article for its appearance
in *Educational Bi-Monthly* 1 (1906), 1–9.

285.8   it shapes] EBM;   shapes
285.15   discussing] EBM;   with discussing
286.5   sovereignty] EBM;   sovereinty
286.6   worthy,] EBM;   worthy for human life,
286.11   signboards] EBM;   sign boards
286.18   goods] EBM;   good
286.19   not valuable intrinsically—] EBM;   intrinsically
           not-valuable;
286.20   aim is to live a life of] EBM;   aim of human life is
286.21   the final] EBM;   final
286.25   Such] EBM;   But such
286.25   buttressed] EBM;   butressed
286.34–35 which is the aim] EBM;   the aim
286.38   which have] EBM;   having
287.7   except] EBM;   unless
287.13   for enjoying] EBM;   enjoying
287.22   secure] EBM;   secure to them
287.29   class.[1] ∧Educational] W;   ~.∧ [1]~
287n.3   at business] EBM;   in business
287n.4   their being] EBM;   being
288.1   was for use] EBM;   is for use
288.1–2   was for culture] EBM;   is for culture
288.6   objectionable] *stet* ATA;   objectional EBM

288.8   mental] EBM;   mental and bodily
288.11   fierceness] EBM;   the fierceness
288.15   cast‸iron] EBM;   ~-~
288.37   requires at hand] EBM;   requires
288.37   labor.] EBM;   labor at hand.
288.40   recruits] EBM;   facile recruits
289.2–3   these shall . . . required] EBM;   these qualities shall
            be secured more than is required
289.8   but somewhat] EBM;   but a life of somewhat
289.9   is] EBM;   shall be
289.18–19   the world commerce] EBM;   world commerce
289.20   has] EBM;   have
289.29   for] EBM;   in
289.30   exchange] EBM;   distribution
290.5   as] EBM;   to be
290.7   dependence upon applied science of] EBM;   depend-
            ence of
290.8   distribution renders] EBM;   distribution upon applied
            science renders
290.8   a] EBM;   the
290.14   plane] EBM;   place
290.24   the charge] EBM;   charge
290.25   that free] EBM;   due
290.26   them a maximum] EBM;   the maximum
290.34   which] EBM;   in which
290.35   permitted] EMB;   indulged
291.1   factor] EBM;   factors
291.3–4   at once] EBM;   both
291.15–16   dying, or dead,] EBM;   dying
291.37   the play time] EBM;   play
292.14   freed] EBM;   free
292.15   human and scientific] EBM;   their human and their
            scientific
292.17   artistic plane,] W;   artistic, plane EBM;   artistic,
292.21   or] EBM;   of
292.27   satisfaction] EBM;   own satisfaction
292.31   life] EBM;   emotional life
292.31   conditions] EBM;   external conditions
292.32   signs] EBM;   signs of its presence
292.32   symmetry] EBM;   symmetery
292.34   the degree in which] EBM;   which
292.34–35   inner joyful] EBM;   joyful
292.35   outward control] EBM;   control
292.35   nature's forces.] EBM;   nature.
293.11   in] EBM;   of
293.12   be] EBM;   will be
293.14   pretense] EBM;   pretence
293.18   which,] EBM;   ~‸

293.23   so ministering] EBM;   it so ministers
293.24   of thought] EBM;   that
293.26   technique.] EBM;   technique of control and aim.

Remarks on Soldan

294.17   undoubtedly] W;   undoubtodly
296.11   school] W;   schools

Review of Place of Industries by Dopp

309.21   reports] W;   report

Review of World Views by Benedict

311.11   asceticism] W;   ascetism

Review of Humanism by Schiller

315.35   materialist's] W;   materalist's
316.29   necessity] W;   necesity

Review of The Life of Reason by Santayana

320.10   ∧for "a] W;   '~ ∧~

"The Organization and Curricula of the College of Education"

333.5   the] W;   he
333n.1   is] W;   s
334.23   Total] W;   [not present]
334n.2   accordingly] W;   accord-
337.26   Meteorology] W;   Meterology
340n.2   languages] W;   languag

"The School of Education: The Building"

342.5   Court] W;   court
342.6   Avenues] W;   avenues
344.15   building] W;   buildlng

"The Psychology of Judgment"

351.15   is] W;   in

LIST OF 1946 VARIANTS IN "LOGICAL CONDITIONS OF A SCIENTIFIC TREATMENT OF MORALITY"

Substantive changes made in "Logical Conditions of a Scientific Treatment of Morality," *Investigations Representing the Departments*, Decennial Publications 3 (Chicago: University of Chicago Press, 1903) when it was collected in PM: *Problems of Men* (New York: Philosophical Library, 1946) appear below after the square bracket which signals the end of the reading in the present volume.

3.6	in this article] I; here PM
5.22	already] I; other PM
5.23–24	judgment is] I; judgments are PM
5.25	any one] I; one of them PM
5.33	that do] I; which do PM
6.38	thought essentially] I; often supposed PM
8.22; 10.4; 31.14; 35.11	universal] I; general PM
10.6	universal] I; proposition PM
10.12	universal] I; such PM
11.7	analyzed] I; unanalyzed PM
12.30	concerned] I; engaged PM
12.31	psychical reality] I; existence PM
13.32	act] I; action PM
13.35	absolutely] I; wholly PM
14.2	case] I; cases PM
14.8	a given case] I; given cases PM
14.19	possibilities] I; alternatives PM
18n.6	unreal] I; abstract PM
19.24	judger] I; situation PM
19.27	or] I; of PM
19.33	motive] I; habit PM
19n.1; 20n.1,7	Peirce] W; Pierce I PM
20.9,n.5; 26.13–14; 28.19; 36.35; 37.16	psychical] I; mental PM
20n.2	psychically] I; physically PM
21.14,31; 22.7	motive] I; interest PM
22.2	hence] I; thence PM

22.30	conscious] I; express PM
23.6	with] I; in PM
23.7	a definitive element in] I; in PM
23.7–8	determination is] I; determination PM
23.9	judging.] I; judging is a factor. PM
23.12	act] I; [*ital.*] PM
23.34	reality] I; structure PM
24.27–28	methods;] I; methods$_\wedge$ as PM
25.25	ultimate] I; basic PM
26.32	as affecting] I; as it affects PM
27.34	psychical] I; active PM
29.24; 31.17,21	psychic] I; mental PM
29.33	specific] I; special PM
30.26	an ideal] I; as an ideal PM
34.31	metaphysics] I; philosophy PM
35.17–18	conscious] I; human PM
36.8	conscious] I; [*ital.*] PM
36.31	conscious] I; explicit PM
37.3	psychical] I; total PM
38.5	activity] I; behavior PM
39.6–7	or experience] I; of experience PM
39.10	conscious change] I; deliberate change PM

Changes made in the 1940 edition of Dewey's article "Ethics" in *Encyclopedia Americana* (New York: Americana Corporation, 1940)—the further deletion of text at the end of the article (the 1918 original deletion is recorded in the Emendations List) and the revision and updating of bibliographical references—appear below.

57.25–36   and end. . . . those situations.] A04;   and end. A40
57.37–58.8   Consult the . . . 1901).] A18;   Bibliography.—Adler, F., 'An Ethical Philosophy of Life' (New York 1918); Baxter, G., 'Of Sanction' (Norfolk, Va. 1923); Brandt, C., 'The Vital Problem' (New York 1924); Carr, H. W., 'Changing Backgrounds in Religion and Ethics' (London 1927); Croce, B., 'The Conduct of Life' (New York 1924); Dawson, M. H., 'The Ethics of Socrates' (New York 1924); Dewey, J., 'Human Nature and Conduct' (New York 1927); Durkheim, E., 'L'Éducation Morale' (Paris 1925); Fuller, Sir B., 'The Science of Ourselves' (London 1921); Givler, R. C., 'The Ethics of Hercules' (New York 1924); Groves, E. R., 'Moral Sanitation' (New York 1916); Hirst, E. W., 'Self and Neighbor' (London 1919); Hobson, J. A., 'Free Thought in the Social Sciences' (New York 1926); Hocking, W. E., 'Human Nature and Its Remaking' (New Haven 1923); Hudson, J. W., 'The Truths We Live By' (New York 1921); Jung, E., 'Le Principe Constitutif de la Nature Organique' (Paris 1923); MacKaye, J., 'The Logic of Conduct' (New York 1924); Thomas, E. E., 'The Ethical Basis of Reality' (London 1927); Sharp, F. C., 'Ethics' (1928); Schweitzer, A., 'Philosophy of Civilization' (2d ed., 1929); Taylor, A. E., 'Faith of a Moralist' (New York 1937); Tuker, M. A. R., 'Past and Future of Ethics' (New York 1938). A40

I. *Copy-text list.*

The following are the editorially established forms of possible compounds which were hyphenated at the ends of lines in the copy-text.

10.10	self-sufficing	196.22	straightforward-
18.21	presupposes		ness
26.14	subject-matter	197.13	re-choose
35.20	non-ethical	198.10	pre-condition
63.15	self-evident	226.11	high-school
70.8	beefsteak	231.4	public-school
73.16	self-consciousness	231.29	non-expert
76.11	offhand	247.7	subject-matter
90.36	thorough-paced	250.15	subject-matter
115.20	self-demanded	263.23	subject-matter
124.7	extra-empirical	265.19	subject-matter
126.21	preconceived	267.24	everyday
135.31	supernaturally	295.21	misdirection
139.5	overweening	322.4	underestimates
156.37	predetermined	326.24	pre-eminently
159.7	horse-dealer	344.19	dark-stained

II. *Critical-text list.*

In transcriptions from the present edition, no line-end hyphens in ambiguously broken possible compounds are to be retained except the following:

22.10	subject-matter	62.23	non-contradiction
37.4	pre-classified	71.15	full-fledged
45.11	free-thinkers	80.3	self-consciousness
51.36	anti-scientific	80.8	self-consciousness
53.20	self-seeking	80.20	sub-sense
53.40	non-theological	80.23	self-consciousness
57.11	self-regulation	103.17	ditch-digger
62.6	to-day	104.7	extra-scientific

114.19	self-contradictory	238.22	clay-modeling
120.13	extra-empirical	242.21	subject-matter
129.17	non-being	246.35	text-book
134.27	psycho-physical	256.26	subject-matter
135.33	supra-empirical	263.23	subject-matter
169.30	self-rectifying	266.18	subject-matter
170.5	self-evident	267.16	subject-matter
175.27	subject-matters	267.19	subject-matter
178.12	non-knowledge	268.9	subject-matter
178.16	wind-curtain	272.22	subject-matter
198.10	pre-condition	291.36	pre-eminently
209.16	self-organizing	296.11	time-wasting
217.17	extra-logical	343.12	group-work
227.37	subject-matter	344.6	work-rooms
229.13	cross-purpose	347.25	text-book
237.7	ready-made		

CORRECTION OF QUOTATIONS

Dewey represented source material in varying ways, from memorial paraphrase to verbatim copy, sometimes citing his source fully, in others mentioning only authors' names, and in still others, omitting documentation altogether.

To prepare the critical text, all material inside quotation marks, except that obviously being emphasized or restated, has been searched out and the documentation has been verified and emended when necessary. Steps regularly used to emend documentation are described in Textual Principles and Procedures (*Middle Works of John Dewey*, 1:347–60), but Dewey's substantive variations from the original in his quotations have been considered important enough to warrant a special list.

All quotations have been retained within the texts as they were first published, except for corrections required by special circumstances and noted in the Emendations List. Substantive changes that restore original readings in cases of possible compositorial or typographical errors are similarly noted as "W" emendations. The variable form of quotation suggests that Dewey, like many scholars of the period, was unconcerned about precision in matters of form, but many of the changes in cited materials may have arisen in the printing process. For example, comparing Dewey's quotations with the originals reveals that some journals housestyled the quoted materials as well as Dewey's own. In the present edition, the spelling and capitalization of the source have been reproduced.

Dewey's most frequent alteration in quoted material was changing or omitting punctuation. He also often failed to use ellipses or to separate quotations to show that material had been left out. No citation of the Dewey material or of the original appears here if the changes were only of this kind—omitted or changed punctuation, including ellipses. In the case of omitted ellipses, attention is called to short phrases; if, however, a line or more has been left out, no attention has been called to the omission.

Italics in source material have been treated as accidentals. When Dewey omitted those italics, the omission is not noted, though Dewey's added italics are listed. If changed or omitted accidentals have substantive implications, as in the capitalization of some concept words, the quotation is noted. The form of listing the quotations, from Dewey as well as from his source, is designed to assist the reader in determining whether Dewey had the book open before him or was relying on his memory.

Notations in this section follow the formula: page-line numbers from the present text, followed by the text condensed to first and last words or such as make for sufficient clarity, then a square bracket followed by the symbol identifying the Dewey item. After a semicolon comes the necessary correction, whether of one word or a longer passage, as required. Finally, in parentheses, the author's surname and shortened source-title from the Checklist of Dewey's References are followed by a comma and the page-line reference to the source.

The sources for Dewey's quotations at 95.7–8, 95.18–21, 109.10–12, and 185.9–10 have not been located.

In three instances, the opening quotation mark has been moved to reflect accurately the exact beginning of quoted material: 147.18, 177.3, and 320.10. In six other cases (130.34, 185.31, 191.16, 197.25–26, 205n.19, 217.4) the text has been emended on the authority of Dewey's source; these nine emendations appear in the Emendations List.

"Ethics"

42.32   as the] Ao4;   the (Bentham, *Principles of Legislation*, cccviii.8)

42.34–35   *to instruct*] Ao4;   [*rom.*] (Bentham, *Principles of Legislation*, cclxviii.5)

"The Terms 'Conscious' and 'Consciousness' "

79n.5   another . . . together.] JP; another. (Murray, Dic-
          tionary, 2:847.100)

"Beliefs and Existences"

85n.4   existed] PR; existence (Tolstoï, Essays, 399.27)
85n.7   and feeling] PR; or sensations (Tolstoï, Essays,
          399.29–30)

"Experience and Objective Idealism"

131.3   observation employed either about] PR; any simple
          idea not received in by his senses from (Locke, Essay,
          71.31–32)
131.3–4   external sensible] PR; external (Locke, Essay, 71.32)
131.4   about] PR; by reflection from (Locke, Essay, 71.32–
          33)
131.4   the internal] PR; the (Locke, Essay, 71.33)
131.4   our] PR; his own (Locke, Essay, 71.33)
131.4   minds] PR; mind (Locke, Essay, 71.33)
131n.10   Memory] PR; memory (Hobbes, Elements, 3.15)
132n.16   and] PR; or (Murray, Dictionary, 3:430.26)
132n.16   consciously affected] PR; consciously the subject of
          a state or condition, or of being consciously affected
          (Murray, Dictionary, 3:430.50–51)
132n.17   act] PR; event (Murray, Dictionary, 3:430.52)
142n.1   of] PR; of a (James, "A World of Pure Experience,"
          536.22)

"The St. Louis Congress of the Arts and Sciences"

146.9   relation] S; relations (Münsterberg, "St. Louis Con-
          gress," 674:1.23)
147.39   on] S; on the (Münsterberg, "St. Louis Congress,"
          678:1.14)

"The Knowledge Experience and Its Relationships"

172.4   account] JP; account of experience (Woodbridge, "Of
          What Sort . . . ," 576.29–30)

172.5   be‿] JP; ～, (Woodbridge, "Of What Sort . . . ,"
            576.30)
174.18   *we . . . about*] JP; [*rom.*] (Woodbridge, "Of What
            Sort . . . ," 576.8)
176.11   sorts] JP; sorts of experience (Woodbridge, "Of What
            Sort . . . ," 575.33)

"Emerson: The Philosopher of Democracy"

184.19   There is] IJE; Senates and sovereigns have (Emerson,
            Works, 4:21.5)
184.19   compliment like] IJE; compliment, with their medals,
            swords and armorial coats, like (Emerson, *Works*,
            4:21.5–6)
184.20   of] IJE; of a (Emerson, *Works*, 4:21.7)
184.21   heights‿] IJE; height, (Emerson, *Works*, 4:21.8)
185.9   and] IJE; or (Emerson, *Works*, 2:291.24)
185.21–22   grammar and no plausibility] IJE; logic or of oath
            (Emerson, *Works*, 2:145.7)
185.22–23   evidence . . . arguments.] IJE; evidence. (Emer-
            son, *Works*, 2:145.8)
186.8   detail] IJE; details (Emerson, *Works*, 3:223.13)
188.23   not, because] IJE; not, whatsoever fame and authority
            may attend it, because (Emerson, *Works*, 2:320.19–20)
188.27   Kant, is] IJE; Kant, or whosoever propounds to you a
            philosophy of the mind, is (Emerson, *Works*, 2:321.7–
            8)
188.28–29   consciousness. Say,] IJE; consciousness which you
            have also your way of seeing, perhaps of denominating.
            Say (Emerson, *Works*, 2:321.10–11)
188.32   not] IJE; no (Emerson, *Works*, 2:321.17)
188.32   natural‿] IJE; natural, common (Emerson, *Works*,
            2:321.18)
191.13   the] IJE; a (Emerson, *Works*, 7:283.15)
191.15   sensibilities‿ and] IJE; sensibilities, those fountains
            of right thought, and (Emerson, *Works*, 7:283.18–19)

"The Philosophical Work of Herbert Spencer"

195.26   them has] PR; them in the interest of plausible fiction
            has (Henry James, "Zola," 198:1.50)

"The Psychological and the Logical in Teaching Geometry"

218.11   with] ER;   with our (Halsted, "Teaching of Geometry,"
         457.22)
218.12   and] ER;   and our (Halsted, "Teaching of Geometry,"
         457.22)

Review of Humanism

313.3   is only the starting∧point] PB;   is the only natural
         starting-point (Schiller, Humanism, xvii.31–32)
313.6   experiences∧] PB;   experience, (Schiller, Humanism,
         xviii.1)
318.25   mental character] PB;   mental life generally (Schiller,
         Humanism, 8.9–10)

CHECKLIST OF DEWEY'S REFERENCES

Titles and authors' names in Dewey references have been corrected and expanded to conform accurately and consistently to the original works; all corrections appear in the Emendations List.

This section gives full publication information for each work cited by Dewey. When Dewey gave page numbers for a reference, the edition he used was identified exactly by locating the citation. Similarly, the books in Dewey's personal library have been used to verify his use of a particular edition. For other references, the edition listed here is the one from among the various editions possibly available to him that was his most likely source by reason of place or date of publication, or on the evidence from correspondence and other materials, and its general accessibility during the period.

A number of works published after 1918 appear in this Checklist; these are Dewey's references for the article "Ethics," in the 1918 and 1940 editions.

Adler, Felix. *An Ethical Philosophy of Life Presented in Its Main Outlines.* New York: D. Appleton and Co., 1918.

Annual Register, 1901–1902. Chicago: University of Chicago Press, 1902.

Bakewell, Charles Montague. "The Issue between Idealism and Immediate Empiricism." *Journal of Philosophy, Psychology and Scientific Methods* 2 (1905): 687–91.

———. "An Open Letter to Professor Dewey concerning Immediate Empiricism." *Journal of Philosophy, Psychology and Scientific Methods* 2 (1905): 520–22. [*The Middle Works of John Dewey, 1899–1924,* edited by Jo Ann Boydston, 3:390–92. Carbondale: Southern Illinois University Press, 1977.]

Baxter, Garrett. *Of Sanction.* [Norfolk, Va.]: The Economic Press, 1923.

Benedict, W. R. *World Views and Their Ethical Implications: A Syllabus of Lectures in Advanced Ethics.* Cincinnati: Cincinnati University Press, 1902.

Bentham, Jeremy. *An Introduction to the Principles of Morals and Legislation*. London: T. Payne and Son, 1789.

Bode, Boyd Henry. "Cognitive Experience and Its Object." *Journal of Philosophy, Psychology and Scientific Methods* 2 (1905): 658–63. [*Middle Works* 3:398–404.]

Bradley, Francis Herbert. *Appearance and Reality*. 2d ed. New York: Macmillan Co., 1902.

———. *The Principles of Logic*. London: Kegan Paul, Trench and Co., 1883.

Brandt, Charles. *The Vital Problem; the Path to Health, Wisdom and Universal Peace*. New York: B. Lust, 1924.

Carr, Herbert Wildon. *Changing Backgrounds in Religion and Ethics; a Metaphysical Meditation*. London: Macmillan and Co., 1927.

Chambers, Robert. *Vestiges of the Natural History of Creation*. London: J. Churchill, 1844.

Cicero, Marcus Tullius. *The Letters of Cicero*. 4 vols. Translated by Evelyn S. Shuckburgh. London: George Bell and Sons, 1899–1900.

Clifford, William Kingdon. *The Scientific Basis of Morals*. New York: J. Fitzgerald and Co., 1884.

Colvin, Stephen Sheldon. "Is Subjective Idealism a Necessary Point of View for Psychology?" *Journal of Philosophy, Psychology and Scientific Methods* 2 (1905): 225–31. [*Middle Works* 3:382–89.]

Croce, Benedetto. *The Conduct of Life*. Translated by Arthur Livingston. New York: Harcourt, Brace and Co., 1924.

———. *Philosophy of the Practical*. London: Macmillan and Co., 1913.

Dante Alighieri. *The Divine Comedy of Dante Alighieri*. Translated by Charles Eliot Norton. Rev. ed. Boston: Houghton Mifflin Co., 1902.

Dawson, Miles Menander. *The Ethics of Socrates*. New York: G. P. Putnam's Sons, 1924.

Dewey, John. *Human Nature and Conduct: An Introduction to Social Psychology*. New York: Henry Holt and Co., 1922; 9th printing, 1927.

———. *Studies in Logical Theory*. University of Chicago, The Decennial Publications, second series, vol. 11. Chicago: University of Chicago Press, 1903. [*Middle Works* 2:292–375.]

———. "The Evolutionary Method as Applied to Morality." *Philosophical Review* 11 (1902): 107–24, 353–71. [*Middle Works* 2:3–38.]

———. "Notes upon Logical Topics." *Journal of Philosophy, Psychology and Scientific Methods* 1 (1904): 57–62. [*Middle Works* 3:62–72.]

———. "The Postulate of Immediate Empiricism." *Journal of*

Philosophy, Psychology and Scientific Methods 2 (1905): 393–99. [*Middle Works* 3:158–67.]

———. "The St. Louis Congress of the Arts and Sciences." *Science*, n.s. 18 (1903): 275–78. [*Middle Works* 3:145–50.]

———, and Tufts, James H. *Ethics*. New York: Henry Holt and Co., 1908.

Dopp, Katharine Elizabeth. *The Place of Industries in Elementary Education*. Chicago: University of Chicago Press, 1903.

Durkheim, Émile. *L'éducation morale*. Paris: F. Alcan, 1925.

Emerson, Ralph Waldo. *Emerson's Complete Works*. Riverside ed. 12 vols. Boston: Houghton Mifflin Co., 1895.

Fuller, Sir Bampfylde. *The Science of Ourselves*. London: Oxford University Press, 1921.

Givler, Robert Chenault. *The Ethics of Hercules: A Study of Man's Body as the Sole Determinant of Ethical Values*. New York: A. A. Knopf, 1924.

Gordon, Kate. *The Psychology of Meaning*. Chicago: University of Chicago Press, 1903.

———. "Feeling and Conception." *Journal of Philosophy, Psychology and Scientific Methods* 2 (1905): 645–50.

———. "The Relation of Feeling to Discrimination and Conception." *Journal of Philosophy, Psychology and Scientific Methods* 2 (1905): 617–22.

Green, Thomas Hill. *Prolegomena to Ethics*. Edited by A. C. Bradley. Oxford: Clarendon Press, 1883.

———. *Works of Thomas Hill Green*. 2d ed. 3 vols. Edited by R. L. Nettleship. New York: Longmans, Green, and Co., 1889–90.

Grotius, Hugo. *Hugonis Grotii de jure belli et pacis libri tres*. Paris: Nicolaus Buon, 1625.

Groves, Ernest Rutherford. *Moral Sanitation*. New York: Association Press, 1916.

Halsted, George Bruce. "The Teaching of Geometry." *Educational Review* 24 (1902): 456–70.

Helvétius, Claude Adrien. *De l'esprit*. Paris: A. Durand, 1758.

———. *De l'homme, de ses facultés intellectuelles et de son education*. 2 vols. London: Société typographique, 1773.

Hirst, Edward Wales. *Self and Neighbor, an Ethical Study*. London: Macmillan and Co., 1919.

Hobbes, Thomas. *The English Works of Thomas Hobbes*. Edited by William Molesworth. Vol. 1: *Elements of Philosophy*. London: John Bohn, 1839.

———. *Leviathan; or the Matter, Form and Power of a Commonwealth, Ecclesiastical and Civil*. 4th ed. Introduction by Henry Morley. London: George Routledge and Sons, 1894.

Hobson, John Atkinson. *Free-Thought in the Social Sciences*. New York: Macmillan Co., 1926.

Hocking, William Ernest. *Human Nature and Its Remaking*. Rev. ed. New Haven: Yale University Press, 1923.

Holbach, Paul Henri Thiry, baron d'. *Système social, ou principes naturels de la morale et de la politique*. 3 vols. London, 1773.

Hudson, Jay William. *The Truths We Live By*. New York: D. Appleton and Co., 1921.

James, Henry. "An Appreciation of Émile Zola." *Atlantic Monthly* 92 (1903): 193–210.

James, William. *The Principles of Psychology*. 2 vols. New York: Henry Holt and Co., 1890.

———. *The Will to Believe*. New York: Longmans, Green, and Co., 1894.

———. "Does 'Consciousness' Exist?" *Journal of Philosophy, Psychology and Scientific Methods* 1 (1904): 477–91.

———. "The Essence of Humanism." *Journal of Philosophy, Psychology and Scientific Methods* 2 (1905): 113–18.

———. "A World of Pure Experience." *Journal of Philosophy. Psychology and Scientific Methods* 1 (1904): 533–43.

Jung, Édouard. *Le principe constitutif de la nature organique*. Paris: F. Alcan, 1923.

Kant, Immanuel. *Critique of Pure Reason*. Translated by Francis Haywood. London: W. Pickering, 1838.

King, Irving Walter. *The Psychology of Child Development*. Chicago: University of Chicago Press, 1903.

Leighton, Joseph Alexander. "Cognitive Thought and 'Immediate' Experience." *Journal of Philosophy, Psychology and Scientific Methods* 3 (1906): 174–80.

Lloyd, Alfred H. "The Personal and the Factional in the Life of Society." *Journal of Philosophy, Psychology and Scientific Methods* 2 (1905): 337–45.

Locke, John. *Essay concerning Human Understanding*. New rev. ed. Edited by Thaddeus O'Mahoney. London: Ward, Lock, and Co., 1881.

MacKaye, James. *The Logic of Conduct*. New York: Boni and Liveright, 1924.

Mackenzie, John Stuart. *A Manual of Ethics*. 4th ed. New York: Hinds and Noble, 1901.

McMurry, Charles Alexander, and McMurry, Frank M. *The Method of the Recitation*. Bloomington, Ill.: Pantagraph Publishing Co., 1897.

Mead, George Herbert. *Definition of the Psychical*. Chicago: University of Chicago Press, 1903.

Mezes, Sidney Edward. *Ethics: Descriptive and Explanatory*. London: Macmillan and Co., 1901.

Mill, John Stuart. *An Examination of Sir William Hamilton's Philosophy and of the Principal Philosophical Questions Dis-*

cussed in the Writings. London: Longman, Green, Longman, Roberts, and Green, 1865.

Moore, Addison Webster. "Some Logical Aspects of Purpose." In *Studies in Logical Theory.* University of Chicago, The Decennial Publications, second series, 11:341–82. Chicago: University of Chicago Press, 1903.

Moore, Eliakim Hastings. "On the Foundations of Mathematics." *Science,* n.s. 17 (1903): 401–16.

Münsterberg, Hugo. "The International Congress of Arts and Science." *Science,* n.s. 18 (1903): 559–63. [*Middle Works* 3:374–81.]

———. "The St. Louis Congress of Arts and Sciences." *Atlantic Monthly* 91 (1903): 671–84. [*Middle Works* 3:352–73.]

Murray, James A., ed. *A New English Dictionary on Historical Principles.* Vols. 2, 3, 5. Oxford: Clarendon Press, 1893, 1897, 1901.

Palmer, George Herbert. *The Field of Ethics.* Boston: Houghton Mifflin Co., 1901.

Paulsen, Friedrich. *A System of Ethics.* Edited and translated from the 4th rev. and enl. ed., by Frank Thilly. New York: Charles Scribner's Sons, 1899.

Peirce, Charles Sanders. "The Law of Mind." *Monist* 2 (1892): 533–59.

———. "Mr. Peterson's Proposed Discussion." *Monist* 16 (1906): 147–51.

Plato. *The Dialogues of Plato.* 4 vols. Translated by B. Jowett. Boston: Jefferson Press, 1871. [*Protagoras,* 1:97–162; *The Republic,* 2:1–452; *Theaetetus,* 3:301–419; *Laws,* 4:1–480.]

Royce, Josiah. *The Philosophy of Loyalty.* New York: Macmillan Co., 1908.

———. *The World and the Individual.* First Series: The Four Historical Conceptions of Being. New York: Macmillan Co., 1900.

———. *The World and the Individual.* Second Series: Nature, Man and the Moral Order. New York: Macmillan Co., 1901.

———. "Recent Logical Inquiries and Their Psychological Bearings." *Psychological Review* 9 (1902): 105–33.

Santayana, George. *The Life of Reason, or the Phases of Human Progress.* Vols. 1–5. New York: Charles Scribner's Sons, 1905–6.

Schiller, Ferdinand Canning Scott. *Humanism: Philosophical Essays.* London: Macmillan and Co., 1903.

Schweitzer, Albert. *The Philosophy of Civilization.* Translated by C. T. Campion. 2d ed. rev. London: A. and C. Black, 1929.

Sharp, Frank Chapman. *Ethics.* New York: Century Co., 1928.

Sidgwick, Henry. *The Methods of Ethics.* 4th ed. London: Macmillan and Co., 1890.

Sorley, William Ritchie. *Recent Tendencies in Ethics*. Edinburgh: William Blackwood and Sons, 1904.

———. "Ethics." In *Dictionary of Philosophy and Psychology*, edited by James Mark Baldwin, 1:346–47. New York: Macmillan Co., 1901.

Spencer, Herbert. *An Autobiography*. 2 vols. New York: D. Appleton and Co., 1904.

———. *Essays Scientific, Political, and Speculative*. 3 vols. New York: D. Appleton and Co., 1901.

———. *First Principles of a New System of Philosophy*. London: Williams and Norgate, 1862.

———. *The Proper Sphere of Government*. London: W. Brittain, 1843.

———. *Social Statics; or, The Conditions Essential to Human Happiness Specified, and the First of Them Developed*. London: John Chapman, 1851; *Social Statics, Abridged and Revised; together with The Man versus the State*. New York: D. Appleton and Co., 1892.

———. *Various Fragments*. New York: D. Appleton and Co., 1898.

Stephen, Leslie. *The Science of Ethics*. London: Smith, Elder and Co., 1882; 2d ed. New York: G. P. Putnam's Sons, 1907.

Stuart, Henry Waldgrave. "Valuation as a Logical Process." In *Studies in Logical Theory*. University of Chicago, The Decennial Publications, second series, 11:227–340. Chicago: University of Chicago Press, 1903.

Tacitus, Caius Cornelius. *The Germania and Agricola of Caius Cornelius Tacitus*. Edited by W. S. Tyler. New York: D. Appleton and Co., 1878.

Taylor, Alfred Edward. *The Faith of a Moralist*. New York: Macmillan Co., 1937.

Thilly, Frank. *Introduction to Ethics*. New York: Charles Scribner's Sons, 1900.

Thomas, Evan Edward. *The Ethical Basis of Reality*. London: Longmans, Green, and Co., 1927.

Tolstoï, Lyof N. *The Works of Lyof N. Tolstoï*. Vol. 12: *Essays, Letters, and Miscellanies*. New York: Thomas Y. Crowell Co., 1899.

Tuker, Mildred Anna Rosalie. *Past and Future of Ethics*. London and New York: Oxford University Press, 1938.

Venn, John. *The Principles of Empirical or Inductive Logic*. London: Macmillan and Co., 1889.

Woodbridge, Frederick James Eugene. "The Field of Logic." *Science*, n.s. 20 (1904): 587–600.

———. "Of What Sort Is Cognitive Experience?" *Journal of Philosophy, Psychology and Scientific Methods* 2 (1905): 573–76. [*Middle Works* 3:393–97.]

————. "The Nature of Consciousness." *Journal of Philosophy, Psychology and Scientific Methods* 2 (1905): 119–25.

————. "The Problem of Consciousness." In *Studies in Philosophy and Psychology*, pp. 137–66. Boston: Houghton Mifflin Co., 1906.

Wundt, Wilhelm Max. *Ethics.* 3 vols. London: Swan Sonnenschein and Co., 1897–1901.

Young, Ella F. *Scientific Method in Education.* The Decennial Publications, first series, 3:143–55. Chicago: University of Chicago Press, 1903.

INDEX